D1237198

RESEARCH IN
THE SOCIOLOGY
OF ORGANIZATIONS

Volume 2 • 1983

RESEARCH IN
THE SOCIOLOGY
OF ORGANIZATIONS

A Research Annual

Editor: SAMUEL B. BACHARACH
*Department of Organizational
Behavior
School of Industrial and
Labor Relations
Cornell University*

VOLUME 2 • 1983

 JAI PRESS INC.

Greenwich, Connecticut   *London, England*

Copyright © 1983 JAI PRESS INC.
36 Sherwood Place
Greenwich, Connecticut 06830

JAI PRESS INC.
3 Henrietta Street
London WC2E 8LU
England

All rights reserved. No part of this publication may be reproduced, stored on a retrieval system, or transmitted in any form or by any means, electronic, mechanical, photocopying, filming, recording or otherwise without prior permission in writing from the publisher.

ISBN: 0-89232-203-9

Manufactured in the United States of America

CONTENTS

LIST OF CONTRIBUTORS

Samuel B. Bacharach

New York State School of Industrial
and Labor Relations
Cornell University

Stewart Clegg

School of Humanities
Griffith University, Australia

Paul Goldman

Department of Organizational Studies
Pitzer College

Leonard Greenhalgh

The Amos Tuck School of Business
Administration
Dartmouth College

Edward J. Lawler

New York State School of Industrial
and Labor Relations
Cornell University

Bruce H. Mayhew

Department of Sociology
University of South Carolina

Lynne G. Zucker

Department of Sociology
University of California, Los Angeles

PREFACE

This volume presents a series of papers which in many ways are on the cutting edge of organizational research. All the papers suggest new theoretical direction for future research. Lynne Zucker's presents an important perspective for examining organizations as institutions. Paul Goldman's suggests how Marxists theory and organizational analysis can intersect. Lawler and Bacharach examine Weber's concept of action and integrate it with a political model of organizations. Stewart Clegg presents a cogent argument for the need for a phenomenological perspective in the analysis of organizations. Bruce Mayhew presents an extensive formal analysis of hierarchical differentiation. The last paper by Leonard Greenhalgh presents a broad theoretical discussion of organizational decline. It is hoped that the papers in the volume will provide new theoretical and research direction for the sociological study of organizations.

Samuel B. Bacharach
Series Editor

ORGANIZATIONS AS INSTITUTIONS

Lynne G. Zucker

I. INTRODUCTION

Organizations are the preeminent institutional form in modern society. They organize and structure the daily activities of most people. This pervasive quality of organizations has frequently been noted (e.g., Aldrich and Pfeffer, 1976; R. H. Hall, 1971; Etzioni, 1964; Presthus, 1962). Organizations are everywhere, involved in almost every possible sphere of human action. Manufacturing firms, schools, grocery stores, churches, and even "social movement organizations," structure segments of life at some point. Not only do organizations have direct effects on the lives of people, they in many senses can be treated as "corporate actors," which have grown to have "immense size and immense power" over "natural persons" (Coleman, 1974:35).

Despite widespread recognition of the central position and role of organizations in modern life, scant attention has been paid to the power that organizations

Research in the Sociology of Organizations, vol. 2, pages 1–47
Copyright © 1983 by JAI Press Inc.
All rights of reproduction in any form reserved.
ISBN: 0-89232-203-9

1

have to alter the forces which affect them, whether internal or environmental. With few exceptions (Pfeffer, 1981; Pfeffer and Salancik, 1977), the effects of key factors—ranging from size to domain to suppliers—on the structure and performance of the organization have been investigated, rather than the power the organization exerts over these same factors.[1]

For clarity, two terms central to the argument that organizations are institutions need to be defined at this point. First, institutionalization is both a process and a property variable: it is a phenomenological process by which certain social relationships and actions come to be taken for granted, that is part of the "objective situation", while at the same time it is the structure of reality defining what has meaning and what actions are possible. Despite their social origin, highly institutionalized elements are experienced as part of the intersubjective world consisting of resistant objective structures independent of any particular actor (Zucker, 1977). Second, both general social forms, such as roles, and particular enactments of those forms, such as "judge", can vary in the degree to which they are institutionalized. Organizational form, here referring to rational hierarchical bureaucratic organization, has varied historically in its degree of institutionalization, as have various specific aspects of organizational form, such as personnel procedures.

The purpose of this paper is to explore some of the sources of organizational power, sources not based primarily on control of resources, but on control of basic institutional structure and process. Following this discussion, the focus will be on institutional transformation: the emergence of a work-based institutional system from a kin-based one. Hence, most of the new data assembled here are historical.

Since institutional structures are highly resistant to change (Zucker, 1977), for change to occur the taken-for-granted quality must be brought into question. While transformations of institutional structure can occur quite rapidly, e.g., in revolutions or through social movements, these changes generally involve the reallocation of individuals among existing institutional definitions, rather than the creation of new definitions (for examples, see Tilly et al., 1975, on proactive violence, especially pp. 233–6; for a laboratory demonstration, see Zucker, 1980a). Such transformations can alter behavior considerably, and redistribute resources and rights [including citizenship (see Marshall, 1977)] among groups in a society, for example by allowing some new groups to vote or by making welfare benefits available to additional recipients. However, transformations of institutional structure which in fact alter fundamental institutional definitions— and hence involve cognitive restructuring (Zucker, 1981)—take place incrementally, and with substantial initial integration of the prior and newly emergent institutional structure. It is this type of transformation which will be explored here, since it is this process of institutionalization which best explains the gradual transformation from a family-based to an organization-based institutional system.

After a brief review of major perspectives in organizational theory, the institutional approach to organizations will be explicated. The view that organizations are constrained by the larger institutional structure will be delineated and compared with the view that organizations are themselves institutions. Evidence concerning the institutionalization of the organizational form is presented, examining the pattern and extent of diffusion and the subsequent stability of organizations. The paper concludes with a detailed historical analysis of the institutionalization of the organizational form, examining the mechanisms of institutional integration and cognitive representation. The analysis focuses specifically on: (1) the early articulation of work systems with kinship systems, as well as their gradual divorce from kin relations; and (2) the massive cognitive changes, reflected in linguistic structures, which resulted from the institutional eclipse of family by organizations. Implications are drawn concerning the control, both direct and indirect, which organizations exert over modern life.

II. MAJOR PERSPECTIVES ON ORGANIZATIONS

Organizations, even though pervasive, are commonly viewed as relatively powerless, or at least at the mercy of internal necessity or of external environmental forces over which they have little control. Earlier approaches to organizations focused on internal structure and process, ignoring the environment. In contrast, current approaches most frequently focus on the effect of uncontrolled (or partially controlled) environmental forces on the organization's structure and function, and in some cases on its very survival. In both approaches, however, the role of the organization *qua* organization is minimized: emphasis is on forces affecting the organization, rather than on forces affected by the organization.

Two major approaches have focused primarily on internal organizational structure and process, emphasizing the effects of internal variables on organizations, despite attempts to control them. In the rational model, the central question is (Thompson, 1967:1): "Organizations act, but what determines how and when they will act?" It is answered most basically in terms of goal specificity and formalization, but also in terms of technology/tasks, organizational design, and administrative structure (Scott, 1975, 1981:Ch. 3). In this model, the major dimensions explored derive largely from the internal features of organizations, ranging from decision-making processes to formal rules (Simon, 1957; Weber, 1947).[2] Internal necessity is seen as the central determining feature; organizations are constrained by the nature of their technology and by their need for efficiency. Control over task-relevant functions is always problematic; the environment is reacted to, not defined by, the organization.

In the social systems approach, organizations are also seen as driven by their internal structure. Developed in part as a critique of the rational systems approach, it also asks how organizations act, but answers in terms of characteristics organizations share with other social groups, rather than focusing on distinctive elements (see Gouldner, 1959). The actual behavior of organizational participants is explored and is often found to be at variance with the formal rules designed to structure behavior (see Roethlisberger and Dickson, 1939; Dalton, 1959). Though the success of the organization is often determined by the informal structure—providing successful leadership or not, providing maximum task efficiency or not—the organization can do little to shape or control informal interaction patterns.

While both the rational and human systems model still are being investigated in current research on organizations, the open systems approach, which focuses on the effects of the organizational environment, is the stimulus for the bulk of current work (Pondy and Mitroff, 1979). Specific subtheories abound. One of the major subtheories, contingency theory, asserts that internal organization features must match the demands of the environment for the organization to perform well—design decisions are contingent on environmental conditions (Lawrence and Lorsch, 1967).

The resource dependence and the natural selection models, two other important subtheories, specify more precisely the expected effects of the environment. In the natural selection approach, the question ''why are there so many kinds of organizations?'' (Hannan and Freeman, 1977:956) is answered by identifying environments which differentially select organizations for survival on the basis of the fit between organizational structure and environmental characteristics (see also Aldrich, 1979; McKelvey, 1982). Forces in the environment, not internal technology or structure, determine why certain forms (or ''species'') of organizations survive and grow, whereas other types decline and die. Once again, the relatively powerless position of the individual organization is stressed. In the closely related resource dependence model, the key to organizational survival and growth is *adaptation* to the environment. Here, the organization is not a passive captive of its environment but is ''active, and capable of changing, as well as responding to, the environment. Administrators manage their environments as well as their organizations . . .'' (Aldrich and Pfeffer, 1976:83). The resource dependence perspective specifically identifies the power of the organization to shape the forces that affect it (see Pfeffer, 1981).

In many areas of social science, a brief review of major approaches could conclude by indicating which is dominant. However, as Starbuck (1974) has reported, perhaps a bit tongue in cheek, there are about 6.7 paradigms per organization theorist! The only consistent defining element—with the exception of the resource dependence perspective—is that the organization as a unit does not wield effective power over either internal structure and process or the external environment. The institutional approach, to be discussed in the next section, as presently formulated, contains this same element: the external institutional environment constrains the organization, determining its internal structure, its growth or decline, and often even its survival. After a review of the effects that the institutional environment has on organizations, the institutional approach is developed further to begin specifying the institutional sources of organizational power.

III. INSTITUTIONAL THEORY AND ORGANIZATIONS

Attention has been drawn in the past to the institutional aspects of organizations, but exclusively in a rationalistic rather than a phenomenological frame. From the rational perspective, institutions consist of distinctive values that are conscious and explicitly articulated by all organizational participants: schools are guided by educational values, governments by political values, and so on. Since participants are also aware of alternatives to these values, deviance is common (Selznick, 1957). In contrast, the taken for granted quality of institutions in the phenomenological approach espoused here implies that participants are not conscious of their central values and that the common understandings are seldom explicitly articulated. Institutionalization simply constructs the way things *are;* alternatives may be literally unthinkable.

The concept "institution" has commonly been applied to the study of organizations in a vague fashion, referring loosely to the pressure of the institutional environment (Selznick, 1948:25), the infusion of "value beyond the technical requirements of the task at hand" (Selznick, 1957:17), and the relative institutional status of types or classes of organizations (Clark, 1956). Generally, "institution" has been underspecified, sometimes used as a causal force originating outside of the organization, sometimes as a consequence of the particulars of an organization's history. Most commonly, the early work on institutions and organizations has focused on constructing explanations *exposing* the role of a particular organization's history in causing changes in its operative goals (e.g., Selznick, 1957 and Clark, 1956). Basically, the organization abandons its *true* goals "in order to survive or grow" (Perrow, 1979:182), leading to an understanding of deviance, not conformity.

The current approach to understanding the sources of institutionalization and its effects on organizational structure and process has very different roots, and hence radically different implications for organization theory. To begin with, institutionalization is rooted in conformity—not conformity engendered by sanctions (whether positive or negative), nor conformity resulting from a "black-box" internalization process, but conformity rooted in the taken-for-granted aspects of everyday life (Zucker, 1977). Within an organization, institutionalization operates to produce common understandings about what is appropriate and, fundamentally, meaningful behavior. They may involve common response to authority, adoption of "reasonable" task-related practices and procedures, and other, as yet unexplored, internal aspects of organizations (Zucker, 1977). The key question here (Zucker, 1977:728) is to what extent are organizations as-

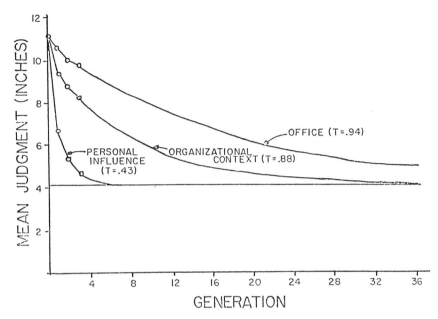

Figure 1. Extrapolated Response Levels Based on Transmission Coefficients Determined by the First Three Generations in Each Condition. (Source: Zucker, 1977.)

sumed to be more "formal," so that "acts will be more regularized and . . . interaction will be more definitely patterned"? This question has been answered in a laboratory experiment (Zucker, 1977). Utilizing an ambiguous situation, it was found that subjects were more likely to accept influence from another when the context was defined as organizational, and were even more receptive to influence from another when that person was defined as holding a specified organizational position (a named office, but not carrying authority or special knowledge). Figure 1 presents the basic results.

Institutional effects can be observed not only within organizations, but also in their environments. Institutionalization, when external to an organization, leads to adoption of common practices: "purposes, positions, policies, and procedural rules that characterize formal organizations" (Meyer and Rowan, 1977:346). Hence, educational institutions with very different student populations and/or educational objectives come to accept as necessary common teacher certification and achievement testing systems. Here, the key question is the extent of the impact of the external institutional environment on organizations (Meyer and Rowan, 1977:346): What determines the degree to which externally impacted "organizations structurally reflect socially constructed reality"? It is typically answered by examining the effect of legal (primarily legislative) and/or fiscal

control over the development of new elements of organizational structure—
ranging from the emergence of specific occupations and service units in schools
from 1930 to 1970 (Rowan, 1982) to the proliferation of evaluation units in
school districts in the 1970s (Zucker, 1982a). Since much of this literature is just
beginning to appear, the next section of this paper will summarize the major
findings and implications of the research on institutions. Again, the emphasis so
far has been principally on the effects of external institutional forces on organizations; following a review of these findings the argument will turn to the effects of
organizations themselves as institutional forces altering other aspects of the
social system.

IV. EFFECTS OF THE INSTITUTIONAL ENVIRONMENT ON ORGANIZATIONS

Recent applications of institutional theory to organizations emphasize the impact
of the external institutional environment on organizations. The effects of societal
growth of "rationalized institutional structures" on organizations are traced
(Meyer and Rowan, 1977:342, 346), with the central idea that rules and controls
of agencies in the social environment shape organizational structures, so that
structures of regulated organizations over time become isomorphic with the rules
of environmental agencies. Four major empirical tests of this approach have been
conducted: one on the adoption of civil service procedures, 1880–1935; a second
on the spread of innovations, 1930–1970, in California school districts; a third
on the development and function of evaluation units in schools; and a fourth on
effects of the interaction of a major institutional change (California's Proposition
13, 1978) with preexisting rules and controls enacted by the state and federal
government on local decision making. The wide variety of empirical contexts
provides a broad base of support for the basic argument that the institutional
environment affects organizations; at the same time, each of these studies further
specifies the conditions under which the institutional environment has an effect.

First, a recent study (Zucker and Tolbert, 1981) investigated the adoption of
civil service reform by government organizations, 1880–1935. The major results
of this study show that one element of formal structure of organizations (civil
service procedures) was gradually institutionalized over the time period. In the
early stages of the adoption process, cities adopted slowly, largely dependent on
the proportion of immigrants in the city's population. As the procedures became
institutionalized, organizations adopted them simply because they were legitimated, regardless of any specific characteristics of the city. In order to appear
"modern, efficient and rational," even when the procedures were not particularly functional, cities adopted civil service. Evidence is provided in a logistic
analysis of civil service adoption which shows that city characteristics were good
predictors of civil service reform initially, but as the reform measure spread and

Table 1. Logistic Analysis of Civil Service Adoption Over Time, 1885–1935[a]

Time Period	Intercept	Percent Foreign Born	Percent Illiterate	Resid. No. of Mfg. Wage Earners	Resid. Municipal Expend.	Log Size	Age	$-2 \log l$	Model Chi-square	Model D	Predictive Accuracy Coefficient
1885–1904 (N = 83)	−25.0849	12.1090 (4.9915)	aa	−.5351 (.9778)	−1.9347 (1.1955)	.3897 (.4027)	.0098 (.0194)	43.00	13.98	.15	.63
1905–1914 (N = 74)	−6.6312	8.8957 (3.6517)	−.0733 (.0962)	−.2089 (.7118)	.1892 (.8126)	.4234 (.3415)	.0015 (.0117)	73.47	18.25	.21	.28
1915–1924 (N = 52)	−27.9152	3.2065 (3.6146)	−.3079 (.1517)	.8064 (.9765)	.5291 (1.5921)	.2111 (.4783)	.0146 (.0147)	52.65	9.83	.18	.27
1925–1934 (N = 39)	15.0216	3.0032 (5.1595)	−.0040 (.1928)	−.3409 (.8706)	−1.7141 (1.9815)	−.7987 (.7139)	−.0072 (.0173)	37.53	2.05	.06	.31

[a] Standard errors in parentheses.

aa Missing data; no estimate possible.

*p < .01; **p < .05; ***p < .10.

8

became legitimated, with cities under more external pressure to adopt, city characteristics were no longer good predictors of adoption. Table 1 presents the basic findings.

The second study (Rowan, 1982) also examined the spread pattern of innovations. In this case, external sources (state and federal government) instituted requirements for local educational organizations. As these requirements became more generally accepted by all educational organizations, the adoption patterns accelerated rapidly. Persistence patterns also differ widely, providing evidence that some innovations became much more highly institutionalized than others (Zucker, 1977). Specifically, instructional elements in educational organizations fail to become institutionalized, continually giving way to new innovations. Rowan (1982:261) argues that institutionalization is more easily maintained in areas "where technical procedures are highly certain and standards of evaluation easy to formulate."

The third study (Zucker, 1982a) more explicitly deals with the effects of definitions and requirements established by government organizations at higher levels (federal and state) for government organizations at lower levels (local). In this research, establishment and function of evaluation units in school districts is investigated. Though the separate organizational units themselves are not required, extensive federal requirements for local evaluation of Title I programs (and legislative requirements in some states) cause an increase in evaluation activity in districts that effected the development of a specific unit. Hence, most of the evaluation units have been established since 1970. The percent of districts with evaluation units have also increased sharply with increasing state regulation and/or funding of local education (see Table 2). In addition to this direct effect of legislation, the expected overall impact of the unit on local decision making has generally not been found in most school districts. Often cited as an example of loose coupling in organizations (where tasks are not monitored at higher levels),

Table 2. Extent of State Regulation and Funding of Local Public Schools and Presence of Evaluation Units (N = 1321)*

Regulation/Funding	# Districts with EU	Percent	N
High State Involvement	226	45.0	502
Moderate State Involvement	136	25.7	529
Low State Involvement	47	16.2	290

*Universe of 750 districts with enrollments of 10,000 or more; 50% sample of districts with 5,000 to 9,999 students (573). Response rate of 100% for larger districts (n = 750); 81% for smaller districts (n = 464). Table total n of 1321 must reflect telephone follow up results.

it instead appears to be a consequence of the external focus of the unit: the staff correctly perceives the reason for its existence to be the provision of evaluation information for federal and state consumption, regardless of whether the information is used. The evaluation unit typically functions as a boundary unit, not primarily as an internal assessor of task performance. It provides the best possible "organizational face" so that outside support will continue; it does not provide "real" tough evaluation information designed to reassess internal teaching functions.

The fourth study (Zucker, 1982b) also addresses the issue of the effects of multiple levels of institutional environment on the local organization. However, here the focus is on the complex interactive effects of multiple institutional requirements in the context of a natural experiment (Proposition 13). Predictions concerning likely decisions on resource reduction in local organizations are made based on the institutional definition—through legislation and administrative requirement—of what is required or optional in the county provision of service, and of what is reimbursed to the county and what is not (see Table 3). It was found that the institutional forces did set the parameters for local organizational change. For example, requirements for county health care effectively caused increases in county health expenditures; reductions resulting from Proposition 13 implementation were effectively blocked by state legislation.

Based on the evidence collected so far, the effects of the institutional environment operate largely through: (1) the gradual legitimation of a new procedure, position, or element of structure; and (2) the requirements established by a hierarchically superior element of the institutional environment (generally another organization). Both of these mechanisms produce a number of secondary effects. For example, since the federal and state government organizations have to exercise control even though they can have no direct surveillance of organizational activities ("long range control systems"), formal elements of local organizational structure are often created to provide the information needed by the other organizations to assess performance and rule compliance. There is clearly much more research needed on these processes in order to specify more fully the conditions under which they occur and the consequences for the organizations they effect.[3]

Before turning to a discussion of the effect of organizations on institutions, some general comments on the studies just reviewed need to be made. One is that while some of the results obtained can be explained using other approaches, the newly developed institutional approach adds significant dimensions to our understanding of organizations: it differentiates the relevant environment, so that all controls and resources are not equated. It makes it clear that some controls designed to impact organizations will have more success than others, because as some become institutionalized, organizations accept their legitimacy. For example, it is now literally unthinkable to open a new bank which would not be covered by federal deposit insurance; by 1940 failure to adopt civil service

Table 3. California Legislative Changes in Funding and Percent Changes in Net County Costs for Health Care (N = 35)

Fiscal Year	Legislative Change	Net County Costs* Inpatient, Outpatient, Public Health (thousands)	Incremental % Change in Net Costs	County Share of Medi-Cal Costs	Incremental % Change in Total County Costs
1966-67	Medicare/Medicaid Implementation	$62,177	—	$180,334	—
1969-70	State Limits $ for "County Option"	$102,838	65.4%	$193,279	22.1%
1972-73	Medi-Cal Reform Act Implemented	$243,496	136.8%	$227,750	59.1%
1973-75	Beilenson Provisions; Medi-Cal Reimbursement Rates Increase	$362,643	48.9%	$290,669	38.6%
[1977-78]**	Counties Curtail Health Services	$363,658	.3%	$322,643	5.1%
1978-79***	SB 154 Implements Proposition 13	$389,454	7.1%	—	—

*Costs which the county must bear itself, after all reimbursement is obtained from state and federal sources.

**Put in, out of series, to make separable the effects of earlier requirements and SB 154.

***Planned expenditures, less than actual. Based on the 35 counties for which time series data is available.

Source: California Department of Health, Office of Planning and Program Analysis, Health Care Costs and Services in California Counties (Sacramento, February 1978). Totals presented above differ slightly from those in the source because the analysis was limited to counties with full information on county net costs for the 1966–67 fiscal year.

procedures was at best evidence of poor government management, with civil service a taken-for-granted element even in local government. In contrast, federal and state laws designed to affect public schools met with much more mixed success (Rowan, 1982): the ethos of "local control" of schools led to considerable resistance to some elements, even though heavily subsidized by the federal and state government (e.g., employment of psychology staff, curriculum planners, and supervisory instructional personnel), while other elements were rapidly adopted (e.g., health personnel). That these differences in adoption reflected underlying institutional process is indicated by the degree to which these elements, once adopted, are resistant to later change (Zucker, 1977). While 80 percent of the schools maintained local positions in health which survived over ten years (Rowan, 1982:Table 7), significantly fewer of the schools retained the other positions listed above over 10 years (62 percent in psychology, 41 percent in both curriculum and instruction).

While the research on the effects of the institutional environment on organizations contributes considerably to knowledge of factors affecting organizations, it generally ignores some important issues which need to be addressed in the continuing work on institutionalization. First, the rational institutional structures in modern societies are most often themselves organizations, commonly government organizations. The expansion of modern institutional structures, as defined in one major approach (Meyer and Rowan, 1977) is thus highly related to the expansion of the government structure. Government employment as a percentage of all employed workers increased from 4.1 percent in 1900 to 12.4 percent in 1949 (Fabricant, 1952:14) and by 1970 was approaching 20 percent (U.S. Bureau of the Census, 1972). Even in the 1970s, government employment was still identified as the most rapidly growing economic sector (Lowenberg and Moskow, 1972). Second, organizations are not simply constrained by the institutional environment: they often define their own position in it. An organization can define itself as a training institute and garner federal funds for veterans, or it can define itself as an educational institution and gain tax-exempt status. Resource dependence theorists can readily explain each option in resource terms, as well as the choice between them, but cannot explain the initial fact that these two alternatives are available. Explanations which focus on the consequences of institutional position, as in Selznick's early work (e.g., 1948, 1957), can describe the dysfunctions this choice may create for the organization's internal functioning. But both of these approaches beg the real question of the process by which these alternatives are constructed.

V. EFFECTS OF ORGANIZATIONS ON THE INSTITUTIONAL ENVIRONMENT

Organizations *largely,* not only on occasion (see Pfeffer and Salancik, 1978), construct the institutional environment—if not their own environment, then the environments of other organizations. This is not news to the interorganizational theorists, but they typically focus on resource exchange, not on institutional structure (for the classic approach, see Levine and White, 1961; for exceptions, see Turk, 1973, and Turk and Zucker, 1981).

The central question posed here is: What are the sources of organizational power over the institutional environment? It has been answered, albeit implicitly, by Coleman, pointing out the place of the modern corporation in law (1974:14) and the replaceability of individual actors in the corporate context (1974:36). It is answered in this paper by assessing the place of the organizational form in the institutional structure as a whole, arguing that the organizational form serves as the focal defining institution in modern society (also see Zucker, forthcoming). Organizational pervasiveness, stability and change, emergence of new internal organizational structure and process, and even environmental advantages and constraints, are often effects, not sources, of the defining power of organizational form.

Coleman (1974) asserts what interorganizational theorists have long been trying to demonstrate (e.g., Turk, 1973; Levine and White, 1961): organizations interact primarily with other organizations. In Coleman's argument (1974:73), which focuses largely on the problems that the individual actor faces in achieving his/her interest in large organizations, such interaction is the product of the need to create "countervailing corporate actors to offset the power of existing ones". Historical evidence does not provide much support for this argument. One of Coleman's major examples, labor unions, appears to support his argument because they are generally established in times of conflict (e.g., in 1908 in Massachusetts, about 50 percent of all strikes were over the issue of unionization). However, once formed, unions reduce such conflict: in 1909, and continuing for at least three more years, conflicts deriving from the countervailing position of unions in Massachusetts declined to less than 25 percent of all strikes (see Gettermy, 1915). During the same time period (1908–1915), the total number of strikes in Massachusetts increased threefold.

Arguments which are grounded in loss of individual rights fail to account for the rush by individuals to place themselves in an organizational locus. As will be documented in the discussion which follows, the rush to create organizations cannot be explained either by the need to counterbalance the power of existing organizations *or* by any distinct advantage inherent in organizational form (such as increased production efficiency). Rather, the rapid rise and continued spread of the organizational form is best interpreted as an instance of institutionalization: early in the process of diffusion, the organizational form is adopted because it has unequivocal effects on productivity, while later it becomes seen as legitimate to organize formally, regardless of any net benefit. Indeed, the activity may be viewed as "on the margins" of the system, as somehow less important, if it does not occur in a formal organization. Hence, late in the process, plumbers who work out of their homes feel marginal, and may be viewed by others such as contractors as marginal, and wish to incorporate as a business and rent commercial space to replace their garage as storage. Associated management problems may actually reduce the productivity of the plumber; the overhead clearly increases costs. In this case, the organizational form does little positive except to increase legitimacy.[4]

Evidence for the increasing institutional character of organizations must be drawn from a myriad of largely historical sources. The evidence can only be summarized briefly here.[5]

A. Rise in Incorporation and Decline in Nonorganizational Employment

Manufacturing enterprises emerged as formal organizations primarily after 1790 (Davis, 1917:26,32). Manufacturing accounted for only about 15 percent of all exports as late as 1880, and it was not until 1920 that its share rose to 50 percent (Fabricant, 1949). Rise in incorporations was dramatic, as shown in Figure 2 (from Evans, 1948); manufacturing firms account for close to or over half of all incorporations throughout the time period. The same pattern held in England, though a bit earlier (Hunt, 1936). The labor force employed by manu-

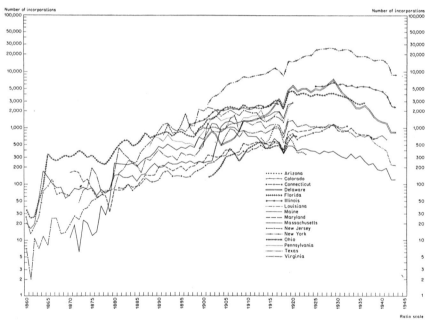

Figure 2.   Business Incorporations, 16 States Annually, 1860–1943. (Source: Evans, 1948.)

Table 4. Change in Self-Employment Rates, 1800 to 1970*

Date	Percent Self-Employed	Percent Wage & Salary Workers
1800	57	12
1860	37	40
1910	22	78
1940	26.1	71.0
1950	21.2	77.2
1960	15.7	83.8
1970	10.2	89.0

*Source for 1800, 1860, 1910: Stanley Lebergott, 1961:292.
**Source for 1940–1970: U.S. Bureau of the Census, 1972:Table 80, 1–374.

facturing firms stayed relatively stable after 1917/18 (Fabricant, 1942:5–6); incorporations also stabilized at about the same period (see Figure 2). Also, there was rapid growth in private production income in manufacturing from the late 1800s until 1920, when the growth peaked; salaries and wages from manufacturing also peaked during the 1920s (Martin, 1940:49,79).

Composition of the labor force during this period also reflected some of the same forces (Fabricant, 1942:5–6, Chart 2): "Entrepreneurs . . . declined both in relation to the total of manufacturing employment and absolutely: there were only half as many factory proprietors in 1937 as there had been in 1899." Fabricant attributes this change to the rapid incorporation between 1899 and 1937. However, it is important to note that during the early period of rapid incorporation in France, the number of proprietors did not drop (see Levy-Leboyer, 1975:90).

Paralleling the rapid rise in incorporation is a systematic decrease in the proportion of self-employment. Table 4 presents data from 1800 to 1970, showing a steady decline from over 50 percent self-employed in 1800 to about 10 percent in 1970. The general explanation for this decrease is the rise of the organizational form; specific forces accounting for the change involve a shift of workers among industries. Workers moved out of agriculture, heavily self-employed, and into manufacturing in the early period and services in the later periods (see Browing and Singelmann, 1978; Singelmann, 1978). But perhaps the story is clearer if the proportion of wage and salary workers is examined. Looking again at Table 4, those earning wages or salaries jumps to 78 percent in 1910 from only 12 percent in 1800, though farming employment was still high. The effects of the rapid rise of incorporation, especially in manufacturing and utilities, is clear. By 1910 the organizational form is dominant; later shifts occur from its gradual diffusion into other areas of the economy.

However, it was not until "home work" was prohibited by law that the organizational form received complete legitimation. As late as 1914 in Massachusetts, there was substantial employment by factories of part-time workers who worked at home [in a survey of 134 factories in Massachusetts, home workers constituted 57.8 percent of the work force (see Massachusetts Bureau of Statistics, 1914)]. According to the Massachusetts data, home work was not confined to a few industries in 1914, but occurred in a wide range, from clothing to jewelry to paper goods. While the home workers were paid wages, the wages were significantly lower than for those employed in the factory. The problem of child labor was significantly greater, with over 20 percent of those employed at home under the age of 14. State statistical reports during this period referred to the "evils of home work." Yet in 1914 only 12 states had any regulation of homework, with only 8 requiring licensing of the places in which such manufacture took place. Few establishments actually obtained the required licenses, since the law was not enforced (see Griffin, 1892; Elkus, 1913; Commons, 1901). Continued abuses of the home work system led to aggressive monitoring of these workers and to extensive lobbying for legislative action. Realizing the ineffectiveness of the regulations already passed, abolition of homework in manufacturing was finally accomplished.[6] At the same time, many persons in the service sector continued to work out of their homes, including professionals such as doctors and lawyers. The movement of such groups into organizations is relatively recent, occurring gradually.

Such changes did not occur without resistance. Incorporations rose dramatically, self-employment dropped, and home work was eliminated, but each change met resistance from institutionalized structures already in existence. It was in the newer areas of industry and, especially, in the newer cities, where less prior institutionalization stood in the way of adoption of the organizational form (see Zucker, 1980b, for a more detailed discussion of new elements as sources of change in highly institutionalized systems). The most compelling evidence on this point is provided by Williamson and Swanson (1966) in their quantitative study of the growth of cities in the northeastern United States from 1820 to 1870. The growth of population during this period, especially 1840–1860, was due "almost entirely to the growth of manufactures" (Bidwell, 1917:834); the cities growing most rapidly were not the older cities (in fact, age was slightly negatively related to growth), but the new cities which were "born" in the preceding decade (Williamson and Swanson, 1966:Table 4.3.A). Williamson and Swanson (1966:57) summarize their principal results as follows:

> The older cities . . . have had a much reduced likelihood of obtaining the growth which young cities enjoyed, since their age implies a set of industrial characteristics and social overhead facilities which are removed from recent technological change. . . . The greater the historical discontinuity in structural and technological change in a specific decade, the more likely that newly-formed cities will have an advantage over the old and that older cities will

suffer from an *equal* disadvantage regardless of age. The latter proposition will be true since all the older cities were "born" during decades of relatively stable cost structures, demand mixes and production functions.

B. Improved Efficiency from Organizational Form

Evidence for the improved efficiency resulting from adopting the organizational form is available for manufacturing. While technological improvements accounted for part of the increase in output per worker, economists studying early manufacturing unanimously attribute much of the gain to organizational factors, including "efficient arrangements of work" (Fabricant, 1942:75; see also Browning and Singelmann, 1978), deriving in part from the assembly line (Ford, 1923; Stone, 1938). Gains in efficiency have also been attributed to "scientific plant and labor management that has permeated industry fairly generally since the 1890s" (Fabricant, 1942:75). The early work of Frederick Taylor (1911) was instrumental in encouraging changes in the organization of plants and in altering activities of workers in a wide spectrum of industries. For example, incentive wage plans were operating in 37 industries by 1924 (Alford, 1928). Implementation and improvement in the organizational form during this early period is thus viewed as "playing an important role in increasing the productivity of industry" by eliminating "waste and the reduction of time and effort" (Fabricant, 1942:76).

It is important to note that the most significant gains per worker in output occurred early in the period—for about four decades after 1899—despite the fact that hours worked per week also dropped dramatically (Fabricant, 1942:46–57), from an average of about 60 hours per week in 1909 (low of 47, high of 66 in different industries) to an average of about 40 in 1937 (low of 33, high of 45).

One way to view the emergence of the social systems and open systems approaches to the study of organizations is to see them as an *apologia* for the limitations of the organizational form: indeed, productivity increases—at least those which were a by-product of organizational form—had nearly reached their limit. So the investigations of the reasons began (see Roethlisberger and Dickson, 1939), with the goal of increasing productivity clearly in mind. Soon these studies gave way to ones investigating the barriers to efficient organizational performance with no special concern for improving performance (e.g., Selznick, 1957; Gouldner, 1959). Uncertainties of the environment then emerged as the major reason why organizations did not perform as expected (e.g., Lawrence and Lorsch, 1967). The lack of organizational control over relevant variables became, as discussed above, the central theme in organizational work, culminating in a denial of the importance of the organization—performance link, replacing it with an organization—personal "well-being" link (see especially Ouchi and Johnson, 1978; Ouchi and Jaeger, 1978). In this latter approach, the key variables became those protective of the workers, including no layoffs, group decision making, informal control, and wholistic concern, rather than firm productivity or innovative capacity (Ouchi and Gibson, 1980:Table 3).

Historical evidence suggests that this shift in focus was not a product simply of changes in the intellectual zeitgeist, but primarily of changes in the gains to be realized from adopting the organizational form. There are two principal aspects of these changes. First, activities which most directly benefited from formal organization were those incorporated first [e.g., manufacturing and public utilities, but not construction, agriculture or service (see Evans, 1948:Ch. 7, Table 23)]. This follows the pattern already demonstrated for initial adoption of innovations which later became institutionalized (Zucker and Tolbert, 1981).

C. Spread of the Organizational Form

The gradual diffusion outward following the initial adoption in manufacturing, as the organizational form became institutionalized, affected areas of human activity which had less to gain directly from the organizational mode of operation, though most gained indirectly through its legitimating properties. At the same time, formally organizing often entials considerable costs for these later adopters.

One example is particularly striking. Social movements, often loose collectivities directed toward social action and change, have increasingly adopted the organizational form. The writings about social movements clearly reflect this trend, with the early work emphasizing the collective character (e.g., Turner and Killian, 1957; Smelser, 1963a) and later work emphasizing the organizational properties (see especially McCarthy and Zald, 1973 and 1977; Snow et al., 1980).[7] Once again, this change in emphasis reflects historical change. Using the sample of nonprofit organizations listed in the *Encyclopedia of Associations* (1961, 1964, 1968, 1970, 1972, 1974), it is clear that these groups increasingly adopt formal structures, with dramatic increase in the size of paid staff over the 1961–1974 time period. Further, McCarthy and Zald (1973:16) report an increase in specialized training of social workers as staff for positions in social movement organizations, with an absolute increase of over 300 percent in the yearly supply between 1965 and 1969. Such increases in staff and professionalization may entail real costs for social movements—costs which may not be offset by gains in legitimacy given that the goals of the group are often at variance with those in society at large. These costs might range from the purely economic (e.g., replacing volunteer labor with paid staff) to the symbolic (e.g., rapid routinization of charisma).

Another example will serve to clarify the general point that the organizational form, after initial adoption, diffused outward to structure associations which were not obviously in need of the formal patterning characteristic of manufacturing firms. Local government in the late 1800s was more like a social movement than a formal organization: it was designed to reflect public opinion and to represent the dominant political interests, with minimal service delivery functions (Griffith, 1974a). The initial stimulus for change in government structure was its rampant corruption (in the form of political machines) and widespread dissatisfaction with government performance (Wiebe, 1967:4–5; Wheeler, 1885). The call for change was picked up as a major platform by the Progressive Movement (Griffith, 1974b:15), which because of its emphasis on Scientific Management [again derived from Taylor (1911)] attempted to change the conception of a city from a "political body" to a "business corporation," with the city "a joint stock affair in which the taxpayers are the stockholders" (Crandon, 1886/7:524; Clinton, 1886). As in the case of industries, cities with the most to gain from change of practices adopted such features early, specifically civil service procedures. Early adoption (1885–1904), as discussed above, is predicted by the percent foreign born and by the complexity of municipal structure, but later adoption (1915–1934) is not predicted by city characteristics (Zucker and Tolbert, 1981). In the case of cities, the adoption of formal structure derived from scientific management principles altered the basic premise of local government, from representation to service delivery, preceding a phenomenal rise in employment in local government (see Fabricant, 1952).

Hence, following the initial adoption of the organization form in manufacturing and utilities, it diffused outward as a "scientific" innovation which legitimated the practices of local governments and, eventually, even more loosely organized collectivities—social movements. Many features of modern society can be traced from the early organizational transformations of government, which initiated the most significant change in the industrial structure: the rise of the service sector (Browning and Singelmann, 1978; Singelmann, 1978). Once the ideology of government as an efficient business enterprise was entrenched, the functional areas of service delivery multiplied rapidly at all levels. Government services expanded rapidly and steadily beginning in 1900, through the spread of old services and the addition of new, at all levels of government (Fabricant, 1952:58):

> In not a single major function of the federal government, the state governments, or the several types of local government did expenditures fall, or even rise less than prices over the 40 or 50 years [1900–1949]. . . . In not a single function of the federal government, the cities, or New York and Vermont, two states for which we have detailed records, did the number of workers actually decline.

Social services not under direct governmental authority also expanded continuously during this period, with the rate of growth accelerating in each decade since 1920. This expansion can be attributed principally to state action in health and education, and only to a minor degree to demographic change (Browing and Singelmann, 1978). The expansion of the service sector, both governmental and nongovernmental, coupled with its focus on social action in the 1960s (War on Poverty), probably contributed substantially to the observed change in paid staff size and professionalization in social movements, as discussed above. Such collective action groups as the Mission Coalition Organization in San Francisco became transformed during the mid-1960s from a loosely organized, participatory action group pushing for more services for Latinos to a highly structured, formal organization with paid staff and heavy direct involvement in delivery of social services (Weissman and Zucker, 1975).

D. Stability of the Organizational Form

Initially, organizational form was adopted rationally to handle large-scale production and to create predictable conditions of work, as the evidence provided previously suggests. As long as the organization was efficient/effective, it survived; but if it faltered, there was no rescue attempt: it died, merged, or otherwise lost its identity.[8] However, as the organizational form gained legitimacy and diffused outward to organize most economic, political, and (later) collective activities, it became a taken-for-granted element, so that it was unthinkable for a new business or political activity to take place *not* located in an organizational structure. Hence, corporations and government agencies both proliferated, and at the same

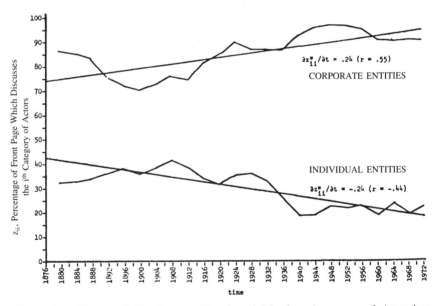

Figure 3.   Slopes of Continuous Trend and Moving Averages of Attention Given to Individual vs. Corporate Entities from 1877 to 1972. (Slopes are corrected as demonstrated in Appendix C and moving average of time t is the arithmetic average of the four-year interval of t with the four-year intervals before and after t.) (Source: Burt, 1975.)

time became institutionalized both objective and exterior (see Zucker, 1977). Further support for this trend comes from the analysis of mass media records (the front page of the *New York Times*) from 1877 to 1972 (see Figure 3, reproduced from Burt, 1975). Increasing attention is given to corporate actors and decreasing attention is given to persons, so that by 1972, corporate entities dominate the front page (85–95 percent), while individual entities are discussed only 20–30 percent of the time. The 1920s again appears to be the critical turning point, where corporate entities begin a more stable increasing pattern, and individual entities begin a more stable decreasing pattern. Indeed, a number of economic historians have pointed to this period as a critical one for the corporation (Chandler, 1969; Galambos, 1966; Edwards, 1975).

Major consequences of institutionalization of any element of culture are maintenance of it over time and resistance to change (Zucker, 1977). Hence, if the organizational form became institutionalized during the 1920s, then increasing stability in firms should be observed. Table 5 summarizes the major results from a series of studies on corporate stability, showing that prior to 1917 the failure rate of firms was substantially greater than the failure rate after 1917 (Edwards, 1975). As shown in column 2, few exits were caused by merger in the pre-1917 period, but a much higher proportion of exits were caused by "failure to grow" and "liquidation." Firms failed at least eight times more frequently in the pre-1917 than in the post-1917 period. The same general trend holds true for nonmanufacturing firms (Edwards, 1975:Appendix Table III, p. 446).

Kaplan's (1964) data provide especially clear support for the hypothesized critical character of the 1920s. He found that only 31 firms in the top 100 in 1909 survived to the 1960 list; 69 failed to do so. But of these 69, 55 percent (38) had moved off the list permanently by 1919. As Edwards (1975:432) has pointed out, "if the sixty-nine failures had been spaced evenly over the fifty-one-year span, only 13.5 would have been expected to fail by 1919 versus the thirty-eight that actually failed." More limited evidence is available for failure rates among the top 50 firms between 1906 and 1950 (Friedland, 1957). Almost 60 percent of the 1906 group were not included in the 50 largest for 1928; in sharp contrast, only 28 percent of the 1928 group were not included among the 50 in 1950. There is also some evidence from other countries of high rates of business failure among all sizes and types of organizations. For example, high rates of failure have been documented for England before 1900 (Hunt, 1936:157).

It should be noted that the common explanation for the increasing stability— increasing concentration—does not explain changes in overall stability, since the concentration of production and distribution by a few large firms occurred only in some industries. In leather and leather products, publishing, lumber, furniture, and apparel, there is very little evidence of concentration in the twentieth century (Chandler, 1969:Chart 1). In industries with a moderate degree of concentration (textiles, paper, and fabricated metal), most of this change came after 1940, so an explanation of the changes in failure rate observed from the 1920s forward

Table 5. Stability of the Organizational Form: Reasons for Exits from List of Top 100 Industrial Firms, 1903–1969*

Time Periods and Source	(1) Total Exits	(2) Exits by Merger**	(3) Exits by Dissolution	(4) Exits by Failure to Grow	(5) Exits by Liquidation	(6) Col. 4–5/years	(7) Col. 5/years
1903–1917 (Edwards 1975)	34	7	0	18	9	1.93	0.64
1909–1917 (Kaplan 1965; Collins & Preston 1961)	35	3	1	27	4	3.88	0.50
1917–1967 (Navin 1970)	32	25	0	2	5	0.14	0.10
1917–1967 (Forbes 1967)	31	23	0	1	7	0.16	0.14
1919–1960 (Kaplan 1964)	25	16	0	4	5	0.22	0.12
1919–1958 (Collins & Preston 1961)	25	16	0	5	4	0.23	0.10
1919–1969 (Edwards 1975)	40	30	0	2	8	0.20	0.16

Source: Modified from Edwards, 1975:Table 3.
*Studies using a base different from the top 100 were adjusted (Navin base, 101; Forbes, 98; Kaplan, 98; Collins and Preston, 97; Edwards, 110). See references for full sources.
**French data on mergers, based on all firms listed on the Paris stock exchange, is strikingly similar: low prior to 1920 (varying from 1.6 to 9.6), jumping to 19 in 1920–24, and to 29.4 in 1925–29 (Houssiaux, 1958:340). The largest French firms were nationalized and are not included.

22

cannot be provided. Finally, in industries with relatively high degrees of concentration, the 1920s actually saw a decrease in the percentage of concentrated industrial groups. Only electrical machinery and instruments showed substantial increases, with a substantial drop in the percent of product value attributed to concentration in electrical machinery (Chandler, 1969:Charts 1 and 2).

The rate of organizational "exits" from the top 100 is a compelling index of stability, despite the common misinterpretation that it reflects increasing concentration. However, because of its traditional interpretation, another index of firm stability will be examined here. The interindustry wage structure is extremely stable, especially so since the early 1900s. An examination of 84 industries indicates that the correlation of the structure of earnings from 1899 to 1950 is extremely high, ranging from .72 to .94 (Cullen, 1956:359, Table II). Table 6 presents the basic results concerning dispersion of the wage structure over this time period. The general impression is one of overall stability, with generally

Table 6. Dispersion of Structure of Annual Earnings, 1899–1950

Date	Interquartile Range − Median × 100	High-Low Percent Differential*	High Vs. Low Wage 1899 Industries Percent Differential**
1899	27.4	162	162
1904	30.0	163	162
1909	25.7	159	153
1914	25.1	160	153
1919	23.5	172	155
1921	21.7	155	141
1923	23.2	159	148
1925	24.2	155	145
1927	25.5	153	146
1929	24.8	158	155
1931	21.1	151	133
1933	22.3	153	135
1935	19.8	160	139
1937	27.9	175	163
1939	30.1	175	153
1947	25.7	151	143
1949[a]	23.0	156	143
1950[aa]	25.4	156	149

Source: Modified from Cullen, 1956:Table III. 84 industries in each year, except as noted.

*For each year, the median of the average annual earnings in those industries forming the top quarter of the earnings structure divided by the median of the average annual earnings in those industries forming the lowest quarter of the earnings structure.

**For each year, the differential between the median earnings in the 21 industries which ranked highest in 1899 and the 21 which ranked lowest in 1899—regardless of the relative position of these industries in subsequent years.

[a]70 industries.

[aa]76 industries.

less stability at the turn of the century. The high–low earnings differential shows higher differences prior to 1921, with generally decreasing differentials except in the late 1930s.

The federal government agency structure reflects these same stabilizing forces. Agencies which deal with industrial and commercial development or regulation originated and remained as small agencies, with high turnover prior to 1920 (Fabricant, 1952:66–77). Many of the permanent powerful agencies dealing with industrial and commercial development or regulation were established in the early 1900s: Bureau of Standards (1901); Bureau of Foreign and Domestic Commerce (1912); Tariff Commission (1916); Board of Governors of the Federal Reserve System (1913); Federal Trade Commission (1914); National Advisory Committee for Aeronautics (1915); Food and Drug Administration (1928). Agencies dealing with labor relations also emerged during this period (e.g., Employees' Compensation Commission, 1916), though most of the major agencies did not appear until after 1930 (e.g., National Labor Relations Board, 1935). Except for labor relations, the government was proactive, not reactive, stepping in officially *before* the organizational society really emerged (for support, see Caves, 1964:Ch. 4; for the counterargument, see Coleman, 1974).

The history of the organizational form since the 1920s records many attempts by the federal government to increase organizational stability through deliberate action. These attempts were primarily indirect before 1940, including federal insurance of bank deposits, but since then have become increasingly direct and frequent, ranging from covering the railroad bad debts to recent direct loans to major corporations (Lockheed, Chrysler). Very recently, states have taken an active role, designed to protect employment in their states; several states in the Midwest have made major loans to Chrysler.

E.   Overview

Organizations not only are pervasive but also have largely redefined modern society. The initial adoption, closely linked to improved efficiency in manufacturing and utilities, succeeded in legitimating formal, rational structure. Seen in objective, nonpersonal terms, and as an exterior, taken-for-granted element of the social system, organizational form became institutionalized. It diffused outward to other kinds of collective activity, including political systems and, most recently, social movements. Further, once institutionalized, organizations became highly stable. Before 1917, the largest organizations frequently failed to grow or were liquidated; after 1917 the failure rate decreased dramatically. Interindustry wage stability provides additional evidence for the expected maintenance of institutional structure and its resistance to change once established.

Organizations, then, transformed their environment in the United States. However, little evidence has been provided so far in this discussion concerning the processes by which this transformation took place. In the next two sections of this paper, the mechanisms of institutional integration and cognitive representation will be delineated. As has been argued elsewhere, explaining change in institutional structures must rest on the same aspects which predict their stability (Zucker, 1980b); change rests on the integration of the new structure with the old. Also, institutionalization is fundamentally a cognitive process. In order for an element of culture to have both objective and exterior qualities, there must be cognitive representations so that for things to be otherwise is *literally* unthinkable (Zucker, 1977, 1981).

VI.   INSTITUTIONAL INTEGRATION: FAMILY AND FORMAL ORGANIZATIONS

A fundamental aspect of the cultural system of any society is its system(s) of classification (Durkheim and Mauss, 1903). With any sweeping institutional change, then, the classificatory systems can also be expected to change. The basic argument here is that it is necessary for the old and new classificatory systems to be integrated, at least to some degree, for successful institutionalization of the new classification.

The stratification system is commonly identified as the most pervasive classification system in any society. Stratification systems have conventionally been treated as conveyers of prestige, and less centrally, as task (role) allocation mechanisms (see Parsons, 1954; Tumin, 1967). Because of the generally functional approach—stratification exists to allocate and reward (see Davis and Moore, 1950) societal tasks—change in stratification systems has been seen as a response to change in the nature of the tasks to be allocated, and as a rational process of reallocation of societal rewards and resources (see Smelser, 1963b). The changes are generally described as rapid, sudden, and transforming.

However, systems of societal classification are generally quite resistant to change, with common intersubjective understandings of them (on kinship, see Radcliffe-Brown, 1952; on occupations, see Balkwell et al., 1980). Institutional structures are transformed, but slowly. The dual character of societies undergoing transition, generally through economic development, has been noted in the literature (Boeke, 1930; Hoselitz, 1966). But this dualism has been perceived largely as a function of particular societal values—*Gemeinschaft* societies—and thus only are applicable to a small range of social systems (see, for example, Boeke, 1947; Barber, 1961).

Here it is argued that societal systems of classification (leaving aside, for the present, the question of evaluative content) are indeed very resistant to change, and that only gradually is one classification replaced by another, with remnants or vestiges of the previous system present for long periods of time. Ogburn (1924), in his theory of cultural lag, took a similar position. However, here the lag is not seen as dysfunctional, and (as the examples below will clarify) the old

LIBRARY OF MOUNT ST. MARY'S COLLEGE EMMITSBURG, MARYLAND

system of classification quickly becomes integrated with the new, in this case at least in a supportive fashion. To be more specific, the traditional kinship system in the United States was quickly folded into the occupational system that emerged with modern economic systems (prior to industrialization). The new stratification system (based on occupation) was initially subordinated to the old [based on kinship; note that in other cultures it was based on tribes and clans (see Cohen, 1969)]. The process of change, then, is expected to involve the integration of pre-existing societal classification systems with emergent classification. emergent classification.

In fact, there are some cases where the new classification system, at least temporarily, is isomorphic with the old. This phenomenon has been over-generalized in some anthropological work—viewed as the customary process instead of the extreme case—producing expectations that all classifications are integrated into a unitary whole (see Radcliffe-Brown, 1951; Fortes, 1969; and Durkheim and Mauss, 1903). Evidence to support the pervasive integration of classification has been drawn largely from the Australian primitive peoples, and yet even this limited evidence has been extensively challenged. It is likely that in the extreme case, societal classifications may form a unitary system. However, more commonly, articulation between these classifications is rough, with exceptions the rule (for a classic statement, see Hughes, 1945). More complete integration probably occurs in the early stages of change in classification systems. Here it is argued that the emergence of the organizational form produced a new classification—a classification which initially was isomorphic with the old kinship system. In early economic organization, kin ties served as the fundamental organizing principle (P. D. Hall, 1977:40):

> The family was . . . the center of economic activity, for there were no banks, insurance companies, corporations, or other formal organizations. . . . Because of the intimacy of the relationship of partners, the personal nature of capital, and the fact that the survival of the individual merchant and his family was at stake in all business transactions, it is hardly surprising that primary commercial ties were concentrated within a small circle of kin.

Table 7 summarizes data available in more detail in P. D. Hall (1977:41,49). Indeed, at the end of the seventeenth century "economic organization was domestic organization" (Laslett, 1965:3–4), but the dramatic change over time is apparent in Table 7. By 1750, business partners were significantly less likely to be kin, and by 1800 less than half of the sons of the business elite were selecting business as their career. The era of widespread occupational inheritance was over, though the effects of family—mediated through educational attainment, as the educational system began to expand rapidly (Kaestle, 1973; Schultz, 1973; J. W. Meyer et al., 1979)—remain a significant determinant of occupational attainment to the present (for a recent statement, see Duncan et al., 1972).

As might be expected, such integration and rapid transformation did not occur in most societies. In France, for example, kin relations remained of fundamental

Table 7. Kin Partnership, 1690–1779, and Inheritance of Occupation, 1680–1839, Among the Boston Brahmins

Birth Cohorts of Fathers	Business Partnership*		Choice of Same Occupation As Father**		
	Kin Partner Percent	Alone or Non-kin Percent	Business Percent	Law and Medicine Percent	Other*** Percent
1680–1719	92	8	88.6	11.4	—
1720–1759	83.9	16.1	78.3	7.4	2.6
1760–1779	80.4	19.4	54.9	10.7	2.6
1780–1799	—	—	51.6	9.1	2.7
1800–1819	—	—	40.5	12.4	1.8
1820–1839	—	—	29.5	13.1	5.7

Source: Modified from Hall, 1977.

*Families included are: Cabot, Higginson, Jackson, Lee, and Lowell.

**Families included are: Amory, Cabot, Codman, Higginson, Jackson, Lawrence, Lee, Lowell, and Peabody.

***Data is so scattered among occupations that it is best to interprete these percentages as showing a lack of significant relation (no time trend).

importance in economic relations even in 1962 (Levy-Leboyer, 1975). Firms in France remained smaller than in most industrial countries in both the 1800s and 1900s, even when controlling for industry. For example, in 1962 the percentage of the labor force working in small (fewer than 100 worker) firms is 27 percent for automobile, engineering, and shipbuilding sectors, in sharp contrast to 15 percent in Germany and 16 percent in the United States.

Much slower transformation has occurred in other countries. Various explanations have been offered for this finding, with two principal explanations emerging: (1) a cultural explanation, with certain societies "based on social principles antithetical to those of modern society" (Hoselitz, 1966); and (2) a domination explanation, asserting that it is the direct interference from the outside at a critical stage of development that prevents "modernization" (Moulder, 1977). A much broader explanation based on institutionalization can be offered: when, for one of a large number of reasons, the existing institutionalized classification system fails to become integrated with the new classification system, change will occur much more slowly and in a disjoint fashion. General conditions under which this will occur include: (1) supplanting of traditional classification system(s) in such a way as to invalidate the old system [e.g., through extensive missionary activity such as occurred in China (see Moulder, 1977)]; and (2) sudden transformation through rapid "modernization," causing segmental change, so that one part of the population retains the old traditional classifications while another part adopts the new classifications, with no overlapping categories [the rapid migration often accompanying modernization exacerbates the problems (see Cohen, 1969)].

As classification complexity increases, so does potential for change. Fundamentally, change begets change. Any new classification system which emerges not only creates new categories, but also modifies existing categories simply by posing problems of interrelation: change accelerates to the extent that two or more classification systems are integrated, since alteration in any element(s) of one classification produces change in the related element(s) of the other classification(s). The rate of change should be at a minimum when only one societal classification system is in use, or when multiple systems are in use but are unrelated to each other; the rate of change should be at a maximum when the classification systems are hierarchically arranged, so that when one element changes it alters not only those other elements with which it is directly related, but also all those elements to which it is hierarchically superior. For example, change was minimal in the Virginia Company settlement at Jamestown as long as organizational status served as the sole classification system. But as other systems emerged, change was accelerated until finally "statuses outside the organization came largely to dictate . . . behavior" (Diamond, 1958:473).

If the emergent classification system is caused by or causes transformation in the societal normative system, then the emergent classification system will become intersubjective rapidly, and over time may erode or eclipse the importance

Table 8. Social Involvement of Organizations and the Extent to Which They Incorporate Elements of Bureaucratic Rationality*

Social Involvement	None	Limited Objectives	Segmental Participation	Performance Emphasis	Specific Job Assignment	Task Specialization	Compensatory Rewards	Central Management
Political Ascription	2	0	4	3	0	0	0	0
Kinship Ascription	0	1	1	0	0	0	0	0
Compulsory Reciprocity	0	0	4	1	0	1	0	0
Self-commitment, Socially Required	0	0	0	0	6	3	0	0
Voluntary Self-commitment	0	0	0	0	0	0	2	6

Source: Udy, 1962.

*The values reported are the actual number of organizations (societies) with the means of determining organizational position cross-tabulated with the organizational scale type. Udy reports a $X2 = 62.79$ (p < .001), collapsing the first three social involvement categories and the organizational scale type (first four categories, then the next two, and then the final two).

of the pre-existing bases for stratification. One indicator, independent of classification, is the redefinition of the value of rewards (and costs) distributed in the society. In the past, members of the cultural system may have been rewarded highly for loyalty to the family unit, which included injunctions against secrecy among family members; currently, they are rewarded more for loyalty to the workplace, with secrets (confidential documents, most especially government classified as secret) expected and even required by law to be kept from family members. Culture change takes place through an initial integration of preexisting classification systems, followed by a reduction in their taken-for-granted intersubjective support, and eventually a replacement or modification of them through the predominance of a new classification system that becomes intersubjective.

A study of early bureaucratic development clarifies this point. In a study of thirty-four production organizations in thirty-four nonindustrial societies, it was found that "socially involved organizations" (those where participation rested on ascriptive criteria external to the organization such as kinship) had fewer of the criteria posited by Weber as characteristics of rational bureaucracy (Udy, 1962). Table 8 summarizes Udy's major findings, where rationality forms a Guttman scale with a coefficient of reproducibility of .95 (that is, if an organization has "segmental participation" it also has "limited objectives," but does not necessarily have "specific job assignment"). The real "breaking point" in Table 8 occurs with specific job assignment: as organizational members are classified in the organization, the other bases of classification external to the organization become much less significant. The findings indicate that as organizational classifications become predominant, classifications based on other, particularly ascriptive, characteristics decline in importance.

A. Methods of Obtaining Jobs

One of the clearest examples of the integration of and change in the kinship and occupational stratification systems involves the method by which people obtain jobs. As discussed above, Udy's (1962) results highlight the transition from kin classification to organizational (occupational) classification. Only when occupation is present do the ascriptive aspects of social involvement disappear, and the self-commitment aspects emerge.

Job search has always—to varying degrees—involved the use of kin. As emphasized above, until the 1800s job search was limited in the majority of cases to the kin network, especially in business (refer again to Table 7). In early industrial development in most societies, persons are allocated to jobs either because of their kin relationships [e.g., in family businesses (see Marris and Somerset, 1971; Geertz, 1969)] or through personal networks using a patron–client system (Wolf, 1966). In the United States by the 1900s there were few family businesses; kin (and friends) assumed the function of job referral. The following quotes from workers who had quit or had been laid off from a textile mill illustrate the role of relatives and friends (Myers and Shultz, 1951:48–9):

> There was a woman working in the mill, and she was working with my father-in-law. . . . Dad saw her one day and . . . found out where she was working. I went to see the woman, and asked her if she thought I could get a job there. . . .

> My brother-in-law is a foreman at the shoe shop. . . . He said he could get me in with no trouble at all. So I went there straight off.

> My wife heard about my job through a friend of hers, who learned it from a sister-in-law who works there. You have to have all your friends on the lookout to find a job now.

Table 9 summarizes the results of some of the major studies on job search, asking comparable questions, from 1930 to 1970. Generally, the role of relatives has not been separated from the role of friends in the research reports. However, the examples given above, drawn from one of the earlier studies (Myers and Schultz, 1951), heavily emphasize kin relations, even though one case above would be coded in the "friend" category. [Some additional evidence on the role of kin in a neighboring town, Manchester, N.H., during an earlier time period can be found in Hareven (1978). Over 75 percent of the workers had at least one member of the family working in the textile mill at some time]. A later study, conducted by the U.S. Department of Labor (1973), did categorize friends and relatives separately. These data are not reported in Table 9 because of its complexity. This study found that relatives were significantly less likely to be used to gain the present job than were friends (17.9 percent of the cases involved friends; only 8.3 percent involved relatives).

There are two conclusions that can be drawn directly from the data in Table 9, the first more uniformly supported than the second: (1) Relatives and friends (most commonly those already working in the firm) serve as an important contact in job search throughout the thirty-five years examined, with the role especially significant earlier in the time period; (2) Over time, there has been a diminishing role for relatives and friends (the Reynolds study being an exception), largely in favor of increased direct application to the employer at the firm or through newspaper ads. Figure 4 graphs these trends. Dividing the time period into three major blocks, the values for both use of family/friends and for direct contract with the employer were significantly different (by chi-square, $p < .01$).

These findings also suggest that kin ties not only are important in early industrialization, but continue—until perhaps very recently—to be a basis for recruitment, though to a gradually declining degree. The importance of these findings are not so much to challenge the prevailing sociological theories of family breakdown under the impact of industrialization (see Smelser, 1959)—Anderson (1972) has already done that—but rather to identify a transformation of the kin role. Kin classification systems are of less importance, to be sure, but they survived well beyond industrialization as bridges to the occupational structure.

Table 9. Methods of Finding Present Job, 1930 to 1972*

| | | | | Relatives/Friends | | Direct Contact with Firm | | | | |
| | | | | | | At Gate | | Newspaper Ads | | |
Study	Date	Labor Market	City Size (000)	Percent	(N)	Percent	(N)	Percent	(N)	Total N
de Schweinitz	1930	Philadelphia	2,000	58	(2320)	23	(900)	3	(120)	4,000
Myers-Maclaurin	1937	Fitchberg, Pa.	60	39	(273)	33	(230)	2	(14)	694
Reynolds and Reynolds-Shister	1947	New Haven, Conn.	350	28	(221)	31	(235)	9	(77)	800
Myers-Shultz	1948–49	Nashua, N.H.	50	39	(73)	18	(30)	6	(6)	195
Miernyk	1951–52	Small towns	80–100	46	(336)	32	(253)	9	(50)	733
Wilcock-Franke	1960–62	Midwestern towns	70–670	43	(595)	27	(371)	—	—	1383
Sheppard-Belitsky	1963	Erie Cnty., Penn.	130	56	(76)	14	(19)	4	(5)	136
Lurie-Rayack	1964	Middletown, Conn.	39	32	(84)	47	(125)	3	(7)	250
Zubrow et al.	1969	Denver, Col.	610	17	(284)	37	(586)	12	(68)	1349
Dept. of Labor	1972	National	—	26	(2735)	35	(3643)	15	(1566)	10437

Sources: See reference for each entry in table.

*Stern and Johnson, 1968, and Granovetter, 1974, also report data concerning methods used to find present job; however, both deal with atypical labor market processes—rapid upward mobility in the first case, and heavily academic employment, often in new positions, in the second case.

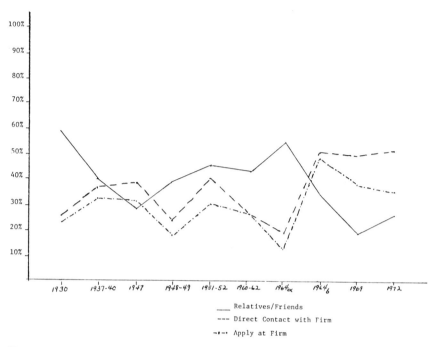

Figure 4. Methods of Finding Present Job, 1930–1972.

This was one way in which integration of the two classification systems was achieved.

Before turning to linguistic evidence reflecting the kin to occupation change, a very brief summary of two of the other indicators of family–job interrelationships provides some additional support for the main point: (1) Immigrants rely heavily on family for job placement and other support (Hareven, 1978), especially those with blue-collar occupations and rural origins (Tilly and Brown, 1967); and (2) Marriage patterns have shifted from first-cousin marriage and sibling exchange (the marriage of two children in one family to two children in another family), common in the 1700s (P. D. Hall, 1977:42–6), to broad family alliances (the making of kin "connections"), to general similarity in socioeconomic background of families, to—most recently—occupational attainment (Skolnick, 1973). Again, both the integration of kin and occupational structure and the increasing shift toward occupational classification as the basis for stratification can be seen.

B. Linguistic Changes in Kinship and Occupational Terminology

One of the most basic indicators of cultural centrality is the structure of the language itself. The more elaborate classification systems are, the more important those elements of culture are thought to be (Durkheim and Mauss, 1903). There is a growing body of evidence that the shorter the expression is, the greater the intersubjective understanding (Zucker, 1981), the more likely it is to be remembered [high recall (see Brown and Lenneberg, 1964)], and the more frequently it is actually used in everyday expression (Rose, 1965). Language, then, plays a central role in cultural expression and perhaps in cultural definition (Kluckhohn and Leighton, 1947:197):

> Every people has its own characteristic classes in which individuals pigeonhole their experi-
> ence. These classes are established primarily by the language through the types of objects,
> processes, or qualities which receive special emphasis in the vocabulary. . . . The language
> says, as it were, "Notice this," "Always consider this separate from that," "Such and such
> things belong together." . . . Every language has an effect upon what the people who use it
> see, what they feel, how they think, what they can talk about.

A great deal of attention has been focused on kinship in the anthropological literature. For the past twenty years or more, the effort has been concentrated on the attempt to discover a set of fundamental principles by which every known kinship system can be described. This has led to the formation of a number of well-known types (e.g., the Crow type). Hence, the philosophic approach has been reductionist to reduce the confusing array of terms to their common elements. The approach taken here is just the opposite. Three principles are used to differentiate types of kinship systems: (1) the degree to which the classification system differentiates kin types (e.g., daughter of sister vs. daughter of brother); (2) the length of the term or expression; and (3) whether the term or expression is compound, that is, composed of another kin term, plus a modifier (such as brother-in-law or stepmother). Each of these elements is expected to reflect (and possibly effect) the cultural centrality of the classification system and its related terminology: the most central classification systems contain more terms for differentiating members of the culture—terms which are briefer than those used in other classification systems.

Because of the interest among anthropologists in reducing all kinship terminology to a common small number of relationships, there have been few studies of change in kinship terminology over time. Indeed, it is not uncommon to cite studies done twenty or thirty years apart to justify the description of a particular kinship system, with any differences attributed to observer error or observation of a slightly different subtribal area. Hence, the evidence has to be largely cross-cultural, comparing societies which do not have elaborate occupational structures to those which do.

The evidence is compelling, but because of its complexity it can can only be briefly summarized here (see Zucker, forthcoming, for a more detailed analysis). Table 10 presents the results. Societies which do not have extensive occupational classifications have kinship classification systems which are two to three times as complex as societies which have extensive occupational classifications.[9] Further,

Table 10. Complexity of Classification Systems:
Comparing Kinship and Occupational Terminology
(N = 20)*

Occupational Terms	Kinship Terminology			
	High Complexity		Low Complexity**	
	Percent	(N)	Percent	(N)
High Complexity	16.7%	(2)	62.5%	(5)
Low Complexity	83.3%	(10)	37.5%	(3)

Source: See Zucker, forthcoming.
*Chi square = 7.18, p < .01. Complexity determined by the number of kin terms, and number of occupational terms, in a society, standardized for complexity of the language (e.g., by dividing number of kin terms by the total number of words in the native language dictionary).
**The curvilinear hypothesis (Blumberg and Winch, 1972) would lead to the expectation that differences in this column would be less striking: societies at a low level of complexity have neither detailed kin nor occupational categories.

the kinship terms of the former societies appear to be shorter, though because of the difficulty the variety of languages poses, number of letters rather than the preferable number of syllables is the measure. The case for compound terms is clearer. Societies without extensive occupational terminology use fewer compound terms—measured as a percent of all kin terms—though some compound terms are found in most societies.

The richness of occupational terminology has not been as thoroughly studied as kin terminology by others. Most of those interested in occupational terminology have been concerned with the status of occupations, often looking over time and across nations to examine occupational ranking (see Treiman, 1975). However, one study did examine changes over time in both the number of occupations and the distribution of individuals across these occupations for the United States, 1900–1950 (Labovitz and Gibbs, 1964). Table 11 (modified form of their Table 1), reports the Gibbs–Martin (1962) measure of degree of division of labor $[D = 1 - \Sigma X^2 /(\Sigma X)^2]$, where D is the degree of division of labor and X is the number of individuals in each occupational category. To compute D, data on occupations were derived from census reports and detailed occupations were analyzed in two ways: (1) as "constant," using all occupations reported in 1900 for each census year; and (2) as "variable," using all occupations reported in any given census year. Again, the results in Table 11 support the contention that the greatest amount of institutional change occurred early in the 1900s, becoming significantly more stable after 1920. This is especially true if the change in complexity of the classification system is taken into account (see column 2).

Table 11.   Change in the Degree of the
Division of Labor in the United States,
1900–1950

	Measures	
	(1)	(2)
	Constant	*Variable*
Date	*Occupations**	*Occupations***
1900	.918	.918
1910	.943	.955
1920	.953	.962
1930	.963	.970
1940	.968	.975
1950	.974	.981

Source: Labovitz, 1964: Table 1.
*The D measure for each year is based on the occupational
categories reported in 1900.
**The D measure is based on the occupations reported in each
census year, i.e., 253 in 1900, 308 in 1910, 313 in 1920, 316
in 1930, 372 in 1940, 372 in 1950.

One more piece of evidence should be cited. This is the striking decrease in the word length of corporate names from 1880 to 1960 (Boddewyn, 1967:41): "The first eight manufacturing firms to be incorporated (1789 to 1800) had names almost twice as long (6.4 words) as those of corporations in 1960." Early corporations tended to be explicit about their activities, so that only 4 percent of the firms incorporated by 1860 failed to mention product, process, or function in their name. Table 12 shows once again that most of the change occurred prior to

Table 12.   Changes in Corporate Names,
1800 to 1960*

Date	*No. of Words per Firm*	*Proportion With No Reference to Product or Activity*
1800	6.4	—
1880	4.1	14%
1900	—	29%
1920	—	32%
1940	3.2	33%
1960	3.5	43%

Source: Data from Boddewyn, 1967.

1920; relative stability obtains after that early period. The shortening of the name, largely by elimination of a description of activity, indicates the increasing common understanding of corporate identity, so that "shorthand" expressions suffice.

VII. CONCLUSIONS

A wide array of evidence has been assembled here to demonstrate that organizations are institutions—indeed, the central defining institution of modern cultural systems. No one piece of the evidence is convincing by itself; there are counterarguments already available in the literature in some of the areas. However, taken as a whole it provides a basis for asserting that the organizational form has become institutionalized.

Organizations are intersubjectively defined, with most elements being taken for granted as part of the "way things are." They are seen as nonpersonal—the "ideal type" of a cultural element defined independently of personal characteristics. Offices, located in organizations, are seen as fundamentally divorced from personal characteristics, and any action by incumbents is thought to be potentially repeatable by others if they occupy the same position without changing the meaning of the action. One indicator of the role that organizations play is their rapid emergence as important forms (corporate actors, not individual actors) and their stability, which suddenly increased when organizations became defined intersubjectively as important institutional forms. A second indicator of the defining role that organizations play is the power of redefinition which organizational context has. A simple shift in organizational context radically and suddenly redefines the normative structure and hence the appropriate action for members to take. Another indicator is the power of new organizational positions in changing the status of individual organizational members.

Finally, organizational classifications have become fundamental to the classification systems in modern industrial societies. After an initial period of kin dominance in occupational structures, the kin and occupational systems were integrated, with occupational systems gradually coming to define relationships which were previously seen as kin based. The job search literature provides evidence on this point. But the cognitive importance of organization-based as opposed to kin-based terminology becomes apparent only when examining the structure of language itself: kin classifications are much more elaborate in cultures with few occupational titles.

The purpose of this paper is not to provide the final evidence for a theory of organizations as institutions. Rather, it is designed to indicate the basic outlines which such a theory might take, to stimulate additional work on the general theory of institutionalization, and to make explicit a research agenda on organizations which takes into account their institutional character.

ACKNOWLEDGMENTS

This essay is part of a larger project in preparation of a book, Organizations As Institutions: Restructuring the Social Order, which has been supported by a grant from the Committee on Research, Academic Senate, UCLA, and by a University of California Regents Faculty Fellowship. I am grateful for comments by Marshall Meyer, Bill Roy, John Meyer, Herm Turk, and Pam Tolbert; their recommendations were followed where feasible in this paper and will be more fully incorporated in my book.

NOTES

1. Weick's work (1979) also presumes that the effects of the environment vary widely because organizational response to the environment is variable: organizations selectively attend to environmental features. Organizations may gain control over the environment by attending to some parts of it, ignoring others.

2. While the rational approach emphasizes that organizations take action to gain internal control, ability to control environmental constraints has also received some attention (Thompson, 1967; Thompson and McEwen, 1958). Still, organizations do not shape the environment; they simply attempt to buffer or otherwise handle its effects.

3. Some earlier studies can be reinterpreted to provide additional support for the institutional approach. For example, Marshall Meyer (1978) found that when leadership is stable, other aspects of the organizational structure (e.g., size, number of divisions) are likely to be stable; when there is turnover in leadership, these aspects of structure are not as stable. See Pfeffer (1981:308–10) for a more complete discussion.

4. Of course, incorporation may increase business with contractors, who may associate the organizational form with stability.

5. The evidence for the increasing institutionalization of the organizational form is analyzed in more detail in Zucker, forthcoming.

6. The battle against home work continues even now. An editorial in the *Los Angeles Times* (May 25, 1981:II, 8) criticizes Secretary of Labor Raymond J. Donovan for proposing to repeal the federal government regulations against homework: "one thing he should do here is talk to the state inspectors for California's Concentrated Enforcement Program. They work hard to close down local sweatshops and they could tell Donovan in graphic terms how serious the homework abuse problem is in the garment trade."

7. This does not imply that social movements are without structure: one of the earliest assumptions made in the literature is that if a social movement is to survive, then it must develop a structure. Generally, this is conceptualized as a more or less formal leadership structure (see Shils, 1954).

8. At this point, population ecology models fit especially well. Note that high turnover does not necessarily indicate competitive conditions: an industry which is in the process of being monopolized may have a very high turnover rate, as the would-be monopolist destroys and absorbs competitors (Friedland, 1957).

9. Table 9 reports preliminary analysis, using native language dictionaries, of 20 societies. Kinship terminology has been widely studied, hence data are readily available. These data have been coded for 123 societies, but comparable occupational data are generally missing from anthropological reports. Hence, the time-consuming process of coding occupational terms from dictionaries must be completed. (This technique was suggested by Morris Zelditch, Jr., Stanford University.) Additional control variables are also being drawn from the Human Relations Area Files. Full results will be reported in Zucker, forthcoming.

REFERENCES

Aldrich, Howard
  1979   Organizations and Environments. Englewood Cliffs, N.J.: Prentice-Hall.
Aldrich, Howard and Jeffrey Pfeffer
  1976   "Environments and Organizations." Pp. 79–105 in A. Inkeles, J. Coleman and N. Smelser (eds.), Annual Review of Sociology, Vol. 2. Palo Alto, Calif.: Annual Reviews, Inc.
Alford, L. P.
  1928   Laws of Management Applied to Manufacturing. New York: Ronald Press.
Anderson, Michael
  1972   Family Structure in Nineteenth-Century Lancashire. Cambridge: Cambridge University Press.
Balkwell, James W., Frederick L. Bates, and Albeno P. Garbin
  1980   "On the intersubjectivity of occupational status evaluations: a test of a key assumption of the 'Wisconsin Model' of status attainment." Social Forces 58:865–81.
Barber, William J.
  1961   The Economy of British Central Africa. Stanford, Ca.: Stanford University Press.
Berger, Peter and Thomas Luckmann
  1967   The Social Construction of Reality. New York: Doubleday.
Bidwell, Percy W.
  1917   "Population growth in Southern New England." Publication of the American Statistical Association 15:831–38.
Blau, Peter M.
  1970   "A formal theory of differentiation in organizations." American Sociological Review 35: 201–18.
Boddewyn, J.
  1967   "The names of U.S. industrial corporations: a study in change." Journal of American Name Society 15:39–52.
Boeke, Julius H.
  1930   Dualistische Economie. Leiden: S. C. van Doesburgh.
  1947   Oriental Economics. New York: Institute of Pacific Relations.
Brown, R. W. and E. H. Lenneberg
  1954   "A study in language and cognition." Journal of Abnormal and Social Psychology 59:454–62.
Browning, Harley and Joachim Singelmann
  1978   "The transformation of the U.S. labor force: the interaction of industry and occupation." Politics and Society 8:481–509.
Burt, Ronald S.
  1975   "Corporate society: a time series analysis of network structure." Social Science Research 4:271–328.
Caves, Richard
  1964   American Industry: Structure, Conduct and Performance. Englewood Cliffs, N.J.: Prentice-Hall.
Chandler, Alfred D., Jr.
  1969   "The structure of American industry in the twentieth century: a historical overview." Business History Review 43:255–98.
Clark, Burton R.
  1956   Adult Education in Transition. Berkeley: University of California Press.

Clinton, Spencer
1886   "Reform in municipal government." Paper read before The Cleveland Democracy of Buffalo (Buffalo, New York):101–116.
Cohen, Abner
1969   Custom and Politics in Urban Africa: A Study of Hausa Migrants in Yoruba Towns. Berkeley: University of California Press.
Coleman, James S.
1974   Power and the Structure of Society. New York: W. W. Norton and Co.
Collins, Norman and Lee Preston
1961   "The size structure of the largest industrial firms, 1908–1958." American Economic Review 51:986–1003.
Commons, John R.
1901   "Tenement-house work and legislation regarding it." Pp. 369–84 in Industrial Commission Reports, v.15. Washington, D.C.: U.S. Government Printing Office.
Crandon, Frank P.
1886   "Misgovernment of great cities." Popular Science Monthly 30:521–4.
1887
Cullen, Donald E.
1956   "The interindustry wage structure, 1899–1950." The American Economic Review 46:353–69.
Dalton, Melville
1959   Men Who Manage. New York: John Wiley.
Davis, Joseph Stancliffe
1917   Essays in the Earlier History of American Corporations: Eighteenth Century Business Corporations in the United States. Cambridge, Mass.: Harvard.
Davis, Kingsley and Wilbert E. Moore
1956   "Some principles of stratification." American Sociological Review 10:22–31.
deSchwinitz, Dorothea
1935   How Workers Find Jobs. Pennsylvania, PA: University of Pennsylvania Press.
Diamond, Sigmund
1958   "From organization to society: Virginia in the seventeenth century." American Journal of Sociology 63:457–75.
Duncan, O. D., D. L. Featherman, and B. Duncan
1972   Socioeconomic Background and Achievement. New York: Seminar Press.
Durkheim, Emile and Marcel Mauss
1903   Primitive Classification. Chicago, IL: University of Chicago Press (1963).
Edwards, Richard C.
1975   "Stages in corporate stability and the risks of corporate failure." The Journal of Economic History 35:428–57.
Elkus, Abram I.
1913   "Social investigation and social legislation." Annals of the American Academy 48:56–58.
Evans, George Heberton
1948   Business Incorporation in the United States: 1800–1945. New York: National Bureau of Economic Research.
Etzioni, Amitai
1964   Modern Organizations. Englewood Cliffs, N.J.: Prentice-Hall.
Fabricant, Solomon
1942   Employment in Manufacturing, 1899–1939: An analysis of its Relation to the Volume of Production. New York: National Bureau of Economic Research.
1949   "The changing industrial distribution of gainful workers: some comments on the American decennial statistics for 1820–1940." In Studies in Wealth and Income, Vol 11. New York: National Bureau of Economic Research.

1952 The Trend of Government Activity in the United States since 1900. New York: National Bureau of Economic Research.

Forbes Magazine
1967 "Management." Sept. 15.

Ford, Henry
1923 My Life and Work. New York: Doubleday Page.

Fortes, Meyer
1969 Kinship and the Social Order. Chicago: Aldine.

Friedland, Seymour
1957 "Turnover and growth of the largest industrial firms, 1906–1950." The Review of Economics and Statistics 39:79–83.

Galambos, Louis
1966 "Business history and the theory of the growth of the firm." Explorations in Entrepreneurial History 4:3–16.

Geertz, Clifford
1969 Peddlers and Princes: Social Change and Modernization in Two Indonesian Towns. London: Routledge and Kegan Paul.

Gettermy, Charles F.
1915 The Massachusetts Bureau of Statistics, 1869–1915. Boston: Wright and Potter.

Gibbs, Jack P. and Walter T. Martin
1962 "Urbanization, technology, and the division of labor: international patterns." American Sociological Review 27:667–77.

Glasser, Carrie and Bernard N. Freeman
1947 "Work and wage experience of skilled cotton-textile workers." Monthly Labor Review 64: 8–15.

Gouldner, Alvin W.
1959 "Organizational Analysis." Pp. 400–428 in Robert K. Merton, Leonard Broom, and Leonard S. Cottrell, Jr. (eds.), Sociology Today. New York: Basic Books.

Griffin, John E.
1892 "Operations of the law in Massachusetts regarding the 'sweating system'." Pp. 87–92 in Proceedings of Sixth Annual Convention of the International Association of Factory Inspectors. Detroit, Aug. 31–Sept. 2.

Granovetter, Mark S.
1974 Getting a Job: A Study of Contacts and Careers. Cambridge, MA: Harvard University Press.

Griffith, Ernest
1974a A History of American City Government: The Conspicuous Failure, 1870–1900. New York: Praeger Publications.
1974b A History of American City Government: The Progressive Years and Their Aftermath, 1900–1920. New York: Praeger Publications.

Hall, Peter Dobkin
1977 "Family structure and economic organization: Massachusetts merchants, 1700–1850." Pp. 38–163 in Tamara K. Hareven, Family and Kin in Urban Communities, 1700–1930. New York: New Viewpoints.

Hall, Richard H.
1977 Organizations: Structure and Process, 2nd ed. Englewood Cliffs, N.J.: Prentice-Hall.

Hannan, Michael T., and John Freeman
1977 "The population ecology of organizations." American Journal of Sociology 82: 929–964.

Hareven, Tamara K.
1978 "The dynamics of kin in an industrial community." American Journal of Sociology 84.

Supplement: Turning Points, Historical and Sociological Essays on the Family. John Demos and Sarane Spence Boocock (eds.):S151–S182.

Hoselitz, Bert F.
1966   "Interaction between industrial and pre-industrial stratification systems." Pp. 177–193 in Neil J. Smelser and Seymour Martin Lipset (eds.), Social Structure and Mobility in Economic Development. Chicago: Aldine.

Houssiaux, Jacques
1958   Le Pouvoir des Monopoles: Essai sur les Structures Industrielles des Capitalisme Contemporaine. Paris.

Hughes, Everett C.
1945   "The dilemmas and contradictions of status." American Journal of Sociology 50:353–359.

Hunt, Bishop Carleton
1936   The Development of the Business Corporation in England, 1800–1867. Cambridge, Mass.: Harvard.

Kaestle, Carl F.
1973   The Evolution of an Urban School System: New York City, 1750–1850. Cambridge, Mass.: Harvard University Press.

Kaplan, A. D. H.
1964   Big Enterprise in a Competitive System. 2nd ed. Washington, D.C.: The Brookings Institution.

Kluckhohn, C. and D. Leighton
1947   The Navaho Cambridge, Mass.: Harvard U. Press.

Labovitz, Sanford and Jack P. Gibbs
1964   "Urbanization, technology, and the division of labor: further evidence." Pacific Sociological Review 7:3–9.

Laslett, Peter
1965   The World We Have Lost. New York: Prentice-Hall.

Lawrence, Paul R. and Jay W. Lorsch
1967   Organization and Environment: Managing Differentiation and Integration. Boston: Graduate School of Business Administration, Harvard University.

Levine, Sol and Paul E. White
1961   "Exchange as a conceptual framework for the study of interorganizational relationships." Administrative Science Quarterly 5: 583–601.

Levy-Leboyer, Maurice
1975   "Innovation and business strategies in nineteenth- and twentieth- century France." Pp. 87–135 in Edward C. Carter II, Robert Forster and Joseph N. Moody (eds.), Enterprise and Entrepreneurs in Nineteenth and Twentieth Century France. Baltimore: Johns Hopkins University.

Lowenberg, J. Joseph, and Michael H. Moskow
1972   Collective Bargaining and Government. Englewood Cliffs, N.J.: Prentice-Hall.

Lurie, Melvin, and Elton Rayack
1967   "Racial differences in migration and job search: a case study." The Southern Economic Journal 33:81–95.

McCarthy, John and Mayer Zald
1973   The Trend of Social Movements in America: Professionalization and Resource Mobilization. Morristown, N.J.: General Learning Press.
1977   "Resource mobilization and social movements: a partial theory." American Journal of Sociology 82:1212–41.

McKelvey, Bill
1982   Organizational Systematics: Taxonomy, Evolution, Classification. Berkeley: University of California Press.

Marris, Peter, and Anthony Somerset
1971 African Businessmen: A Study of Entrepreneurship and Development in Kenya. London: Routledge and Kegan Paul.
Marshall, T. H.
1977 Class, Citizenship and Social Development. Chicago: University of Chicago Press.
Martin, Robert F.
1940 National Income in the United States, 1799–1938. New York: National Industrial Conference Board, No. 241.
Massachusetts Bureau of Statistics
1914 Report on the Statistics of Labor. Boston, Mass.: Wright and Potter.
Meyer, John W., and Brian Rowan
1977 "Institutionalized organizations: formal structure as myth and ceremony." American Journal of Sociology 83: 340–363.
Meyer, John W., David Tyack, Joane Nagel, and Audri Gordon
1979 "Public education as nation-building in America: Enrollments and bureaucratization in the American States, 1870–1930." American Journal of Sociology 85: 591–613.
Meyer, Marshall W.
1978 "Leadership and organizational structure." Pp. 200–32 in Marshall W. Meyer and Associates (ed.), Environments and Organizations. San Francisco: Jossey-Bass.
Meyer, Marshall W. and M. Craig Brown
1977 "The process of bureaucratization." American Journal of Sociology 83: 364–385.
Miernyk, William H.
1955 Inter-Industry Labor Mobility: The Case of the Displaced Textile Worker. Boston, Mass.: Northeastern University, Bureau of Business and Economic Research.
Moulder, Frances V.
1977 Japan, China and the Modern World Economy: Toward a Reinterpretation of East Asian Development ca. 1600 to ca. 1918. Cambridge: Cambridge University.
Myers, Charles A. and W. Rupert MacLauren
1942 The Movement of Factory Workers: A Study of a New England Industrial Community, 1937–1939 and 1942. New York: John Wiley and Sons.
Myers, Charles A. and George P. Shultz
1951 The Dynamics of a Labor Market: A Study of the Impact of Employment Changes on Labor Mobility, Job Satisfactions, and Company and Union Policies. New York: Prentice-Hall.
Navin, Thomas R.
1970 "The 500 largest industrials in 1917." Business History Review 44:360–86.
Ogburn, William Fielding
1924 Social Change with Respect to Culture and Original Nature. New York: Viking Press.
Ouchi, William G. and David B. Gibson
1980 "Control and Commitment in Industrial Organizations." Unpublished manuscript, Graduate School of Management, UCLA.
Ouchi, William G. and A. M. Jaeger
1978 "Type Z organization: Stability in the midst of mobility." Academy of Management Review 3:305–14.
Ouchi, William G. and J. B. Johnson
1978 "Types of organizational control and their relationship to emotional well being." Administrative Science Quarterly 23:293–317.
Parnes, Herbert S.
1954 Research On Labor Mobility: An Appraisal of Research Findings in the United States. New York: Social Science Research Council, Bulletin 65.
Parsons, Talcott
1954 "A revised analytical approach to the theory of social stratification." Essays in Sociological Theory. Glencoe, Ill.: Free Press.

1956   "Suggestions for a sociological approach to the theory of organizations. I." Administrative Science Quarterly 1: 63–85.

Perrow, Charles
1979   Complex Organizations: A Critical Essay. Glenview, Ill.: Scott, Foresman.

Pfeffer, Jeffrey
1981   Power in Organizations. Marshfield, Mass.: Pitman.

Pfeffer, Jeffrey and Gerald R. Salancik
1978   The External Control of Organizations. New York: Harper and Row.

Pondy, Louis R. and Ian I. Mitroff
1979   "Beyond open system models of organization." Pp. 3–39 in Barry M. Staw (ed.), Research in Organizations, vol. 1. Greenwich, Conn.: JAI Press.

Presthus, Robert
1962   The Organizational Society. New York: Knopf.

Pugh, D., D. J. Hickson, C. R. Hinings, and C. Turner
1969   "The context of organizational structures." Administrative Science Quarterly 14:91–141.

Radcliffe-Brown, A. R.
1951   "Murngin social organization." American Anthropologist 53:37–55.
1952   "The study of kinship systems." In A. R. Radcliffe-Brown, Structure and Function in Primitive Society. New York: Free Press. First published in the Journal of the Royal Anthropological Institute 74 (1941):1–18.

Reynolds, Lloyd G.
1951   The Structure of Labor Markets: Wages and Labor Mobility in Theory and Practice. New York: Harper and Brothers.

Reynolds, Lloyd G., and Joseph Shister
1949   Job Horizons: A Study of Job Satisfaction and Labor Mobility. New York: Harper and Brothers.

Roethlisberger, F. J. and William J. Dickson
1939   Management and the Worker. Cambridge, Mass.: Harvard University Press.

Rose, E.
1965   "Uniformities in culture: ideas with histories." Pp. 154–76 in N. F. Washburne (ed.), Decisions, Values and Groups. New York: Macmillan.

Rowan, Brian
1982   "Organizational structure and the institutional environment: the case of public schools." Administrative Science Quarterly 27:259–279.

Schultz, Stanley K.
1973   The Culture Factory: The Boston Public Schools, 1789–1860. New York: Oxford University Press.

Scott, W. Richard
1975   "Organizational Structure." Pp. 1–25 in Alex Inkeles (ed.), Annual Review of Sociology, Vol. 1. Palo Alto, Calif.: Annual Reviews, Inc.
1981   Organizations: Rational, Natural, and Open Systems. Englewood Cliffs, N.J.: Prentice-Hall.

Selznick, Philip
1948   "Foundations of the theory of organization." American Sociological Review 13:25–35.
1957   Leadership in Administration. New York: Harper and Row.

Sheppard, Harold L. and A. Harvey Belitsky
1965   The Job Hunt: Job Seeking Behavior of Unemployed Workers in a Local Economy. Report Prepared by the Upjohn Institute for Employment Research for the Office of Manpower, Automation and Training, U.S. Department of Labor.

Shils, E. A.
1954   "Authoritarianism: Right and left." Pp. 24–49 in R. Christie and M. Johoda (eds.),

Studies in the Scope and Method of 'The Authoritarian Personality.' Glencoe, Ill.: The Free Press.

Simon, Herbert A.
1957 Administrative Behavior. (2nd ed.) New York: Macmillan.

Singelmann, Joachim
1978 From Agriculture to Services: The Transformation of Industrial Employment. Beverly Hills: Sage.

Skolnick, Arlene
1973 The Intimate Environment: Exploring Marriage and the Family. Boston, Mass.: Little, Brown.

Smelser, Neil J.
1959 Social Change and the Industrial Revolution. Chicago: University of Chicago Press.
1963a Theory of Collective Behavior. Glencoe, Ill.: Free Press.
1963b "Mechanisms of change and adjustment to change." In Bert F. Hoselitz and Wilbert E. Moore (eds.), Industrialization and Society. The Hague: Mouton.

Snow, David A., Louis A. Zurcher, Jr., and Sheldon Ekland-Olson
1980 "Social networks and social movements: A microstructural approach to differential recruitment." American Sociological Review 45:787–801.

Starbuck, William H.
1974 "The current state of organization theory." Pp. 123–39 in J. McGuire (ed.), Contemporary Management. Englewood Cliffs, N.J.: Prentice-Hall.
1976 "Organizations and their Environments." Pp. 1069–1123 in Marvin D. Dunnette (ed.), Handbook of Industrial and Organizational Psychology. New York: Rand McNally.

Stern, James L. and David B. Johnson
1968 Blue- to White- Collar Job Mobility. University of Wisconsin: Industrial Relations Research Institute.

Stinchcombe, Arthur L.
1965 "Social Structure and Organizations." Pp. 142–93 in J. G. March (ed.), Handbook of Organizations. Chicago: Rand McNally.

Stone, N. I.
1938 Productivity of Labor in the Cotton Garment Industry. Washington, D.C.: Bureau of Labor Statistics, Bulletin 662.

Taylor, Frederick W.
1911 Principles of Scientific Management. New York: Harper.

Thelen, David P.
1972 The New Citizenship: Origins of Progressivism in Wisconsin, 1885–1900. Columbia, Missouri: University of Missouri Press.

Thompson, James D.
1967 Organizations in Action. New York: McGraw-Hill.

Thompson, James D. and William J. McEwen
1958 "Organizational goals and environment: goal setting as an interactive process." American Sociological Review 23:23–31.

Tilly, Charles and C. Harold Brown
1967 "On uprooting, kinship, and the auspices of migration." International Journal of Comparative Sociology 8:139–64.

Tilly, Charles, Louise Tilly, and Richard Tilly
1975 The Rebellious Century, 1830–1930. Cambridge, Mass.: Harvard University Press.

Treiman, Donald J.
1975 Occupational Prestige in Comparative Perspective. New York: Seminar Press.

Tumin, M.
1967 Social Stratification: The Forms and Functions of Inequality. Englewood Cliffs, N.J.: Prentice-Hall.

Turk, Herman
   1973   Interorganizational Activation in Urban Communities: Deduction From The Concept of
          System. Rose Monograph Series. Washington, D.C.: American Sociological Review.
Turk, Herman and Lynne G. Zucker
   1981   "Interorganizational perspectives on stability and change: Institutional persistence and
          macrosocial complexity." Unpublished manuscript.
Turner, Ralph H. and Lewis M. Killian
   1972   Collective Behavior. Englewood Cliffs, N.J.: Prentice-Hall.
Udy, Stanley H. Jr.
   1962   "Administrative rationality, social setting, and organizational development." American
          Journal of Sociology 68:299–308.
Ullman, Joseph C. and David P. Taylor
   1965   "The information systems in changing labor markets." Pp. 276–96 in Gerald G. Somers
          (ed.), Proceedings of the Eighteenth Annual Winter Meeting, New York. Madison,
          Wisconsin: Industrial Relations Research Association.
U.S. Bureau of the Census
   1972   Characteristics of the Population, General Social and Economic Characteristics, Vol. 1.
          Washington, D.C.: U.S. Government Printing Office.
U.S. Department of Labor, Bureau of Labor Statistics
   1975   Jobseeking Methods Used By American Workers. Washington, D.C.: U.S. Government
          Printing Office.
Weber, Max
   1947   Theory of Social and Economic Organization. New York: Free Press.
Weick, Karl E.
   1979   The Social Psychology of Organizing. 2nd edition. Reading, Mass.: Addison-Wesley.
Weinstein, James
   1968   The Corporate Ideal in the Liberal State. Boston: Beacon Press.
Weissman, Stephen R., and Lynne G. Zucker
   1975   "External constraints and internal responses in urban social programs." In Steven A.
          Waldhorn and Joseph Sneed (eds.), Restructuring The Federal System: Approaches to
          Accountability in Post-Categorical Programs. New York: Crane-Russak.
Wheeler, Everett P.
   1885   "Civil service reform." Civil Service Record 4:65–68.
Wiebe, Robert
   1967   The Search for Order, 1877–1920. New York: Hill and Wang.
Wilcock, Richard C. and Walter H. Franke
   1963   Unwanted Workers: Permanent Layoffs and Long-term Unemployment. Glencoe, Ill.: Free
          Press.
Williamson, Jeffrey G. and Joseph A. Swanson
   1966   "The growth of cities in the American Northeast, 1820–1870." Explorations in En-
          trepreneurial History 11 (Supplement):1–101.
Wolf, Eric R.
   1966   "Kinship, friendship, and patron-client relations in complex societies." Pp. 1–22 in The
          Social Anthropology of Complex Societies, Michael Banton (ed.). London: Tavistock.
Zubrow, R. A., W. D. Kendall, E. S. Burgess, and P. L. Miller
   1969   Poverty and Jobs: A Study of Employment and Unemployment and Job Vacancies in the
          Denver Labor Market. Report prepared for the Mayor of the city of Denver and the
          Economic Development Administration, U.S. Department of Commerce.
Zucker, Lynne G.
   1977   "The role of institutionalization in cultural persistence." American Sociological Review
          42:726–43.

1980a "Effects of sudden redefinition of institutional structure on 'demand characteristics' in experiments." Presented at the West Coast Conference for Small Group Research, San Francisco, May 1980.

1980b "Sources of change in institutionalized systems: Generating and applying a theory of occupational mobility." Revised version of a paper presented at the annual meeting of the American Sociological Association, Chicago, 1978.

1981   "Typifying interaction: action, situation and role." Revised paper presented at the annual meeting of the American Sociological Association, Boston, 1979.

1982a "Institutional structure and organizational processes: the role of evaluation units in schools." Pp. 65–86 in Evaluation in Schools: Theory and Practice, Adrianne Bank and Richard C. Williams (eds.), Los Angeles, CA: Center for the Study of Evaluation. Monograph No. 10.

1982b The Impact of Proposition 13 on Public Funding and Services for Education and Health in California. California Policy Seminar Monograph Number 15. Berkeley, CA: Institute of Governmental Studies, University of California.

Forth-
coming Organizations as Institutions: Restructuring the Social Order. Unpublished monograph, UCLA.

Zucker, Lynne G. and Carolyn Rosenstein
1981   "Taxonomies of institutional structure: dual economy reconsidered." American Sociological Review, December.

Zucker, Lynne G. and Pamela Tolbert
1981   "Institutional sources of change in the formal structure of organizations: the diffusion of civil service reform, 1880–1935." Paper presented at the annual meeting of the American Sociological Association, Toronto.

THE LABOR PROCESS AND THE SOCIOLOGY OF ORGANIZATIONS

Paul Goldman

I. INTRODUCTION

The 1960s and 1970s saw the rapid development of Marxist scholarship in the United States. During that period Americans experienced sharp social conflict, and many evinced a new awareness of their society's contradictions. Neither conventional liberal wisdom nor mainstream social science adequately explained, much less resolved, the questions rasied by the war in Indochina, ghetto uprisings, the student movement, Watergate, liberation struggles throughout the Third World, and in the 1970s an economy that simultaneously exhibited inflation, unemployment, and the persistence of poverty. For many social scientists Marxism's emphasis on economic factors and on relations between social classes provided a more coherent approach to larger social phenomena.

In recent years Marxist social science has gained some acceptance and considerable intellectual credibility, even in a cultural climate where anti-communism

Research in the Sociology of Organizations, vol. 2, pages 49–81
Copyright © 1983 by JAI Press Inc.
All rights of reproduction in any form reserved.
ISBN: 0-89232-203-9

is for many a reflexive response. This newfound, and still tenuous, respectability has been justified by substantial contributions to our knowledge about class structure and the politics of class; imperialism, racism, and militarism; the role of women; and a wide range of economic issues such as the business cycle, urban economics, and so on. In most of these areas, the work of Marxists has challenged traditional orthodoxies and stimulated sustained debate.

Until recently, however, American and even European Marxists have been relatively silent about the organization of work in capitalist societies and about the more general question of modern industrial bureaucracy. For a century Marxists did not follow up on Marx's (1967) discussion of the division of labor and hierarchy in the first volume of *Capital*. Gramsci (1971:303) made some trenchant observations about "Fordism" in industry, but his remarks were more critique than analysis. Lenin (1969) used *State and Revolution* to prescribe how the Bolshevik party might transform society from capitalism to socialism, but although quite impressed with Taylorism in the early 1920s, he wrote little about the labor process.[1] More recent generations of Marxists, especially those in the United States, have assumed that industrial bureaucracy reinforces the status quo in capitalist systems, but few have actually attempted to describe the internal workings of bureaucratic systems and the ways in which they do or do not maintain capitalist hegemony. The challenge of combining bourgeois social science's interest in bureaucracy and Marxism's concern with class relations has not seemed intellectually attractive.

This neglect is rooted, at least partially, in the lack of intersecting traditions in Marxism and organizational analysis.[2] The latter has been the province of sociology, or at least of a "sociological" approach, for over three decades, although academics in business administration and psychology add their own flavor to the discipline. At the risk of some oversimplification, we can say that mainstream practitioners share a very strong presumption that bureaucracy, although imperfectable, is both inevitable and desirable (Jacoby, 1973; Weber, 1947). Most theory and research explain the effectiveness or ineffectiveness of specific bureaucratic strategies or procedures within that context. The business school tradition stresses executive behavior and especially the process of decision making. Sociologists, particularly those employing field methodologies, have been more inclined to study relations between managers and rank and file (Gouldner, 1954, 1955; Blau, 1955; Crozier, 1964). Their emphasis on the "human factor" finds few parallels in classical Marxist theory.[3] Generally, Marxists within sociology have had some difficulty finding an intellectual voice that synthesizes *both* the Marxist and the sociological tradition; nowhere has this been more evident than in studies of work organization.[4]

During the mid-1970s a number of widely read articles raised issues that showed organizational analysis could benefit from an infusion of radical political economy. This work took its concepts, categories, and modes of analysis more or less directly from Marx and Engels. Historical analysis is fundamental to

Marxism, and it is not surprising that this research examined historical themes and tied the labor process to emerging organizational forms (Stone, 1974; Marglin, 1974; Davis, 1975; Edwards, 1975; Palmer, 1975). More important still, Harry Braverman's (1974) monumental treatise, *Labor and Monopoly Capital,* had its roots in Marx's theories of the labor process. Braverman attempted to bring *Capital* up to date by employing a Marxist analysis of Taylorism as both an historical and as a contemporary phenomenon.

Note my shift in terminology. Mainstream organizational analysts discuss "bureaucracy," "organization," "management," or, less frequently, "labor relations"; Marxists refer to the "labor process." They define this concept as both the "activities that transform raw materials into useful objects . . . with the assistance of instruments of production" and the relations of workers with management and with one another (Burawoy, 1979:15). The term signals an appreciation of *the workplace* as the cornerstone of the capital accumulation process and as the starting point for discussions of organizations. Emphasis on the labor process allows researchers to stress the immediate activities and concerns of the working class, while examining such broader issues as the dynamics of organizational power, the relationship of broader economic conditions to the structure of work, and trends in union activities.

During the past five years, the surge of published work on labor process has provided fresh perspectives that form the beginnings of a Marxist theory of organization. This research has been theoretical and empirical. Several journals have devoted special issues to the labor process.[5] Recent monographs demonstrate the diversity of Marxist (or neo-Marxist) research on the labor process. Kusterer (1978) studied a variety of work settings and discovered that even "unskilled" workers possess relatively sophisticated knowledge about the labor process at their workplaces. Kraft (1978) and Greenbaum (1979) described the evolution of the labor process in the data processing industry. Noble (1977) examined the engineering profession's assimilation of corporate goals and its penetration into corporate life, a crucial development for the actual design of the forces of production.

Finally, the authors of three subsequent books, each using a different methodology, have tried to provide a more general picture of the capitalist labor process. Richard Edwards (1979) used economic data, some company records, and interviews to look at changes in work during the course of this century. Michael Burawoy (1979) employed a participant observation approach and analyzed a metal working establishment where he worked. His research had an unexpectedly historical dimension as he fortuitously learned that he was replicating the work of Donald Roy who had observed the same shop more than 30 years earlier. Dan Clawson (1980) used historical data, especially legislative hearings, to study changes between 1860 and 1920 and to test explicitly many of the propositions suggested by Braverman.

Attempts to integrate Marxism and organizational analysis are not limited to the United States. A number of recent English (and continental) books and articles suggest that the effort to join the two traditions is a concern of a growing number of scholars in the developed world (Allen, 1975; Burrell and Morgan, 1979; Boreham, 1980; Boreham and Dow, 1970; Clegg, 1975, 1979; Clegg and Dunkerley, 1980; Hyman, 1977; Kouzmin, 1979; Palloix, 1976; Pignon and Querzola, 1976). Most of these workers are, however, general, and do not treat the labor process as a central concern. One exception is Friedman's (1977) *Industry and Labour*.

These works reflect a new awareness that Marxists can draw successfully from organizational analysis' long traditions. Existing research data may be reinterpreted and provide insights and information even for those who start with contrary assumptions. No synthesis of the two paradigms has yet appeared—and none is likely—but it is clear that contemporary Marxists have begun to deal with issues previously confined to the mainstream and have been influenced by its traditions.[6]

II. MARXISM, ORGANIZATIONS, AND THE LABOR PROCESS: ELEMENTS OF A WORLD VIEW

Before outlining the Marxist's emerging analysis of the capitalist labor process and its implications for the study of bureaucratic organization, a discussion of how Marxists view the world is useful. Any such characterization lends itself to caricature, because complex issues are necessarily reduced to simple generalizations and assumption of consensus ignores the atmosphere of debate. Nevertheless, certain themes are sufficiently frequent in the labor process literature that we may take them as common understandings among those who deal with this question. Seldom spelled out explicitly, they represent points of departure and combine values, assumptions, and past research findings. Four topics stand out: (1) the Marxist characterization of economic process in capitalist economies; (2) the dialectics of conflict and change in organizations (and in societies); (3) the Marxist vision for the future; and (4) the nature of organizational environments.

First, the economics of capitalism: Much of Marx's mature work discussed the creation of value in commodities, usually under the rubric of the "labor theory of value." This theory asserts that the value (not the price) of a commodity is best expressed by the labor time required to produce it. The original exposition—much less subsequent elaboration and critique—cannot be summarized here, but the basic message is that workers, through their labor, not capitalists or entrepreneurs, create value. Most Marxists accept this definition or variants of it, although several recent arguments suggest important modifications (Gough, 1972; Braverman, 1974:230,410; O'Connor, 1975; Burawoy, 1978). In capitalist systems, wages are (usually) set by the capitalist who pays the worker only what is required to sustain his or her family. During part of the working day each laborer works for himself or herself, and for the rest of the day he or she works for the capitalist. What is produced during the latter period is *surplus value,* and as Marx (1967:331) himself suggested:

> the directing motive, the end and aim of capitalist production, is to extract the greatest possible amount of surplus value, and consequently to exploit labour-power to the greatest possible extent.

It is, therefore, in the interests of the capitalist to obtain as much effort from the worker as possible without necessarily increasing wages.

The persistence of organizational and social conflict constitutes a second area of consensus for Marxists and follows directly from the firm's need to extract surplus labor from workers. Neoclassical, Keynesian, and monetarist economics traditions see capitalism as a system capable of almost unlimited expansion potentially benefiting capitalist, worker, and public alike. Marxists see capitalism as a zero-sum game (or very close to it). What workers achieve in terms of improved wages, benefits, less demanding or demeaning jobs, autonomy, job safety, and the like, employers lose—and vice-versa. On these issues, the interests of capital and those of labor inevitably clash and form the basic contradiction of capitalist society. The workplace, then, is a battlefield, or to use Richard Edwards' apt phrase, a "contested terrain." Struggles can be found at several levels: in the formal atmosphere of trade union–management conflict; in coordinated actions by groups of workers; or in individual sabotage or withdrawal that denies management what *it* defines as a "fair day's work." Marxists studying the labor process have looked for, and have generally located, substantial tension and conflict.

It is occasionally assumed that the worker *should* be militant and angry when at times he or she is not. Concrete worker actions result from mixed motives— mainly anger at a system that expropriates labor, makes meaningless daily work activity, and engenders insulting and aggravating relations of authority. Research cannot always disentangle these from one another or from attitudes workers bring to the job.

The perpetual nature of organizational contradiction and conflict is nonetheless significant. New solutions may engender new problems, and the battle for management is never over. For example, initiatives to increase productivity and to increase the intensity of labor frequently stimulate adverse worker response— perhaps a new attempt to organize a union, a strike, random sabotage, and so on (Watson, 1968; Aronowitz, 1973; Rothschild, 1973; Yellowitz, 1977; Zimbalist, 1979b). Conversely, workers' organizing drives, or demands for improved wages and/or working conditions encourage management's latent or manifest antilabor tendencies, and may move them to try busting the union or move production facilities (Goldman and Van Houten, 1980b). This tug-of-war has existed as long as there have been capitalists and wage laborers. Marx and Engels themselves had the opportunity to observe it. Struggles today differ from, but also parallel, those of mid-nineteenth-century England and turn-of-the-century America. Changing issues and changing tactics should not obscure structural similarities. Marxist historians have been markedly successful in bringing out this point.[7]

A third aspect of the Marxist world view is the hopeful vision of work organizations in the future. This outlook corresponds to a conception of human nature that goes back to Marx's (1964) early writings. For Marx it is work—the conscious, organized transformation of nature to meet needs for material sustenance—that most frequently distinguishes humans from animals. This materialist philosophic orientation leads directly to the presumption that work is the most important of human activities. Jobs that are alienating either because tasks are degraded or because workers are powerless to control their work lives are thus violations of human rights and, indeed, of the human spirit. This position might be qualified. Most contemporary Marxists appreciate that an adequate intellectual approach, not to say a radical politics or a Marxist psychology, must extend beyond the boundaries of material production and working life. This insight, while raised by Marxism's critical theory traditions, has been brought home most sharply by writings coming out of women's movement of the 1960s and 1970s. Nevertheless, the nature of work organization remains a central concern of Marxists.

Specific prescriptions for the ideal work organization vary, but there is agreement about the desirability of eliminating hierarchy and status differences, sharing technical knowledge and expertise to the greatest extent possible, and democratizing critical decisions such as selection of managers and supervisors.[8] Dan Clawson (1980:16–17) succinctly describes the requirements of communist work organization:

> Communism involves total democracy, with the election of anyone beyond the level of ordinary worker, with no fixed hierarchy and no one having the right to give commands (except insofar as this right is temporarily delegated, with the commands always subject to review by the group as a whole). Moreover, instead of a plethora of rules and an illusory focus on bureaucratically defined expertise, in communism regulations are reduced to a minimum, freedom is maximized, and everyone becomes technically competent to do the work.

Few work situations meet these exacting standards, but some models suggest that the highly bureaucratized and hierarchical work structures typical in capitalist economies are not the only way to organize production. Maoist China is certainly the most significant large-scale illustration of this point.[9] Yugoslavia exhibits some characteristics of producer democracy.[10] Sweden has drawn attention from the American Left community because national debate increasingly focuses on issues of industrial and economic democracy.[11]

These examples indicate that societies and work organizations based on greater equality and participation are humanly possible as well as morally defensible. Even in the United States there is growing evidence that workers at all levels possess the individual and collective potential to take charge of their jobs. Several generations of participant observation studies note the degree to which workers have sophisticated knowledge about the machines and materials with which they work, even if they frequently hide this ability from supervisors (Roethlisberger and Dickson, 1939; Roy, 1952, 1954, 1958; Gouldner, 1954, 1955; Kusterer, 1978; Burawoy, 1979; H. Mills, 1979; Zimbalist, 1979b; Mulcahy and Faulkner, 1979; Shapiro-Perl, 1979). Even more significant are contemporary experiments in workplace democratization. Many of these are joint labor–management projects; others are worker co-ops that survive where capitalist firms have failed. All suggest that relatively large organizations can function effectively with considerable participatory input.[12] One project was so successful that management called it off when it became evident executives could not deal with their own dispensibility (*Business Week,* Mar. 28, 1978:78–81).

It is in this area, however, that the Marxist world view is somewhat vulnerable to both internal uncertainty and external attack. We can catalog the damage resulting from capitalism and from organizations in the capitalist world: inequality in both income and power; continued racism and sexism; exploitation in the Third World; and so on. The record of socialism is mixed, and while more equal standards of living do exist in the socialist world, political and economic power is not widely diffused. While nationalized industry and state planning is a common feature of socialist economies and in principle is more democratic than private ownership, one cannot argue that workers control shopfloor production in the Soviet Union or East Germany.[13] Recent (Fall, 1980–1981) demonstrations in Poland indicate problems with the organization of that nation's industry and economy. Even if the record of Algeria, Cuba, and Yugoslavia seems very encouraging, socialism as practiced has not necessarily resulted in internal democracy or equalitarianism.

We can partially explain the slow development of truly socialist institutions in nominally socialist states by the weight of presocialist cultural traditions, economic backwardness at the time state power was captured, and the military threat from the West which discouraged experimentation. These arguments are cogent, but less than fully satisfying. It is possible that the *Gemeinschaft* and community solidarity that seems an essential part of the revolutionary process, especially in the Third World, is not easily adaptable to the building of a modern economy, especially when the socialist nation depends on exchange in world markets. Moreover, the problem of scale also seems to be a factor. Small countries and small factories or other workplaces are more amenable to nonbureaucratic, nonhierarchical, participative organizational structures. A less competitive national and international economy, an important feature of a truly socialist world order, would make these issues less disturbing, but it is likely that socialists will always have some concern for productive efficiency.

American Marxists have also had difficulty explaining (or explaining away) the lack of militance shown by the American working class. By whatever measure—voting behavior, sanctioned and wildcat strikes, demands—workers and their unions are not perched on the precipice of all-out class war. Workers are frequently as angry at their unions as they are at employers. The labor movement has been slow to reach out to new organizing targets (frequently workplaces employing women). We do see very real anger, occasionally bitter rather than token strikes, and informally organized or individual slowdowns, but most workers have been quite resistant to socialist appeals. We can plausibly explain these phenomena by referring to the highest standard of living for any working class in history (even if not all workers share in it), to strong but not particularly radical trade unions, and to a culture stressing individualism. Moreover, schools and the media have for generations glorified capitalism, social mobility, and "the American way," and have derided socialism. Finally, labor market segmentation and organizational strategies designed to reinforce it tend to divide fractions of the working class from one another. The United States has always been heterogeneous, and it has proven difficult for workers differing in race, ethnicity, sex, and skill to organize collectively and effectively. In sum, while there is optimism about democratizing work, Marxists are aware of the many obstacles to its potential realization.

The fourth characteristic of the Marxist world view involves organizational environments. With few exceptions [notably Benson (1975), Clegg and Dunkerley (1980), and Karpik (1977, 1978)], Marxists have devoted little attention to environments in the sense that the term is conventionally used by organizational sociologists. Nevertheless, some assumptions—namely, those about science and about the state—differentiate Marxists very sharply from mainstream organizational theorists. Marxists do not believe in a "free" science, where research is guided by unworldly curiosity. The directions of scientific discovery, particularly in what Karpik (1977:46) calls the "science of transformation," are politically (in the largest sense of the term) inspired and politically actuated. Clawson (1980:66) claims, "capitalists have the resources and the rewards. They decide what technology is to be developed and adopted. Therefore, they shape this technology." Because capitalists directly control or indirectly influence (through the state) the funding of science, we should not be surprised that enormous effort will be placed on developing techniques and equipment that can increase managers' control over workers.

Employers have always been concerned with the political uses of technology. Henry Ford used to talk about his friend Tom Edison who "invented" himself out of a difficult labor situation by devising a machine that eliminated the jobs of striking skilled workers (Sward, 1968:114). Other less dramatic historical examples can be cited (Rosenberg, 1976b:119ff.). The inventiveness that reduces the market power of skilled labor is often marked by an ideology of productivity rather than by inventors' conscious desires to de-skill workers. Recent research by Shaiken (1979) and Noble (1979), however, suggests the invention and application of computer-based, numerically controlled machine tools came about for the express purpose of minimizing the leverage of strongly unionized machinists. Computer technology generally reduces the size of a labor force wherever it is used and de-skills affected occupations, especially clerical and other jobs typically held by women (Kraft, 1978; Greenbaum, 1979; Hacker, 1979). There is no question that most of this research, and the dissemination of the more general Marxist assumptions about science, has come about largely through the impact of Braverman's work. It is ironic, however, that in the economic crisis of the late 1970s (and presumably of at least the early 1980s) many employers seem fearful of new investment. Research and development, and even equipment purchase, is expensive and risky; even if it potentially increases management's control over labor, it may be less immediately profitable than other types of financial outlay (Goldman and Van Houten, 1980a).

Lastly, Marxists see the state as playing a very special environmental role for corporations and for the business community as a whole. The precise nature of this role, and even of the boundaries between state and corporation, is the subject of intense controversy among Marxists.[14] Here, however, we are concerned with elements of agreement. There is consensus that the state *apparatus* is *not* a neutral arbiter of class interests and that it *does* serve as guarantor of the capitalist economy and of the capitalist corporation (Clegg and Dunkerley, 1980:489). Specifically, the state subsidizes the training of the labor force, funds (often through the military budget) national research and development expenditures, engages in countercyclical economic policies, buffers (large) corporations in trouble, and advances the overseas interests of corporations through foreign and military policy (Szymanski, 1978a:183). As Block (1977) suggests, the state plays a primary role in maintaining "business confidence." The considerable overlap in background, recruitment patterns, and belief systems between state and corporate managers, as well as job mobility between the two sectors, reinforces the symbiotic relationship between state and corporation.

This relationship is not without stress and contradiction. State policies are not always effective. Sometimes they help some corporations or industry sectors at the expense of others. At other times they result in delegitimation of the governing political coalition or of the state apparatus itself (Block, 1977). State actions, or their effects, may even anger substantial labor or citizen groups who struggle to improve *their* access to the state (Esping-Anderson et al., 1976). Nevertheless, the power of capital to organize in order to protect and expand their interests is usually felt in the formulation and implementation of legislation and policy (Domhoff, 1978).

III. THE LABOR PROCESS

Study of the capitalist labor process has become a cornerstone of contemporary Marxist analysis of organizations. Harry Braverman (1974:9) lamented that, in the century following the publication of *Capital*, there was "no continuing body of work in the Marxist tradition dealing with the capitalist mode of production in the manner in which Marx treated it." The situation has changed dramatically, partially as a result of *Labor and Monopoly Capital*. Braverman's popularity and influence comes not *just* from his deep understanding of technology and its relationship to skilled labor, or from his penetrating critique of Scientific Management. His work is important because he pioneered the effort to apply and adapt the conceptual framework laid out by Marx himself. Thus, he sees organizational practice and the structure of work as the natural result of employers' desires to increase capital accumulation by controlling workers.

Braverman's (1974:86–138) description of Scientific Management is especially important because he ties the logic of specific technique to the logic of capitalism itself. Braverman argues that the Taylorist practice of "separating conception from execution" was a particularly critical step in the evolution of capitalist industry. It paved the way for the "degradation of work" by making workers passive objects following commands and directives, not active subjects. Once traditional craft knowledge is lost, workers' ability to use judgment on the job is also greatly diminished. Braverman contends that Scientific Management, especially as it de-skilled workers and appropriated productive knowledge (by planners), has become embedded in the capitalist labor process. Mechanization, especially the development of increasingly versatile and sophisticated machinery, is tied to Scientific Management and the detailed division of labor. One turn-of-the-century manager claimed that "I want machines so simple in their operation that any fool can run them" (Tolman, 1909:2). Braverman implies that the natural consequence of divided, repetitive work is an atomized, dependent working class which lacks resources to combat managerial hegemony. However, he gives this issue little explicit attention.

Braverman's argument appeals to contemporary researchers, however, because it goes well beyond the World War I era factory. Separation of conception from execution, hierarchical distinctions between those who plan and those who do, and specification of each step of the labor process has continued, not abated, during the subsequent six decades. Workers now are unlikely to understand the details of how a complex product is made and are less infrequently asked to exercise individual or collective discretion. Moreover, Scientific Management and the degradation of labor are not confined to the manufacturing industry. Braverman (1974:293–374) describes comparable processes in service occupations, retail trade, and clerical work. Therefore, recent American trends away from industry towards these occupations do not mitigate the force of his argument.

Braverman's general argument is accepted by most Marxists, albeit not wholeheartedly. Critiques of *Labor and Monopoly Capital* see its focus on technology and Taylorism as static, one-dimensional, overly reliant on management theory, and, above all, as too pessimistic.[15] Two types of criticism have been quite widespread. The first concerns Scientific Management. Braverman's argument depends largely on Taylor's and his disciples *writings*, rather than on analysis of management's actual actions (Edwards, 1978:109). The evidence supporting this critique is not entirely conclusive. Taylor was influential and controversial; debates on Scientific Management dominated the business press during the century's first two decades (Goldman and Van Houten, 1979:109–10). Moreover, the vitality of that press, its wide readership, and contributions to it by eminent businessmen suggest that magazines such as *Factory, Systems,* and *Industrial Management* reflect actual practice as well as belief systems (Clawson, 1980:32–3; Goldman, 1981). At the same time, Edwards (1978:109ff.), Palmer (1975:33–5), Friedman (1977:80), and Goldman and Van Houten (1979:114–20) argue that the movement towards industrial efficiency was itself widespread and that the Taylor *system* did not necessarily play a major role. On balance, this view may underestimate Taylor's impact. Employers *were* moving towards rationalization of *all* aspects of the workplace, including the labor process. The banner of Taylorism gave aspects of that historical process considerable visibility and affected the consciousness even of those who had little interest in adopting the Taylor system. Thus, the fact that the full system was used in at most a few hundred companies, and that many of these were small metalworking firms, is not important in itself (Nelson and Campbell, 1979). The unresolved issues are clearly compounded by the inability to agree upon what exactly constitutes Scientific Management.

A second set of critiques react to Braverman's apparent conception of workers and working-class struggle. Braverman's own crafts background and his focus on trades that were at one time highly skilled implied that the nineteenth-century working class consisted primarily of skilled laborers (Littler, 1978; Szymanski, 1978b; Montgomery, 1979b). Braverman's concern for organizational and technical innovation also suggested that workers have been more or less passive victims of changes initiated by management (Edwards, 1978:109; Clawson, 1980:33–4; Sattel, 1978; Ehrenreich and Ehrenreich, 1976). This characterization covers the historical epoch, when worker resistance was strong, and the contemporary period, when worker movements have been relatively quiescent. A number of writers argue that changes in the labor process partially, if not primarily, result from management's need to institute practices that weaken the strength of worker resistance (Clawson, 1980:51–70; Edwards, 1979:48–71; Goldman and Van Houten, 1979:108; and Stark, 1980:98–101). In some respects, Braverman defines the issue from a rationalist, managerialist perspective. He leaves us with "the impression of an inexorable *force* that somehow operates without serious interference or resistance. In this sense Braverman . . . indicates a less than fully dialectical understanding of power" (Sattel, 1978:37).

Braverman did not stress worker culture and the ways it incubates both adaptation and resistance. Burawoy (1979:15) suggests that the labor process is *relational* as well as *practical,* and that the interactions of workers with one another are central to, and help structure, the labor process. Workers have a clear capacity to act in their own behalf—learning and transmitting skills, slowing down production individually or collectively, making a game out of daily work lives (Burawoy, 1979:81–95; Kusterer, 1978). Working out effective relationships with one another, with first-line supervisors, and with higher managers is an ongoing process.

Recent analyses of the labor process have expanded upon these critiques in amplifying and modifying Braverman's thesis. While they can be approached in several ways, four issue areas seem particularly important. Together they show the work's breadth and depth and relate the Marxist conception of the labor process to organizations. I include in this list: (1) technical efficiency and social control; (2) class conflict and the struggle for organizational control; (3) Scientific Management, technology, and the devaluation of labor; and (4) labor market segmentation. Before discussing each in turn, two caveats bear mention. First, the issues selected are not mutually exclusive; lines or argumentation overlap their boundaries. Second, the capitalist labor process is complex and shows considerable variation between work settings. Some of the studies discussed below attempt to deal with these differences explicitly, others do so implicitly, and still others not at all.

IV. TECHNICAL EFFICIENCY AND SOCIAL CONTROL

Marxist analyses of capitalist organizations focus on a persistent, paradoxical dilemma of the capitalist labor process. They distinguish between two related conceptions: efficiency and control. One dimension refers to the requirement that any large-scale production process must be authoritatively coordinated and utilize technologies that minimize labor time and effort. The other dimension refers to the organizational control necessary in a capitalist system that depends on exploitation and which triggers worker resistance and class struggle. An effective labor process must deal with both technical efficiency *and* social control (Goldman and Van Houten, 1979:110–14).[16]

Different writers have utilized various terminology to express these dual aspects of the labor process. Heydebrand (1977) uses the traditional "forces" and "relations" of production. Gartman (1978:103) speaks specifically of "basic" control, which is necessary for large-scale production of use values, and "surplus" control, which overcomes worker resistance to produce surplus value. Some writers emphasize technologies. Noble (1979:30) asserts that there is "a distinction between productive technology which directly increases output per person-hour and technology which does so only indirectly by reducing worker resistance." Clawson (1980:63) notes that "the technical advantages of machinery are crucial, but the social control advantages are no less important."

Palmer (1975:32) claims that superior technique is "quantitative, raising output and increasing productivity . . . [which] creates a qualitative transformation, elevating capital's status as a hegemonic force." Gordon (1976:22) also focuses on the notion of "efficiency," distinguishing between "quantitative" and "qualitative" efficiency; the latter "maximizes the ability of the ruling class to reproduce its domination of the production process." Finally, several authors use a conception of managerial strategy to analyze the two aspects of the labor process. Marglin (1974:39) suggests that early capitalists eschewed efficient practices in order to divide-and-conquer workers. Burawoy (1979:81-6) suggests that the capitalist labor process, as it actually functions at the shopfloor level, simultaneously "secures" surplus value, while "obscuring" that phenomenon from workers. Edwards' (1979) distinction between "simple," "technical," and "bureaucratic" control and Friedman's (1977) similar description of "direct control" and "responsible autonomy" imply historical evolution, allow comparisons between firms, and suggest some degree of managerial choice.

The relationship between these two general concepts is not always clear. Both represent important managerial priorities. Rising efficiency suggests a secular trend: over time the labor process becomes more efficient in that less human labor is required to produce manufactured goods.[17] Social control is more complex. One interpretation suggests that efficiency—embodied in Scientific Management, mechanization, and fractionation of work—*increases* social control by individualizing work and evaluation, atomizing the worker, and destroying crafts traditions. Goldman and Van Houten (1977:111-4) and Marglin (1974:39) argue that efficiency is attractive to managers primarily *because* it has this effect. The emphasis on efficiency not only reduces the effects of human variability, but also encourages workers to seek individualistic rather than collective solutions to their alienation. Stone (1974) provides one example in her discussion of how job ladders co-opt workers.

Gordon's perspective is a bit different. He suggests, if skeptically, that capitalists may have to *choose* between greater or lesser emphases on efficiency and social control (Gordon, 1976:24). This is a plausible hypothesis. Complete disregard for workers' physical capabilities, traditions, or human dignity can result in sabotage or strike, offsetting the advantage of low labor costs. Conversely, high turnover or low productivity may induce employers to stress quality-of-work issues that may reduce some elements of management control. Goldman and Van Houten (1980a, 1980b) suggest that contemporary managers seem poised between humanistic management and an intensive war on labor. Pre-1930 managerial strategy sometimes involved a choice between welfare work and efficiency, posing some of the same dilemmas (Nelson, 1975; Edwards, 1979; Goldman and Van Houten, 1979).

The concern with efficiency and social control is a significant aspect of the Marxist approach to organizations. It stresses managerial *intentionality* in the design of organizational structure and the labor process. In doing so, Marxists attack the view that organizational technique is the result of a slow process in which the primary concern is gradual rationalization of production and improved coordination. Social control is more long-term, since it necessarily involves how to keep labor from fundamentally challenging the prevailing organization of capital.

V. CLASS CONFLICT AND CONTROL OVER THE LABOR PROCESS

For Marxists the struggle between capital and labor is epic and heroic. The Molly McGuires; Haymarket Strikes; Homestead Steel Strike; strikes of shoemakers, garment workers and textile workers in New York and New England; the Ludlow Massacre; and the strike wave of 1919 and the sit-ins of the 1930s are frequently cited examples. Three demands were paramount: the right to form unions and bargain collectively; reduction of the length of the working day; and wages allowing workers to live at or above minimum standards of human decency. Significantly, these issues are *still* part of today's labor–management negotiations as economic issues are contested by both sides.

Braverman emphasizes management's conscious effort to assert its control over the details of the labor process itself. It is easy to take this for granted: in contemporary industrial societies it seems natural that management sets tasks and that conflicts involve supervisory practice at the micro level and economics at the macro level. In short, we tend to accept what employers see as ''management rights'' and look at increasingly specialized division of labor and introduction of machinery as a sign of naturally evolving industrial progress.

Braverman and others have transformed the issue of shopfloor control by *politicizing* it. *Labor and Monopoly Capital* suggested that control is as much a part of industrial politics as economic issues or union security. Others, influenced by this work, go further and contend that changes in productive technique result from potential or actual class conflict and are designed to reduce the workers' collective leverage. The labor process, technology, even bureaucracy itself are thus *consequences of class struggle,* not of a depoliticized evolutionary process (Goldman, 1978:22).

The historical research of Montgomery, Clawson, and others substantiates this point. Montgomery (1976:485ff.) stresses the moral aspects of traditional craftsmen's social codes. Workers knew what constituted ''a fair day's work'' and enforced standards on slaggards as well as on ratebusters. Time study symbolized ''the theft of [the craftsman's] knowledge by his employers and an outrage against his sense of honorable behavior at work'' (Montgomery, 1979b:115). Nineteenth-century workers, especially in the skilled trades, were remarkably productive, whether they were employed directly by capital or through the popular inside sub-contracting system (Clawson, 1980:71–165).

"Whether the question was one of speed or quality, workers were not simply maximizing their individual pleasure. . . . Workers did not earn power and respect either in the work group or the community by producing inadequate amounts of inferior quality goods" (Clawson: 1980:153). Moreover, *workers* themselves pushed for standardization when employers demanded flexibility in work rules, staffing requirements, and rates (Montgomery, 1979b:113).

The political issue was who would control the shopfloor and details of production. Paternalism and welfare capitalism left this problem untouched (Bernstein, 1972:187; Edwards, 1979:131). Business unionism, whereby management agreed to negotiate economic issues in exchange for worker acceptance of "management rights," facilitated and consolidated a political solution but was not itself decisive. Piecework did not produce basic changes as long as workers monopolized shopfloor knowledge and could keep management ignorant of how, and how quickly, a job could be done (Clawson, 1980:214). Unions protected worker knowledge through a code of mutuality, not individualism (Montgomery, 1972a:9). Only when the attack on unions was joined with the efficiency movement (of which Taylorism was a major part), could employers claim true control over the workplace. In industry after industry, labor struggles centered on the issue of control. Braverman tended to ignore this political dimension and its roots in class conflict, but his reconceptualization of Taylorism pointed subsequent researchers to the connection.

The virtual destruction of skilled trades as they existed in the nineteenth century represented a major victory for capital. But, as Montgomery (1979a:10) puts it:

> even in the setting of modern technology and large scale production, it was possible to have collective direction of the way in which jobs were performed. . . . Such direction required not only a struggle against management's efforts to control the work, but also a rejection of individualistic, acquisitive behavior.

Marxists today see evidence that control continues to be (or at least is resurfacing as) a factor in industrial relations (Boreham, 1981:20). In some cases, the printing and longshore industries for example, strong unions and the limitations of prior technologies combined to delay fundamental struggles until after World War II. Each technological change provokes intense conflict, in part because the progressive erosion of skilled crafts also severely damages workers' long-standing social and cultural patterns (H. Mills, 1979: Zimbalist, 1979a).

Even where the labor process separates mental and manual labor and where the work of most employees is relatively simple and repetitive, we seen shopfloor politics. Recent studies indicate that how to do a particular job and the appropriate time each job should take are still points of contention between labor and management (Burawoy, 1979:167ff.; Kusterer, 1978; Mulcahy and Faulkner, 1979; Lamphere, 1979; Shapiro-Perl, 1979). If workers can guard *some* of their know-how from management and have informal organizations that limit output and/or transmit knowledge from worker to worker without supervisory intervention, struggle over *control* can continue.

Management has become increasingly sophisticated in dealing with workers' commitment to one another rather than to the company. Friedman (1977:116) argues that:

> Top managers will often spend considerable effort directly counter-attacking worker resistance. They will also try to accommodate this resistance by pursuing policies which limit its effect. To co-opt union leaders, to maintain relations with small suppliers, to lay off poorly-organized workers before well-organized ones; these strategies—as "scientific" as Taylorian scientific management—largely reflect the reality of worker power within production in advanced countries, and top managers' recognition and accommodation of that reality.

The current attack on the American labor movement using "preventive labor relations" is a common alternative strategy, as are plant closures and movement of facilities to locations where labor is unlikely to unionize (Goldman and Van Houten, 1980b). This tactic is dangerous, as the creation of homogeneous work experiences in an already homogeneous community has in the past led to worker struggle (Friedman, 1977:50ff.).

Some employers have tried to recognize and *use* worker concern for control as a means of increasing productivity through co-optation. Programs to improve the "quality of working life" may include job redesign, job rotation, or a shift to quasi-autonomous work groups to improve skills and job satisfaction. However, "job recomposition never really calls the division of labor into question . . . because it builds into the functioning of small work groups the fact that they are a subordinate part of the collective" (Palloix, 1976:64). Similarly, plans for formalized worker participation at the shopfloor level—whether work teams, suggestion systems, or gripe sessions—usually are attempts to improve workers' "sense" of control without interfering with basic decision making and planning processes (Zimbalist, 1975; Nord, 1978; Marglin, 1977; Sennett, 1979; Goldman and Van Houten, 1980a).

VI. SCIENTIFIC MANAGEMENT, TECHNOLOGY, AND THE DEVALUATION OF LABOR

Students of the capitalist labor process contend that Scientific Management was a crucial component in the battle for organizational control.[18] The destruction of traditional crafts was an obvious consequence, and, of course, was a source of skilled trade worker militancy. Management's new capacity to substitute poorly-paid for well-paid labor and to maintain flexibility in staffing, however, had more long-term impact. Scientific Management involved more than mere separation of manual from mental labor, planning ahead of work, or even the stopwatch. It represented the triumph of rationalization on management's own terms and improved both efficiency and social control.

Scientific Management justified and intensified the already growing detailed division of labor. If workers were to be instructed in the "one best way," tasks had to be narrowly limited and repetitive. In theory, at least, reducing set-up time, sequencing operations, and accomplishing each task more quickly compensate for many material transfers and for the number of people who carry them out. Specialization, in the sense that workers repeatedly perform the same operation, helps management supervise and count every worker's individual output.

Braverman saw other advantages to the detailed division of labor, especially when it was allied with Scientific Management. He resuscitated the "Babbage principle," long a dead proposition in the sociology of organizations, which specifies that employers will try to substitute cheap labor for expensive labor (Braverman, 1974:79–83). Routinization justifies wage cuts and/or hiring of unskilled labor as it is "irrational" to use expensive labor to run preset equipment or assemble parts. In the early 1900s, wage specialist Frank Ericsson saved International Harvester money by firing machinists, millwrights, and pattern-makers whenever he could (Ozanne, 1967:61–9). During the same period, the wage differential between skilled and unskilled workers began to shrink (Shergold, 1977).

The implications of the Babbage principle are enormous and involve labor management as well as work management. Flexibility in labor deployment is possible if hiring, training, and break-in time are short. Labor turnover is a lesser concern if the external labor market provides sufficient new applicants. The transition from craft to mass production took place at a time when European immigration provided a seemingly endless flow of new workers. Rationalization of production and the integration of immigrant labor were symbiotic; when combined, they gave management substantial relative power vis à vis labor.

Today's worker has far less leverage than his or her forebear of just a few generations ago. Productive knowledge is more limited than when most manufacturing was performed by crafts workers; even the meaning of skill itself has changed (Braverman, 1974:430ff.). A skilled worker may have considerable esoteric knowledge without necessarily knowing very much about how an item is made, what makes a finished good tick, or how to manufacture a product from start to finish. Skills may be unique to a particular firm or industry. Workers may easily be replaced and are trapped by internal or external labor markets. Moreover, de-skilling reduces the ability of individuals, small groups, or even unions to disrupt the production process to win a labor dispute (Friedman, 1977:95). Telephone companies, newspapers, and other industries can maintain at least minimum production using only supervisory personnel and a few strikebreakers. In a tight labor market, workers may have to work harder and put in longer hours.

De-skilling is related to mechanization, and the relationship is a major theme of several discussions of the labor process (Braverman, 1974; Rosenberg, 1976a, 1976b; Gartman, 1978, 1980; Noble, 1979; Clawson, 1980). Two issues emerge. One, the impact of technology on the labor process, is straightforward. The other, historical causality, is controversial and unsettled as I note below.

What does mechanization do? Machines can overcome human physical limitations since, unlike us, they are capable of indefinite improvements in speed and accuracy and may reduce or actually eliminate back-breaking toil (Rosenberg, 1976b:131–2).[19] Gartman (1980) lists additional advantages: machines limit discretionary time; allow mechanical or time study pacing and predetermined output; make work more continuous; reduce handlings; and allow recruitment of unskilled workers who are more compliant. More critically, machinery structures production independently of workers whose contribution is more routine (Clawson, 1980:61ff.). Sophisticated technology introduces into the shopfloor equipment that cannot easily be understood by workers and which further symbolizes and legitimates the separation of mental and manual labor. Mechanization often individualizes production and raises the effectiveness of supervisory surveillance. Finally, expensive machinery encourages employers to run their establishments around-the-clock.

There are two Marxist explanations of why mechanization, technological innovation, and Scientific Management have been so closely related. Both suggest that employers and/or inventors saw the ability to invent and innovate as part of a political struggle with labor. One school of thought follows the logic set out by nineteenth-century manufacturer Andrew Ure, who claimed that "when capital enlists science in her service, the refractory hand of labor will always be taught docility" (cited in Rosenberg, 1976b:118). Rosenberg (1976a, 1976b) and Noble (1977, 1979) seemingly take this position. They document a few cases where employers consciously attempted to use new technology specifically to weaken well-organized workers.

There is a different approach. Marglin (1974:46–9) suggests that the technological changes associated with the English industrial revolution were shaped by, rather than caused, the rise of the factory. Hierarchy and discipline were for him the crucial variables. Clawson (1980:55ff.) takes an even stronger position, claiming that Scientific Management itself generated conditions that encouraged increased mechanization. He suggests (1980:60) that:

> it is the organization of work that has changed—now each worker does only one detail operation over and over, and the whole is controlled and coordinated by capital. There has been an organizational revolution, but no technical revolution. It is not the technological change which has forced industry to adopt a certain form of organization; not that machinery, independently developed following an inner technological imperative, has required organizational innovations in order to be successfully used; rather, capitalism has selected and developed a certain form of organization which fits its purposes. The new capitalist organization of work "creates the material conditions for the existence of machinery." Technological development takes place within the framework of a capitalist organization of production.

Additional historical and contemporary evidence will elaborate the relationship between organizational and technological changes. The utility of the Marxist position is that it suggests that there *is* a relation and that innovation and change are both influenced, perhaps even determined, by management's need to subdue and control labor.

Resulting changes are irreversible and, as Braverman suggested, extend not only to most corners of industry but to work in the service, clerical, and retail sectors as well. Nevertheless, in solving old contradictions, a labor process built upon divided tasks and complex technology almost simultaneously generates new ones. Class struggle may take on different forms and even have different meanings, but seemingly cannot be eradicated. De-skilled jobs are correlated with low morale and low organizational commitment and high absenteeism and turnover as the recent business press reports. This is a crisis for individuals who are dissatisfied and alienated from their jobs, for firms which devote increased resources to supervision and/or mollification of workers, and for a society which worries about worker productivity and economic distress (Goldman and Van Houten, 1980a). De-skilled labor can be seen in a context of ever-increasing organizational size and complexity. Product design and even general details of the labor process itself are no longer accessible to management, and few, if any, scientists or technicians can fully grasp the full range of technical knowledge used by a company. Long feedback loops and overloaded information circuits may cause poor decision making. Moreover, progressive de-skilling means that in *some* industries skill differentials among workers lose their traditional meanings and *by themselves* serve poorly as managerial devices to divide and conquer (Gartman, 1978:106). Finally, a labor process dependent on extreme fractionation of work means individuals, work groups, departments, and even whole factories are highly interdependent. Relatively small groups of workers can, at least for short periods, paralyze production schedules affecting many times their number (Friedman, 1977:95).[20]

VII.   LABOR MARKET SEGMENTATION

Marxists have never viewed organizations as closed systems. The growth of scholarly work on minorities and women has had an impact on the development of a Marxist sociology of organizations. One question has seemed particularly important: why do some groups—women, minorities, and especially minority women—have poorer occupations and/or jobs than white men? Why are their salaries, working conditions, status, and power on the job so relatively inferior? This is an enormously complex question and any reasonably adequate answer must take into account historical, cultural, psychological, and political factors, as well as economic and organizational variables (Hartmann, 1976). Marxists, particularly those writing in the political economy tradition, sometimes eschew "human factor" and other individual-based explanations and, instead, focus on institutional issues such as theories of the dual labor market and of labor market segmentation.[21]

A crucial determinant of life chances for all employees is the ability to use a particular job as the foundation for building a lifelong career either in the same organization or in a different one. Ideally, each job provides the opportunity to build and deploy growing skills and knowledge, whether a career moves up rungs of a civil service ladder or a corporate hierarchy, or from apprentice to journeyman to master of a skilled trade. Labor market segmentation theory suggests that the crucial variable in determining career mobility is the *employer,* and that differences in organizational size, market power, and stability account for variations in individual opportunity. Some employers—those in the public sector, large organizations, unionized companies, firms with monopoly power, corporations in growing economic sectors—both provide advancement opportunities and pay comparatively high wages. This is the "primary" labor market, and white males are disproportionately represented within it. Small manufacturing firms, agribusinesses, companies specializing in services, fast-food franchises, and some firms employing retail and clerical workers constitute the "secondary" labor market.[22] The marginal status of these employers, combined with lack of union protection, low wages, and few promotion opportunities, make jobs in these sectors dead ends. A vicious circle results, since workers have no chance to develop transferable skills or seniority, and the company has little incentive to retain workers who may demand higher wages or make long-term claims.

Edwards (1979) and, to a lesser extent, Friedman (1977) attempt to show the relationship between labor market characteristics and management's strategies of organizational control. Edwards (1979:16–22) suggests that firms may show one of three types of control. "Simple control" is exemplified by the small, entrepreneurial firm; "technical control" by large size and a technology that paces work; and "bureaucratic control" by an internal rule of law and the internalization of norms. Friedman (1977:88–107) characterizes the first two patterns as "direct control" and the third as "responsible autonomy," implying a single continuum rather than a more multifaceted approach.

Edwards makes more of these distinctions, claiming that the types of control represent an historical evolution that is pervasive, but incomplete, leaving remnants of older types in various corners of the economy. Furthermore, he suggests that there is a "package," linking types of control to segments of the labor market (Edwards, 1979:163–83). For example, firms using labor from the secondary market—women, minorities, youths—stress simple control since workers seldom have union protection or, given the nature of the jobs, long-term organizational commitment. Edwards divides the primary market into two subcategories, the "subordinate" and the "independent."[23] Technical control is tied to the subordinate primary market as union contracts and job ladders encourage mutual commitment and allow remote control, yet discourage arbitrary supervision. Despite alienating job content, the reward structure encourages, but does not guarantee, co-optation and legitimacy. Skills of workers in the independent primary labor market may transcend a particular workplace or industry, and firms thus tend to use bureaucratic control and allow workers increased autonomy.

Friedman's (1977:109ff.) work fills some of the gaps in Edwards' logic. He notes that firms operate in more than one labor market, especially if they maintain regular, but not necessarily permanent, relations with subcontractors. Moreover, many firms employ a wide range of workers in different departments or plants, and strategies are not as clear-cut as Edwards intimates. Nevertheless, it would appear plausible that control and labor market differences *within* a firm would correspond to his typology.

There are some limitations to the labor market segmentation approach as it applies to organizations. It provides some sense of process, but does not fully explain why *initial* recruitment patterns are so different for women and minorities. These groups' apparent "willingness" to work for lower wages and benefits is the explanation, but clearly other factors are at play. Edwards' work, and that of others writing in the political economy tradition, seems to underestimate some of the day-to-day *dynamics* of organizational careers for blue- and white-collar workers, and for men, women and minorities.[24] Moreover, we have too little data on the ways in which employers intentionally use differences between these groups to divide and conquer and to keep wage levels from rising. Hacker (1979) has shown that AT&T very consciously used putative affirmative action compliance tools to control strategically sex ratios at various levels of the organization. My own research (Goldman and Van Houten, 1980b; Goldman, 1981) indicates that employers attempt to use a buyer's market for labor both to reassert organizational control and to break unions. Labor markets and control strategies *are* connected, but more research, particularly from within the executive suite itself, is needed.

VIII.   CONCLUSION

Stripped to essentials, the Marxist concentration on the labor process is simple and has required little, if any, *fundamental* change since the publication of *Capital*. To accumulate capital, employers seek a labor force that is both cheap and tractable. This goal shapes the development of technologies and administrative strategies, but both nurture conflicts of one sort or another. Capitalism's systemic contradictions, especially economic cycles and uneven development, activate latent conflicts.

What does this approach tell us about *organizations* and about common boundaries between the Marxist perspective and traditional ways of looking at organizations? First, it suggests that the need to control labor is embedded in organizational structure. A case can be made that *bureaucracy*, as we think about it today, is a consequence of class struggle (Clawson, 1980; Goldman and Van Houten, 1979). Rules and regulations, the growth of a technical staff, increased supervisory personnel, and a growing clerical component develop *in part* as adjuncts to Scientific Management and fractionated work which originally are strategies to control workers. It follows that organizational researchers need look carefully at the relationship between power, the labor process, and characteristics of bureaucracy. Marxists hypothesize that this basic relationship is built into the capitalist system and has changed little during the past 100 years. In this regard the Marxist approach seems to confront some of the issues Hirsch (1975) raised when he lamented the disjuncture between the fields of complex organizations and industrial sociology.

Second, Marxists have a very different view of executives and managers than do mainstream organizational theorists. The latter seem often to view today's executive, or management team, as constantly struggling with external and internal uncertainties and as generally testing the limits of rationality. The Marxist analysis is very different, contending that managers know exactly what they are doing—trying to accumulate capital by maximizing the exploitation of workers given the constraints of time, place, and industry. At times, however, there is a tendency to take a demonic view and perceive managerial actions as based upon sophisticated perceptions of the political economy and concern for long-term system maintenance. This oversimplifies, because managers are often trapped by short-term issues and by the limitations of a narrowly conceived ideology. Moreover, executives within a firm may differ in how they conceptualize the "labor problem" and in their solutions to it. There can be sharp differences between shop management, who deal directly with workers, and higher management, who worry mainly about profits (Burawoy, 1980:176). Similar conflicts may arise between those, frequently in personnel, who prefer humanistic management, and others, often in operations, who want more hard-nosed tactics (Goldman and Van Houten, 1980a:86; 1980b:280). Research on managerial decision making and conflict might then benefit from more concentration on the labor process and on labor relations strategies. Examining the tension between technical efficiency and social control may help clarify the dynamics involved in such terms as "maximize," "satisfice," and "muddling through."

Third, concentration on the labor process can sharpen our notions of the distinction between open and closed systems. Edwards (1979:163–83), for example, suggests that the relationship between bureaucracy and labor market, between organization and environment, is active, not passive. This observation becomes more compelling if we realize that multinational corporations have the ability to dominate, change, or even move their environments physically.[25] The symbiotic relationship between corporate needs and both technological development and government policy (for example in regulatory activity) can be more completely understood when we start by looking at the labor process. Furthermore, the Marxist focus suggests a potential shift in traditional conceptions of the "unit of analysis," moving it from the plant or corporation to the technology, labor, force employed, industry sector, or conceivably, to the mode of production itself.

Mainstream social science has yet to arrive at a single satisfying, or even adequate, "theory of organization." Instead, there are competing perspectives that explain portions of organizational phenomena. The research theory discussed in this paper constitutes an emerging paradigm that has developed very rapidly in just a few years. It holds the possibility that to the rich, but often limited, understanding of traditional analysis may be added Marxism's historical scope, theoretical breadth, and concern for workers.

ACKNOWLEDGMENTS

This paper has benefited from my several years of contact and collaboration with Don Van Houten. Virtually all of the ideas in this paper derive from, or became part of, our several times weekly discussions. Neither he, nor others who kindly read and commented on the paper—Mimi Goldman, Steve Deutsch, Stewart Clegg, Nancy DiTomaso, and Sandra Albrecht—are at all responsible for the logic of presentation or any errors in the final version. I would also like to thank John Jermier and Walt Nord who encouraged me to present a preliminary sketch of the ideas at the 1979 Academy of Management meetings, and W. Richard Scott who invited me to give a very different version to Organizations Training Seminar at Stanford in 1980. A penultimate draft was presented at the 1980 American Sociological Association meetings. Thanks too to the clerical staff at the University of Oregon Department of Sociology, especially Barbara Kosydar and Vicki Van Nortwick.

NOTES

1. Chapter 5 of Erik Wright's *Class, Crisis and the State* compares Lenin's and Weber's views on bureaucracy and the state. Also see Merkle (1981).

2. Elsewhere I have speculated on this issue, suggesting that the implicit social control aspect of organizational sociology partially explains Marxists' disinterest in the topic (Goldman, 1978:27).

3. Some exception to this general statement is found in the "early" Marx (1964), especially in the *Economic and Philosophical Manuscripts of 1844*.

4. Two exceptions are Blauner (1964) and Zwerman (1970). In *White Collar*, C. W. Mills (1951) shows the influence of both traditional approaches to the sociology of occupations and an implicit critical Marxism.

5. *Monthly Review* (July–August, 1976); *Politics and Society* (Summer, 1978); *The Insurgent Sociologist* (Winter, 1978; Spring–Summer, 1979); *Economic and Industrial Democracy* (Fall, 1980). These journals, as well as *Working Papers for a New Society, Radical America, Socialist Review*, and *Review of Radical Political Economics*, regularly print articles on the labor process.

6. Gouldner (1976:273ff.) comments on the importance of this "marriage." DiTomaso (1979) notes that power structure research could gain substantially by more attention to organizational

issues. Two papers at the 1979 American Sociological Association (ASA) meetings, one by Form and the other by Colignon and Cray, assess the potential of Marxist approaches to organizations in critical, but not unfriendly terms. A recent reader edited by Zey-Ferrell and Aiken (1981) further suggests the reciprocal effect of Marxism and organizational analysis. Also see Burrell (1979) and Nord (1974). At the same time this impact can easily be overestimated. Scott's (1981) review of organizational research between 1960 and 1980 mentions only Braverman (and only in passing at that) among Marxists who have contributed to the field.

7. Most of this research is summarized in Goldman and Van Houten (1979) and in Brecher et al., (1979). In addition to the works discussed in the text, Marxists studying the labor process have been heavily influenced by historians who have studied working-class life, especially Thompson (1964), Hobsbawm (1964), and Gutman (1976).

8. General treatments of the "requirements" for workers' control can be found in Blumberg (1968), Hunnius et al. (1973:Part IV), Vanek (1975:Part I), Bernstein (1976), Pateman (1976), and Abrahamsson (1978:Ch. 11–15).

9. Hearn (1978) attempted to assess the relationship between Maoist practice and Marxist theories of bureaucracy. A non-Marxist approach may be found in Whyte (1973). The Chinese' recent retreat from their earlier position, as exemplified by the cultural revolution, appears to have resulted from problems that were only partially related to the effectiveness of past practice.

10. Blumberg (1968) and Hunnius (1973) provide overviews of institutional self-management in Yugoslavia while Deutsch (1977) reviews recent literature by Yugoslavian sociologists currently available in English.

11. Carnoy and Shearer (1980) explicitly use Sweden as a model from which Americans might and should draw useful lessons. However, they are more interested in Sweden's socialization of social welfare than in its efforts to change the work environment and broaden worker participation.

12. There has been a growing literature on workers' control during the past decade. Rothschild-Whitt (1979) summarizes work on producers' co-ops, Zwerdling (1978) provides a case book of (largely) worker-initiated projects within capitalist firms, and Davis and Cherns (1975:Vol. 2) have collected a comparable casebook of management-sponsored programs. General critiques of the prespective represented by Davis and Cherns can be found in Zimbalist (1975), Gomberg (1976), Nord (1978), Marglin (1977), Sennett (1979) and Goldman and Van Houten (1980a).

13. Europeans have been particularly interested in this subject. See Lefort (1972) and Bahro (1977).

14. A useful, if somewhat out-of-date review of the literature can be found in Gold et al. (1974). See also Holloway and Picciotto (1978).

15. Specific reviews include Aronowitz (1978), Baxandall et al. (1976), Coombs (1978), deKadt (1975), Ehrenreich and Ehrenreich (1976), Goldman (1975), Gordon (1976), Littler (1978), Sattel (1978), Szymanski (1978b). Edwards (1978), and Clawson (1980) discuss Braverman at length in their work.

16. This distinction, of course, has parallels in discussions of informal organization and humanistic management that have been a strand in organizational analysis for more than half a century. The Marxist approach differs in its suggestion that management strategy is geared to eradicating situations in which the human factor might play a vital role.

17. Efficiency is an imprecise, and possibly misused, term. Haber (1964:ix) defines no less than four frequent definitions, including a firm's input–output ratio of dollars, which is probably the most common usage among businesspeople today. This definition is quite close to the term "productivity." Even where the term denotes a rather broad concept, as in Gordon's notion of "qualitative efficiency," the unit of analysis is usually the firm, although Gordon does imply that his definition refers to broader capitalist system maintenance. Seldom in the mainstream literature does efficiency refer to what might be "efficient" for individual workers, for instance a safe and healthy workplace, interesting work, location proximate to place of residence, and so on. Similarly, definitions of

efficiency rarely deal with the *social* costs (pollution, for example) for strategies that may be internally efficient.

18. It seems also to have represented a victory of one historic trend over another. The crafts organization of production, including the inside contracting system, was as efficient as mass production operated on an enormous scale, and was quite technologically innovative (Clawson, 1980:71–125). In addition to direct attacks by management, it may have lost ground because of its inability to absorb large number of immigrant workers into the system and because of tensions between skilled crafts and unskilled workers (Clawson, 1980:165–6; Montgomery, 1979b:103–8).

19. It is easy to make a fetish of mechanical equipment. Gartman (1980) notes that skilled machinists may in some instances be more accurate than even the most sophisticated machines. In work requiring enormous precision, the most advanced machines usually must be operated by highly skilled, strongly motivated crafts workers. For heavy work, or for highly repetitive yet not unusually precise tasks, machines may be superior. Nevertheless, most mechanical equipment, like workers, is subject to fatigue and breakdown.

20. Moberg (1978:64) reminds us that there are limits to the degradation of labor and that works may act affirmatively even in the most routinized situations. He analyzes the Lordstown GM Assembly Plant strike in 1972 as follows:

> If workers behaved according to management's image of them as mindless, programmed automatons, then production would decline in quality or even halt. It was a reminder to the corporation, and a reaffirmation to themselves, that individual concrete labor and imagination were needed even on the assembly line, where corporate policy over the years had attempted to approximate in real life the abstraction upon which capitalism is founded in theory.

Watson (1968) relates a similar set of responses in the auto plant he worked during the mid-1960s, and Clawson (1980:136) points out that it is *workers* who first diagnose, and often correct, flaws in the assembly process that have been overlooked by technicians.

21. The literature on labor market segmentation, especially on wage differences between white male and other workers, is voluminous. It is also somewhat unusual in that Marxists and non-Marxists have shared some assumptions and most techniques. Reich et al. (1973) lay out many of the theoretical issues and Edwards et al. (1975) contains case studies using several different methodological approaches. Important quantitative studies include Beck, et al. (1979), Bibb and Form (1977), Bonacich (1972), and Wolf and Rosenfeld (1978). See also Baron and Bielby (1980).

22. Rothschild (1981:13–4) notes that these areas are (by far) the fastest growing sectors of the American economy.

23. See Durham et al. (1980) for an empirical test of Edwards' "package."

24. More research seems to have been done on women in organizations than on minorities. See, for instance, Acker and Van Houten (1974), Acker (1978), Glenn and Feldberg (1977, 1979), Feldberg and Glenn (1979), and Kanter (1976).

25. Colignon and Cray (1980) develop this point.

REFERENCES

Abrahamsson, Bengt
1977 "Bureaucracy or participation: the logic of organization." Beverly Hills, CA: Sage Publications.
Acker, Joan
1978 "Issues in the sociological study of women's work." Pp. 134–161 in A. Stomberg and S.

Harkness (eds.), Women Working Theories and Facts in Perspective. Palo Alto, CA: Mayfield Publications.

Acker, Joan and Donald R. Van Houten
1974 "Differential recruitment and control: the sex structuring of organization." Administrative Science Quarterly 17 (June): 152–163.

Allen, V. L.
1975 Social Analysis. London: Longman

Aronowitz, Stanley
1973 False Promises: The Shaping of American Working Class Consciousness. New York: McGraw-Hill.

Aronowitz, Stanley
1978 "Marx, Braveman and the logic of capital." The Insurgent Sociologist 8 (Fall):126–146.

Bahao, Rudolf
1977 The alternative in eastern Europe. New Left Review 106 (Nov.–Dec.):3–37.

Baron, James and William Bielby
1980 "Bringing the firms back in." American Sociological Review, 45 (Oct.):766–786.

Baxandall, Rosalyn, Linda Gordon, Susan Reverby
1976 "The working class has two sexes." Monthly Review, 26 (July–Aug.):1–9.

Beck, E. M., D. Horan and C. Tolbert
1978 "Stratification in a dual economy: a sectoral model of earnings determination." American Sociological Review 43 (Oct.):704–720.

Benson, J. Kenneth
1975 "The interorganizational network as political Economy." Administrative Science Quarterly, 20 (Sept.):229–249.

Bernstein, Irving
1960 The Lean Years: A History of the American Worker, 1920–1933. Boston, MA: Houghton-Mifflin.

Bernstein, Paul
1976 Workplace Democratization: Its Internal Dynamics. Kent, OH: Kent State.

Bibb, Robert and William H. Form
1977 "The effects of industrial, occupational, and sex stratification on wages in blue collar markets." Social Forces, 55 (June):974–996.

Blau, Peter M.
1955 The Dynamics of Bureaucracy. Chicago, Il: University of Chicago Press.

Blanner, Robert
1964 Alienation and Freedom: the Factory Worker and His Industry. Chicago, Il: University of Chicago.

Block, Fred
1977 "The ruling class does not rule: notes on the Marxist theory of the state." Socialist Revolution 7 (May–June):6–28.

Blumberg, Paul
1968 Industrial democracy: the sociology of participation. New York: Schocken.

Bonacich, Edna
1972 "A theory of ethnic autogonism: the split labor market." American Sociological Review, 37 (Oct.):547–559.

Boreham, Paul and Geoff Dow (eds.)
1980 Work and Inequality: Ideology and control in the Capitalist Labour Process. Melbourne, Australia: MacMillan.

Braverman, Harry
1974 Labor and Monopoly Capital: The Degradation of Work in the Twentieth Century. New York. Monthly Review.

Brecher, Jeremy et al.
 1979 "Uncovering the hidden history of the American workplace." Review of Radical Political Economics 19(Winter):1–23.
Burrell, Gibson
 1979 "Radical organization theory." Pp. 90–107 in David Dunkerley and Graeme Salaman (eds.), The International Yearbook of Organization Analysis. London: Heineman.
Buraway, Michael
 1978 "Contemporary currents in Marxist theory." The American Sociologist 13 (Feb.):50–64.
Buraway, Michael
 1979 Manufacturing Consent: Changes in the Labor Process under Monopoly Capitalism. Chicago, Il: University of Chicago Press.
Carney, Martin, and Derek Shearer
 1980 Economic Democracy. New York: M. E. Sharpe.
Clawson, Dan
 1980 Bureaucracy and the Labor Process: The Transformation of U.S. Industry, 1860–1920. New York: Monthly Review.
Clegg, Stewart
 1975 Power, Rule and Domination. Boston, MA: Routledge and Kegan Paul.
Clegg, Stewart
 1979 The Theory of Power and Organization. London: Routledge and Kegan Paul.
Clegg, Stewart and David Dunkerley
 1980 Organization, Class and Control. London: Routledge and Kegan Paul.
Colignon, Richard and David Cray
 1979 "New approaches to organizational research: a critique." Paper presented at the Annual Meeting of the American Sociological Association, Boston.
Colignon, Richard and David Cray
 1980 "Critical organizations." Organization Studies 1:349–366.
Coombs, Rod
 1978 "Labor and monopoly capital." New Left Review, 107:79–96.
Crozier, Michel
 1964 The Bureaucratic Phenomenon. Chicago, Il: The University of Chicago.
Davis, Lewis and Albert Cherns (eds.)
 1975 The Quality of Working Life. 2 vols. New York: Free Press.
Davis, Mike
 1975 The Stop Watch and the Wooden Shoe: Scientific Management and the Industrial Workers of the World. Radical America 9(Jan.–Feb.)69–95.
deKadt, Maarten
 1975 "A review of labor and monopoly capital." Review of Radical Political Economics, 7:84–90.
Deutsch, Steven
 1977 "Sociological currents in contemporary Yugoslavia." The American Sociologist, 12:84–90.
DiTomaso, Nancy
 1979 "The contributions of contemporary sociology to power structure research." The Insurgent Sociologist 9 (Aug.) 136–142.
Domhoff, G. William
 1978 The Powers That Be. New York: Vintage Press.
Durham, T. R., Judy Morgan, Barbara Larcom, and Chris Chase-Dunn
 1980 "Labor markets segments and the quality of employment." Paper presented at the Annual Meetings of the Society for the Study of Social Problems. New York.

LIBRARY
OF
MOUNT ST. MARY'S
COLLEGE
EMMITSBURG, MARYLAND

Edwards, Richard C.
1975   "The social relations of production the firm and labor market structure." Politics and Society 5(Summer):83–108.
Edwards, Richard C.
1978   "Social relations of production at the point of production. The Insurgent Sociologist 8(Fall): 109–125.
Edwards, Richard C.
1979   Contested Terrain: The Transformation of the Workplace in the Twentieth Century. New York: Basic.
Edwards, Richard, Michael Reich and David Gordon
1975   Labor Market Segmentation. Lexington, MA: Heath
Ehrenreich, John, and Barbara Ehrenreich
1976   "Work and consciousness." Monthly Review 28(July–Aug.):10–18.
Esping-Anderson, Gosta, Roger Friedlander, and Erik Wright
1976   "Modes of class struggle and the capitalist state." Kapitalistate 4–5:186–220.
Feldberg, Roslyn and Evelyn Glenn
1979   "Male and female: job versus gender models in the sociology of work." Social Problems 26 (June):524–538.
Form, William
1979   "Resolving ideological issues on the division of labor." Paper presented at the American Sociological Association Annual Meeting, Boston.
Friedman, Andrew
1977   Industry and Labour: Class Struggle at Work and Monopoly Capital. London: MacMillan.
Gartman, David
1978   "Marx and the labor process: an interpretation." The Insurgent Sociologist 8:(Fall)109–125.
Gartman, David
1980   "Basic and surplus control in capitalist machinery: the case of early mechanization in the U.S. auto industry." Unpublished manuscript.
Glenn, Evelyn and Rosyln Feldberg
1977   "Degraded and deskilled: the proletarianization of clerical work." Social Problems 25(Oct.)152–163.
Glenn, Evelyn and Roslyn Feldberg
1979   "Proletarianizing clerical work: technology and Organizational control in the office. In A. Zimbalist (ed.), Case Studies on the Labor Process, New York: Monthly Review 51–72.
Gold, David, Clarence Lo and Erik Wright
1975   "Marxist theories of the state." Monthly Review 26(Oct.) 29–43 and (Nov.) 51–72.
Goldman, Paul
1975   "Review of labor and monopoly capital." The Insurgent Sociologist, 6: 98–100.
Goldman, Paul
1978   Sociologists and the study of bureaucracy: a criticism of ideology and practice." Insurgent Sociologist, 8:21–30.
Goldman, Paul
1981   "Managerial ideology and labor in the aftermath of World I." Paper presented at the Annual Meetings of the Society for the Study of Social Problems, Toronto, Canada.
Goldman, Paul and Donald R. Van Houten
1977   "Managerial strategies and the worker: a Marxist analysis of bureaucracy." Sociological Quarterly 18 (Winter):108–125.
Goldman, Paul and Donald R. Van Houten
1979   "Bureaucracy and domination: managerial strategy of turn-of-century American industry." 1977 International Yearbook of Organization Studies, 108–141.

Goldman, Paul and Donald R. Van Houten
1980a "Uncertainty, conflict, and labor relations in the modern firm I: productivity and capitalism's 'human face'." *Economic and Industrial Democracy: an International Journal* 1 (Winter):63–98.

Goldman, Paul and Donald R. Van Houten
1980b "Uncertainty, conflict, and labor relations in the modern firm II: the war on labor." *Economic and Industrial Democracy: An International Journal* 1 (Spring):263–287.

Gomberg, William
1976 "The impact on labor of more 'science' in management." *Conference Board Record* 13 (June):28–31.

Gordon, David M.
1976 "Capitalist efficiency and socialist efficiency." *Monthly Review* 28 (July–Aug.):19–39.

Gough, Ian
1972 "Marx's theory of productive and unproductive labor." *New Left Review* 76 (Nov.–Dec.):47–74.

Gouldner, Alvin W.
1954 *Patterns of Industrial Bureaucracy.* New York: The Free Press.

Gouldner, Alvin W.
1955 *Wildcat Strike: A Study in Worker-Management Relationships.* Yellow Springs, Ohio: Antioch Press.

Gouldner, Alvin W.
1976 *The Dialectic of Ideology and Technology.* New York: Seabury.

Gramsci, Antonio
1971 *Selections from the Prison Notebooks.* New York: International Publishers.

Greenbaum, Joan
1979 *In the Name of Efficiency: Management Theory and Shopfloor Practice in Data-Processing Work.* Philadelphia: Temple University Press.

Gutman, Herbert G.
1976 *Work, Culture and Society in Industrializing America.* New York: Knopf.

Haber, Samuel
1964 *Efficiency and Uplift: Scientific Management in the Progressive Era.* Chicago: University of Chicago.

Hacker, Sally
1979 "Sex stratification, technology and organizational change: a Longitudinal study at AT&T." *Social Problems* 26 (April):539–557.

Hartmann, Heidi
1976 "Capitalism, patriachy, and job segregation by sex." *Signs: A Journal of Women in Culture and Society* 1 (Spring):137–169.

Hearn, Francis
1978 "Rationality and bureaucracy: Maoist contributions to a Marxist theory of bureaucracy." *Sociological Quarterly* 19 (Winter):37–54.

Heydebrand, Wolf
1977 "Organizational contradictions in public bureaucracy: towards a Marxian theory of organization." *Sociological Quarterly,* 18(Winter):83–107.

Hirsch, Paul
1975 "Organizational analysis and industrial sociology: a case of cultural lag." *The American Sociologist* 19 (Feb.):3–10.

Holloway, John and Sol Picciatto
1978 *State and Capital: A Marxist Debate.* Austin: University of Texas.

Hobsbawm, Eric
1964 *Labouring Men: Studies in the History of Labour.* London: Weidenfeld and Nicolson.

Hunnius, Gerry, G. David Garson and John Case.
1973   Worker's Control: A Reader on Labor and Social Change. New York: Vintage.
Hunnius, Gerry
1973   "Workers and Self-Management in Yugoslavia." Pp 268–321 in Gerry Hunnius et al.
       (eds.), Worker's Control: A Reader on Labor and Social Change. New York: Vintage.
Hyman, Richard
1975   Industrial Relations: A Marxist Introduction. London: MacMillan.
Jacoby, Henry
1973   The Bureaucratization of the World. Berkeley: University of California.
Kanter, Rosabeth Moss
1977   Men and Women of the Corporation. New York: Basic Books.
Karpik, Lucien
1977   "Technological Capitalism." In S. Clegg and David Dunkerley, Critical Issues in Organi-
       zation. London: Routledge and Kegan Paul.
Karpik, Lucien
1978   "Preface." Pp. 1–12 in Lucien Karpik (ed.), Organization and Environment: Theory,
       Issues and Reality. London: Sage.
Kouzmin, Alexander
1979   "Control in organizations: the lost politics." 1979 International Yearbook of Organization
       Studies 1:56–89.
Kraft, Philip
1978   Programmers and Managers: The Routinization of Computer Programming in the United
       States. New York: Heidleberg Science Library.
Kusterer, Kenneth
1978   Know-How on the Job. Boulder, Colorado: Westview.
Lamphere, Louise
1979   "Fighting the piece-rate system: new dimensions of an old struggle in the apparel indus-
       try." Pp. 257–276 in A. Zimbalist (ed.), Case Studies on the Labor Process. New York:
       Monthly Review.
Lefort, Claude
1975   "What is bureaucracy." Telos, 22 (Winter):310–365.
Lenin, V. I.
1969   "State and Revolution." Selected Works. One Volume Edition. New York: International.
Littler, Craig
1978   "Understanding Taylorism." British Journal of Sociology, 29 (May):185–202.
Marglin, Stephen A.
1974   "What the bosses do: The origins and functions of hierarchy in capitalist production." The
       Review of Radical Political Economics, 6 (Summer):33–60.
Marglin, Stephen
1977   "Catching flies with honey: an inquiry into management initiatives to humanize work."
       Unpublished manuscript.
Marx, Karl
1964   The Economic and Philosophical Manuscripts of 1844. New York: International.
Marx, Karl
1967   Capital. New York: International.
Merkle, Judith A.
1981   Management and Ideology: The Legacy of the International Scientific Management Move-
       ment. Berkeley: University of California.
Mills, C. Wright
1951   White Collar: The American Middle Classes. New York: Oxford.

Mills, Herb
  1979   "The San Francisco waterfront: The social consequences of industrial modernization." Pp.
         127–155 in A. Zimbalist (ed.), Case Studies on the Labor Process. New York: Monthly
         Review.
Moberg, David
  1978   "No more junk: Lordstown workers and the demand for quality." The Insurgent Sociolo-
         gist, 8 (Fall):63–69.
Montgomery, David
  1976   "Workers control of machine production in the nineteenth century." Labor History Re-
         view, 17 (Fall):485–509.
Montgomery, David
  1977   "Immigrant workers and managerial reform." Pp. 96–110. In Richard Erlich (ed.), Immi-
         grants in Industrial America, 1850–1920. Charlottesville: University Press of Virginia.
Montgomery, David
  1979a "The past and future of worker's control." Radical America, 13 (Nov.–Dec.):7–23.
Montgomery, David
  1979b Worker's Control in America. New York: Oxford University Press.
Mulcahy, Susan and Robert Faulkner
  1979   "Person and machine in a New England Factory." Pp. 228–241 in A. Zimbalist (ed.),
         Case Studies on the Labor Process. New York: Monthly Review.
Nelson, Daniel
  1975   Managers and Workers: Origins of the New Factory System in the United States,
         1880–1920. Madison: University of Wisconsin.
Nelson, Daniel and Stuart Campbell
  1972   Taylorism versus welfare work in American industry: h.l. Gantt and the Bancrofts."
         Business History Review (Spring):1–16.
Noble, David F.
  1977   America by Design: Science, Technology and the Rise of Corporate Capitalism. New
         York: Knopf.
Noble, David F.
  1979   "Social choice in machine design: The case of automatically controlled machine tools."
         Pp. 18–50 in A. Zimbalist (ed.), Case Studies on the Labor Process. New York: Monthly
         Review.
Nord, Walter
  1974   "The failure of applied behavioral sciences: a Marxian perspective." Journal of Applied
         Behavioral Science.
Nord, Walter
  1978   "Dreams of humanization and the realities of power." Academy of Management Review,
         3:674–679.
O'Connor, James
  1975   "Productive and unproductive labor." Politics and Society, 5 (May):297–336.
Ozanne, Robert
  1967   A Century of Labor-Management Relations at McCormick and International Harvester.
         Madison: University of Wisconsin.
Palloix, Christian
  1976   "The Labour process: from Fordism to neo-Fordism." Pp. 46–47. In Conference of
         Socialist Economists Pamphlet, 1: The Labour Process and Class Strategies. London:
         State 1.
Palmer, Bryan
  1975   "Class, conception and conflict: the thrust for efficiency, managerial views of labor and

the working class rebellion." The Review of Radical Political Economics, 7 (Summer): 31–49.

Pateman, Carole
1975 "A contribution to the political theory of organizational democracy." Pp. 9–30 in G. Garson and Michael Smith (eds.), Organizational Democracy: Participation and Self-Management. Beverly Hills, CA.: Sage.

Pignon, Dominique and Jean Querzola
1976 "Dictatorship and democracy in production." Pp. 63–99. In Andre Gorz (ed.), The Division of Labour: The Labour Process and Class Struggle in Modern Capitalism. Atlantic Highlands, N.J.: Humanities Press.

Reich, Michael, David Gordon and Richard Edwards
1973 "A theory of labor market segmentation." American Economic Review, 63 (May):359–365.

Rosenberg, Nathan
1976a "Marx as a student of technology." Monthly Review 29 (July–Aug.):56–77.

Rosenberg, Nathan
1976b Perspectives on Technology. New York: Cambridge University.

Roethlisberger, Fritz and William Dickson
1939 Management and the Worker. Cambridge: Harvard.

Rothschild, Emma
1973 Paradise Lost: The Decline of the Auto-Industrial Age. New York: Random House.

Rothschild, Emma
1981 "Reagan and the real America." New York Review of Books. (Feb. 5)13–18.

Rothschild-Whitt, Joyce
1979 "The collectivist organization: an alternative to rational-bureaucratic models." American Sociological Review 44 (Aug.):509–27.

Roy, Donald
1952 "Quota restriction and goldbricking in a machine shop." American Journal of Sociology, 57 (May):427–452.

Roy, Donald
1954 "Efficiency and the fix: Informal intergroup relations in a machine shop." American Journal of Sociology, 60 (Nov.):255–266.

Roy, Donald
1958 "Banana time: Job satisfaction and informal interaction." Human Organization 18 (Winter):158–168.

Salaman, Graeme
1979 Work Organizations: Resistance and Control. London: Longman.

Sattel, Jack
1978 "The degradation of labor in the 20th century: Harry Braverman's sociology of work." The Insurgent Sociologist 8 (Winter):35–39.

Scott, W. Richard
1981 "Developments in organization theory, 1960–1980." American Behavioral Scientist 24 (Jan.–Feb.):407–422.

Sennett, Richard
1979 "The 'boss' new clothes." New York Review of Books 26 (Feb.22):42–46.

Shaiken, Harley
1979 "Numerical control of work: Workers and automation in the computer age." Radical America 13 (Nov.–Dec.):25–38.

Shapiro-Perl, Nina
1979 The Piece rate: Class struggle on the shop floor. Evidence from the costume jewelry industry in Providence, Rhode Island." Pp. 277–298 in A. Zimbalist (ed.), Case Studies on the Labor Process. New York: Monthly Review.

Shergold, Peter R.
   1977   "Wage differentials based on skill in the United States, 1899–1919: A case study." Labor History 18 (Fall): 485–508.
Stark, David
   1980   "Class struggle and the transformation of the labor process: A relational approach." Theory and Society 9 (Jan.):83–130.
Stone, Katherine
   1974   "The origins of the labor process in the steel industry." Review of Radical Political Economics 6 (Summer):61–97.
Sward, Keith
   1948   The Legend of Henry Ford. New York: Holt, Rinehart and Winston.
Szymanski, Albert
   1978a The Capitalist State and the Politics of Class. Cambridge: Winthrop.
Szymanski, Albert
   1978b "Braverman as a neo-Luddite?" The Insurgent Sociologist 8 (Winter):45–50.
Thompson, E. P.
   1964   The Making of the English Working Class. New York: Vintage.
Tolman, William H.
   1909   Social Engineering: A Record of Things Done by American Industrialists Employing Upwards of One and One-Half Million People. New York: McGraw-Hill.
Vanek, Jaroslav (ed.)
   1975   Self-Management: Economic Liberation of Man. Baltimore: Penquin.
Watson, Bill
   1971   "Counter-planning on the shopfloor." Radical America 5 (May–June):77–85.
Weber, Max
   1947   The Theory of Social and Economic Organization. New York: Free Press.
Whyte, Martin King
   1972   "Bureaucracy and modernization in China: The Maoist critique." American Sociological Review 38 (April):149–163.
Wolf, Wendy and Rachel Rosenfeld
   1978   "Sex structure of occupations and job mobility." Social Forces 56 (March):823–844.
Wright, Erik Olin
   1978   Class, Crisis and the State. London: New Left Books.
Yellowitz, Irwin
   1977   Industrialization and the American Labor Movement, 1850–1900. Port Washington, N.Y.: Kennikat.
Zwerman, William
   1970   New Perspectives on Organizational Theory: A Reconsideration of the Classical and Marxian Analysis. Minneapolis: Greenwood.
Zimbalist, Andrew
   1957   "The limits of work humanization." The Review of Radical Political Economics 7 (Summer):50–60.
Zimbalist, Andrew
   1979a Case Studies on the Labor Process. New York: Monthly Review.
Zimbalist, Andrew
   1979b Technology and the labor process in the printing industry." Pp. 103–126 in A. Zimbalist (ed.), Case Studies on the Labor Process. New York: Monthly Review.
Zwerdling, Daniel
   1978   Democracy at Work. Washington: Association for Self-Management.

POLITICAL ACTION AND ALIGNMENTS IN ORGANIZATIONS

Edward J. Lawler and Samuel B. Bacharach

I. INTRODUCTION

In recent years, organizational scholars have begun to resurrect the broad image of organizations implied by Dalton's (1959) classic case study and Cyert and March's (1963) early theoretical work—namely that organizations are political systems in which individuals and subgroups vie for power and influence (Zaleznik, 1970; Baldridge, 1971; Pettigrew, 1975; Abell, 1975; Kipnis, 1976; Tushman, 1977; Bacharach, 1978; Bacharach and Lawler, 1980; and Pfeffer, 1981). Few would question that organizational politics should be a major concern, but, at the same time, few have taken seriously the implications of a political image or model of organizations. Porter et al., (1981) noted that a survey of basic texts in organizational behavior and related fields found that only .2 percent of the page content dealt with organizational politics. In light of the fact that practitioners, themselves, emphasize the role of politics in organiza-

Research in the Sociology of Organizations, vol. 2, pages 83–107
Copyright © 1983 by JAI Press Inc.
All rights of reproduction in any form reserved.
ISBN: 0-89232-203-9

tional decision making (see Madison et al., 1980), the relative neglect of organizational politics is surprising.

Organizational politics may be incorporated into the literature on organizational theory as a limited and complementary perspective or as an alternative perspective. To date, most efforts treat organizational politics as a supplement or complement to more traditional lines of work on organizations. This legitimizes organizational politics as a theoretical or research topic while incorporating it within prevailing images of organizations (March and Simon, 1958). For example, Pfeffer (1981) conceptualizes politics as a distinct facet or category of decision making that complements those emphasized in the literature on organizations. To Pfeffer (1981), work on organizational politics is important to account for and understand departures from rational decision making. Mayes and Allen (1977) suggest that politics is the management of *non*sanctioned means and ends, and still others construe politics as relevant primarily to how actors use discretion or to upward, rather than downward, influence in organizations (Porter et al., 1981). Efforts to clearly distinguish political from nonpolitical spheres and to interweave the political with existing foci have implicitly retained the connotation that "politics" in organizations is limited, irrational, unfair, or illegitimate.

The second, less prevalent, approach to organizational politics is to offer it as a model which contrasts with prevailing models of organizations. By a model, we mean a perspective or set of concepts, propositions, foci, and questions around which to organize empirical work and with which to recast work, ostensibly outside the emerging area of organizational politics. A political model of organizations suggests a fundamental change in the way scholars approach and analyze organizations, including: (1) a shift in the unit of analysis from the total organization to actors within the organization; (2) a conceptualization of organizational structure as, at once, a result of power struggle and a set of conditions or parameters underlying future power struggle; and (3) a treatment of coalitions as the major tactical mechanisms for gaining, maintaining, and using power in organizations (Bacharach and Lawler, 1980). This paper falls within this second approach and is designed to further develop the political model of organizations.

In the context of a political model, "politics" is a primitive term referring to the efforts of social actors to mobilize support for and/or opposition to policies, rules, goals, and means in which they have some stake. This notion of politics must be applied broadly if we are to realize the explanatory potential of a political model. That is, this definition implies that politics is not restricted to the boardroom decisions of the higher echelons, but is also incorporated into the day-to-day activities at all levels. While suggesting that organizational politics involves actors at all levels of the organization, this definition also implies that politics crosses all decision spheres. That is, politics is not limited to arenas of discretionary decision making nor to subtle upward influence attempts (Mayes and Allen, 1977; Porter et al., 1981) but may also occur in spheres of formal decision making. Most important, within this definition, organizational politics is not a separate category of decision making that forces departures from rationality (Pfeffer, 1981); rather, it becomes the process through which the rationality of decision making is defined. What is rational for one group need not be rational for another; organizational politics is essentially the struggle of different groups to impose their standards and criteria of rationality on spheres of decision making.

A political model of organizations implies an emphasis on *action* and *alignments*. Political action consists of the tactics actors use to deal with opposition and to maximize their influence. Political alignments refer to the network of coalitions within which action takes place at a particular time. Political action and political alignments are interrelated. Alignments emerge from action, action modifies existing alignments, and the prevailing alignments constrain and channel political action. The importance of action suggests that a political model be grounded in social-action theory (Weber, 1947; Parsons, 1937; and Schutz, 1967), since political action can best be construed as a type of social action. The "fact" that alignments emerge from political action suggests, further, that we identify basic types of political action and show how these lead to different types of political alignments in organizations.

This paper, specifically, argues that: (1) political action, whether at the individual or subgroup level, is the most appropriate unit of analysis for organizations; (2) a political analysis, grounded in social-action theory, suggests a treatment of rationality as a *form* of thought (not to be confused with the content of thought, particular organizational procedures, or specific inputs to a decision); (3) an analysis of political action requires a tactical approach to power and conflict, such that tactics and countertactics become the critical elements of the political process; (4) "absorption" and "insulation" are the broadest categories for examining tactical action by subunits in an organization; (5) these tactics—absorption and insulation—are grounded in actors' subjective evaluation of power; and (6) tactics of absorption and insulation lead to different types of political alignment. This paper interrelates social-action theory (Weber, 1947; Parsons, 1937) with the political model of organizations (Bacharach and Lawler, 1980) and, in this context, conceptualizes absorption and insulation as political processes giving rise to various political alignments. We will begin by discussing the implications of social-action theory.

II. SOCIAL-ACTION THEORY

Social-action theory can and has been used as the foundation for very different approaches to organizations. Phenomenologists use the notion of social action as a starting point for understanding the interpretive, symbolic processes of actors in organizations. The emphasis is on the construction of social order (Weick, 1979; Schutz, 1967). Functionalists, on the other hand, begin with social action and move to the analysis of total organizations as inherently cooperative systems with a life of their own (Parsons, 1937, 1956; Perrow, 1979). In contrast to phenomenologists, functionalists stress the conceptualization of "order already constructed." Even the political economy–approach of Mayer Zald and associates can be construed as implicitly grounded in Parsons' theory of social action (Zald, 1970; Zald and Berger, 1978). Social-action theory is at least a subtle theme underlying much organizational theory. Derivations from social-action theory, however, have missed one of the most fundamental points in Weber's original analysis of social action—namely, that social action, conflict, power, and politics are inextricably bound together. It is Weber (1947) rather than Parsons (1937, 1956) who takes the initial step toward a perspective that fuses elements of what today we call social-action theory and the political model of organizations.

The Weberian approach to organizations has too often been associated with a narrow focus on the formal structure of bureaucracy. Organization theorists typically treat Weber's concept of bureaucracy as if it is his concept of social system and neglect the role of social action in Weber's theory. A broader examination of Weber's work indicates that political strife among subgroups is a central characteristic of social systems at both the societal and organizational levels. The subgroups have incompatible interests based primarily on their power and status, and social action is the key construct for understanding the patterns of interaction between conflicting subgroups. Thus, it is not structure as "social form" that is the unit of analysis but rather the social action of subgroups; and, it is the notion of action that integrates the particular social actor and the structural context of action. Without a close examination of Weber's notion of social action and related concept of social system, one is left with the impression that Weber construes organizations as static, formal entities removed from rather than reflecting, emergent from, and sustained by component actors. As Collins (1975) indicates, the field of organizations has essentially turned Weber's theory on its head.

Given that organizations to Weber are arenas of political struggle, the structure of organizations is a social-control mechanism made necessary not only by continual conflict but also by the fact that the outcomes of any interest groups are rarely consistent with their expectations and desires (Collins, 1975). The first important element in Weber's notion of structure is that it develops from the calculative decisions of organizational actors (individuals and/or interest groups)—it is not an evolutionary phenomenon outside of the immediate direction of powerful actors in conflict with other actors. The second basic element of Weber's structure is captured by his analysis of legitimacy. Legitimacy is the major means of controlling actors in the organization and, thereby, constraining the boundaries of the conflict between interest groups. From this interpretation of Weber, organizations must be understood as dialectical systems in which the "first step" is political action of individuals based on the failure of existing structures to be sustained as legitimate by their supporting interest groups. The "second step" is the institutionalization of action in a newly emergent structure; the "third step' is constraining the boundaries of prior conflict by giving the new structure and concomitant patterns of action an aura of legitimacy. This is the implied dialectical process in Weber, and it leads to an image of organizations in constant, but bounded, tension. It also suggests, as we noted earlier, that political action and political alignments are critical dimensions of organizational politics.

There are two major ideas embedded in Weber's analysis of structure and action: (1) social action is subjective, and (2) social action is rational from the point of view of the actor at the moment action is taken. Action is subjective because it is guided by the set of meanings actors bring to the situation, and different meanings by different actors or the same actor across different times are virtually inevitable given the ambiguity and potential variability in social settings (Bacharach and Lawler, 1980). Order is an imputation of actors rather than an objective feature of the structure, and rationality becomes the mode of thought through which actors attribute meaning and order to the world. As a mode of thought, rationality is simply "means-ends" calculation. The basis and nature of rationality on a concrete level may differ—for example, across actors within an organization, across organizations over time, or across different cultures. It is this form of thought, i.e., means-end calculation, that makes action rational rather than the concrete information or content to which the method of thought is applied. Organizational structure, then, becomes a strategy for objectifying and legitimizing action and the common meanings underlying it. To the degree that organizations and component interest groups face uncertainty and to the degree that political strife cannot be totally enveloped by formal structure, social action remains an important starting point for understanding relations in organizations.

Assumption 1: *Political action is the appropriate unit of analysis.*

The emphasis suggested by this assumption is action, not the actor. Organizational theory has been too concerned with identifying the type of actor or level in the organization that best serves as the unit of analysis. In contrast, this first assumption is based on the idea that actors are important only to the degree that they are the initiator or inhibitor of social action. Particular units—e.g., individuals, departments, divisions, or total organizations—are important, not because of what they are, but because of their decisions to act (or not) and the consequences of their action for themselves and others in the organization. To conceptualize social action as the unit of analysis, therefore, is to leave open the specific unit of greatest importance to a specific context. This flexibility is important because in some contexts or with respect to some issues, the appropriate units could range from departments, divisions, or occupational categories to coalitions of individuals or groups, or even to individuals only tacitly representing different organizational subgroupings. The unit of analysis is simply social action relevant to a particular issue or decision at a given point in time, regardless of the size or identification of the "actors." In this sense, a political model, informed by a social-action perspective, essentially transcends some of the historic debate over the units of analysis in the field of organizations.

Assumption 2:   *Political action in organizations is intentional, i.e., goal directed.*

A central feature of political action is that it is directed to some future state of affairs. However, this implication of social-action theory does not imply a concern with organizational goals. With a political model of organizations, organizational goals are an emergent product of internal political processes; multiple goals at the organizational level are a reflection of a multitude of interests vying for power within the organization; and the difficulty of using goals to analyze organizations reflects the pervasiveness of organizational politics. The concept of organizational goals has little place in the social-action approach to organizational politics.

The goals of interest groups could appear to be particularly crucial to a political perspective. However, the basic tenets of social-action theory, found in Weber (1947) and Parsons (1937) for that matter, suggest that the particular goals of particular actors are less important than the mere fact that action is goal *directed*. It is not necessary to specify the wants, goals, etc. of actors in detail or even clearly; we need only emphasize those processes and contexts where actors are engaged in action directed at some goal, regardless of how unspecified or unarticulated the goal happens to be. Goal-directedness becomes a defining characteristic of political action specifying broad boundaries of investigation, rather than an explanatory construct. Social-action theory, thereby, sidesteps the problem of infinite regression when attempting to explain structure or behavior in terms of goals, and a related political perspective on organizations need not get caught in the web of conceptual debates generated by the goals approach (Georgiou, 1981; Perrow, 1979; Clegg and Dunkerley, 1980) to organizations. Consistent with Weber, it is only important to begin with the understanding that organizations are structures that facilitate, constrain, and channel the goal-*directed* behaviors of interest groups composing the larger organization and of individuals within particular interest groups.

Assumption 3:   *Political action in organizations is conscious choice.*

Political action is choice, and actors are conscious of and reflective about their prospective and actual options. By conscious choice, we simply mean that actors are aware of the fact that they are deciding between two or more lines of action. Other choices may actually be embedded in those actors are conscious of, meaning that an actor choosing between 1 and 2 also might be unknowingly choosing between A and B. The main reason for this is that the choices attended to by actors are not objectively given or presented to them by the environment; the nature of the choice, itself, is the object of interpretive processes of the actor. The choices and options created by actors are as subjectively defined as are their responses to them, and the choices identified by actors do not necessarily exhaust those they are actually making. Furthermore, an actor's definition of available choices and, hence, their actual choice can readily fluctuate over time as a result of successive reevaluations.

A political perspective on organizations suggests that these choice processes are grounded in the actor's interests and, specifically, their conflicting relationships to other actors. Since choices consciously made are intertwined with those not consciously made, both classes of decisions are a part of organizational politics. The tactical value of foresight and anticipation is a reflection of the fact that the choice actually made—because it combines conscious and nonconscious decisions—is often only clear in retrospect. Overall, the incorporation of ideas from social-action theory into a political perspective on organizations leads one to view intentional or conscious and unintentional or nonconscious decision making as inherently imperfect, subjective, and political.

Assumption 4: *Political action in organizations is rational.*

This assumption indicates that actors evaluate choices in a rational manner. Social-action theory suggests that rationality is a form or process of thought not to be confused with the content of decision making. Rationality is simply the use of a means-ends schema to evaluate choices, i.e., it implies the specification of goals or ends, identification of options or means, evaluation of the consequences of different means, and the linking of means to ends (Weber, 1947; Parsons, 1937). It is not the content of decision making, e.g., what particular options are considered or even how particular actors link specific means to specific ends, that determines rationality, but the degree to which decision making follows a rational form or process. Therefore, the use or advocacy of different means or ends by different actors is to be expected, and such differences do not necessarily suggest a difference in the degree to which actors are rational. As a process, rationality can and will serve to justify a range of decisions on any given issue, and the selection among a number of equally rational decision outcomes is a political problem, not a problem of sharpening the rationality of the decision making. Overall, this means that judging the degree of rationality from the decision outcome or identifying a particular outcome as rational is inappropriate. The problem for decision makers and for students of decision making is to evalute how rational principles are translated into concrete means and ends, and a political model of organizations seems imperative to understanding this translation process. It is one of the major bases for conflict and political action, because the specific standards, elements, and inputs underlying rational decision making are likely to be the result of power struggle.

This rationality assumption captures one of the primary differences between our approach to organizational politics and those found elsewhere (Pfeffer, 1981; Allison, 1971; Porter et al., 1981; Mayes and Allen, 1977). With social-action theory as a backdrop, it is misleading to treat organizational politics as nonrational or, in application to decision making, to argue that rational and political elements are distinct or even distinguishable (see, especially, Pfeffer, 1981). Such a conceptualization of organizational politics confuses the form of rationality with the content of decision making. Part of this confusion can be traced to the notion of "bounded rationality" (Simon, 1976; Allison, 1971), for it implies some absolute standard of rationality (e.g., "comprehensive rationality") against which to compare the content of decision making. Our political perspective on organizations does not question the value of this concept, but it suggests that a limited search for options or alternatives (bounded rationality) vs. an unlimited search (unbounded or comprehensive rationality) is primarily a difference in content. The question raised by a political mode is: What determines the "boundaries"? The search for alternatives, as well as the other dimensions of rational decision making, should be constrained by what information and positions an interest group requires to combat adversaries and influence a given decision. In this sense, there is nothing intrinsically nonrational about organizational politics and nothing decidedly rational about "nonpolitical" decision making.

To conclude, the fourth assumption suggests that political action is rational in the broad principles it conforms to or general form it takes. Those engaging in organizational politics can be construed as acting rationally, and organizations that permit the infusion of politics into decision making are not necessarily any less rational than organizations which attempt to remove politics from decision making. The content of decision making and related social action develops in the context of the struggle within which groups contend over how to define and apply standards of rationality for a given decision. The identification of means, evaluation of their consequences, and the linking of means to ends are all embedded in and inseparable from a political process composed of influence tactics and countertactics. Thus, the translation of rationality, as form, into decision making content is a political act with dramatic consequences for subgroups and individuals in the organization and for the organization as a whole.

Tenets of social-action theory, encompassed in the four assumptions, identify the broad parameters and characteristics of political action in organizations. These assumptions represent an initial orientation; beyond them, a political model of organizations must deal more extensively with the *interaction* of actors—specifically, with the tactical nature of this interaction. To expand political perspective in this direction, the remainder of this paper will: (1) examine the nature of relationships between conflicting actors; (2) identify insulation and absorption as the major political processes; and (3) develop a classification of political alignments and show how they are generated by the process of insulation and absorption.

III. CONFLICTING ACTORS

When two or more actors interact, there are various types of social relationships that can develop and be maintained over time. Some relationships induce cooperation, some induce competition, and still others induce a combination of cooperative and competitive lines of action. Any image of organizations makes implicit or explicit assumptions about the predominance of competitive and cooperative *action,* as well as the nature of the *relationship* underlying these patterns of action. In fact, such assumptions represent a point along which traditional cooperative images (Barnard, 1938) contrast with more recent attempts to construct a conflict or Marxist model of organizations (Benson, 1977). To distinguish a political perspective from alternative models, it is important to examine and specify the nature of the relationship among actors in an organization.

A political model of organizations implies that a given subunit in an organization (whether the subunit is an individual or subgroup) will have adversarial relationships with at least some of the other subunits within the organization (Collins, 1975; Tushman, 1977; Bacharach and Lawler, 1980). Any actor will have relationships with a number of other actors. Some of these relationships will be predominantly competitive, and others will be predominantly cooperative. Moreover, the relationship of a given actor to others must be viewed in an issue-specific manner, because within any given relationship the actors are likely to be adversaries with respect to some issues, tacit or explicit collaborators with respect to others, and uninvolved with regard to still others. The overall nature of the relationship on the competitive–cooperative dimension should not obscure the "fact" that there are likely to be both cooperative and competitive tendencies within any given organizational relationship, even though these *tendencies* are not always manifested in the interaction of the actors. In this sense, virtually an intraorganizational relationship is *mixed-motive* in nature.

A mixed-motive relationship must be contrasted with positive-sum and zero-sum types of relationships (Rapoport, 1966). In a positive-sum relationship, both actors can maximize their payoffs by cooperative action; in a zero-sum relationship, actors' payoffs are negatively correlated, and, therefore, there is a strong tendency toward competitive action and little room for voluntary cooperation. On the other hand, a mixed-motive relationship simultaneously contains incentives to cooperate and incentives to compete. Traditional organization theory (see reviews by Perrow, 1979; Clegg and Dunkerley, 1980), portrays intraorganizational relationships in positive-sum terms by assuming that organizations are naturally cooperative systems; conflict theories, developed from the writings of

Karl Marx, treat the relationships as zero sum and view any cooperation of workers with the organization as a function of force, oppression, or false consciousness (see, for example, Benson, 1977; Goldman and Van Houten, 1977; Heydebrand, 1977). A mixed-motive conceptualization of actors' relationship is most compatible with a political perspective on organizations.

Portraying organizational relations as mixed-motive has a number of implications for organization theory. One is that intraorganizational relationships should be treated as explicit or tacit bargaining (Bacharach and Lawler, 1980; Abell, 1975). A positive-sum image suggests that cooperation is natural and inevitable, except where members of the organization are inadequately trained, irrational, or misunderstand their relationship to others. Bargaining between parties, in this context, is unnecessary or superfluous, and conflict resolution is based on education and improvements in communication. A zero-sum image, on the other hand, implies that the conflicting interests embedded in intraorganizational relationships make bargaining, in a strict sense, useless. The only "solution" is for one party to force the other into submission; consequently, the emphasis of Marxist approaches is typically on how management legitimizes the existing relations of production and keeps the workers from disrupting production or from threatening the larger economic system (Benson, 1977; Goldman and Van Houten, 1977). In contrast, a mixed-motive image of organizational relations integrates the implications of traditional theory and Marxist approaches such that bargaining is no longer necessary or useless but intrinsic to the activities of organizations. Given incentives to cooperate and to compete, mixed-motive relationships inherently involve distrust and instability. It is bargaining, tacit or explicit, that keeps conflict within acceptable boundaries and enables actors to continue to deal with each other on a day-to-day basis. Furthermore, the resolution of conflict is likely to be temporary, and intraorganizational relations are likely to require continual renegotiation because of the persistent potential for conflict in mixed-motive situations. The mixed-motive assumption of a political model suggests that tacit and explicit bargaining capture the primary modes of social action in organizations.

A second, and related, implication of a mixed-motive conception is that it suggests more uncertainty and unpredictability in intraorganizational relations than other conceptions. This dovetails with the implications of social-action theory. Actors do not act in terms of the a priori "recipes" embedded in the organizational structure of traditional theory or the political economy of Marxist approaches; they act in terms of subjective predictions they make about others' action and orientation to the situation. The situation is made predictable and the uncertainty of the other's action is reduced only through the interpretive or subjective judgments of the actors in the relationship. If relations were naturally cooperative, as portrayed in traditional organizational theory, then these judgmental processes would not be that important—except insofar as they account for the training or other deficiencies of the individuals; organizational structure, itself, dictates cooperative lines of behavior. If the relationships are zero sum, as portrayed by Marxist theory, the problems of uncertainty and unpredictability are not that salient to actors because the structure of conflicting interests essentially dictates competitive lines of behavior. Only the mixed-motive imagery brings this uncertainty and unpredictability to the foreground and begins to grasp the political nature of problems confronted by actors in the organization.

A mixed-motive conception of intraorganizational relations leads to an emphasis on the tactical nature of political action. Political action becomes a choice among tactics based on how others will respond which, in turn, is based on the actor's evaluation of the power relationship. With regard to any particular issue, therefore, the actor will confront several tasks or questions—for example, it must: (1) anticipate what other actors will support or oppose their position on the issue; (2) anticipate how active or forceful prospective opponents will be; (3) examine tactics for minimizing or overcoming the opposition on this issue; and (4) consider how to use this issue to improve their power position on other issues in the future. Traditional theory fails to raise such questions; Marxist theory detracts attention from such questions by attempting to link, by definition, such matters to larger class-related interests; while a political model takes these as major questions to be addressed. The difficulty of answering these questions with traditional theory and research on organizations and organizational behavior suggests the need for a framework on political action and political alignments in organizations.

IV. POLITICAL ACTION

Bacharach and Lawler (1980) develop a general perspective for analyzing the political nature of organizations. They criticize wholistic approaches to organizations and argue that organizations should be conceptualized in terms of interest groups and coalitions. The initial step for analyzing organizational politics is to identify the major interest groups around which political action tends to develop. Interest groups are natural divisions created by the structure of the organization (e.g., departments, divisions, role or occupational categories, professional groupings) or by stratification in the larger social system (e.g., sex, age, race, social class). Interest groups are grounded in the formal structure, tasks, and manpower intrinsic to the activities of the organization. An emphasis on interest groups, however, is not sufficient to a political analysis because it suggests a primary concern with the relatively static, morphological dimensions of the organization.

The central issue is to understand how interest groups—or individuals explicitly or implicitly representing different interest groups—combine with one another, break apart existing combinations, or recombine in an effort to influence specific decision areas. To Bacharach and Lawler (1980), this implies a focus on coalitions, that is, joint action by two or more interest groups against some target group. Coalitions partition organization members into distinct groups on the basis of common interests. They bind the members with the most common interests together, while pitting those with the most divergent interests in opposition to one another. In any organization, there are likely to be numerous differences among actors, and it is coalitions that crystallize, highlight, and make salient the most critical differences; it is coalitions that represent the primary tactical mechanisms through which individuals and subgroups develop, maintain, and use power. In this sense, coalitions are not just the major units of political action, but also what establishes and defines the political game (Bacharach and Lawler, 1980).

Coalitions in organizational contexts can take many different forms. They may bring together many or only a few interest groups. The alliances may be quite explicit or very subtle or implicit. The coalitions may be short term, deal with only one temporally-bound issue and then disband, or they may involve long-term alliances directed at broad issues that subsume many specific, time-bound issues. Finally, coalitions may combine individuals who explicitly and knowingly represent different interest groups or individuals who only tacitly—or even unknowingly—represent particular interest groups. An image of organizations as a coalition network does not imply that individual actors are unimportant, but rather than the interaction of individual actors should be viewed in the context of the interest groups and coalitions that prevail within the organization (see Dalton, 1959; Cyert and March, 1963; Bacharach and Lawler, 1980). Coalitions constitute the operative organizational structure and represent the basic units underlying the political action of individuals and subgroups.

Any organizational structure contains a prevailing political alignment, created and modified by coalition processes within the organization. The concept of political alignment implies some degree of stability, while the political nature of coalition processes indicates that the stability of a given alignment is limited. Given that political alignments ostensibly emerge from coalitions within, it becomes critical to examine how coalitions affect the relationship of actors within the organization. There are two fundamental affects that coalitions have on actors in the organization: they (1) bind some actors together *within* the coalition, and simultaneously (2) split these actors off from others *outside* the coalition. These dual effects represent different foci or "motivations" for actors partaking in a coalition. Actor A may ally with B to gain control over B or to protect itself from C, an actor who remains outside the coalition. On the most basic level, this suggests that there are two major political processes underlying coalition formation: *absorption* and *insulation*. Absorption deals with the relationship of actors within a coalition, while insulation deals with the relation of actors in the coalition to those outside.

Absorption and insulation refer to the consequences of coalition processes *over time*. We are concerned here with long-term coalitions, a focus that makes considerable sense because such coalitions are likely to have the greatest impact on political alignments in the organization. Absorption refers to the process by which a given actor within the coalition essentially envelops other actors, thereby making others less distinguishable from itself. For example, if A and B maintain an alliance over time, the coalition may come to look more like A than like B due to an absorption process. Absorption welds together the interests originally combined in the coalition to such an extent that the coalition comes to look more like an interest group than a coalition. In the most extreme cases, given actors become virtually indistinguishable from one another.

Insulation processes, on the other hand, generate more distinguishable differences between those within and those outside the coalition. That is, insulation sharpens the lines dividing some actors. Taking the organization as a whole, absorption processes blur the formal distinctions between some subgroupings, while insulation processes sharpen or heighten the salience of some distinctions. The major subgroups and political alignment existing at a given point in time, therefore, can be construed as the result of prior absorption and insulation processes.

The relationship of absorption and insulation should be viewed as an empirical issue. The mere fact of a coalition implies some minimal degree of insulation from outside actors, but the degree of insulation can vary considerably and, beyond this minimal level, insulation essentially becomes a tactical issue for the actors in the coalition. Actors within the coalition can use it to insulate themselves from certain actors to a greater or lesser degree depending on their goals and position in the organization. In contrast, the mere fact of a coalition does not imply absorption of one or some actors by others within the coalition. A coalition may or may not lead to partial or total absorption, depending, once again, on how the actors use the coalition tactically. While absorption captures the process of moving together and insulation the process of moving apart, these processes are not bound together inextricably. Overall, the degree of absorption and insulation, as well as the relationship between these processes, is contingent on the manner in which actors use coalitions in a given context.

The concepts of absorption and insulation raise questions for both the micropolitics and macropolitics of organizations. Micropolitics is concerned with the action of particular actors attempting to deal with opposition from other actors. At the micro level, absorption and insulation are tactics for developing and using power, e.g., one way is to absorb the opposition, another is to absorb third parties to protect oneself against the opposition, and still another is to insulate oneself from the opposition. Such tactics have consequences for the particular actors but also for the organization as a whole. Macropolitics is concerned with the latter—specifically, with the nature and operation of the political alignments embedded in the organizational structure. The major task for bridging these micro and macro concerns, then, is to classify political alignments and understand how they are generated by processes of absorption and insulation. To understand political alignments, one must provide a parsimonious way to analyze the sources (antecedents) of absorption and insulation, as well as the effect (consequences) of these processes for the organization as a whole. The antecedents of absorption and insulation should be found in the structure of the organization, and the consequences of prime concern are the modification or creation of political alignments. This implies a reciprocal relationship of structure and social action that is quite consistent with the "dialectical" elements of Weber's theory, discussed earlier in this paper.

V. POLITICAL ALIGNMENTS

Two dimensions of organizational structure are critical for analyzing the sources and consequences of insulation and absorption: the *number of actors* involved with a given issue or decision area and the *power differentiation* among these actors. Social psychological work on coalitions and sociological analyses of organization dovetail in their historic concern with these dimensions. Social psychologists have developed several theories of coalition formation which attempt to predict how coalition decisions will vary with the number of actors in the situation and distribution of resources across the actors (Murnighan, 1978; Caplow, 1968; Komorita and Chertkoff, 1973; Komorita, 1974). Such theories implicitly cast these dimensions as basic parameters of coalition situations. Similarly, organizational theorists and researchers, through investigations of organizational size, centralization, worker participation and the like, portray related dimensions as basic to the structure of an organization (Perrow, 1979; Clegg and Dunkerley, 1980; Hall, 1982).

A political perspective on organizations implies a particular orientation toward the analysis of the number of actors and power differentiation. The number of actors is not the same as the total number of employees or individuals in an organization but is rather the number of distinct subgroups implicated in an issue or issue area. Traditional measures of organizational size do not qualify as adequate indicators of the number of distinct actors implicated in an issue or issue area. An actor is an interest group or coalition (or individual representing such groupings) that is engaged in distinguishable lines of action on an issue. Social action is the appropriate foundation for identifying relevant actors, and the number of actors will vary across specific issues or decision areas. By power differentiation, we refer to the differences in potential influence among the relevant actors. At the micro level, this is tantamount to the relative power or resources of an actor vis-à-vis prospective allies and adversaries. At the macro level, power differentiation may be viewed in terms of centralization and decentralization. For our purposes, the most critical aspect of power differentiation is the variance of power across the actors. Low variance in power indicates relatively equal power among the multitude of actors vying for influence, while high variance indicates that there are substantial power inequalities among at least some of the actors. The *variance* of power more readily captures the parameters of power struggle than does the *distribution* of power.

The number of actors and power differentiation are important to insulation and absorption for different reasons. The number of actors reflects the range of options available to actors putting together coalitions. With many actors involved in the issue, there are generally more options or prospective allies, but also more potential sources of opposition. Decisions on what coalitions to mobilize and how to use them, therefore, become more complex, and there is greater uncertainty about the ability of adversaries to respond with coalitions of their own. A context with many actors compels actors to consider how coalitions can be used to make the situation more predictable and orderly. Power differentiation, on the other hand, reflects the problems of control within the coalition and influence outside of it. In general, actors will prefer coalitions with lower-power others because they are likely to have more control over the internal affairs of the coalition (see Caplow, 1956, 1968). Also, such power lays the groundwork for absorbing coalition partners. Power inside vs. outside presents a high-power actor with a dilemma. Coalitions with lower-power actors can forestall alliances of lower-power actors against higher-power ones (e.g., subordinate revolts), but they may not allow one high-power actor to overcome the opposition of another high-power actor.

Our purpose is not to predict what coalition will form but to understand how actors tend to use coalitions and the bearing this will have on political alignments in the organization. The first step is to examine the impact of the number of actors and power differentiation on the tendency of actors' to use coalitions as insulating and absorbing mechanisms. Figure 1 schematically presents the basic relationships. Let us emphasize that these are very basic tendencies that will be modified by other aspects of a given context. Our position is that to understand such modifications, one has to specify the broad patterns on an abstract level.

With regard to the number of actors, Figure 1 posits a positive relationship to absorption processes and a negative relationship to insulation processes. In the context of many actors, absorption becomes a means of making decisions in the particular area more manageable and predictable over time by reducing the number of actors. For higher-power actors (the absorber), this has obvious advantages; for the lower-power actors (ones being absorbed), the close affiliation with higher-power ones facilitates some protection from other actors. The more actors in the situation, the more likely it is that the higher-power actors will attempt and the lower-power actors will accept greater levels of absorption. Over time, this leads to a smaller number of coalitional actors, each of which is highly integrated within by absorption processes.

The positive effect of absorption on insulation (Figure 1) reflects the fact that some degree of insulation is an unintentional by-product of absorption processes. The implication is that the way to successful insulation is through absorption

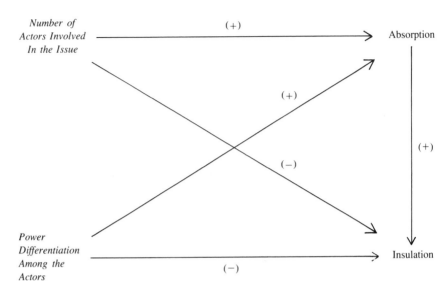

Figure 1.   Impact of the Number of Actors and Power Differentiation Among
the Actors on the Tendency Toward Absorption and Insulation.

when a large number of actors are involved in the decision. In the context of
many actors, insulation as the dominant tactic is likely to be ineffective, because
actors should recognize that their opponents also have several coalitional opportunities and, therefore, that attempts to insulate an adversary will typically lead
to retaliation in kind. A coalition of A and B, designed to insulate the actors from
C, should be unlikely or short lived if C can readily block the impact of the AB
coalition by allying with D. More actors provide all with more opportunities for
coalitional action and, thereby, enable all to protect themselves from insulation
by others. Thus, with many actors involved in an issue, the use of coalitions as
insulating devices should lead to little change over time, that is, they create and
maintain standoffs on specific decisions falling within the general area of concern. To the extent that insulation occurs at all under such circumstances, it is
likely to occur indirectly through prior absorption processes.

  Turning to power differentiation, Figure 1 posits that greater power differentiation among the actors will increase the tendency toward absorption and
decrease the tendency toward insulation. This is based on the assumption that
actors balance two considerations when evaluating their power vis-à-vis others'.
First, actors will prefer coalitions in which they are dominant (see Caplow,
1968). Greater power within the coalition enables them to exert more influence
over the coalition and make fewer concessions to maintain the coalition over
time. Second, actors will prefer smaller to larger coalitions in order to minimize
problems of coordination within the coalition (Riker, 1962; Komorita, 1974).

High power differentiation implies that actors with more power have greater opportunity to act in accord with the first consideration, and this should be their paramount concern. Actors with lower levels of power may be particularly amenable to alliances with higher-power actors due primarily to the second consideration, i.e., the size of available coalitions. With all other things equal, a coalition with a high-power actor may be more beneficial to low-power actors who gain entrance to such a coalition than a larger coalition of actors with actors of less power. Overall, high power differentiation among the actors involved in a decision establishes conditions favorable to coalitions that generate absorption processes.

Insulation is a major foundation for coalitions that develop under conditions of low power differentiation. A situation of low power differentiation leads to coalitions with actors of relatively equal power. Such coalitions will confront serious problems of internal stability over time, because equal power requires members of the coalition to make substantial compromises (see Bacharach and Lawler, 1981 for a discussion of equal vs. unequal power in bargaining relationships). Actors will carefully and continuously weigh the costs of remaining in the coalition vs. the costs of leaving it. In this context, the maintenance of the coalition is less a matter of internal solidarity, per se, and more a matter of what external pressures make the coalition valuable. To the extent that a coalition insulates its members from adversaires, it handles one major source of external pressure. Thus, while the stability of an "absorptive" coalition is based primarily on internal solidarity generated by the absorption process, the stability of an "insulative" coalition is based on the external threat handled by the coalition. Such theoretical reasoning leads to the conclusion that low power differentiation among the actors establishes conditions favorable to coalitions that generate insulation.

To this point, our discussion indicates that actors can use coalitions as tactics of insulation or as tactics of absorption. The choice or emphasis adopted by actors can be predicted from the number of actors involved in the issue and the degree of differentiation among these actors. The more actors or the larger the power differences confronted by the actors, the more inclined they become toward absorption tactics and the less inclined they become toward insulation tactics. However, while we have analyzed the number of actors and power differentiation in isolation, the basic implication is that the combined or interactive effects of these dimensions is most critical. Specifically, our discussion leads to the following proposition: *With few actors and low power differentiation, actors are likely to use coalitions as tactics of insulation; with many actors and high power differentiation, actors are likely to use coalitions as tactics of absorption.* The emphasis placed on these modes of coalitional action is important because it has an impact on the political alignments that emerge from coalitions processes. Essentially, this paper conceptualizes the number of actors and power differentiation as the primary independent variables, insulation and

Table 1.   Type of Political Alignment by
the Number of Actors and the Power
Differentiation Among the Actors

		Power Differentiation	
		Low	*High*
Number of Actors	*Few*	Politics of Confrontation	Politics of Patronage
	Many	Politics of Crisis	Politics of Cooptation

absorption as the intervening variables, and political alignment as the dependent variable.

A cross-classification of the number of actors (few vs. many) and power differentiation (low vs. high) suggests four major types of political alignment: confrontational, crisis, patronage, and co-optational (see Table 1). These types of alignment must be interpreted with reference to the emphasis actors place on absorption and insulation tactics. Insulation leads to either the politics of confrontation or the politics of crisis, while absorption leads to either the politics of patronage or the politics of co-optation. Each of these political alignments is discussed, in turn.

A.   Politics of Confrontation

This form of political alignment develops from the insulation processes that tend to occur when there are few actors of relatively equal power. The prototype is a highly decentralized organization in which there are relatively few interest groups and coalitions. The central characteristics of this political alignment are that: (1) alliances are relatively stable and pit a few major subgroups against one another; (2) the conflict between subgroups is manifested across a large range of issues, e.g., the conflict seems to "pop up" everywhere; and (3) no one group, given the stable alliances, is able to dominate the organization as a whole, although such domination may periodically occur over specific, time-bound issues. The politics of confrontation essentially creates a circumstance where divergent groups and individuals, representing these groups, can and must engage in relatively conscious and explicit bargaining to get things done. Beyond the dominant coalitions defining this form of political alignment, more transient coalitions are likely to develop over specific issues, but these must be viewed in the context of the relatively stable coalitional structure that manifests this form of alignment. Overall, the politics of confrontation give rise to persistent but patterned, predictable, and manageable conflict.

B. Politics of Crisis

This form of political alignment develops when insulation tactics are prevalent in a context containing many actors with relatively equal power. The prototype is the highly decentralized organization in chaos or what Karl Weick (1976) has termed the "loosely coupled" system. The politics of crisis is characterized by unstable, fluid alliances which, because of their instability, are only able to address relatively specific, temporally bound issues. Every specific issue seems to create a new set of alliances, not necessarily predictable from alliances on previous issues. There is some order to the chaos, but it is attributable primarily to the multitude of interest groups created by the formal structure of the organization, rather than to the emergence of a relatively stable coalition structure as in the case of the politics of confrontation. Organizational elites may maintain control over the broadest parameters of the conflict, but the conflict tends to be unpatterned, unpredictable, and unmanageable from the standpoint of the actors, thus creating an "embattled" mentality.

C. Politics of Patronage

This form of political alignment develops from absorption processes when there are large power differences among relatively few actors. The prototype, of course, is the highly centralized organization. The main characteristics are: (1) very stable alliances that crosscut higher and lower levels of the formal organization hierarchy; (2) the appearance of little or no conflict between subgroups, generated by the ability of high-power actors to smooth over differences and subtly "force" consensus on a wide range of issues; and (3) highly constrained, trivialized patterns of conflict. Conflict tends to be attributed to the personalities of the individuals involved rather than to the divergent interest groups or coalitions that they implicitly or explicitly represent. Conflict is kept in the background, and when it does occur, it is specific or made specific and given the appearance of a temporary aberration. The politics of patronage tend to occur when the absorption processes conceal differences and lead to difficulty in identifying different interest groups or coalitions. An organization that appears on the surface to consist only of two coalitions, labor and management, is often one in which key actors have successfully carried the absorption processes in this direction.

D. Politics of Co-optation

This form of political alignment has its source in absorption processes occurring in the context of many actors and high power differentiation. The existence of many actors encourages those with high power to co-opt actors with lower power and, thereby: (1) solidify their competitive position vis-à-vis other high-power actors; and (2) prevent collective revolts by those with less power (Lawler et al., 1978). Co-optation is a tactic for dividing or forestalling potential opposition while increasing the strength of the coalition in its dealings with other coalitions. At the same time, the existence of many actors gives those who are co-opted at one point the option of defecting from the coalitions in the future. Consequently, the politics of co-optation are manifested in: (1) moderately stable alliances that are subject to continual bargaining because of the defection problem; (2) bargaining that is less explicit (i.e., more tacit) than in the politics of confrontation, but more explicit than in the politics of patronage, and (3) the manipulation of symbols of unity or cooperation, which lends legitimacy to the relationship between actors and deemphasizes their divergent interests. Schemes for participative management often create this form of political alignment.

This framework for dealing with political alignments can be applied to the internal dynamics of an interest group or coalition (i.e., to micropolitics) as well as to the organization as a whole (i.e., to macropolitics). In application to the micropolitics of particular subgroups, the scheme suggests that the choice of ally and the organizational structure facilitate one of these forms of political alignment. A coalition between actors of relatively equal power will tend to create internal politics of confrontation or crisis, with the attendant problems of long-term stability. To maintain such a coalition over time and use it to address a wide range of issues, members will have to devote more time and effort to the management of the internal politics of the coalition. On the other hand, coalitions between actors of widely divergent power will tend to create politics of patronage or co-optation, depending on the viability of alternative allies to the lower-power actor, the competition between the high-power actor and others, and the particular direction taken by the processes of absorption. Such coalitions may be stable over time, but as coalitions they may have less strength in dealings with other coalitions containing at least one high-power actor.

The scheme also leads to the inference that the tactics for creating and maintaining coalitions in organizational contexts are different across political alignments. Coalitions with patronage politics are based primarily on coercion and threats, made possible by wide disparities in power among allies. Coalitions with co-optational politics are based primarily on the inducements higher-power actors can offer lower-power ones. The inducements are made necessary by the alternatives available to lower-power actors, and typically include a combination of tangible benefit and the symbolic value of affiliation with the particular high-power actor. Coalitions with confrontational politics are based on explicit bargaining through which actors overcome their differences via substantial, mutual concessions. Finally, coalitions with crisis politics are likely to be based on tacit areas of consensus developed through persuasive argumentation. These tactics for creating and maintaining particular coalitions are also the dominant tactics maintaining political alignments at the organizational or macro level.

At the macro level, the scheme fosters a political perspective on centralization and decentralization. Insulation processes tend to underlie decentralization, which can take the form of either the politics of confrontation or the politics of crisis; absorption processes underlie centralization, which can take the form of patronage or co-optational politics. Centralization and decentralization are thereby construed as the emergent product of political action. However, we have consistently argued in this paper that there is a reciprocal relationship of action and structure, and this is also important to the analysis of centralization. The processes of insulation and absorption do not simply create different levels of centralization, they also occur within some existing level. The foregoing scheme implies that highly centralized organizations tend to create the politics of patronage or co-optation; therefore, they tend to be more stable than decentralized organizations which, in contrast, create confrontational or crisis politics. A centralized organization fosters conditions favorable to political action like absorption, while a decentralized context facilitates action such as insulation. Our framework, thus, suggests the importance of a dynamic, political approach to centralization based on the assumption that the existing structure produces political action that, in turn, reinforces or modifies that structure.

The framework also has implications regarding the prevalence of interest-group politics and coalition politics. Bacharach and Lawler (1980) indicate that organizational politics are most likely to be organized around interest groups when the subgroups in the organization have *both* divergent functional goals and ideologies—for example, when different professions represent major segments in the organization. Coalition politics, on the other hand, are most likely when both the goals and ideologies of some subgroups are compatible. While the types of political alignment identified in the present paper may involve either or both interest group and coalition politics, there is reason to expect the following patterns: interest-group politics will tend to be associated with both confrontational and patronage alignments, while coalition politics will be associated with crisis and co-optational alignments. Confrontational politics implies a situation where irreconcilable differences (e.g., in both functional goals and ideology) are made reconcilable by bringing the conflict to the foreground and explicitly dealing with it. Patronage politics implies a situation where irreconcilable differences are pushed into the background through the ability of a high-power group to absorb a low-power group. Crisis politics implies a situation, not where differences are irreconcilable, but where they are essentially difficult to define and manage. It is not clear exactly which differences are irreconcilable and which are not; it is only clear that there are many differences manifested in so many groups without consistent, regular patterns over a multitude of issues. Coalitions are often born of such chaos and offer the only clear mechanism for self-protection and partial management of the conflict. Co-optational politics similarly implies a situation more complex and uncertain than confrontational and patronage politics for many of the same reasons—one of which is that there is not necessarily a clear divergence on both ideology and functional goals among the many groups implicated in the conflict. Overall, the prevelance of interest group vs. coalition politics should be affected by the existing political alignment in an organization.

VI. CONCLUSION

A political perspective on organizations proposes a particular approach to the analysis of intraorganizational relations. First, it is necessary to identify the relevant actors, that is, those who are involved in or attempt to influence an issue or decision. The actors may be individuals, work groups, interest groups, or coalitions. While we emphasize coalitions, it is not the particular type of actor that is the most critical but what actors are responsible for the major lines of social action relevant to the issue. A political perspective recommends that we be wary of interpreting conflict as a manifestation of personality or focusing on individuals. Individuals in conflict typically represent—if only implicitly—divergent interests of subgroups within the organization. What appear to be personality or individual conflicts are often manifestations of conflict between organizational subgroupings.

Second, a political perspective suggests that organizational politics are issue specific. For each issue within a general decision area and for each decision area, there is likely to be some difference in the set of relevant actors. By the same token, the political alignments may shift across issues or decision areas. This paper has developed a general framework for analyzing political alignments, but its concrete application must take account of the issue specificity of organizational politics. While we believe that there are dominant alignments that pervade an organization, this is ultimately an empirical question because the degree to which a given alignment is maintained across issues is likely to vary within and across organizations. Only by adopting an issue-specific approach can one determine the overall power of given actors and the generality of a particular political alignment.

Third, a political perspective stresses the tactical nature of intraorganizational relations. The relations of specific actors over a given issue are manifested in their efforts to overcome or reduce opposition from others and to maximize their influence over the decision. There are innumerable tactics that might be adopted and also innumerable ways to categorize and conceptualize them (Kipnis et al., 1980; Tedeschi and Bonoma, 1972; Bacharach and Lawler, 1980; Pfeffer, 1981). This paper has treated insulation and absorption as tactics for using coalitions and examined the impact of these on political alignments.

Fourth, the tactical action of concern to a political model must be considered in the context of the organizational structure. This paper treats the number of actors and power differentiation as basic dimensions of the organizational structure within which to examine insulation and absorption tactics. Other facets of organizational structure, such as formalization and complexity, must also be integrated into the concerns of this paper. Our position is not that the number of actors and power differentiation are the only structural dimensions of importance, but that these are the broad parameters to which other dimensions of structure should be related.

Fifth, a political perspective suggests that political alignments condition and channel organizational processes, such as communication, innovation, decision making and conflict management. The traditional foci of organizational work, therefore, should be viewed and interpreted in the context of the political alignments. Communication patterns, innovation, etc. are outcomes of a political process and should reflect the prevailing political alignments. By the same token, the impact of the environment on internal organizational processes should be mediated by political processes and alignments such as those examined in this paper.

REFERENCES

Abell, Peter
  1975   Organizations as Bargaining and Influence Systems. London: Heinemann.
Allison, Graham T.
  1971   Essence of Decision. Boston: Little Brown and Company.
Bacharach, Samuel B.
  1978   "Morologie et processus: une critique de la Recherche intra-organisationnelle contemporaine." Sociologie Du Travail (June).
Bacharach, Samuel B. and E. J. Lawler
  1980   Power and Politics in Organizations. SanFrancisco: Jossey-Bass.
Bacharach, S. B. and E. J. Lawler
  1981   Bargaining: Power, Tactics and Outcomes. San Francisco: Jossey-Bass.
Baldridge, J. V.
  1971   Power and Conflict in the University. New York: Wiley.
Barnard, Chester I.
  1938   The Functions of the Executive. Cambridge, MA: Harvard University Press.
Benson, J. K.
  1977   "Organizations: a dialectical view." Administrative Science Quarterly 22:1–21.
Caplow, T.
  1956   "A theory of coalitions in the Triad." American Sociological Review 21:489–493.
Caplow, T.
  1968   Two Against One. Englewood Cliffs: Prentice-Hall.
Clegg, Stewart and David Dunkerley
  1980   Organizations, Class and Control. London: Routledge and Kegan Paul.
Collins, Randall
  1975   Conflict Sociology. New York: Academic Press.
Cyert, R. M. and J. G. March
  1962   A Behavioral Theory of the Firm. Englewood Cliffs: Prentice-Hall.
Dalton, Melville
  1959   Men who Manage. New York: Wiley.
Georgiou, Petro
  1981   "The goal paradigm and notes toward a counter paradigm." In Complex Organizations: A Critical Perspective, Mary Zey-Ferrell and Michael Aiken (eds.), Glenview: Scott, Foresman and Company.

Goldman, Paul and Donald R. Van Houten
1977 "Managerial strategies and the worker: a Marxist analysis of bureaucracy." The Sociological Quarterly 18 (Winter):108–125.

Hall, Richard H.
1982 Organizations. Englewood Cliffs: Prentice-Hall.

Heyebrand, Wolf
1977 "Organizational contradictions in public bureaucracies: toward a Marxian theory of organizations." The Sociological Quarterly 18 (Winter):83–107.

Kipnis, David
1976 The Powerholders. Chicago: The University of Chicago Press.

Kipnis, D., S. M. Schmidt, and I. Wilkinson
1980 "Intraorganizational influence tactics: explorations in getting one's way." Journal of Applied Psychology 65:440–452.

Komorita, S. S. and J. Chertkoff
1973 "A bargaining theory of coalition formation." Psychological Review 80:149–162.

Komorita, S. S.
1974 "A weighted probability model of coalition formation." Psychological Review 81:242–256.

Lawler, E. J., G. A. Youngs, Jr., and M. D. Lesh
1978 "Cooptation and coalition mobilization." Journal of Applied Social Psychology 8, no. 3:199–214.

Madison, D. L., R. W. Allen, L. W. Porter, P. A. Renwick, and B. T. Mayes
1980 "Organizational politics: an exploration of managers' perceptions." Human Relations 33, no. 2:79–100.

March, J. G. and H. A. Simon
1958 Organizations. New York: Wiley.

Mayes, B. T. and R. W. Allen
1977 "Toward a definition of organizational politics." The Academy of Management Review 2, (4)(October):672–678.

Murnighan, J. K.
1978 "Models of coalition behavior: game, theoretic, social psychological, and political perspectives." Psychological Bulletin 85:1130–1153.

Parsons, Talcott
1956 "Suggestions for a sociological approach to the theory of organizations -I." Administrative Science Quarterly (June):63–85.

Parsons, Talcott
1937 The Structure of Social Action. New York: Free Press.

Perrow, Charles
1979 "Complex Organizations." Glenview, Ill.: Scott, Foresman and Company.

Pettigrew, Andrew M.
1973 The Politics of Organizational Decision Making. London: Travistock.

Pfeffer, Jeffrey
1981 Power in Organizations. Marshfield, Mass.: Pitman Publishing Co.

Porter, L. W., R. W. Allen, and H. L. Angle
1981 "The politics of upward influence in organizations." Pp. 109–149 in B. M. Staw and L. L. Cummings (eds.), Research in Organizational Behavior, vol. 3, Greenwich, Ct: JAI Press.

Rapoport, Antol
1966 Two-Person Game Theory. Ann Arbor, Michigan: University of Michigan Press.

Riker, W. H.
1962 The Theory of Political Coalitions. New Haven, Conn.: Yale University Press.

Schutz, Alfred
1967   Phenomenology of the Social World. Evanston, Ill.: Northwestern University Press.
Simon, H. A.
1976   Administrative Behavior. New York: Macmillan.
Tedeschi, J. T. and T. V. Bonoma
1972   "Power and influence: an introduction." In Social Influence Processes by J. T. Tedeschi, Chicago, Ill.: Aldine-Artherton.
Tushman, Michael L.
1977   "A political approach to organizations: a review and rationale." Academy of Management Journal 2 (April):206–217.
Weber, Max
1947   "The theory of social and economic organization." A. M. Henderson and T. Parsons (eds.), and Translators. New York: Oxford Press.
Weick, K.
1976   "Educational organizations as loosely coupled systems." Administrative Science Quarterly 21:1–19.
Weick, K.
1979   The Social Psychology of Organizations. Reading, Mass.: Addison-Wesley.
Zald, M. N.
1970   Organization Charge: The Political Economics of the YMCA. Chicago: University of Chicago Press.
Zald, Mayer N. and Michael A. Berger
1978   "Social movements in organizations: coup d' etat, insurgency and mass movements." American Journal of Sociology 83(4):823–861.
Zaleznik, Abraham
1970   "Power and politics in organizational life." Harvard Business Review (May–June):47–60.

PHENOMENOLOGY AND FORMAL ORGANIZATIONS:
A REALIST CRITIQUE

Stewart Clegg

I. INTRODUCTION

Organization theory has been characterized as displaying the dominant orthodoxy of the functionalist paradigm (Burrell and Morgan, 1979). Exceptions, which are sometimes constituted in the literature as phenomenological, exist of course, such as Goffman's (1971) dramaturgical sociology of self-survival or Weick's (1969) *Social Psychology of Organizing*. However, these exceptions have not explicitly challenged the *epistemological* presuppositions of the "orthodoxy." It has been left largely to an English writer, David Silverman, to make this challenge by drawing on some well-established resources from the phenomenological critique of positivism which has occurred in the philosophy of the social sciences and in ethnomethodology.[1]

Research in the Sociology of Organizations, vol. 2, pages 109–152
Copyright © 1983 by JAI Press Inc.
All rights of reproduction in any form reserved.
ISBN: 0-89232-203-9

The debate has deep roots in the soil of German Idealism but appears as only a recent seedling to most Anglo-American organization theorists, although it was a central concern of Max Weber and his immediate contemporaries. Silverman draws on one side of this debate, that presented by the protagonists of the *Geisteswissenschaften,* to criticize those who draw from the other side. The "orthodoxy" opposed is one which derives from a conception of social science modeled on the *Naturwissenschaften:* the natural sciences as opposed to the cultural sciences.

This essay will explore the immediate background of this debate in the context of recent contributions to the philosophy of science which render some of the dichotomous positions proposed redundant. First, it will consider how phenomenology developed into social science discourse and became institutionalized there as part of the critique of positivism. Second, it will consider the development of this critique of positivism within the specific field of the sociology of organizations and its implications for organization analysis. Third, it will consider the adequacy of this binary characterization of the field of knowledge as either positivist or phenomenological. In so doing the claims of a "realist" theory of knowledge will be advanced. Fourth, an imaginative sketch for a realist analysis of organizations will be advanced.

The essay will conclude by listing which distinctive features of such an analysis would be compared with either a "positivist" or "phenomenological" one.

II.   PHENOMENOLOGY AND POSITIVISM

Edmund Husserl, who died in 1938, is widely regarded as the progenitor of phenomenology. This movement began in philosophy (and remained there in Husserl's work) but has had some repercussions in the social sciences through the work of Alfred Schutz, a pupil of Husserl's who died in 1959.[2]

I shall begin by characterizing Husserl's phenomenology.

A.   Husserl's Phenomenology

Husserl's phenomenology has as its intention the achievement of certain, absolute knowledge unclouded by the relativities of time, place, perspective, context, class, history, etc. This knowledge could not be the property of any particular subjectivity but would be constitutive of any and all subjectivity; it would be a transcendental subjectivity. Such a knowledge necessarily shakes to the core our mundane belief in the necessity of things—their true, given nature. Husserl refers to our ordinary way of seeing things as the "natural attitude." This is our normal empirical but conventional[3] way of being in the world, of experiencing it as facticity rather than illusion.[4]

Husserl argues that in order to approach phenomenological certitude we must begin by suspending or bracketing (the *éphoche*) this "natural attitude." If the "natural attitude" is our ordinary way of being in the world, then, as Bauman (1978:116) has written, it implies an "extra-ordinary effort" to overcome this comfortable form of life.[5] Indeed, as Bauman goes on to argue, there can be no passage from criticism *in* the natural attitude to criticism *of* the natural attitude. Such a criticism as the latter, necessarily, will be a critique of the consciousness in terms of which the former is located—hence, as it is proposed by Berger and Pullberg (1966), a critique of reification. However, for Husserl (1967), it is not just some modes of being in the world which are "reified" but all such modes. The phenomenological reduction seeks to produce knowledge which will stand independently of the coordinates of existence.

Husserl's (1970) later work does attempt to reconnect consciousness and society, but in a manner which is profoundly unconvincing to anyone with the slightest acquaintance with one of the central concerns of sociology: social conflict. Husserl attempts to bridge the gap by stressing intersubjectivity. The move from subjectivity to intersubjectivity is made on a presumption of social order. This highly consensual and order-oriented conception of the life world enters into sociological phenomenology as well.

B. Schutz's Phenomenology

Alfred Schutz's phenomenological sociology (1962, 1964, 1966, 1967) is grounded in precisely this unsatisfactory resolution of intersubjectivity. The impossibility of transcendental intersubjectivity was remarked by Schutz himself (1970:10):

> I suggest that it is a "scandal of philosophy" that so far a satisfactory solution to the problem of our knowledge of other minds and, in connection therewith, of the intersubjectivity of our experience of the natural as well as the sociocultural world has not been found . . .

Nonetheless, Schutz follows Husserl in "postulating a reciprocated intentional bond between subjectivity and its contents" (Bauman, 1976:52). From a strictly phenomenological point of view this is an illegitimate "solution" to what must prove to be an insoluble problem. Having been bracketed out, reality cannot be legitimately smuggled back in through the space "outside" of subjectivity-in-particular, or through the space between the alleged transcendental subjectivity that I and the other share. [As Lazlo (1966:222) puts it, "inter" presupposes the many, and "subjectivity" connotes the one.]

Schutz's major systematic work is *The Phenomenology of the Social World* (1967), first published in Vienna in 1932. It is from this work that the project of a sociological phenomenology and, more particularly, a "phenomenologically influenced" perspective on organizations has developed. Schutz (1967) agrees with Weber (1968) that the foundation of the philosophy of the social sciences must be a grasp of the nature of human action as governed by subjective meanings. Schutz (1967:6) formulates his project in these explicitly Weberian terms:

> Never before had the project of reducing the "world of objective mind" to the behaviour of individuals been so radically carried out as it was in Max Weber's initial statement of the goal of interpretative sociology. This science is to study social behaviour by interpreting its subjective meaning as found in the intentions of individuals. This aim, then, is to interpret the actions of individuals in the social world and the ways in which individuals give meaning to social phenomena.

But he does so with phenomenological reservations (1967:7–8).

> [Weber] breaks off his analysis of the social world when he arrives at what he considers to be the basic and irreducible elements of social phenomena. But he is wrong in this assumption. His concept of the meaningful act of the individual—the key idea of interpretative sociology—by no means defines a primitive, as he thinks it does. It is, on the contrary, a mere label for a highly complex and ramified area that calls for much further study.

This "much further study" will be accomplished through using Husserl's phenomenological reduction of Weber's concerns as a matter already in hand. Such a use of Husserl, as both Bauman (1976) and Hindess (1977) note, is an abuse. Rather than taking Husserl's rigorous idealism, which seeks to make all phenomena subject to a radical investigation of sense, Schutz (1967) unproblematically accepts Weber's (1968) definition of the problem of sociology without radically questioning it, or bracketing its reliance on the German idealist tradition of the *Geistewissenschaften*. What he does (1967:8) is to argue that Weber's definition of the unit-act of sociological analysis was inadequate:

> Weber makes no distinction between the action, considered as something in progress, and the completed act, between the meaning of the producer of a cultural object and the meaning of the object produced, between the meaning of my own action and the meaning of another's action, between my own experience and of someone else, between my self-understanding and my understanding of another person. He does not ask how an actor's meaning is constituted or what modifications this meaning undergoes for his partners in the social world or for a non-participating observer. He does not try to identify the unique and fundamental relation existing between the self and the other self, that relation whose clarification is essential to a precise understanding of what it is to know another person.

In order to remedy these inadequacies, Schutz (1967) insists that we turn to a "constitutive phenomenology of the natural attitude." This will inquire into the natural (reified) attitude which governs the commonsense or mundane world of everyday life. It will do this by showing how interacting subjects (that "fundamental relation") experience and construct social reality. As Silverman (1972:166) puts it, a phenomenological sociology must "move beyond the experience of any one person in order to reveal shared assumptions about social reality (and the activities associated with them) which generate and sustain such experiences—it must seek to understand the process of experiencing.'' What are these ''shared assumption''? They are ''anthropological universals,'' as Bauman (1976:50) terms them, smuggled into this phenomenology as a priori factors of analysis. These consist of those stable ''background expectancies'' through which actors are able to construct typifications of other persons. These intersubjective anthropological universals are threefold. Schutz (1962) introduces these as the ''reciprocity of perspectives'' and ''interchangeability of standpoints,'' and the ''congruency of relevances.'' In other words, Schutz's phenomenology assumes a priori that the other will see things my way, and that I will see things the other's way, given the interchangeability of our standpoints and the fact that we have congruent relevancies. In short, as Hindess (1977) develops, there is an assumption of liberal tolerance in Schutz, that, writing as one liberal for other liberals, such things as are constitutive of a good fellow may be taken for granted. As Lassman (1974:128) notes, this ''promotes a highly consensual image of the social reality of the ''life world'' and this image has permeated the whole phenomenological approach.'' It has certainly pervaded much of it, if not all (e.g., M. F. D. Young, 1971; Paci, 1972).

This ''constitutive phenomenology of the natural attitude'' can be applied not only to substantive areas of sociological analysis, such as an inquiry into an organization's members' sense of that organization, but also to an understanding of the sense *of their sense* that organization theorists necessarily (and usually tacitly) rely on in order to make their own analysis. It assumes a priori that social explanation can only proceed through relying on the meanings and understandings of the subjects who are under investigation. This proposes a different conception of social science to one which does not recognize the specificity of the social in social science.[6]

C. Natural vs. Social Science

The relationship of the natural and the social sciences and the method and forms of explanation appropriate to each are the terrain on which the phenomenology vs. positivism dispute has waxed and waned. As Benton (1977:46) puts it: ''in the name of the unity of science the positivists have argued for an extension of the methods and forms of explanation developed in the natural sciences into the social sciences and have generally refused to recognize a difference of principle between the approaches appropriate to the two fields of enquiry.'' Schutz (1970:6) certainly formulates his opposition in these terms, charging that ''all forms of naturalism and logical empiricism,'' including positivism, ''simply take for granted . . . social reality, which is the proper object of the social sciences. Intersubjectivity, interaction, intercommunication, and language are simply presupposed as the unclarified foundation of these theories.'' Furthermore, he argues that positivism excludes several important dimensions of social reality from its possible scope of inquiry, such as the effect

of the investigator on the phenomenon under study, its meaning to the participants, possible types of nonaction (i.e., intentional refraining from action),
definitions of the situation, and "action at a distance." The remainder of
Schutz's argument (1970:11) is dedicated to explicating "the fact that there is an
essential difference in the structure of the thought objects or mental constructs
formed by the social sciences and those formed by the natural sciences."

The phenomena studied by the natural sciences have no conception of themselves; atoms, iron filings and magnets, etcetera have no meaning in and of
themselves. On the contrary, the phenomena of social reality have "a specific
meaning and relevance structure for beings living, acting and thinking within
it." Consequently, Schutz (1970:11–2) argues, "The thought objects constructed by the social scientist, in order to grasp this social reality, have to be
founded upon the thought objects constructed by the commonsense thinking of
men, living their daily life within their social world." Because of this, Schutz
believes that the constructs of the social sciences have to be founded on,
grounded in, and agreeable with the commonsense experiences of the social
world. This leads to a concern with typifications as our ordinary way of being-in-
this-world, of negotiating our way through the "stocks of knowledge" which
characterize it and its inhabitants, whom we encounter in more or less degrees of
intimacy and anonymity.

This précis of some of Schutz's central ideas forms much of the basis for
Silverman's (1970) renowned critique of positivist systems' theories of organizations, in terms drawn from phenomenology.

III. PHENOMENOLOGY AND ORGANIZATIONS

Schutz's (1962, 1964, 1967) phenomenology developed a radically subjectivist
sociology which Bauman (1976) aptly characterized as "existentialist" because
of its insistence on the self as an active being-in-the-world who not only is in the
world, but also actively constructs the world he or she is in, as that world which
has meaning for his or herself. The self is both a social constructor of reality and
a socially constructed being, as Berger and Luckmann (1966) were to develop in
their elaboration of some of Schutz's ideas.

This phenomenology is implicit in Silverman's (1970:5) announcement of the
intention of *The Theory of Organizations:* "I will seek to draw out the implications for study and for theory-building of a view of social reality as socially
constructed, socially sustained and socially changed." This involves a critique of
reification in theories of organizations, thus developing a criticism introduced in
an earlier paper (Silverman, 1968:223):

> By treating the "goals" and "needs" of organizations as givens, it seems to us that we are
> attributing apparently human motivations to inanimate objects: in other words, we are reifying

the organization. Instead of attempting to establish empirically the conception of ends and needs held by its members, we begin with a priori notions of an organization's "needs" and then examine the processes through which it secures them.

Silverman (1970) develops his critique of conventional theories of organization, modeled upon the various systems analogies, in the first five chapters of *The Theory of Organizations*. In the sixth chapter he develops "The Action Frame of Reference" as a critique of positivism. This is couched in terms of an elaboration of seven propositions which are axiomatic to his subsequent working out of theoretical and methodological implications of the "action" perspective. These propositions reduce to the following: (1) The familiar phenomenological distinction between natural science and social science is stated: sociology, as a social science, does not just observe behaviors (as, for instance, in observing the pattern of iron filings around a magnet), but understands action; (2) Action is meaningful, and meaning defines social reality; and (3) Meaning is institutionalized in society and is continually reproduced and changed through the routine actions of everyday life. Thus, in the tradition of the *Geisteswissenschaften* (cultural sciences) rather than the *Naturwissenschaften* (natural sciences), "explanations of human actions must take account of the meanings which those concerned assign to their acts; the manner in which the everyday world is socially constructed yet perceived as real and routine becomes a crucial concern of sociological analysis" (Silverman, 1970:127).

The "action frame of reference" requires us to study the "definitions of the situation" of the actors involved in the organization. These "definitions" will be constructed by actors from the "meaning of the social world . . . given to us by the past history and present structure of our society" (Silverman, 1970:132). This meaning will be expressed in "typifications" (Schutz, 1964), which are habituated expectations of how others will behave toward us, or of what certain abstract symbols mean. These typifications are institutionalized and thus become part of our cognitive furnishing of the world, part of that which we take for granted. As such, they are now oriented toward, as if they were objective, "real" phenomena. Meanings thus become institutionalized as social facts. They are socially sustained through this process of reification, continually recreating the fragile web of meaning in the cast-iron form of seemingly objective reality.

Because we ordinarily experience the world as if it were objectively there, we forget that "realization of the drama depends upon the reiterated performance of its prescribed roles by living actors. The actors embody the roles and actualize the drama by presenting it on the given stage. Neither drama nor institution exist empirically apart from this recurrent realization" (Silverman, 1970:133–4; quoted from Berger and Luckmann, 1966:75). That which is socially constructed but objectively experienced continues to be "realized" as such in a double sense; as Bauman (1976:68) puts it:

It is an apprehension of social reality as "reality," and, at the same time, the production of this reality, in so far as individuals, taking its objective nature for granted, ongoingly act toward perpetuating and continually re-creating its objectivity. It is this knowledge which lends institutions the appearance of cohesion and harmony they enjoy; the order of the universe is in the eye of the beholder, and in the habituated action of the actor.

Why should individuals continually recreate these institutionally located and taken-for-granted typifications? Because of existential dread: the fear of uncertainty and chaos that lurks in the world. As Berger and Luckmann (1966:121) put it:

> The legitimation of the institutional order is also faced with the outgoing necessity of keeping chaos at bay. All social reality is precarious. All societies are constructions in the face of chaos. The constant possibility of anomic terror is actualized whenever the legitimations that obscure the precariousness are threatened or collapsed.

In other words, uncertainty is an ontological condition (as it so often is in organization theory). However, it is one which can be put to human purposes, because particular legitimations will be related to the relative power of various actors. Uncertainty can be held at bay or exploited by differentially powerful actors: "He who has the bigger stick has the better chance of imposing his definitions" (Berger and Luckmann, 1966:101; quoted by Silverman, 1970:138).

Where does this leave the analysis of the organization? According to Silverman (1970:147), it provides us not with a theory of organizations but with "a method of analysing social relations within organizations." In the context of a discussion of phenomenological deviance theory, Taylor et al. (1973:193) observe that there are generally "two related methodological imperatives built into a phenomenological orientation. One imperative is to give a correct representation of the phenomenon under study; the other is to show how the phenomenon is constituted or built up." The consequence of these methodological imperatives is to turn attention away from reified conceptions of the phenomenon under investigation to the processes whereby such a reification has been constituted. The thrust will be away from deterministic theories to the study of intentional action. Silverman's discussion of "the origin of organizations" is faithful to these imperatives. First, Silverman (1970:147–8) begins by contrasting deterministic systems' theories of organizations with the action approach to the origin of organization:

> From the Systems point of view it has been argued, in general terms, that organizations (as sub-systems of society) arise as part of an evolutionary process of internal differentiation of system parts. In order to explain the number and nature of organizations that are created at any time, it is necessary, therefore, to consider the stage of development of a society and the kind of environmental conditions to which it must adapt. An explanation in terms of the Action approach, on the other hand, would begin from the fact that organizations are created by a

specific person or group. It therefore becomes necessary to ask: who are these people and what is the nature of the ends and definitions of the situation which cause them to form an organization with a particular goal? How does the pattern of expectations and type of legitimate authority within the organization relate to the stock of knowledge characteristic of the society and to the finite provinces of meaning of its founders?

The environment of the organization has been de-reified, but at the cost of reducing the environment solely to meaningful environment of "stocks of knowledge," "finite provinces of meaning," and "definitions of the situation" as they are subjectively constituted. The environment is now no longer a deterministic constraint under which people labor, because the emphasis has shifted toward the active, constitutive side of people as social constructors of reality. The implications of this process are quite conservative. As Silverman (1970:148) puts it:

> Organizations reflect the prevailing meaning-structures of their time in their internal pattern of social relations. Thus organizations originating within a bureaucratized society will tend to be created with a bureaucratic structure—even when, one might add, they are designed to overturn the political system of that society (e.g., radical political parties, trade unions). This is because the founders of organizations, whatever their aims, will usually take their ideas about efficient organization from the stock of knowledge characteristic of their society at that time.

Given this notion of hegemonic stocks of knowledge, it would be very difficult, for instance, to explain how radical social change might occur other than through some notion of exogenous "stocks of knowledge" being imported into a situation—or rather, its definition—and thus changing that situation's definition. There is no conception here of how the definition may be radically shattered by transforming the situation. Situations, having been built entirely of definitions, seem to possess little solidity. However, Silverman's phenomenological project is not entirely subjective [if it were, it might be a more rigorous phenomenology, but at the expense of being an impossible sociology, as Bauman (1976) argues]; instead, it is concerned, as was Schutz (1967), with intersubjectivity. As regards intersubjectivity, not all definitions of the situation are equivalent. Some are "institutionalized expectations about the likely action of others without which social life cannot proceed" (Silverman, 1970:152). These bulwarks against existential dread are "the rules of the game." Interestingly, Silverman maintains that these persist not because it serves the interests of a dominant class, coalition, or group to make them do so, but because all groups tend to accept them "for the time being, either because they feel they can do nothing to alter them or, more importantly, because of the rewards which stable group relations offer to all those concerned." Again, the conservatism of phenomenology reemerges.

The perspective and the studies which Silverman (1970) endorse have in common a concern with the processes rather than the structure of the organization. This is aptly characterized as a concern with the "rules of the organizational game'' (Silverman, 1970:196). In order to understand the game, one first has to learn the rules as they are understood and used by the participants. For phenomenologists, this injunction is primary. Indeed, phenomenologists would agree with Schutz (1962:44):

> Each term in a scientific model of human action must be constructed in such a way that a human act performed within the life-world by an individual actor in the way indicated by the typical construct would be understandable for the actor himself as well as his fellow-men in terms of common-sense interpretations of everyday life. Compliance with this postulate warrants consistency of the constructs of the social scientist with the constructs of common-sense experience of the social reality.

It follows from this that any scientific account of organizational phenomena, according to phenomenological canons, ought to be one which is reducible to the meanings of the actors in the situation. However, our objectives in studying these phenomena are not necessarily the same as those of the actors who constitute the phenomena to which we then attend (see Taylor et al., 1973:197–9, for a treatment of this with respect to deviancy theory). Although we would have different practical purposes, by phenomenological standards, our accounts would have to share the same common sense as lay accounts. [Thus, for instance, as McHugh (1968) makes quite clear, we could have no concepts such as ''false consciousness.''] For phenomenology, nearly all theoretical concepts of sociology, such as organization and its goals, rules, and environment, are all second-order constructs. In the words of Taylor et al. (1973:197–8):

> [T]hey are constructions at one order removed from any phenomenological typification, for they do not have reference to, neither are they reducible to, everyday taken-for-granted, practically constituted, intentionally created phenomena. Thus there is no guarantee that in extracting these second-order analytical constructs from the totality of social phenomena that they are in any sense homologous or isomorphic with the concrete reality of social existence. In one important sense, then, the process of phenomenological investigation is a radical attack upon the possibility of the very foundations of an etiological social theory itself. For it insists that sociology deals in decontextualized meanings and that there is no guarantee that actors in concrete settings construct their lives and the rules which govern them in a similar fashion.

Silverman (1970:223) recognizes this phenomenological limitation when he states, ''the nature of social life implies that the concepts employed in Sociology should not be applied without taking into account the subjective meanings of those who are being observed.'' It is in obeying this imperative that Silverman suggests that the sociologist should be wary of imposing his or her own definitions on the situation studied. Thus, although sociologists may use a definition of, for example, ''authoritarian supervision,'' which appears to be subjectively meaningful as well as logically consistent, they should also make their concepts conform to the canon of what has been called ''usage-adequacy'' (Clegg, 1975:117). If this were done, then supervision which is apparently authoritarian might be construed as something quite different (Silverman, 1970:224):

The supervisor might see it as the only means of enforcing his wishes on a recalcitrant or uninterested work group, while the workers might interpret it as an illegitimate attempt to limit their just rights. Or, in a society where traditional authority was predominant, both parties might regard such behaviours as a legitimate exercise of authority and would not think of questioning it. It would merely be the customary act of superiors and would not be interpreted as a strategy to obtain personal ends.

In this "weak" version of the canon of usage-adequacy one may detect no particular problems. Sociology at its best has always attempted to make seemingly inexplicable phenomena, meanings, and situations theoretically explicable in another set of terms. Silverman opposes the tendency in (positivistic) sociology to regard this other set of terms as reified social constructs, as different from, and superior to, lay constructs. This practice is characterized by what Cicourel (1964) calls "measurement by fiat."

Silverman's (1972) subsequent work was heralded as one of several papers contributing to *New Directions for Sociological Theory*. The major continuity between these "new directions" and the phenomenologically influenced action perspective is in maintaining a radical distinction between natural and social science, and in refusing to treat the organization as "real" (1972:188):

> The defining processes of social life make social objects and forces different in kind from physical objects and forces. It would, indeed, be absurd if it were not so commonplace to treat the relations between social institutions and human behaviour in the same way as the relations between a magnet and iron filings. The reification of social phenomena—their treatment as objects—is part of the "natural" attitude of everyday life in which the world appears as a collection of objectified typifications both solid and real. A phenomenological consciousness leads to a suspension of belief in the reality of these objects and an analysis of the social processes through which human definitions are objectivated by members. A profession, an organization or an ability range, to take three examples, are no longer treated as "real" things, or as objects which (in the case of the first two) take actions to meet their needs; they are viewed instead as labels which members use to make sense of their activities and as ideologies used to defend their activities to others.

The central subject matter of a phenomenological sociology becomes an account of members' accounts and commonsense practices. This introduces the topic of "indexicality." Indexical expressions refer to the objects they describe in contextual terms, and are thus bound to their occasioned use in contrast to what Garfinkel (1967:4–11) terms "objective expression." These are characterized as being decontextual and typal. To say that an expression is indexical would be to say that it is relative to such contextual matters as who said it, to whom it was said, and in what kind of context, where context invokes such features as the occasion, the social relationships involved, and so on. Garfinkel argues that the substitution by sociologists of objective for indexical expressions is both an "endless" (as necessarily reflexive) and unnecessary practice, in that indexical expressions are rational, accountable, and ordered prior to any sociological reformulation (see Garfinkel, 1967:4–11; Garfinkel and Sacks, 1970;

Wieder, 1974). Instead of this substitution as an "endless" activity, ethnomethodology recommends that the process by which accounts are constructed and given, the "glossing" activity, should become the focus of study. This is the point at which the implications of Schutz's project become most apparent. If a phenomenological study seeks to give a correct representation of the phenomena under study (the "descriptive imperative") and the processes by which the phenomenon is constituted (the "constitutive imperative"), the end result will be a relativistic regress which can only reach bedrock when we accept the version of what it is that they are doing that actors would ordinarily give us. We phenomenologically bracket away until we reach this common sense. Elsewhere (Clegg, 1975), I have developed a critique of the conservative implications of this phenomenology in the context of a discussion of "power" and its possible study by ethnomethodology, in which I concluded that, phenomenologically, other than at the most mundane level (which is, of course, what ethnomethodology aims for), one can say very little about power in everyday life. What one can say is insignificant with respect to the ways in which power is usually conceived. An example of this would be the analysis of turn taking in conversations as an indication of relative power. One either studies relatively trivial phenomena, it would seem, or else one is again involved in phenomenologically unwarranted reifications, such as "power" and "domination" (Clegg, 1975) or "the powerful character of speech" (Silverman and Jones, 1976). It is such reifications that phenomenological bracketing seeks to avoid.

Phenomenological bracketing is simply a methodological device which seeks to set aside all judgments about the (supposed) reality of a phenomenon by suspending these judgments as a prerequisite of analysis. Once belief in the "real" nature of the phenomenon has been bracketed, attention can switch to the ways in which any phenomenon can be treated as if it were real, irrespective of its actual ontological status. This necessitates that the central topic of a phenomenological sociology will be an anlysis of how members' practices constitute the pervasive sense of reality (common sense) which we experience in everyday life. This is what Garfinkel (1967) referred to as "glossing practices." As Silverman (1972:170) puts it:

> Phenomenologists certainly seek to understand common-sense interpretations of social reality but they do so in order to stand outside them more completely. They argue that only by questioning taken-for-granted assumptions about reality (phenomenological reduction) is it possible to surpass common sense. The social world is a topic for study but the assumptions and processes of reasoning of its members must not be used as an unexplicated resource by the observer.

In shifting the focus of sociological investigation to the analysis of the situated practices of everyday life, the American version of sociological phenomenology acquired its name. It is an ethnomethodology, a "folk-methodology" (see Garfinkel, 1974). That is, as Garfinkel (1956:184) puts it, it is an investigation of the everyday methods through which situations of practical, everyday life are socially organized and, as such, are perceived, known, and treated by persons as uniform sequences of actual and potential events which the person assumes that other members of the group know in the same way that he does, and that others, as does he, take for granted.

Prime examples of such "social organization" can not only be found in everyday practices, but also in the practices through which these may be studied. This is because ethnomethodology is not an analysis of any concept or object domain, but of the ways in which all, any, and every domain is constructed. As Garfinkel (1967:viii) states:

> Ethnomethodological studies analyse everyday activities as members' methods for making these same activities visibly-rational and reportable-for-all-practical-purposes, i.e., "accountable" as organizations of commonplace everyday activities.

This treatment of each and every phenomenon as problematic, as not given but as an accomplishment, has been used by Silverman (1975) in furthering his critique of reification in organization theory. He suggests that a part of the "consensus" which "characterizes the current state of organizational analysis" is an "agreement about the subject matter of the study of organizations." The agreement "rests on a commitment, shared by the spectrum of sociological perspectives, from the structural-functionalists to the symbolic interactionists, to a task of describing and explaining organizational structures and relationships" (Silverman, 1975:269–70). A feature of this consensus "is the non-problematic status accorded to the structures and relations which are purportedly being described and explained. The social world . . . is somehow 'out there' and the role of the sociologist is to catch or to 'tap' its component parts which, as it were, await explication . . . the very availability of the phenomenon and of knowledge of its features is not itself an issue" (Silverman, 1975:270). The upshot of this is that "accounts of organizational structures, which, like everyday accounts, propose to describe phenomena which exist separately from anyone attending to them, create the features of a 'real,' 'available' world" (Silverman, 1975:271). The conclusion that Silverman would have us draw from this is that if members of organizations themselves are not attending to a phenomenon, are not involved in its practical accomplishment, then that phenomenon cannot be said to be real: it does not exist unless someone thinks and acts as if it existed. And, if they do that, then it does not matter if it exists at all, because, as the old adage says: "If men define situations as real, they are real in their consequences." A crucial resource for this method in the context of organizational analysis is Bittner's (1965) paper "The Concept of Organization." This can be seen in the following quotation (Bittner, 1973:265):

> In certain presumptively identified fields of action, the observed stable patterns of conduct and relations can be accounted for by invoking some programmatic constructions that define them prospectively. Insofar as the observed stable patterns match the dispositions contained in

the programmes they are instances of formal organizational structure. Whereas, if it can be shown that the programme did not provide for the occurrence of some other observed patterns which seem to have grown spontaneously, these latter belong to the domain of the informal structures. . . . The programmatic construction is itself a part of the presumptively identified field of action, and thus the sociologist finds himself in the position of having borrowed a concept from those he seeks to study in order to describe what he observes about them.

In this context, it is the "borrowing" of concepts which is central to this ethnomethodological approach to organization analysis. This borrowing, in the terms of Zimmerman and Pollner (1971), is a confounding of "topic" and "resource" whereby commonsense "recognitions and descriptions" which are shared by both ordinary members of society and sociological investigators of it are used by the latter as resources to study the phenomena which are "made real" through members' practices, and thus become "topics." Rather than continue this confounding, whereby reified phenomena are attended to as if they were real, Zimmerman and Pollner (1971), as exemplary ethnomethodologists, would advise a displacement of analytic focus. This should shift from the presumptive "thing-in-itself" to the practices whereby this "thingness" is accomplished. These practices are essentially done through the use of "rules." These rules are not part of some external normative order, such as the fabled "central value system" of society, but are a mundane feature of members' situated activities through which they produce the sense of the scenes they are in. The topic is "not social order as ordinarily conceived, but . . . the ways in which members assemble particular scenes so as to provide for one another evidences of a social order as-ordinarily-conceived" (Zimmerman and Pollner, 1971:83). Silverman (1973:270) put it in the following terms in the context of organization:

If one suspends belief in organizational structures as "real things" it becomes possible to develop an alternative posture concerned with the manner in which members use rules to do the work of defining and interpreting actions.

Silverman recommends Bittner's (1965; reprinted 1973) paper as a resource for such an alternative. In particular, he suggests that studies might focus on various facets of the occasioned use of the concept of organization as a commonsense construct, instead of suppressing its resourceful character through either an operational definition or unexplicatedly assuming it. By contrast, "the meaning of the concept, and of all the terms and determinations that are subsumed under it, must be discovered by studying their use in real scenes of action by persons whose competence to use them is socially sanctioned" (Bittner, 1973:270).

In subsequent empirical work these issues were to be directly addressed. The analysis of selection interviews which provides the data for "the construction of 'acceptable' selection outcomes" (Silverman and Jones, 1976:27–60) is accomplished in terms of an investigation of how candidates are judged as either "acceptable" or "abrasive," the two key lay terms used in producing selection decisions. The analysis displays that such terms cannot and do not stand apart from the contexts in which they are used. Indexicality is affirmed, and it can be seen that the use of such terms provides a "rhetoric through which outcomes are made accountable" (Silverman and Jones, 1976:60). Their use is itself grounded in a much wider collection of implicit, taken-for-granted rules, known more or less in common between candidates and interviewers. The degree of "know-in-commonness" becomes the crucial variable for a candidate's being selected. One gathers from the transcripts and the treatment of them that these rules are a feature of class practices. However, as no specific theoretical model informs the analysis (indeed, in its own terms, it would have been illegitimate if it had done so), these rules are not particularly apparent. Nor do they become so in much of the subsequent descriptive parts of the study.

Three consequences of the preceding and any phenomenologically influenced analysis of organizations may be stated. One consequence is that the criteria of an adequate organization analysis will be shifted toward a representational imperative, showing the adequacy of one's representation in terms of the members' knowledge and definition of the situation they are in (e.g., Van Maanen, 1979). Second, one will follow the constitutive imperative and show how the phenomenon is possible: how it is constituted or built up in and through mundane practices (e.g., Silverman and Jones, 1976). Third, and I would argue most important: the epistemological imperative. This consists of a radical skepticism toward the criteria of adequacy at use in the community of science—characterized as positivism—as anything other than more or less conventionalized practices, which, much the same as any other social practices, can be grasped only in their meaning-in-use rather than in their meaning-of-necessity (e.g., Manning, 1979). I have argued that the implications of these imperatives are visible in the development of a phenomenologically influenced sociology of organizations in *The Theory of Organizations* (Silverman, 1970). These implications have recently been restated in quite explicit terms by Peter K. Manning (1979) in the context of a collection of papers in the *Administrative Science Quarterly* (*ASQ*) designed to "introduce" the journal's readership to phenomenologically influenced work on organizations. Other of the papers from the same issue might have served as well, except that Manning's (1979) piece demonstrated the least sociological insularity of the pieces in question. The central issue is clearly stated in the following: "within a phenomenological perspective, there is no single 'correct' reading of the 'external world,' no proper way in which facts must be selected and presented, and no arrangement, employment or presentation, or encodation that is uncontrovertibly correct or valid" (Manning, 1979:660). Most sociologists, argues Manning, suffer from the arrested development contingent upon the "correspondence version of truth." They fail to realize that observers create a domain of interest through concepts and perspectives, affirm it by selective and selected measures, and, in a sense, construct the social world through these actions. The critics raise the specter of solipsism by considering all analyses of the social world to be problematic accounts rather than objective descriptions subject to confirmation or disconfirmation through scientific investigation (Manning, 1979:660).

Manning's (1979) resolution of the "specter of solipsism" is the familiar ethnomethodological displacement of the topic by making "language the locus of analysis." However, because of Manning's strong ethnographic interests, the paper as such does not wholly bear out the implications of his position: we are, thankfully, still left to believe in a "real" world of drug users and enforcers, albeit that its precise status now becomes contingent upon the discourse structure through which "it" is revealed (which leaves the precise status of "it" problematic). It becomes rather more an "occasion" than an event, as one author (Clegg, 1975:10–14) has put it.

The consequences of this phenomenology for the analysis of organizations, or indeed any substantive phenomena, are radical. They go to the root of our usual conception of analysis. What they recommend is not an analysis of things as social facts but of things as nonsocial practices, as invariant interpretive procedures. They are nonsocial because they are constitutive aspects of any socially taken-for-granted phenomenon, irrespective of its social particulars. They are practices because things can no longer be taken to exist independently of the ways in which we constitute their facticity. Facticity becomes rather more a consequence of our ways of seeing things as such and such a type of factual thing rather than any essence of the thing itself. Moreover, these are not particular practices but are invariant: they apply equally to the interpretive procedures of the sociologist as to those studied.

Thus the sociologist's analysis is just another "account" produced through the same invariant practices as those of any "lay person." The reality of organizations is only an effect of our analyses.

IV. BEYOND PHENOMENOLOGY AND POSITIVISM

The battle lines are clear: one may be either a positivist or an antipositivist. To be an antipositivist, it seems, one must be a phenomenologist. On a number of occasions (i.e., Clegg, 1978, 1979a), I have argued that this binary characterization of contemporary sociological debate has been somewhat sterile and indeed even fallacious. As I have put it, they may be "necessary and essential positions in critical debate. But they are not final berths" (Clegg, 1978:83). This view is not purely idiosyncratic on my part. It has become a feature of the recent espousal of a "realist" theory of science [under the general tutelage of Rom Harre's innovations in the philosophy of science (e.g., Harre and Madden, 1975) and Althusser's (1971) innovations in the philosophy of Marxism] which has characterized much of the most interesting of the recent revival of philosophical themes in British social science (i.e., those of Bhaskar, 1975, 1979a, 1979b;

Keat and Urry, 1975; Benton, 1977). In particular, Bhaskar's argument has been most timely and stimulating.

Roy Bhaskar (1975) has argued that in historical terms only three broad positions need to be conceived in the development of the philosophy of science. Elsewhere I have argued for three broad positions to be conceived in the development of sociology as a social science (Clegg, 1978, 1979a). By pulling some elements of our various arguments together and through attempting to construct the implications of Bhaskar's transcendental realist position for inquiry into organization, I hope to be able to propose a firmer foundation for this inquiry than those which have been dissected in detail elsewhere (Clegg and Dunkerley, 1980; Burrel and Morgan, 1979).

A.   Empiricism/Positivism and Science

The first position in the philosophy of science which we can identify is that of classical empiricism. This consists essentially in a belief in the givenness of facts embodied in atomistic events to which it is considered knowledge ought to correspond. Knowledge is thus conceived as an effect of nature. Correct knowledge depends upon correctly reading nature's message where criteria of correctness are embodied in the canons of positivism.

Logical positivism has been the most distinctive form of empiricism in the recent past, with its most significant developments coming from the philosophic position of logical atomism, associated in particular with Wittgenstein's earlier work, the *Tractatus Logico-Philosophicus* (1961). The *Tractatus* is based on the crucial assumption that every proposition has a clear and definite sense, and that this sense lies in that proposition's relation to the world. Propositions refer to the world; the language they are phrased in ought to picture that world. Such a picture can be accurate or inaccurate, true or false, depending on how accurately it agrees or corresponds with reality: "The fact that the elements of a picture are related to one another in a determinate way represents that things are related to one another in the same way" (Wittgenstein, 1961:Par. 2.15).

The proposition serves to depict reality much as a blueprint or map should. To arrive at a determinate sense of a proposition, Wittgenstein suggests that we must define it by means of a logically proper language (which it is philosophy's task to provide), so that understanding a proposition would depend on knowing what would count as verifying or falsifying it: "The sense of a proposition is its agreement and disagreement with possibilities of existence and non-existence of states of affairs" (Wittgenstein, 1961:Par. 1.2).

Philosophy, defined as the *Tractatus* would have it, becomes an "under-labourer," in Locke's phrase, rather than a generative source of inquiry. Its labor is to clarify concepts, because "without philosophy thoughts are, as it were, cloudy and indistinct" (Wittgenstein, 1961:Par. 4.112).

The connection between sociological practice and the philosophy of the *Trac-*

tatus is the historical stream of positivism, into which the latter was merged when it became allied to the contemporary philosophic respect for natural science methodology, which centered around the chair of inductive science at the University of Vienna. At the turn of the century this was occupied by Ernst Mach, who constitutes a link with sociological positivism as it is properly understood, in his respect for the doctrines of Auguste Comte. Mach had argued that all claims to knowledge had to derive from our observation of sense-data, a sensationalism which the members of the Vienna Circle allied to Wittgenstein's conviction that a proposition was a representation of reality, to be considered meaningful when empirical and when rendered in the elementary propositions of more complex statements. Each elementary proposition was to contain terms ostensibly defined by association with empirical sense-data. In this way, then, the correctness of, for example, Newtonian dynamics would reside in the statements of the abstract formal axioms being taken to be empirical demonstrations of the natural world as we perceive it (see Janik and Toulmin, 1973; Passmore, 1957).

Given the positivist emphasis in Mach on sense-data, an epistemological reliance central to the Circle's position, it is hardly surprising that in their reading of the *Tractatus* they should have taken his representational model not so much as a plausible and elegant formal ensemble of possibilities, but rather as actually existing bedrock data open to the senses. The latter reading depends on an immediate relationship between the elementary proposition and that which it corresponds to; this is an isomorphism which is found lacking in use in empirical instances. Where it does occur, it may be taken as a practical accomplishment of reasoning rather than as the providence of nature.

It could be the case that those sociologists who do arbitrarily achieve this isomorphism by using operational measurement and definition might be taken as being warranted in their use by Wittgenstein's remark that "we make models for ourselves" and that a model is "laid against reality like a measure" (Wittgenstein, 1961:Pars. 2.1, 2.1512). One could then proceed as do many sociologists who assert operationalism as a creed. That is, they assume that what is modeled is representational, and then treat that assumption as if it were proven. But this proof can never be forthcoming. It is based on the assumption that the correct structure of language is propositional. This assumption is the basis of a further one, which is that the real world is describable in such a way. And about such assumptions one can offer no proof and can only remain silent.

A further difficulty is that which has been identified by Benton (1977:50), when he notes that "the operationalist theory of meaning requires that the meaning of any empirical concept be exhausted in some finite set of operations, whereas the development of scientific knowledge involves the progressive introduction of new techniques for measuring the properties referred to by existing scientific concepts in a way that is not specifiable in advance." This in turn leads to further problems. If "the meaning of a statement is its method of verification" (Benton, 1977), then method can and has outstripped observable sense-data, which, as Benton elaborates, is the source of further and insuperable problems for positivism. Indeed, in light of Kuhn's (1962) investigations in the history of science, it is clear that any account of scientific explanation in terms of either a verificational or confirmational principle is logically inadequate, because all such explanations can be shown to be theory dependent. Their theoretical dependence produces the meaningful frame for their application, on a gestalt principle. In other words, objects of analysis are always theoretically constituted as such.

Bhaskar (1979a:107) would claim that the foundation of the naturalist view of a unified science is based "in the last instance" on the Humean notion of law. In its modern interpretation, this implies that a scientific prediction is couched as an explanation in terms of antecedent conditions, the statement of which enables the description of an event, which is an effect of these conditions. The deduction of the event, where its deduction is not falsified through scientific practice and where it can thus be observed not to be empirically disconfirmed, is taken to be an explanation. As Benton (1977:55) puts it, "the description of an event to be explained or of an event to be scientifically predicted constitutes the conclusion of a deductive argument including at least one universal law amongst its premises." It is Bhaskar's (1979a) argument that the characterization of a naturalist position as entailing deduction from empirical invariances which, in turn, depend upon the availability of constant conjunctions of events, is incorrect. This identifies naturalism—a commitment in principle to the essential unity of method between the natural and the social sciences—with positivism. This entails the additional assumption that there is an identity of subject matter (a reductionist argument) as well as of method (a scientistic argument). Naturalism, Bhaskar (1979a) maintains, is committed to the scientific possibility of social explanation, though not to its reduction to natural explanation.

The subject matter of social science is quite different from that of natural science. This is largely due to the impossibility of effecting closure in experimental situations in the social sciences analogously with experiments in the natural sciences. Hence, in the social sciences there is no possibility of experimentation leading to successful prediction. But this does not rule out the possibility of a naturalist model for the social sciences which is not founded on a fallacious positivism.

If positivism is an inadequate characterization of natural science practice, then much of the power of the phenomenological critique in sociology is deflected. There is little point in mounting a research program on a critical position whose major thrust is founded on fallacious criticism, because its object of critique (positivism) is an effect of its own knowledge-producing practices rather than of an objectively correct representation. This is the import of Bhaskar's (1975) argument for the social sciences.

What, if not positivist stipulations, are the constitutive features of science? The realist argument rejects the Humean causal law postulate as an inadequate grounding for scientific practice because of the gestalt problems of identifying necessary and sufficient causal conditions, independent either of effects (see Clegg, 1979:50–4) or of a prior conceptual framework of possible (as opposed to impossible) causes (Harre and Madden, 1975). In its place it argues that such an identification of necessary and sufficient conditions is possible only through the effect of an investigator in constructing ingeniously closed experimental situations in which causal laws may be "analyzed as tendencies, which are only necessarily manifest in empirical invariances under relatively special closed conditions" (Bhaskar, 1979a:109). Causal laws are *not* empirically grounded in nature but in experiment. That such causal knowledge can be produced is not an effect of the experiment itself. Rather, the effect of an experiment is to reveal the real structure of an intransitive nature through transitive knowledge-producing practices.

B.   Idealism/Phenomenology and Science

Bhaskar's (1975, 1979a, 1979b) positions open up the possibility of a critique of positivism which is not committed to the legacies of nineteenth-century idealism. It is this legacy, in the form of transcendental idealism, which has provided the epistemological resources for the revolt against positivism (Hughes, 1962) that surfaced in organization theory in work derived from Schutz (1967) and his pupils, as well as in the philosophic critique of Winch (1958). In recent years this transcendental idealism has been best known through the work of Kuhn and associated philosophies of science, as well as through the more explicitly sociologically oriented contribution cited above. The principal idea of transcendental idealism is not that knowledge ought to correspond to the necessity of nature, but that in fact the necessity of nature is a more or less coherent and conventional effect of knowledge. In the past decade these ideas have been worked through to perhaps their most consistent position as a critique of positivist methodology by Derek Phillips (1973).

The critical potential of transcendental idealism is significant. Indeed, although he probably was not aware of having done quite this, Peter McHugh (1971) employed a transcendental idealist position to signal the "failure of positivism." Incidentally, this article is a further example of the way in which positivism has been constituted as *the* naturalist position. Additionally, as positivism has been so frequently identified as the particular "discipline" of empiricism, his remarks are useful in this context.

McHugh regards positivism as asserting "that a proposition is true if there is an object corresponding to the proposition" (McHugh, 1971:323). However, he rejects this on the grounds that "no institution can go outside itself to a world of independent objects for criteria of knowledge, since there is no other way except by its own rules to describe what's being done with regard to knowledge" (McHugh, 1971:335). He argues this through a distinction between the activity of "sensing," which is essential to any representational model, and the activity of "ascribing" truth, which is "warranted by socially organized criteria" (McHugh, 1971:329). This "warranting" is a separate and subsequent question to one which asks whether or not we can have knowledge by sense observation. This latter knowledge, of whatever sort it may be, is achieved through an individual's sense perceptions, which are inherently incoherent, as the psychology of perception demonstrates.

Agreement over and above individual differences in sense observation results from collectivity phenomena. Agreement is a social process in a way that sense observation is not. To know that our sense perceptions cohere with, or correspond to, those of some other person's perceptions, is a feature of linguistic activity which is both public and communal, whereas sense observation is argued to be private and individual. Because "truth," as McHugh (1971:232) proposes it, is what is collectively conceded to be he can submit that:

> a finding is true (or false or ambiguous) . . . only after applying to it the analytic formulation of a method by which that finding could have been understood to have been produced. . . . [A]n event is transformed into the truth only by the application of a canon that truth seekers use and analysts must formulate as providing the possibility of agreement.

With its insistence on the fact that knowledge is a social product produced by social practices where the means of production of these practices are already-produced knowledges, it seems to me that this critique is substantially irrefutable—no other view of scientific production is plausible. However, as I argued in *Power, Rule and Domination,* while inquiry is necessarily acquired and organized through our conventional ways of doing that inquiry, if only "because one 'looks' through speech as the means of articulation of our knowledge of things," it produces "a knowledge which is revealed by discourse but which is not dependent on this discourse" (Clegg, 1975:37). What I was attempting to formulate in that work was a conception of inquiry as a social practice producing a social product whose status was not wholly subjective, intersubjective, or irrational. In other words, I was proposing a conception of inquiry in which some reason for the knowledge produced could be maintained independently of that production and not just simply as a natural effect.

Transcendental idealism will not allow that this position is tenable. In so doing, it in turn adopts an equally untenable position, inasmuch as it is only ever able to locate rationality in the effects of its own practices. When wholly consistent, it can have no conception of a universal reason underlying the rationality of knowledge: other rationalities may exist. If they do so, they do so more or less incommensurably: they are an effect of different practices (see Burrell and Morgan, 1979). And this becomes, in theory at least, almost all we can say about them. To be consistent, we would have to argue only from within those practices from which and by which we speak. We could not at the same time reason between competing perspectives; in fact, we would have to argue against there being such a thing as a perspective, because it is not at all clear what thing it could be a perspective of. There could be no neutral and mutually acceptable ground on which debate could proceed. What might be ceded to be "rational" debate would flourish only within specific communities. As I have remarked previously, "this would be nihilism with a vengeance" (Clegg, 1975:30). It would also be an empirically impossible depiction of the history of the production of knowledge, despite the practices of some of the more obscure and esoteric cults in sociology which have been such as to make one blink at the specter, if not the reality. And reality is what is at issue. In transcendental idealism, reality is reduced to an effect of knowledge-producing practices. In sociological variants of this, "situations" disappear into the wings and their "definition" occupies center stage in a theater of the absurd. Consequently the real action takes place elsewhere, while we admire the shadow play of its shifting definition. This was the sort of thing which gave medieval metaphysicians a bad name, and in my experience it has not done sociology much good either.

C.   Realism and Science

In light of the preceding discussion, how should we constitute the relationship between what I have termed method and sociological discourse (Clegg, 1978, 1979a)? How does one actually analyze the historical development of a sociological discourse on a topic if one is not simply to read it as an empiricist reflection or idealist fancy? One solution that I have proposed is to argue that discourse has its own internal dialectic of moments of evolution and transcendence of knowledge by knowledge (Clegg, 1978, 1979a). When this was applied to a historically specific debate concerning the concept of power, it was argued that the nature of the debate developed not simply in an internal dialectic of its own language game, although that is some of the truth of the matter, but it also developed as a dialectical reflection *on* (not of) an evolving material reality, albeit a process of reflection which could only grasp that reality through its own knowledge-constituting practices.

At this level—the level of the practice of knowledge—it is knowledge's inability to resolve either internal contradictions in the knowledge it has produced or the relationship of this knowledge to our experience of "the ways of acting of things" (Bhaskar, 1975:14) which generates social changes in knowledge. And this social change is a never-ending open-ended dialogue of knowledge with its own practices and products and with the material conditions which support them. Hence, to coin a phrase, "theorizing is a twin dialogue" (Clegg, 1975:37). It is a dialogue between a structured and differentiated knowledge and a structured and differentiated world, which it is possible to come to account for through scientific work in thought. Knowledge is thus only produceable by means of knowledge. What knowledge seeks to produce is a theory of the real world: that is, a model with an existential commitment (Bhaskar, 1975:192). Such a theory would be an explanation of the structures that sustain (social) reality, a reality of structures which are in fact visible in their effects. Theoretical knowledge thus is an identification of the nature of things, an explanatory dialectic "between knowledge of what things there are and knowledge of how the things there are behave" (Bhaskar, 1975:211).

The objects of a science, in this conception, are things which can be constituted as "the reason for some pattern of normic behaviour" (Bhaskar, 1975:212). As will become apparent, this implies a notion of generative structure and structural causality.

The notion of explanatory dialectic is neither radical nor ideal; such a conception of "dialogue" is stock-in-trade of the historian's practice, as witnessed by Thompson (1978:235–6), for example:

> Historical practice is above all engaged in this kind of dialogue; with an argument between received, inadequate, or ideologically-informed concepts or hypotheses on the one hand, and fresh or inconvenient evidence on the other; with the elaboration of new hypotheses; with the testing of these hypotheses against the evidence, which may involve interrogating existing evidence in new ways, or renewed research to confirm or disprove the new notions; with discarding those hypotheses which fail these tests, and refining or revising those which do, in the light of this engagement.
>
> Insofar as a notion finds endorsement from the evidence, then one has every right to say that it *does* exist, "out there", in the real history. It does not of course actually exist, like some plasma adhering to the facts, or as some invisible kernel within the shell of appearances. What we are saying is that the notion (concept, hypothesis as to causation) has been brought into a disciplined dialogue with the evidence, and it has been shown to "work"; that is, it has not been disproved by contrary evidence, and that it successfully organizes or "explains" hitherto inexplicable evidence; hence it is an adequate (although approximate) representation of the causative sequence, or rationality, of these events, and it conforms (within the logic of the historical discipline) with a process that did in fact eventuate in the past. Hence it exists simultaneously both as a "true" knowledge and as an adequate representation of an actual property of those events.

According to my earlier accounts (Clegg, 1978, 1979a), one element of this dialogue occurs between different moments of a dialectic immanent to the production of sociological knowledge. I termed these moments "logocentric" and "sociocentric" to signal their differing principles of production of knowledge. Logocentrism is organized around the ideal *logos* of a positivistic empiricism, while sociocentrism is organized around the ideal *socio*linguistic community of a hermeneutic or phenomenological empiricism. As moments each is located within a "transcendental framework" (Habermas, 1974).

Empiricism, when it is conceived logocentrically as positivism, occupies the space defined by the knowledge interest of instrumental action: experience is invoked as the sole ground of knowledge. The basis of scientific knowledge is regarded as being the ability to control experience through the production of predictive statements about the necessary relationship of the events which constitute experience.

Transcendental idealism is not concerned with producing such a logocentrically monadic natural knowledge. Lacking a conception of the determinate nature of material reality, it regards experience of events not as pure and given but as idealized representations of knowledge produced through knowledge's own social practices. We can come to understand these through grasping our "community" with their "tradition." Thus, it is sociocentric in regarding both its own social practices and those that constitute the data of empirical experience that it attends to as the grounds of any possible knowledge. In *The Theory of Power and Organization* (Clegg, 1979a) an attempt was made to break out of this transcendental framework.[7]

Transcendental realism can be shown as a way of achieving a more real and less purely formal transcendence than this earlier attempt, by relating the "realist" position to an actual attempt at a decisive break with the constitutive framework in the area of organization analysis. If as a result of this we arrive at a more adequate scope and method for the analysis of organizations as real objects, then this will have proved worthwhile.

D.   The Realist Theory of Science and Social Analysis

We can begin by identifying the fundamental argument of a realist view of science. First, against positivistic empiricism and with transcendental idealism, it is argued that "knowledge is a social product, produced by means of antecedent social products"; but, in addition, and this is to depart from the idealist argument, "the objects of which, in the social activity of science, knowledge comes to be produced, exist and act quite independently of people" (Bhaskar, 1975:16–7). In the natural sciences we may refer to these as a transitive and intransitive dimension. The transitive dimension refers to the knowledge domain in which the theoretical object is produced. The intransitive dimension refers to the real object, structure, or mechanism which "exists" and acts quite "independently" of people and of the theoretically or naturally produced conditions which allow people access to it.

In the social sciences we have to be somewhat more guarded about the intransitive dimension if we are not to become Durkheimian reifiers. Clearly, in dealing with a socially constructed reality, a history that people inhabit, albeit not always nor even usually under conditions of their own choosing, we cannot hold that this world would exist without people. Social reality cannot endure other than through our reproduction of it, and occasionally, through our transformation of it.

Social reality differs from natural events in that while the latter's structures are intransitive, those of the former are not. Social structures exist only inasmuch as they endure; they endure only inasmuch as there are social practices which reproduce them. Inasmuch as there are social practices which reproduce them, then these structures exist. In this respect the structures are visible through their effects. To turn once more to Bhaskar (1979a:122):

Because social structures are themselves social products, they are themselves possible objects of transformation and so may be only relatively enduring. And because social activities are interdependent, social structures may be only relatively autonomous. Society may thus be conceived as an articulated ensemble of such relatively independent and enduring structures; that is as a complex totality subject to change both in its components and their inter-relations.

One implication to be drawn from this is that social structures, because of their realization in practices, cannot meaningfully be said to exist independently of the conceptions of those agents involved in those practices. This does not mean, however, the uncritical acceptance of some canon of usage-adequacy. While agents may know they are doing something and may have some idea of what they are doing in their practices, this does not mean that their own knowledge, their self-conceptions, are incorrigible. Furthermore, although agents may be doing something competently, according to public knowledge, they may be unable to formulate the basis of that knowledge, as for instance, in the common example of grammatical competence. Additionally, agents' actions and reasons for acting may have functional consequences that they are quite unaware of, for many different possible reasons of time, space, and understanding. While agents have understandings of their actions, it is not to these that an independent science of society should be responsible. Any such understanding must have social conditions of existence. These are the standing conditions that sustain them, the relatively enduring relationships and practices which are the real, not just reified and taken for granted, framework of existence.

The system in which these standing conditions operate is in principle and practice uncontrollable, owing to its uniqueness (the system being the totality of social relations and interdependencies) and to its relative unboundedness. In consequence, social prediction must remain chimerical. Explanation through explanatory understanding must be social science's forte. Necessarily such explanation must always remain incomplete, at the level of hypothetical knowledge as it were, because of the ontological openness of social possibilities. Only tendencies—not laws—are possible products of social explanation; they always remain open to empirical correction. What form might such a realist social science take in its explanations? It will seek to analyze the tendencies visible in social practices as they have evolved. These are most readily visible through their effects as discrete breaks, interventions, and ruptures in social practices. Discrete breaks, interventions, and ruptures exemplify the variable selectivity of social practice, the capacity to innovate and do things otherwise. When this capacity for innovation—concretized in discrete interventions, innovations, and breaks in social practices—becomes widely distributed and generalized in a population, then we can look to the environmental standing conditions that sustain this selection, variation, and retention.

These capacities formed as interventions, breaks, and ruptures will be formulated here as *selection rules*. These are the underlying tendencies of observable social practices: the "deep structure" underlying "surface appearance" (Clegg,

1975). Tendencies may be conceived of as the underlying generative mechanisms and structures, formulated as selection rules, which produce the relatively enduring objects of our knowledge that we grasp as real objects by means of the theoretical objects of our knowledge-producing practices. The theoretical objects are useful only because they enable us to grasp the process and structure of the real objects. This can only be expressed in and through knowledge, but its nature does not depend upon nor is contingent upon our knowledge of it.

V.   REALISM AND ORGANIZATIONS

A.   Assumptions

What might a realist analysis of organizations be? I will propose that it would be one which could explain the real structure of actual organization as an empirical effect of the mechanisms of organization as a tendency.

What are the mechanisms of organization as a tendency? They are the evolution of organizations as complex structures-in-motion, the analytic focus of which is the control of the labor process. This control is conceptualized in terms of different "rules" operative at different levels of the class structure (in its ethnic and sexual composition) in organizations. Rules can be related in a causal argument to the "long waves" of economic life. It is these long waves that propel the structure-in-motion which are the motive force of its tendency to more or less reproduce or transform itself over any given period.

A realist notion of organization entails, at a minimum, the following five assumptions: (1) Organizations are the site of the social relations of production which define class structure. (2) Different types of organization are constructed at different levels of class structure. (3) Different levels of the organization are constructed at different levels of the class structure. (4) Consequently, different types of control tend to evolve in a specific relationship to different levels of the class structure, both intra- and interorganizationally. (5) Different intraorganizational control rules evolve at different times and at different stages of functional complexity. Earlier rules may persist at specific levels in the organization despite the development of more complex rules at a later date. They may be represented as a superimposed series, layered on top of each other. Given the indeterminate nature of social reality and social agency, the articulation of relations between the different levels of complexity may produce not only unanticipated consequences but also contradictions. The layers exist in a dynamic relationship with each other. The metaphor most apt for representing this is drawn from geology: sedimentation.

B.   Representation

Any given sedimentation is a record of historically evolved structure. The social coordinates of structural space are the strata of society. Classes provide

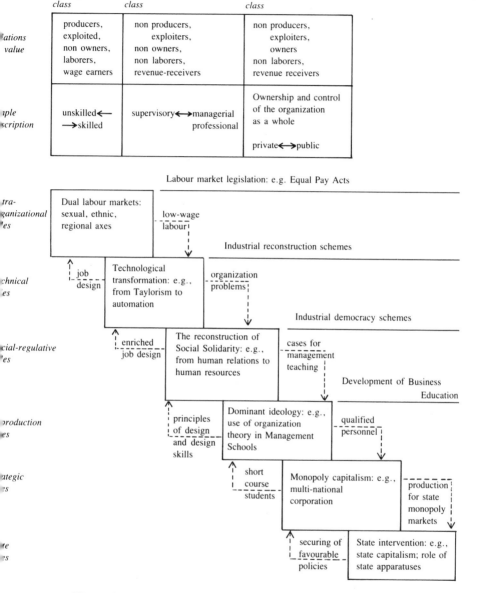

Figure 1. The Sedimented Structure of Selection Rules.

Note: The figure is a diagonal matrix. The stepped series represent the intersection of types of rules and levels of class structure of the organization. Hatched lines represent the articulation between levels while the solid lines represent the effect of the state.

these coordinates. They may be represented in an ideal and abstract form through a series of categorical distinctions. These are depicted below in Figure 1 as the definition of the working class, the middle class, and the ruling class.

The definition hinges on the relationship to value of different categories of agents. Simple descriptions of the typical range of occupations are also provided. These class categories run horizontally across the page. The concrete history of organizational strategic calculations and of management techniques and practices provide the temporal coordinates of the vertical axis. These are the "rules" which represent ways of formulating decisive "breaks" or "interventions" in principles of organization. In their moment of dominance they may be related to the development of "long waves" in the world economy. They become dominant at particular moments because they represent strategies appropriate to the conjunctural possibilities of accumulation.

As such, the locus of their decision making may be either intraorganizational to the focal organization or outside it. The locus is less important than the effects registered in the structure of social relations of production. These constitute the organizations' structure through introducing the different rules of control.

Read the figure as a matrix: the diagonal-stepped series running across the page represents the level of the class structure at which the rules operate in their greatest specificity. Although historical in conception, they persist and endure at different levels of the organization. Developments in strategic calculations and in management techniques and practices transform the evolving task-discontinuous organization.

Different interventions are specific to different levels of the class structure as it is produced, reproduced, and transformed in organization structures. These interventions have their dominant "moments," but they may persist and endure as residues of earlier practices. As I conceive of these rules as selecting what is enacted for the organization, I call them *sedimented selection rules*.

The role of the state as the overall rule-making, -defining, and -enforcing agency of organizational life is not neglected. In the most recent post-war era of the post-Keynesian "managed" economy, the role of the state has become dominant, particularly in the monopoly, and, of course, state capitalist sectors (see Clegg and Dunkerley, 1980:Ch. 13). The effects of the state have a feedback function at all levels of organizational practice, with specific state interventions having specific effects at specific levels.

Finally, as we are dealing with a sedimented structure, we need to look at the interrelationship between levels. These are represented in the diagram by the dashed lines, depicting the interrelations between the rules. (For instance, dual labor markets generate low wage labor which can be utilized through job design which de-skills more complex elements of the labor process; such de-skilling, particularly in full-employment conditions, can generate "organization problems" of absenteeism, turnover, etc. These are remedied through "enriched" job design, whose principles are taught as part of the dominant ideology of organization theory in, for instance, business schools, whose students, drawn primarily from the ranks of the state and monopoly capital sectors, learn through studying "cases" drawn from the literature of organization problems. Those students who survive the corporate race to executive positions then become the nexus between the state (as "regulator" and as market) and monopoly capital.

C. Standing Conditions and Selection Rules

The general character of a whole era may be determined as one of relatively fast or slow accumulation. Accumulation depends on the rate of profit. A heightened rate of profit leads to a relatively fast period of accumulation. The relationship of fast to slow periods of accumulation is one of succeeding cycles of "long waves of accelerated and decelerated accumulation determined by long waves in the rise and decline of the rate of profit" (Mandel, 1975:129). The expansionary, accelerating phase of a long wave occurs when the rate of profit is "triggered" by "triggering factors." These are factors which lower the organic composition of capital or raise the rate of surplus value. As these factors are exhausted, the rate of profit begins to fall because of unfavorable changes in either the organic composition of capital or the rate of surplus value. The long wave moves back into expansion when the rate of profit is once again lifted radically by a further combination of factors.

The movement of these long waves provides the standing condition for the development of organization. New technologies, particularly of energy, have a leading role to play as "triggers." However, as Rowthorn (1976:64) has stressed, the role of social technologies of control should not be neglected in consideration of these cycles. Such "social technologies" would be the generalized adoption of specific practices of organization. Conceived this way, certain speculative possibilities may be sketched for organization analysis.

We can distinguish the following "long cycles" of capitalist development in the past hundred years. The generalized depression which lasted from the early 1870s until the mid-1890s marked the downturn phase of a long wave, with an upturn occurring from the mid-1890s through the First World War. The downturn of this wave persisted through the 1920s to the beginning of the Second World War, which marked the renewal of accumulation on an accelerated scale, persisting until the late 1960s. Since then we have clearly been in a renewed downturn phase.

Each up-phase in accumulation has seen the emergence of institutions which have intervened in, and thus framed, the organization of the labor process. They have been major determinants of renewed accumulation and have been historically sedimented, as depicted.

The upturn phase of the period after the 1890s marked the emergence of attempts at applying formal abstract theories of organization to the labor process, such as F. W. Taylor's Scientific Management. The development of Scientific

Management was incumbent upon a number of radical innovations in technology which bunched together, particularly the development of electricity as an energy source capable of powering new production technologies such as high-speed lathes.

Through such innovations were laid the technological foundations for the erosion of craft and personal skill as a tactical move in the process of class struggle. Taylor's system facilitated this erosion initially in the steel industry, although at a later stage, more generally. We can refer to interventions of this type as *technical rules,* because they stress the rule of technique over the will of the worker.

During the First World War mobilization of skilled male workers the capitalist labor process assimilated many raw recruits, due to the increasingly routinized, simplified, and de-skilled labor process made possible by innovations such as those of Taylor. Most notable among these are women, young people, and aged peasants, who, through the real subordination of the labor process, were able to be rapidly inducted into these new forms of labor. In the postwar period this Taylorist simplification of the labor process was to be extended from the shop-floor to the office, where female labor became increasingly employed as a cheap and unskilled source of commercial work.

During the contracting interwar period, the increasing de-skilling and routini-zation of white-collar office work provided a major device for increasing the efficiency of capital. This created a more homogenous labor process, a less skilled and differentiated labor force recruited from increasingly differentiated labor markets, with the major axes of differentiation being ethnic and sexual divisions which were used to construct institutionalized skill and wage level differences.

We can refer to this form of labor market segmentation as an intervention constructed through utilizing preexisting extraorganizational divisions. Thus they may be termed *extraorganizational rules.* We will discuss these in more detail shortly.

The individual enterprise or organization is not the overall economy. The fully employed war economy, followed by the long postwar boom, posed particular problems for the organization and control of the labor process at the level of specific enterprises. Specifically, it withdrew the coercive domination of the reserve army of the unemployed. In these circumstances, as we might anticipate, the balance of domination became more hegemonic. Mayo's (1975) wartime studies into the breakdown of social solidarity, and their subsequent articulation from "Human Relations" to "Human Resources" and "Work Humanization" during the long postwar boom, may be identified in this context as an interven-tion into the *social regulative rules* of the organization, precisely because of the unavailability of more coercive controls, due to the absence of the reserve army of the unemployed.

A major effect of full employment in the postwar period was the specialization of forms of labor control contingent upon the class structure of occupations. Friedman (1977) has suggested that the two strategies which I have termed technical and social regulative rules may be applied to the labor process not only in different moments of the world economy, particularly as its rhythm has been modulated by two world wars, but also selectively to different elements in the labor process. Technical rules tend to be applied to those workers who are more peripheral to the labor process (less strategically contingent), while social regulative rules tend to be applied to those workers who are more central (more strategically contingent). This differential strategy arises as a way of handling inflexibilities generated by contradictions within each intervention into the labor process.

On the one hand, Taylorist technical rules could not be applied universally. Not everyone could be de-skilled, nor could everyone be a high-wage laborer. In both spheres differentials would have to be preserved for the strategy to work. Second, the "affluent worker" is not necessarily a happy worker. Finally, neither is he or she necessarily a very satisfactory worker in a situation which demands flexible workers with a degree of discretion. It is precisely these types of workers, who are more strategically contingent, that capital will attempt to control through more subtle hegemonic domination; that is, through social regulative rules as a form of control.

This division of the work force can be carried further, through use of what I have termed extraorganizational rules (Clegg, 1979a). The specialization of forms of labor control contingent upon the class structure of occupations can be extended through a sexual, racial, or ethnic division of labor which is extraorganizational in its dividing principle.

Those skills which are not strategically contingent—generally those with low status, relatively low pay, and low job entrance requirements—can be further distinguished from the rest of the labor process. This has the effect of minimizing the possibility of labor's developing a collective consciousness of itself *for* itself. In this way the contradictory possibility that "participation," for instance, might become a collective and liberating catchword would be minimized. This has been achieved by Taylorizing unstrategic skills in the organization. Because of their low social definition in the labor market, such unstrategic skills tend to attract the most socially disadvantaged groups in the labor force—women and ethnic minorities such as blacks or recent migrants—groups which are sexually and racially discriminated against. It has frequently been observed that management will often actively encourage these divisions by overqualifying not only managerial but other strategically contingent skills, or by locating administration and research tasks only where native-born, white male workers can easily get to them.

There is substantial evidence for the above, as Friedman (1977) argues, "from several countries concerning the more volatile unemployment levels for blacks, immigrants and women'' citing Hill et al. (1973), Edwards et al. (1972), and Castles and Kosack (1973) as evidence. These extraorganizational rules relate to the structure of the secondary labor force.

Social regulative rules will tend to be more specifically aimed at workers structurally located in the new middle class which Carchedi (1977) identifies: those workers in contradictory supervisory positions who fulfill functions of both the collective worker *and* the global capitalist. Hypothetically, if this thesis is correct, we would expect to find that controls on the working class will tend largely to be of either technical rules or extraorganizational rules.

Extraorganizational rules, of the dual labor market type, will function through the development of secondary labor markets, largely at the level of relatively unskilled workers. Technical rules, as forms of control, will tend to be developed principally in relation to technological transformations such as Taylorism or automation, which increase the amount of surplus that can be accumulated from skilled workers. It is this phenomenon of interventions by technical rules in the labor process which can generate the limited discretionary powers of decision making identified by Crozier (1964), for instance, with respect to maintenance workers. These discretionary powers are historically sedimented in residual craft skills which escaped rationalization by Scientific Management.

The development of technological capitalism and other forms of monopoly capitalism, as they became dominant in the postwar long boom, necessitated a further kind of intervention in organizations which we can call *strategic rules*. Strategic rules are an intervention in the spheres of both production and circulation, while social regulative rules and technical rules are an intervention only in the production of commodities—not their circulation. As such, they are a one-sided intervention in commodity production with very definite implications for commodity circulation, which necessitates these further forms of intervention of the type of strategic rules.

Any organization based on mass production has to harness its labor power to its machine power for the maximum utilizable time because of the peculiarities of a modern plant economy. The more that such a modern plant is utilized by the organization below its rated capacity, the greater will be the unit cost of its output. Hence, in terms of the production process, economy is achieved and the greatest surplus potentially produced when maximal production is achieved. However, the market has to be able to absorb the increased output.

In a market economy "no intrinsic correlation exists between increased output and the capacity of effective demand to absorb production" (Sohn-Rethel, 1976:31). Consequently, although technical and social regulative rules may maintain productivity, they are not sufficient by themselves. Sometimes they are not even necessary.

It can be appreciated that the previous analysis of the need for such strategies holds most true for developed market economy social formations, in which the national proletariat, on the average, will form part of an international labor aristocracy. (Obviously, there will be gross wage differences within any given social formation.) In low-wage, less-developed social formations—the periphery and semiperiphery of the world economy—hegemonic forms of domination will recede in importance. It is for this reason that a large number [Vernon (1973) estimated it at 187] of U.S., European, and Japanese international firms have established themselves in these more peripheral regions. These enterprises are there precisely because of the reduced cost of the labor process, the possibility of multi-factor supply for core production (e.g., in the United States), and the frequently observed phenomenon of transfer pricing. These firms, as both Karpik (1977) and Adam (1975) have argued, tend to be large technological enterprises. Their control of the labor process, when not assured by work which in the local context offers regular if not high wages, coupled with a large reserve army of the unemployed, can frequently be assured by the policies of the domestic state. This assured quantity is the existence of a compliant work force asserting little or no power.

We can now consider the case of organizations primarily operative in the core states of the world economy, in particular those organizations generated by the upturn of the cycle of accumulation in the postwar era. This developed on the basis of an important bunching of inventions in production and energy use during the interwar period. These were associated in particular with the automobile industry, such that the postwar boom is often referred to as "the age of the internal combustion engine."

Associated with this age was the impact on mass consumption of the development of large-scale electronics and plastics industries. The leading firms in these industries are primarily monopoly capitalist organizations. While for such organizations control of the labor process may be absolutely necessary, it is not sufficient. Intraorganizational interventions into production have to be buttressed and supported by strategic rules, which intervene in the market in an attempt to plan its rational control (Sohn-Rethel, 1978:32; also see Baran and Sweezy, 1968).

The significance of this capacity to plan is apparent when we consider that multinationals controlled 20 percent of industrial output in the capitalist world and 30 percent of world trade in 1970/71. At the same time, they possessed three times the gold and currency reserves of the United States (Mandel, 1975:23). It has been forecast that by the end of this century between 200 and 300 multinationals will control 75 percent of the private assets of the capitalist world (Wheelwright, 1973). Two aspects of this situation of corporate dominance will be discussed; specifically, problems of control by: (1) the corporate organizations of the new, massively expanded, middle-class supervisory, managerial, and professional strata internal to these organizations' own control functions; and (2) the expanded strata of middle-class professional workers in the state apparatuses of the large corporate organizations themselves. This entails a rejection of the classical liberal conception of state–market relations in the face of corporate dominance.

The development of organizations in both the state and private sphere gives rise to whole strata of nonproducers/exploiters/nonowners/revenue-receivers who fulfill, among other types of tasks, the functions of operating extensive controls of, and in, the organization. These agents do not necessarily have the decisive material interest of ownership, in the legal terms of possession, of the means of production which they control. This then poses the question of how they are to be controlled, or in terms of the way the scheme in Figure 1 poses the question, what are the *reproduction rules* of late capitalism and where are they located?

It has been argued elsewhere (Clegg and Dunkerley, 1980) that it is the business and management schools which have become the institutional site for the reproduction of the contemporary dominant ideology of late capitalism (after Marceau ci al., 1978:310). This dominant ideology functions, above all, to control the actions of those organizational agents who enjoy most discretion or least specificity of role prescription, who are not constrained simply by the practices of routinely designed work in organization. As both Marcuse (1964) and Perrow (1972) have argued, this is best achieved through employing agents with rules and rationality "built into them" through educational socialization.

Finally, as has been argued in considerably more detail elsewhere (Clegg, 1979; Clegg and Dunkerley, 1980), we have to consider the role of the state in these interventions into the labor process. The state cannot be conceived of as a polity parallel to and outside of the economy. Its resources are one of the major prizes to be fought over, bribed for, and won among corporate executives. The state, through rule definition, making and enforcement, constitutes the space in which organizations operate. Large organizations that have the power to do so attempt to favorably formulate this constitution in their own interests.

For capitalist organizations operating on the market, the state exists as a potential source of protection from the operation of this market (see McCullough and Shannon, 1977). Polanyi (1957) describes two central features of the market system. First, greater profit accrues to those organizations that possess larger amounts of resources. As a result, there is a continual pressure toward monopolization and the creation of privileged access to resources. In addition, however, the market system is dynamic and creates risks and uncertainties for any specific organization, since new areas of demand and new profit opportunities can be continually exploited, often undercutting and disadvantaging existing organization profit centers. Hence organizations continually attempt to control those contingencies which are strategic for their profit-centered activity, in order to both protect and increase their advantages. This leads organization actors to attempt to use the state to effect the market in their interests, as Wallerstein

(1974:405) has argued, and to secure favorable state interventions in the socialization of costs, risks, and losses.

Additionally, the state becomes the major client of much monopoly production, particularly of "defense" systems and electronic data processing equipment. This process of state–capital interorganization, particularly as it is mediated through taxes and inflation, may well be generative of profound "fiscal crises" (O'Connor, 1973) and "legitimation crises" (Habermas, 1976).

The state is also important because of its role as a "factor of cohesion" and disarticulation of the totality, as depicted in the state's feedback functions in Figure 1. These can have not only anticipated but also unanticipated consequences. An example from Australia is illustrative of this. The Crawford Report (1979), a federal government report on the manufacturing industry in Australia, has argued that it is precisely the provisions of equal pay legislation (at the extraorganizational level) which have forced the rate of adoption of new technology (at the level of technical rules), thus exacerbating both industrial relations conflicts and unemployment, both of which have profound effects at the state level. As the cost of the exchange values involved in the labor process have increased in consequence of such legislation, organizations have attempted to cheapen their labor process by technological substitution of computerized intelligence systems.

VI. CONCLUSION

This exercise in imaginative realism has been highly abstract, at the level of organization-in-general. As such, it offers a simple sketch of complex possibilities encountered at the level of organizations-in-particular. The latter is the world of concrete organizations open to empirical scrutiny and data collection. In order to bridge the gap between organization-in-general as an abstract theoretical object and the concrete world of particular organizations, with its multitude of determinations resistant to abstraction, an intermediate level of analysis is required. This would be the level of uneven development of organizations' labor processes through the dimensions of: (1) time (organized around the modalities of long waves as hypothetical structuring frames for breaks); (2) space [the internal class structure of organizations, the location of the specific organization(s) in particular regions of the world economy with their peculiar histories and role]; and (3) economy (the dominant sector, e.g., monopoly capital, within the particular branch, e.g., coal mining). While space and economy would be dependent variables, the independent variable would be time conceived as the modalities of historically specific long waves.

Holding constant the branch within an industry in which a particular sector of capital dominates, do organizations drawn from the dominant sector display the

same patterns of organization evolution specific to the same internal class structure and across different regions of the world economy? Contingency theory, for
instance, with its emphasis on either internal determination by size or external
determination by environment would suggest so, although it stresses different
aspects of organization than those elaborated here (see, for example, Hickson
and Lammers, 1979, particularly the "Conclusions" section).

The aspects stressed in this framework are the following:

1. Organizations are complex structures-in-motion. Their essence is control.
   Differential controls apply to people involved at different levels of the
   social relations of production: the class structure.
2. The major variable conditioning the general (as opposed to specific) historical determination of these controls is the effect of cyclical and general
   changes in accumulation as they are mediated by the calculations of
   organizationally dominant members: the intraorganizational elite repre-
   sentative of the ruling class.
3. Control is expressed through "rules." These are an analytic construct
   which formulate the discrete principles underlying generalized interventions into the organization of the labor process.
4. Comparative analysis of organization structures should proceed through
   the construction of generalized patterns of organization evolution within
   constant branches, sectors, and regions of the world economy. A realist
   theory would expect variation in structure to be a result of variation of
   sectoral dominance and regional location structuring the possible range of
   calculations of decisive organizational agents.

In conclusion, it should be quite clear that the tendencies (of long waves) and
selection capacities (the evolving sedimented rules) are neither on the surface,
empirically open for inspection and statistical manipulation as variables, nor in
the understandings and usage of the actual agents in organizations. Neither are
they dependent upon the understanding and acceptability of these individuals for
their credence or functioning. Rather like the rules of grammar, they can persist,
endure, and evolve beneath the surface, meaning, and cognition of everyday
social life, yet still have a real, determinate existence and effect on the appearance of this everyday life. Thus, organizations which differ in appearance
may be explained in terms of variation, selection, and retention of control as the
generative structural category. This evolving control is of a labor process whose
limits can be demarcated only by politically resourceful actors engaged in political struggles within a specific economic context (of capital accumulation).

Perhaps a synthesis between the perspective argued for here and that proposed
by Aldrich (1979) is overdue. Indeed, there is good reason to suggest that a
political economy of "natural selection" or population ecology which seeks "to
develop from the actual, given relations of life the forms in which these have

been apotheosized'' is well over 100 years overdue. It was, after all, in 1867 that Marx recommended this study in the following terms (1976 ed.:493):

> Darwin has directed attention to the history of natural technology, i.e., the formation of the organs of plants and animals, which serve as the instruments of production for sustaining their life. Does not the history of the productive organs of man in society, of organs that are the material basis of every particular organization of society, deserve equal attention? And would not such a history be easier to compile, since, as Vico says, human history differs from natural history in that we have made the former, but not the latter?

It might, indeed, be easier to compile if it were not the case that this history is littered with ''abstract and ideological conceptions'' in precisely the terms that Marx designates: analyses ''which exclude the historical process'' (Marx, 1976 ed.:493). Having criticized these elsewhere (e.g., Clegg, 1977), the purpose of this chapter has been to clear the ground a little. Of necessity, only a theoretical space has been secured. How fertile it will prove to be remains to be seen in the fruits of further research.

ACKNOWLEDGMENTS

I would like to acknowledge the institutional support of Griffith University, whose commitment to interdisciplinarity has enabled me to keep chipping away at the concerns expressed in this paper.

Additionally, my Danish friends and colleagues, particularly Kristian Kreiner, were a sympathetic if sometimes puzzled sounding board for my adventures in ''realism,'' whilst I was visiting The Technical University of Denmark in 1979. The space they gave me for wide reading and reflection could not be bettered.

Finally, some of the ideas and arguments in this paper are well rehearsed in earlier works of mine; their production then would not have been possible in that form if I had not had colleagues and friends like David Hickson and David Silverman.

NOTES

1. In the interests of narrative structure, I have decided to construct this account around David Silverman's work. As this work developed after *The Theory of Organizations*, it did so by drawing on a range of American ethnomethodologists.

As I will not have space to discuss them all in text, I am referencing them here. Their developments made David Silverman's later work possible. Notably, these included Garfinkel (1967); Garfinkel and Sacks (1972); Bittner (1965, 1967); Cicourel (1968, 1973); McHugh (1971); Phillips (1973); Sudnow (1973); Zimmerman (1971); and Zimmerman and Pollner (1971).

Perhaps the writer who influenced Silverman (1974a, 1974b; Silverman and Jones, 1976) most during the later period of his interest in organizations was Alan Blum (notably 1971, 1974). Certainly, the ''Speaking Seriously'' papers are only explicable if one has read Blum (1974) and understood the peculiar proclivity for the work of Martin Heidegger that Blum's later work displayed. One early attempt to try and settle accounts with Blum's work was Clegg (1976). The ''Blum effect'' was institutional: David Silverman was (and is) a member of Goldsmiths College, London, which in the early mid-1970s was one of the two bastions of American-inspired ethnomethodology in England. The other was Manchester University—but there the major influence was the "conversational analysis" associated with Harvey Sachs. At Goldsmiths, Alan Blum's extreme version of reflexivity had been particularly influential as a result partly of a period of leave spent there by his colleague Peter McHugh in 1973. During late 1973 and early 1974, the Goldsmiths Group (which included Paul Filmer, David Walsh, Mike Philipson, Barry Sandywell, Maurice Roche, Chris Jencks, David Silverman and Stewart Clegg as participants at various times) met in and around London to prepare a series of papers for the 1974 British Sociological Association Conference. These were written around the theme of "stratifying practices" and were later to be published as *Problems of Reflexivity and Sociological Enquiry* (1974). These represent the nadir of phenomenological sociology in Britain.

Since that time the trend has moved in other directions. Any reader of *Problems of Reflexivity and Sociological Enquiry* would have an extremely good idea why this should be so. My own earlier work [particularly Clegg (1975, 1976, 1977)] was unfortunately influenced in this manner.

2.   There is neither a fetish of necrophilia nor of chronology at work here. The foundation of phenomenology belongs to a much earlier period than either its reception in sociology or its subsequent articulation into formal organizations. It is also worth noting that the articulation of phenomenology into formal organizations has been very partial. It has not, for instance, drawn on the work of phenomenological Marxists such as Enzo Paci (1972) and the writers associated with the journal *Telos*. I have not addressed this literature here. Readers who wish to do so may refer to Barry Smart's (1976) *Sociology, Phenomenology and Marxian Analysis*.

3.   The implications of this are radical indeed—far more radical than even that champion of scepticism, Popper, allows. For it is not that our knowledge can only ever be a series of conditional approximations to true knowledge, minutely and laboriously achieved. We are obliged to reject the notion of truth at all and instead resign ourselves to a world in which we must always doubt and in which no possible grounds for the dissolution of doubt exist as Bauman (1978:112–3) and Kolakowski (1975:28–9) have argued. This leads to the "conventionalist" position (see Clegg, 1975:Ch. 1).

4.   The suggestion of "illusion" presents the possibility of a critique of reification being generated from transcendental idealism. Such a critique, of course, is historically well established through the work of Lukacs (1971) and its subsequent developments into sociology (i.e., Berger and Pullberg, 1966).

5.   The choice of the term "form of life" is deliberate. While not exclusively associated with Wittgenstein (1968), for similar formulations are to be found in other outcrops of German idealism [i.e., Marx and Engels' (1965 ed.) *The German Ideology* and Marcuse's (1955) *Reason and Revolution*], it is in Wittgenstein that the term is most frequently referenced (i.e., Winch, 1958; Clegg, 1975). Part of the thrust of some of my earlier work (as Burrell and Morgan, 1979:321 allude) was in fact to seek a way of "showing" how this ordinary form of life might be opened up for analysis. Whether or not this was achieved remains contestable. Nonetheless, the import of that earlier work was indeed to attempt to "show" the constraint exercised in and through the natural attitude upon our (lack of) understanding of the taken for granteds of both inquiry and everyday life. Much of the analysis elaborated in this paper has developed from concerns broached in the second section of the second chapter (pp. 30–41) of that earlier work and revised and extended subsequently (Clegg, 1976, 1978, 1979). In the present stage of formulation these earlier positions are effectively negated. (Although this may not be true of the totality of *The Theory of Power and Organization*, it would seem to be true of the chapter specifically devoted to these issues, chapter two).

6.   It would not be unduly biographical to observe that it was precisely this revolt against positivism which initially so attracted some of the late-60s generation of British sociologists, of which I am one. Given the nature of British sociology and its development (see Rex, 1974:Introduction; Rex, 1973:Ch. 1, 5, 8, 16), the reception of European phenomenology was largely mediated through the United States, notably Cicourel (1964); Berger and Luckman (1966); and Garfinkel (1967). For many of us, the originals came later.

Perhaps Ogburn (1950) should be resurrected with respect to the role of the ASQ in delimiting the field of organization theory. Certainly it strikes an English sociologist, as reader, as bizarre that at a time when phenomenology and its influence had waxed and waned in other substantive fields [e.g., education, where it reached its high point in the Young (1971) critique (see Clegg, 1979b) or criminology, where it reached its high point in the early days of the National Deviancy Conference, and was roundly criticized by Taylor et al. (1973) in *The New Criminology*] that it should only now be making an impact in the ASQ. Perhaps by 1990 some impact on the field may have been made (on an approximate 10-year lag) by the revival of Marxist social theory in the post-Althusserian 1970s. Or, to reecho an older debate, are we just dealing here with the "peculiarities" of the Americans? Or, is it that free enterprise in thought favors a restricted marketplace of ideas on the basis of an "elective affinity"?

7. These rather formal distinctions between sociocentrism and logocentrism were not so much a prolegomenon to a conclusion already secure and achieved but might rather more correctly be characterized as a means of production. Through the process of construction a formal structure I was manufacturing a scaffolding, an organizing device, in which to support the subsequent argument. Part of this argument stressed the necessity of transcending the formal dialectic I had constructed. Perhaps formal dialectics are only capable of producing formal transcendence; certainly the "critical sociology" that was proposed did not consist of anything other than a suspension of judgment as to the reality of the perceived nature of our ordinary experience and our received categories of intellectual experience, such as, for instance, organization theory. Whether or not the knowledge that was subsequently produced achieved any such transcendence in any less formalist way is a matter for judgment (Clegg, 1978, 1979a).

REFERENCES

Adam, G.
  1975 "Multinational corporations and worldwide sourcing." Pp. 89–104 in H. Radice (ed.), in International Firms and Modern Imperialism. Harmondsworth: Penguin.
Aldrich, H.
  1979 Organizations and Environments. Englewood Cliffs: Prentice-Hall.
Althusser, L.
  1971 Lenin and Philosophy and Other Essays. New Left Books.
Baran, P. and P. Sweezy
  1968 Monopoly Capital. Harmondsworth: Penguin.
Bauman, Z.
  1976 Toward a Critical Sociology. London: Routledge and Kegan Paul.
Bauman, Z.
  1978 Hermeneutics and Social Science. London: Hutchinson.
Benton, T.
  1977 The Philosophical Foundations of the Three Sociologies. London: Routledge and Kegan Paul.
Berger, P. and T. Luckmann
  1966 The Social Construction of Reality. New York: Doubleday.
Berger, and P. S. Pullberg
  1966 "Reification and the sociological critique of consciousness." New Left Review:35:56–71.
Bhaskar, R.
  1975 A Realist Theory of Science. Leeds: Basic Books.
Bhaskar, R.
  1979a "On the possibility of social scientific knowledge and the limits of naturalism." Pp.

107–137 in J. Mepham and D. H. Ruben (eds.), Issues in Marxist Philosophy. Hassocks: Harvester Press.

Bhaskar, R.
1979b The Possibility of Naturalism. Brighton: Harvester Press.

Bittner, E.
1965 "The concept of organizations." Social research 32:239–255.

Bittner, E.
1973 "The police on skid-row: a study of peace-keeping." ASR 32:699–715.

Bittner, E.
1973 "The concept of organizations." Pp. 264–276 in G. Salaman and K. Thompson (eds.), People in Organizations. London: Longman.

Blum, A.
1971 "Theorizing." Pp. 301–319 in J. D. Douglas (ed.), Understanding Everyday Life. London: Routledge and Kegan Paul.

Blum, A.
1974 Theorizing." London: Heinemann.

Burrell, G. and G. Morgan
1979 Sociological Paradigms and Organizational Analysis. London: Heinemann.

Carchedi, G.
1977 On the Economic Identification of Social Classes. London: Routledge and Kegan Paul.

Castles, S. and G. Kosack
1973 Immigrant Workers and Class Structures in Western Europe. Oxford: Oxford University Press.

Cicourel, A.
1964 Method and Measurement. New York: Wiley.

Cicourel, A.
1968 The Social Organization of Juvenile Justice. New York: Wiley.

Cicourel, A.
1973 Cognitive Sociology. Harmondsworth: Penguin.

Clegg, S.
1975 Power, Rule and Domination: A Critical and Empirical Understanding of Power in Sociological Theory and Organizational Life. London: Routledge and Kegan Paul.

Clegg, S.
1976 "Power, theorizing and nihilism." Theory and Society 1 (3):65–87.

Clegg, S.
1977 "Power, organization theory, Marx and critique." Pp. 21–40 in S. Clegg and D. Dunkerley (eds.), Critical Issues in Organization. London: Routledge and Kegan Paul.

Clegg, S.
1978 "Method and sociological discourse." Pp. 67–90 in P. Brenner, P. Marsh, and M. Brenner (eds.), The Social Contexts of Method. London: Croom-Heim.

Clegg, S.
1979a The Theory of Power and Organization. London: Routledge and Kegan Paul.

Clegg, S.
1979b "Sociology of power and the university curriculum." Pp. 25–53 in M. R. Pusey and R. E. Young (eds.), Control and Knowledge. Canberra: Australian National University Press.

Clegg, S. and D. Dunkerley
1980 Organization, Class and Control. London: Routledge and Kegan Paul.

Crawford Report
1979 Study Group on Structural Adjustment. Canberra: Australian Government Publishing Service.

Crozier, M.
1964 The Bureaucratic Phenomenon. London: Travistock.

Edwards, R. C., M. Reich, and T. E. Weisskopf
1972   The Capitalist System. Englewood Cliffs: Prentice-Hall.
Fox, A.
1966   Industrial Sociology and Industrial Relations. Research Paper 3, Royal Commission on Trade Unions and Employers Associations. London: HMSO.
Friedman, A.
1977   "Responsible automony versus direct control over the labour process." Capital and Class 1:43–57.
Garfinkel, H.
1956   "Some sociological concepts and methods for psychiatrists." Psychiatric Research Report 6 (October):191–195.
Garfinkel, H.
1967   Studies in Ethnomethodology. Englewood Cliffs: Prentice-Hall.
Garfinkel, H.
1974   "Origins of the term 'Ethnomethodology'." Pp. 15–18 in R. Turner (ed.), Ethnomethodolgy. Harmondsworth: Penguin.
Garfinkel, H. and H. Sachs
1970   "On the formal structures of practical actions." Pp. 337–366 in J. C. McKinney and E. A. Tiryakian (eds.), Theoretical Sociology: Perspectives and Developments. New York: Appleton Crofts.
Goffman, E.
1971   The Presentation of Self in Everyday Life. Harmonsworth: Penguin.
Habermas, J.
1974   Knowledge and Human Interests. London: Heinemann.
Habermas, J.
1976   Legitimation Crisis. London: Heinemann.
Harre, R. and E. H. Madden
1975   Causal Powers. Oxford: Blackwell.
Hickson, D. G. and Lammers, C.
1979   Organizations Alike and Unalike, London, Routledge and Kegan Paul.
Hill, M. J., R. M. Harrison, A. V. Sargeant, and V. Talbot
1973   Men Out of Work. Cambridge: Cambridge University Press.
Hindess, B.
1977   Philosophy and Methodology in the Social Sciences. Hassocks, Sussex: Harvester Press.
Hughes, H. S.
1962   Consciousness and Society. London: Mac Gibbon and Kee.
Husserl, E.
1967   Ideas. London: Allen and Unwin.
Husserl, E.
1970   Cartesian Mediations. The Hague: Martinus Nijhoff.
Janik, A. and S. Toulmin
1973   Wittgenstein's Vienna. London: Weidenfeld and Nicholson.
Karpik, L.
1977   "Technological capitalism." Pp. 410–471 in S. Clegg and D. Dunkerley (eds.), Critical Issues in Organizations. London: Routledge and Kegan Paul.
Keat, R. and J. Urry
1975   Social Theory as Science. London: Routledge and Kegan Paul.
Kolakowski, L.
1975   Husserl and the Search for Certitude. New Haven: Yale University Press.
Kuhn, T.
1962   The Structure of Scientific Revolutions. International Encyclopedia of Unified Sciences 2 (2): University of Chicago Press.

Lassman, P.
1974   "Phenomenological perspectives in sociology." Pp.125–144 in J. Rex (ed.), Approaches to Sociology. London: Routledge and Kegan Paul.

Lazlo, E.
1966   Beyond Scepticism and Realism. The Hague: Martinus Nijhoff.

Lukacs, G.
1971   History and Class Consciousness. London: Merlin Press.

McCullough, A. E. and M. Shannon
1977   "Organizations and protections." Pp. 72–85 in S. Clegg and D. Dunkerley (eds), Critical Issues in Organizations. London: Routledge and Kegan Paul.

McHugh, P.
1968   Defining the Situation. Indianapolis: Bobbs-Merrill.

McHugh, P.
1971   "On the failure of positivism." In J. D. Douglas (ed.), Understanding Everyday Life. London: Routledge and Kegan Paul.

Mandel, E.
1975   Late Capitalism. London: New Left Books.

Manning, P. K.
1979   "Metaphors of the field: varieties of organizational discourse." American Science Quarterly 24 (4):660–671.

Marceau, J., A. B. Thomas, and R. Whitely
1978   "Business and the state: management education and business elites in France and Great Britain." Pp. 128–157 in G. Littlejohn, B. Smart, J. Wakeford, and N. Yuval-Davis (eds.), Power and the State. London: Croom-Helm.

Marcuse, H.
1955   Reason and Revolution. London: Routledge and Kegan Paul.

Marcuse, H.
1964   One Dimensional Man. London: Routledge and Kegan Paul.

Marx, K. and F. Engels
1965   The German Ideology. London: Lawrence and Wishart.

Mayo, E.
1975   The Social Problems of an Industrial Civilization. London: Routledge and Kegan Paul.

O'Connor, J.
1973   The Fiscal Crisis of the State. New York: St. Martins Press.

Offe, C.
1976   Industry and Inequality. London: Edward Arnold.

Ogburn, W. F.
1950   Social Change with Respect to Culture and Original Nature. (revised edition) New York: Viking Press.

Paci, E.
1972   The Function of the Sciences and the Meaning of Man. Evanston, Ill,: Northwestern University Press.

Passmore, J.
1957   A Hundred Years of Philosophy. London: Duckworth.

Perrow, C.
1972   Complex Organizations. Glenview, Ill,: Scott Foresman.

Phillips, D.
1973   Abandoning Method. San Francisco: Jossey-Bass.

Polanyi, K.
1957   The great Transformation. Boston: Beacon Press.

Rex, J. (ed.)
1973   Approaches to Sociology: An Introduction to Major Trends in British Sociology. London: Routledge and Kegan Paul.

Rex, J.
1974   Discovering Sociology. London: Routledge and Kegan Paul.
Rowthorn, B.
1976   "Review article: late capitalism." New Left Review 98:59–83.
Sandywell, B.; M. Phillipson; P. Filmer; D. Walsh; M. Roche and D. Silverman
1974   Reflexivity and the Problems of language. London: Routledge and Kegan Paul.
Schutz, A.
1953   Collected Papers. Volume 1, edited by M. Natanson, The Hague: Martinus Nijhoff.
Schutz, A.
1964   Collected Papers. Volume 2, edited by A. Broderson, The Hague: Martinus Nijhoff.
Schutz, A.
1966   Collected Papers. Volume 3, edited by I. Schutz, The Hague: Martinus Nijhoff.
Schutz, A.
1967   The Phenomenology of the Social World. Translated by G. Walsh and F. Lehnert. With an Introduction by G. Walsh. The Hague: Evanston, Ill.: Northwestern University Press.
Schutz, A.
1970   "Concept and theory formation in the social sciences." Pp. 1–19 in D. Emmet and A. MacIntrye (eds.), Sociological theory and Philosophical Analysis. London: Macmillan.
Silverman, D.
1968   "Formal organizations or industrial sociology; towards a social action analysis of organizations." Sociology 2:221–238.
Silverman, D.
1970   The Theory of Organizations. London: Heinemann.
Silverman, D.
1972   "Some neglected questions about social reality." Pp. 165–182 in P. Filmer, M. Phillipson, D. Silverman, and D. Walsh (eds.), New Directions in Sociological Theory. London: Collier-Macmillan.
Silverman, D.
1974a "Speaking seriously." Theory and Society 1:1–15.
Silverman, D.
1975   "Accounts of organizations: organizational 'structures' and the accounting process." Pp. 269–302 in J. B. McKinlay (ed.), Processing People: Cases in Organizational Behaviour. London: Holt, Rinehart and Winston.
Silverman, D. and J. Jones
1976   Organizational Work. London: Collier-Macmillan.
Smart, B.
1976   Sociology, Phenomenology and Marxian Analysis. London: Routledge and Kegan Paul.
Sohn-Rethel, A.
1976   "The dual economics of transition." Pp. 26–45 in CSE Pamphlet No. 1, The Labour Process and Class Strategies. London: Stage 1.
Sohn-Rethel, A.
1978   Intellectual and Manual Labour: A Critique of Epistemology. London: Macmillan.
Sudnow, D.
1973   "Normal crimes: sociological features of the penal code in a public defender office." Pp. 346–357 in G. Salaman and K. Thompson (eds.), People and Organizations. London: Longman.
Taylor, I., P. Walton, and J. Young
1973   The New Criminology. London: Routledge and Kegan Paul.
Thompson, E, P.
1978   The Poverty of Theory. London: Merlin Press.
Van Maanen, J.
1979   "The fact of friction in organizational ethnography." American Sociological Quarterly 24, (4):539–550.

Vernon, R.
   1973   "Multinational enterprise in developing countries: issues in dependency and interdependence." Pp. 40–62 in D. E. Apter and L. W. Goodman (eds.), The Multinational Corporation and Social Change. London: Praeger.

Wallerstein, I.
   1974   The Modern World System: Capitalist Agriculture and the Origins of the European World Economy in the Sixteenth Century. London: Academic Press.

Weber, M.
   1968   Economy and Society: An Outline of Interpretive Sociology. 3 vols. edited with an introduction by G. Roth and C. Wittich. New York: Bedminister Press.

Weick, K. E.
   1969   The Social Psychology of Organizing. Reading, Mass.: Addison-Wesley.

Wheelwright, E. L.
   1973   "International capitalism - the sourcerers apprentice?" Meanjin Quarterly 32:2.

Wieder, D. L.
   1974   "Telling the code." Pp. 144–172 in R. Turner (ed.) Ethnomethodology. Harmondsworth: Penguin.

Winch, P.
   1958   The Idea of a Social Science. London: Routledge and Kegan Paul.

Wittgenstein, L.
   1961   Tractatus Logico-Philosophicus. London: Routledge and Kegan Paul.

Wittgenstein, L.
   1968   Philosophical Investigations. Oxford: Blackwell.

Young, M. F. D., (ed).
   1971   Knowledge and Control. New Directions for the Sociology of Education. London: Collier-Macmillan.

Zimmerman, D.
   1971   "Record-keeping and the intake process in a public welfare organization." Pp. 63–95 in S. Wheeler (ed.), On Record: Files and Dossiers in American Life. New York: Russell Sage Foundation.

Zimmerman, D. and M. Pollner
   1971   "The everyday world as aphenomenon." Pp. 80–103 in J. Douglas (ed.), Understanding Everyday Life. London: Routledge and Kegan Paul.

HIERARCHICAL DIFFERENTIATION IN IMPERATIVELY COORDINATED ASSOCIATIONS

Bruce H. Mayhew

I. INTRODUCTION

Georg Simmel (1894:499) suggested that sociology has as its distinctive task the study of social forms. And, certainly one of the most important areas of inquiry concerns forms of domination or control (Simmel, 1907). In this essay, I discuss certain forms of domination that emerge in "imperatively coordinated associations" (Weber, 1922:29).[1] These associations coordinate activity through imperative statements or *commands* issued by persons occupying positions of authority. Although imperatively coordinated associations include a very broad range of organizational types, perhaps most of them appear as bureaucracies, or *instrumental formal organizations* (Thompson, 1967).

This essay confines attention to the hierarchical properties of administrative

Research in the Sociology of Organizations, vol. 2, pages 153–229
Copyright © **1983 by JAI Press Inc.**
All rights of reproduction in any form reserved.
ISBN: 0-89232-203-9

control relations in human social systems, usually, but not exclusively, to control relations in formal organizations. The principal thesis will be that administrative hierarchies tend to assume one general form, ordinarily called "unity of command" (Fayol, 1917:25). Explication of this thesis includes offering an account of the emergence of unity of command as a property of administrative systems, as well as showing that available data agree with it. Additional hierarchical properties are a consequence of unity of command, and these properties permit the definition of variables which enter into explanation of structural variation in organizations. I will suggest that the hierarchical properties examined here are a major part of the explanation for some of the most important variations in the structure and operation of formal organizations. In particular, the emergence of an administrative elite in the form of minority rule can be explained by these properties. However, structural properties of hierarchy do not account for all dimensions of control in organizations. Consequently, this essay can offer no more than a *first approximation* to a theory of vertical control in organizations.

Although formal organizations are the principal variant considered here, others are relevant to the extent that they face similar environments and ultimately become transformed into instrumental formal organizations. Thus, a tribe of pastoral nomads may assume a military posture and establish a conquest state (Grousset, 1939), or a bandit gang may initiate a shipping line for piracy, trade, or both (Bono, 1964). In any case, instrumental organizations operate on their environments in direct and active ways. They are task oriented and are work organizations in that their members ordinarily hold positions on a full-time basis (Weber, 1922:651). Instrumental organizations range across the entire political and economic spectrum of society, from the smallest hamburger stand to the largest corporation and from the smallest post office branch to the largest multinational empire. They include armies and hospitals, police departments and restaurants, universities and factories, post offices and banks, local governments and supermarkets, national governments and high schools, barber shops and bakeries, insurance firms and battleships. The task of these organizations is to get something done in the empirical world within a finite period of time. They are, therefore, subject to significant environmental constraints, constraints which have important implications for their internal structure and operation.

Control hierarchies are one form of vertical order in social systems and are subsumed under theories of social stratification (Eisenstadt, 1971:11). In complex societies, however, control hierarchies in organizations are the paramount form of vertical order; many other systems of stratification are no more than derivatives of organizational hierarchies (Collins, 1975:41). But hierarchy can assume diverse configurations, ranging from microstructural dominance relations in discussion groups (Bartos, 1967) to macrostructural semilattices spanning leviathans (Friedell, 1967). The present focus is on hierarchical structures mapped by unity of command, and this involves only one type of semilattice. While other forms may enter into consideration for purposes of illustrative contrast, they are not a central concern. Dominance structures as well as more generalized power inequalities among humans in face-to-face interaction are relevant to a theory of vertical order, but have been treated elsewhere (Mayhew and Gray, 1971, 1972; Mayhew and Levinger, 1976a). The relations which define hierarchical control in organizations may connect persons in face-to-face interaction as well as persons and groups located in distant macrostructural units of the organization. But this inquiry will avoid an exclusive concern with microstructural phenomena. The conditions of face-to-face interaction attenuate, rather than accentuate, the stresses which produce unity of command. If all organizations were small groups, unity of command would still emerge under environmental constraint, but much less often than it does in spatially dispersed organizations. The contingencies which arise in coordinating macrostructural relations, relations between work groups and larger units, provide the strongest impetus toward unity of command. And—contrary to received opinion—the fundamental problems of system survival are located in macrostructural interaction.

II. UNITY OF COMMAND

The mathematical realization of unity of command is given by what graph theorists call an "aborescence" (Berge, 1958:13) or an "out-tree" (Harary, 1969:201). All distinct, nonisomorphic, out-trees of order six are shown in Figure 1. As this figure illustrates, an out-tree is a connected diagraph consisting of a set of points and a set of directed lines. The points correspond to positions in the authority structure and the lines indicate the direction of authority relations. Only one position has no superior—the chief executive—and all other positions have exactly one immediate superior. The number of points in an out-tree corresponds to the number of personnel in the system. That is, the size of the system corresponds to the order of its out-tree (Harary, 1967:3). Henceforth, unity of command and out-tree will be used as interchangeable terms.

Control hierarchies characterized by unity of command may appear to be quite restrictive in the scope of relations they permit. They are. Nevertheless, unity of command admits more variation than may be apparent upon first consideration. As the size of the organization increases, its potential for variation in the structure of unity of command increases multiplicatively, so that even relatively small organizations have the opportunity to select from a vast array of structural possibilities. This mathematical truism is illustrated in Table 1, which shows the number of possible configurations that unity of command may assume at selected sizes. An organization with only 12 members has almost 5,000 possible forms which its control structure may assume even when constrained to unity of command; an organization with 36 members has more than 179 trillion possibilities.

An organization is, among other things, a set of people connected in a communication network. Hierarchical control in the form of unity of command deals

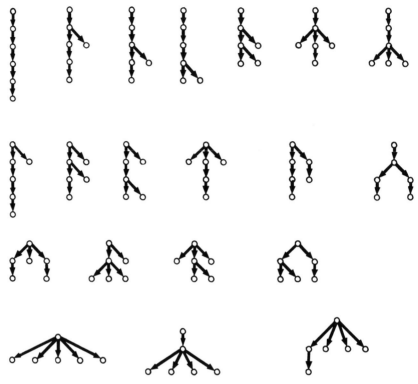

Figure 1. All Distinct (Nonisomorphic) Out-Trees of Order Six.

with only one part of this network. To see this, it is necessary to distinguish between types of information flowing through the organization. Some messages are "declarative" statements: they are purely descriptive and contain no hint of command (Walter, 1966:188). Such statements are not irrelevant to the problem of control, but they should not be confused with "imperative" statements or *commands:* messages which specify outcomes or activities and which must be obeyed (Walter, 1966:189). Unity of command as defined here refers to the communication network along which commands flow through the organization. This is to be distinguished from channels along which more general information moves. Other types of information can flow in all directions, up the hierarchy, down the hierarchy, within levels, and so on. Suggestions, requests, advice, and all sorts of information may flow freely along available channels, without necessarily interrupting a chain of command. But unity of command is a chain of command. Specifically, it is a communication network defined by who-gives-orders-to-whom relations. It is not defined by who-reports-to-whom relations. This point bears elaboration.

A person occupying a lower level position may have as a routine part of his task the obligation to send information up the hierarchy, not only to his immediate superior, but also to other higher level personnel. This does not imply that the same person receives orders from more than one superior. Rather, sending information up the hierarchy along several channels is a standard information-infusion device. Its objective is to apprise higher level personnel of activities occurring in different parts of the organization, activities in which they have an interest but over which they have no direct control. Accordingly, if A reports to B, this in no way implies that B gives orders to A. Failure to appreciate these differences can lead to the worst sorts of confusion in describing hierarchies. An explicit illustration should help to avoid such misunderstandings.

Figure 2 shows some of the network possibilities that may be encountered in the study of administrative hierarchies. Figure 2A is an out-tree through which commands are diffused to subordinates. Figure 2B shows what happens when the directed lines of 2A are reversed to map the infusion of information from subordinates. This second illustration covers the same channels as the first, but maps only the upward flow of reports. The network in 2B is called an ''in-tree'' (Harary, 1969:201). Figure 2C shows a more generalized information-infusion configuration in which some subordinates report upward to more than one person at higher levels. The fundamental point is that neither Figure 2B nor 2C indicate anything about the flow of directives through the system. Only Figure 2A shows that. Of course, if a command structure has the out-tree form of Figure 2A, it is quite likely to have an information-infusion structure covering at least the chan-

Table 1. Number of Distinct (Nonisomorphic) Out-Tree Structures Which are Logically Possible at Selected Organizational Sizes*

Size	Number of Out-Tree Structures	Size	Number of Out-Tree Structures	Size	Number of Out-Tree Structures
2	1	14	32,973	26	5,759,635,456
3	2	15	87,811	27	16,083,730,432
4	4	16	235,381	28	45,007,065,088
5	9	17	634,847	29	126,186,553,344
6	20	18	1,721,159	30	354,426,814,464
7	48	19	4,688,676	31	997,171,462,144
8	115	20	12,826,228	32	2,809,934,118,912
9	286	21	35,221,824	33	7,919,819,299,840
10	719	22	97,055,168	34	22,409,528,737,792
11	1,842	23	268,282,848	35	63,411,719,241,728
12	4,766	24	743,724,800	36	179,655,915,077,632
13	12,486	25	2,067,174,400		

Source: Robinson and Schwenk (1974).

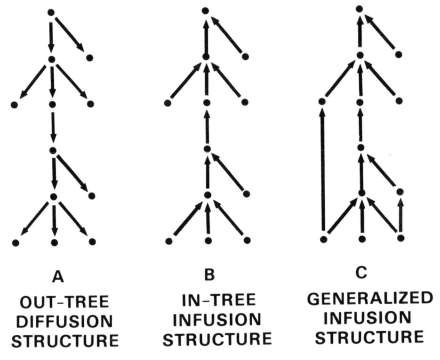

A

**OUT-TREE
DIFFUSION
STRUCTURE**

B

**IN-TREE
INFUSION
STRUCTURE**

C

**GENERALIZED
INFUSION
STRUCTURE**

Figure 2.   Diffusion of Orders Through an Out-Tree (A); Infusion of Information Through an In-Tree (B); and Infusion of Information Through a More
Generalized Set of Channels (C).

nels shown in Figure 2B; however, nothing precludes the possibility that its
information-infusion structure could look like Figure 2C or even some denser
form of network.

When an administrative hierarchy is mapped by unity of command, supervisory personnel send both orders and other types of information down the hierarchy.
Whether persons are in supervisory positions or not, they tend to send information up the hierarchy—possibly along several channels—and they may send it
horizontally within levels. But no one sends orders up the hierarchy or horizontally within levels. A concrete example is the administrative hierarchy of Swat
State described by Barth (1959:129): "Information and appeals travel upwards in
this hierarchy, while instruction and decisions are passed downward and implemented by it." When researchers examine an administrative hierarchy, they may
conclude that it is not characterized by unity of command if, and only if, the flow
of commands is not mapped by an out-tree such as the one shown in Figure 2A.

An underlying assumption of many analyses is that the concrete pattern of
hierarchy is fixed, so that one picture of its broad contours is sufficient to

describe its significant properties. No doubt, some organizations—such as universities—are ossified in one pattern, but the assumption is generally false. Many organizations *routinely* shift their pattern of hierarchy from one configuration to another as they move through activity cycles over time. This may happen, for example, when a local fire station changes its structure as trucks are sent out to fight fires (Stern, 1972). The hierarchical network of command changes when a warship shifts to battle stations. In some large military aircraft, the structure of command on the ground is different from the structure of command in the air, or at least during actual combat conditions. But a full review of such variation is beyond the scope of this essay. A brief illustration must suffice.

Figure 3 provides three pictures of the same administrative hierarchy. In each case, persons are labeled for identification. Figures 3A and 3B show the same organization at two different points in time. The concrete pattern of communication among persons has changed over time, but the form of the hierarchy remains unaltered. Figure 3C shows an organization chart devised by a researcher who was told that position j is a secretary who works for both positions k and w. This hypothetical investigator might conclude that the system under consideration is not characterized by unity of command. He would be wrong. As Figures 3A and 3B illustrate, the movement of a worker from one point to another within a network, or an alteration in the pattern of communication over time, in no way removes unity of command as an operating structure. Secretary j will not receive contradictory orders from superiors because secretary j has only one superior at a time. It is the actual over-time operation of hierarchical structures which is relevant to organizational survival. Summary configurations such as the one shown in Figure 3C are irrelevant.

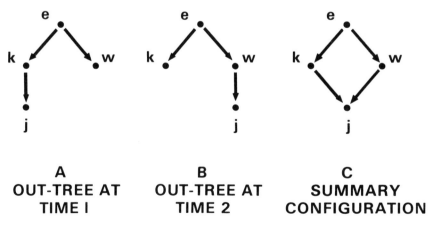

A	B	C
OUT-TREE AT	OUT-TREE AT	SUMMARY
TIME 1	TIME 2	CONFIGURATION

Figure 3. Out-Tree Control Hierarchies at Two Points in Time (A and B), and a Summary Configuration which Ignores Time (C).

III.   PROPERTIES OF HIERARCHY

Figure 4 provides two elementary hierarchies: illustration A with the maximum number of levels and illustration B with the maximum span of control in an organization of size five. The number of hierarchical levels means the length of the longest directed path (Harary et al., 1965:32) through the hierarchy, plus one. In a maximum-level hierarchy, the number of levels is exactly equal to the size of the organization. Figure 4A shows a system of five persons, each occupy ing a different level. By contrast, Figure 4B shows a hierarchy with the minimum possible number of levels. In an organization of size S, the number of levels, L must take on integer values in the range $2 \leq L \leq S$, because S itself is defined in the range $2 \leq S < \infty$. There are no one-person organizations. The span of control refers to the number of immediate subordinates per supervisor. It is therefore defined only for those out-tree positions which have a positive 'outdegree' (Ha rary et al., 1965:16). Positions with an outdegree of zero are not supervisory positions. But all other positions are supervisory, including those with only one immediate subordinate. Figure 4A illustrates the minimum and Figure 4B the

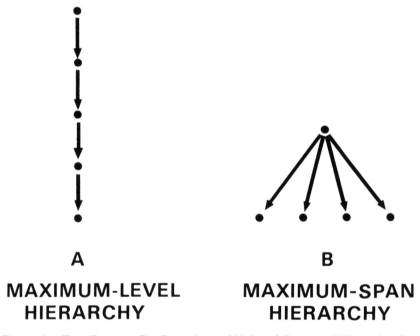

A

MAXIMUM-LEVEL
HIERARCHY

B

MAXIMUM-SPAN
HIERARCHY

Figure 4.   Two Extreme Configurations of Unity of Command Hierarchy: One with the Maximum Number of Levels (A) and One with the Maximum Span of Control (B).

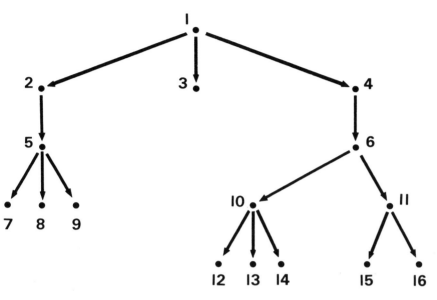

Figure 5. A Unity of Command Hierarchy with Branches of Unequal Length and Variations in Span of Control.

maximum span of control for organizations of size five. For an organization of size S, the average span of control, X, must fall in the range $1 \le X \le S - 1$.

Figure 5 introduces problems. An out-tree can have branches of unequal lengths, and the span of control can vary both within and across levels. A structural variable which supplements understanding of levels and spans is the intensity of indirect control (Starbuck, 1965a:376–80). It is a measure of the extent to which *indirect* control is obtained through the structure of the hierarchy itself. The measure is constructed by assigning to each position a value, j_i, corresponding to the number of subordinates controlled both directly and indirectly. In Figure 5, where each position is identified by a number for the index i, the values of j_i, vary from $j_{16} = 0$ to $j_1 = 15$. While these values are at times of interest in themselves (Blau, 1977), they are here summed to yield a control value, J, for the hierarchy as a whole. In Figure 5, $J = 42$. In that hierarchy, there are a cumulative total of 42 positions controlled both directly and indirectly. The intensity of indirect control, C, is expressed as $C = (J - J_{min})/(J_{max} - J_{min})$, where $J_{min} = S - 1$ and $J_{max} = S(S - 1)/2$ in an organization of size S. Thus, intensity of indirect control is contained in the range $0 \le C \le 1$. It indicates the proportion of indirect control relations that occur in the hierarchy out of all those which can occur at a given size, excluding, as the above expression shows, the minimum number which must be present at each size. For the hierarchy in Figure 5, $C = 9/35$.

The intensity of indirect control is one of the most important features of any administrative hierarchy. As Samuel and Mannheim (1970:218–9) have noted, it has the advantage of "being sensitive to the height of the hierarchy as well as to the cumulative authority and responsibilities of each successive link in the control chain . . . reflecting variations in the span of control within and between levels of supervision." The intensity of indirect control takes on its maximum value of one in hierarchies with the maximum number of levels—as in Figure 4A—where indirect control is maximized. It takes on its minimum value of zero in hierarchies with the maximum span of control—as in Figure 4B—where indirect control is minimized. It provides a measure of the balance between structural proliferation of hierarchical levels and spans of control (Stern, 1972).

Another property of out-trees is the number of major hierarchical divisions. In purely structural terms, this corresponds to the span of control of the chief executive—or the outdegree of the root point in an out-tree. The number of major hierarchical divisions, M, is contained in the range $1 \leq M \leq S - 1$. The two extremes are illustrated in Figure 4, which shows that in these cases M is synonymous with the span of control.

The property of hierarchical symmetry also reflects a dimension of both spans and levels. An out-tree is symmetric if, and only if (1) the branches are all identical in length and (2) the span of control is the same for all supervisory positions. There is no well-defined measure of the degree of hierarchical symmetry, partly because symmetry occurs at both extreme values of the span of control, as shown in Figure 4. Symmetric or near-symmetric out-trees are commonly used in illustrations of other aspects of hierarchical structure (Starbuck, 1965a, 1965b). Whether hierarchies actually tend toward symmetry is an important question, although not necessarily for reasons suggested in the literature (Meyer, 1971).

Possibly the most controversial property of administrative hierarchies is the supervisory ratio, or as it will be defined here: the ratio of supervisory personnel to all personnel. If s is the number of supervisors and S is organizational size, then the supervisory ratio, R, is given by $R = s/S$. In an out-tree, this is the ratio of positions with positive outdegree to all positions. It is contained in the range $1/S \leq R \leq (S - 1)/S$, as may be seen in Figure 4. As a more general theoretical construct, the supervisory ratio corresponds to *the relative size of the controlling component,* for supervisory personnel are those "who occupy positions from which the activity of the organization is directed" (Mayhew, 1973:472).

An out-tree is a type of directed graph consisting of a set of points and a set of directed lines. The points correspond to positions and the lines to communication channels, so that these terms will be used interchangeably. An important property of any digraph is its degree of connectivity (Harary et al., 1965:50–84). There are several categories of connectedness, but only one distinction is required here. In general, a digraph is connected if it has no isolated points or sets of isolated positions. Isolated positions are found only in broken communication networks.

Once a network is broken, or disconnected, it is no longer a unitary communication system and is therefore incapable of concerted action. All out-trees are connected digraphs; no positions are isolated from the stream of directives. However, it is certainly possible and even probable that empirical out-tree hierarchies will be broken from time to time and their networks thereby disconnected. There are two ways to disconnect a digraph: by removing a line or by removing a point. If it is possible to disconnect a digraph by removing a line, the network is said to be "line vulnerable" (Harary et al., 1965:252). If it is possible to disconnect a digraph by removing a point, the network is said to be "point vulnerable" (Harary et al., 1965:252). According to a well-known theorem, if a digraph of size three or larger is line vulnerable, then it is also point vulnerable (Harary et al., 1965:253). For this reason, only point vulnerability need be considered in studying unity of command hierarchies.

If it is possible to disconnect an out-tree by removing a point, the point in question is called a "cutpoint" (Harary, 1967:5–6). All other points in out-trees are called "endpoints" (Harary and Ostrand, 1971:7). Both types of points are illustrated in Figure 6. If a position in an out-tree is a cutpoint, then it is also a supervisory position, although the converse is not strictly true. As Figure 6 shows, when the chief executive has a span of control no greater than one, his position is not a cutpoint. Otherwise, all supervisory positions are cutpoints and all cutpoints are supervisory positions. The minor discrepancy in the instance above need occasion no concern on either practical or theoretical grounds. In all but the smallest out-trees, the difference between the proportion of cutpoints and the proportion of supervisory positions is trivial and will henceforth be ignored.

Human activity rides on the information and energy flowing through communication networks. Disconnected networks directly negate social action and ensure failure—even destruction. Therefore, a certain amount of stress needs to be placed on the remarks in the two preceding paragraphs. They are not merely important, they are critical. If, as I will maintain here, administrative hierarchies tend toward unity of command, then they also have some features which are as

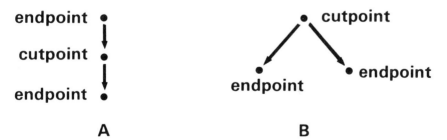

Figure 6. All Out-Trees of Size Three, Showing Location of Cutpoints and Endpoints.

singular as they are problematic. Not all communication networks are point vulnerable. Indeed, as redundancy in significant strands of social structure has survival value, most human communication networks are probably point invulnerable. But all unity of command hierarchies are point vulnerable, and they are point vulnerable by virtue of the supervisory positions they contain. This aspect of unity of command has far-reaching theoretical implications. These implications hinge upon two properties of out-trees.

The first property is, of course, the proportion of hierarchical positions which are cutpoints. Since the supervisory ratio, R, is synonymous with this variable, an additional measure is not required. It is only necessary to note that any increase in the proportion of cutpoints in out-trees magnifies their vulnerability to the paralytic effects of a broken network. Therefore, increases in the supervisory ratio increase the organization's exposure to the risk of disrupted communication and threaten its chances of maintaining concerted action. Such a paradox is instructive. It indicates that different facets of the same structural dimension can have quite contrary effects. Increases in the absolute number of supervisory personnel may at times be necessary to accommodate an expanding scale of operations. But, if the proportion of supervisors also increases, then the positions added to implement coordination can themselves increase the likelihood that unitary action will fail to occur.

A second structural property of cutpoints derives from the fact that some cutpoints have a greater disruption potential than others. Harary and Ostrand (1971:7) have defined the "cutting number" of any position, v, in a communication network, G, as "the number of pairs of points {u,w} of G such that u,w ≠ v and every (communication channel connecting u and w) contains v." In out-trees, the cutting number of endpoints is always zero, so that their values are omitted from Figure 7, which shows how the cutting numbers of cutpoints can be quite variable. As Figure 7 clearly shows, the maximum disruption potential is not necessarily associated with the chief executive. Rather, the cutting number of a cutpoint indicates how many pairs of positions lose contact with one another when a given cutpoint is removed from the network. This excludes pairs involving the cutpoint itself. The loss of a person or position may have quite distinct effects independent of the disruptive consequences for communication. Cutting numbers are defined so as to reflect disruption that occurs above and beyond that attributable to the loss of the individual himself. A cutting number assesses purely structural aspects of out-trees.

As Figure 7 shows, the cutting number of a hierarchical position may provide a conception of intraorganizational power very much in the terms suggested by Hickson et al. (1971). That is, cutting numbers measure the strategic position of personnel insofar as the hierarchy itself is concerned. While only this structural aspect is involved, the "strategic contingencies" view of Hickson et al. (1971:216) is a sound basis for suggesting cutting numbers as one measure of relative power in organizations. For administrative hierarchies, the strategic

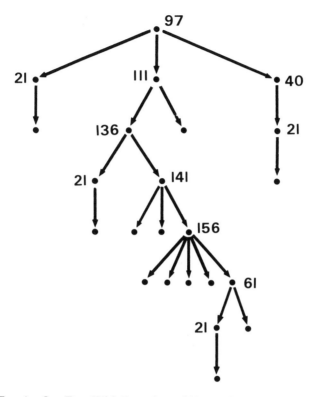

Figure 7.   An Out-Tree With Branches of Unequal Length, Showing the
Cutting Number of Each Supervisory Position.

contingencies in question are information and the control of information (Wirsing, 1973). At the same time, a person's ability to disrupt many lines of communication simply by withdrawing from interaction provides him with a strong
bargaining position (Blau, 1964).

To gain some perspective, it is convenient to define the "cutting center"
(Harary and Ostrand, 1971:7) of an out-tree. The cutting center of any connected
graph is the set of positions with the largest cutting number. In some networks,
the cutting center involves more than one point. In terms of the strategic contingencies rationale mentioned above, the cutting center is the most powerful
position, or set of positions, in an out-tree. That is, on purely structural grounds,
the cutting center is the most powerful part of the network. As shown in Figure 7,
the chief executive will not necessarily be the cutting center, but it is instructive
to consider the conditions under which he will be. Figure 8B shows the hierarchical configuration under which the chief executive will have not only the highest
cutting number, but also the maximum possible cutting number in an organiza-

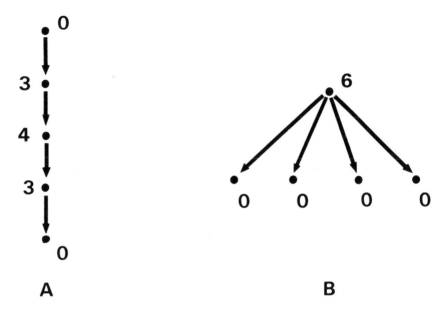

Figure 8.   Two Extreme Out-Tree Configurations Showing the Cutting Number
of Each Point.

tion of given size: when the span of control takes on its maximum value of $S - 1$.
More generally, the chief executive will always be the cutting center of an out-
tree when both of two conditions hold: the span of control is greater than one and
the hierarchy is symmetric. Furthermore, under these same conditions, the larger
the span of control, the greater the chief executive's cutting number will be—
again, see Figure 8. Given the relative power implications of cutting numbers, it
is easy to see that chief executives might prefer to keep hierarchies as symmetric
as possible and spans of control as large as possible. However, the whims of
chief executives do not enter into sociological explanations.

Discussion of the chief executive's relative strength merely illustrates conditions which assume their greatest significance upon being generalized to the total
supervisory component. The implications of hierarchical symmetry and large
spans of control for the chief executive carry over to all other supervisory
positions. In general, the more nearly symmetric a hierarchy and the larger the
average span of control, the larger will be the cutting numbers of supervisory
positions in organizations of a given size. Thus, minimizing the number of
hierarchical levels, expanding the span of control, and—in consequence—maintaining near symmetry are strategies with far-reaching implications for the entire
supervisory component, not just for the chief executive. Such conditions magni-

fy the structural basis of power for the supervisory component as a whole and have, therefore, direct implications for system survival.

The final system property of unity of command hierarchy is the average cutting number of its positions. This average cutting number is a measure of the magnitude of the system's disruption potential. For out-trees of size S, let n_i be the cutting number of point i, for $i = 1, 2, 3, \ldots, S$. If N is the sum of these cutting numbers, the *the magnitude of the hierarchy's disruption potential*, D, is given by $D = N/S$. As this value is defined across all positions in an out-tree, it has implications for the entire system, not just for supervisory positions. And, it is not obvious just what forms of out-trees will have the larger or smaller values of D, so consider Figure 8. The out-tree in Figure 8A has a value of $D = 2$, while the out-tree in Figure 8B has a value of $D = 1.2$. This type of differential holds generally. If a tall hierarchy experiences the random removal of a person, the effects will on the average be more disruptive of communication than in a system with fewer levels. Therefore, hierarchies can minimize the magnitude of their disruption potential under exactly the same conditions which both minimize the number of supervisory personnel and magnify the cutting numbers of such supervisory personnel as do exist. There are, then, considerations above and beyond mere power structure that press hierarchies in that direction.

To briefly summarize the out-tree properties which bear upon disruption of communication and coordination, an out-tree will have a value of R and a value of D. R, the relative size of the controlling component, is synonymous with the proportion of cutpoints. Hence, R measures the likelihood that a randomly removed position will disrupt communication in the hierarchy. For this reason, R is called the disruption potential of a unity of command hierarchy. D, the average cutting number of an out-tree, measures the *magnitude* of the system's disruption potential. It indicates the average degree of communicative chaos that will occur following the random removal of a position. D is called the magnitude of the hierarchy's disruption potential.

IV. OBSERVATIONS ON THEORY

Following Blau (1970) and Segraves (1974), a theory constitutes an explanation under specific conditions. A theory is a set of propositions which state relations between variables. The variables are general concepts, such as size and disruption potential. An empirical phenomenon is explained when its occurrence is deduced from a theoretical proposition. The general proposition predicts the occurrence of the concrete empirical regularity. Thus, explanation always means that particular events are deduced from more general concepts and relations. Explanation has no other meaning. As Popper (1935:75) observed, it is not possible to explain one concrete event by reference to another concrete event. Such attempts are no more than loose talk; they are not explanations.

In observational sciences, theoretical propositions are probabilistic and do not assume the archaic notion of necessary connection or so-called "causality." Informed opinion rejects the use of a term like causality (McFarland, 1970) for the same reason it was rejected in physics (Waissman, 1959). Since Hume's (1739) critique of the idea of necessary connection in nature, theoretical propositions have come to be viewed in a contingent or probabilistic sense (Pearson, 1911:174), and explanation is construed in purely logical or instrumental terms. As expressed by von Schlick (1931:158):

> "A determines B" can mean nothing else than: B can be calculated from A. And this means: there is a universal formula, which attests to the occurrence of B, when certain values are substituted for the initial conditions A and in addition definite values are assigned to such variables as time t. . . . The word "determined" thus means exactly what is meant by "predictable" or "calculable in advance."

This is not to deny that there may be necessary connections in nature, but only to say that assuming such connections—for they can only be assumed—does nothing to enhance explanation and does much to create misunderstandings. Accordingly, in observational sciences, theoretical propositions are probabilistic; they are explanatory in a purely logical and instrumental sense.

A theory of hierarchical structure is a sociological theory. It is stated in terms of sociological variables, because hierarchy is a property of social systems. Hierarchy is a form of organization which emerges from interaction within a human population and primarily as a result of the relation between that population and its environment. For this reason, the theoretical propositions will refer to system structure, to environmental conditions, and to system–environment relations. A point which bears emphasizing is that a theory of administrative hierarchy is not about individuals, their behavior, or individual characteristics. Individual characteristics are irrelevant to understanding the emergence and development of structure in social systems (Mayhew, 1980, 1981). However, as some social scientists appear to be unaware of this, a few remarks in clarification are appropriate. Organizations are designed by nature, not by people. People are only one part of nature, not its prime mover (White, 1948). Their activities do not assume a special significance in understanding the emergence of social structure.

A different view is prevalent in some quarters. Social psychologists generalize the great man theory of history to the masses. Their view implies that all men are great and their actions significant. The opposite is true. Humans are puny and their actions are insignificant. In illustration, the claim by W. I. Thomas that: "If men define situations as real, they are real in their consequences" (Thomas and Thomas, 1928:572), is merely misleading, for as Goffman (1974:1) has pointed out:

This statement is true as it reads but false as it is taken. Defining situations as real certainly has consequences, but these may contribute very marginally to the events in progress; in some cases only a slight embarrassment flits across the scene in mild concern for those who tried to define the situation wrongly.

Group structure is the prime determinant of individual action. Individuals do not dominate social situations; social situations dominate individuals. As Goffman (1974:1–2) noted further:

> Presumably, a "definition of the situation" is almost always to be found, but those who are in the situation ordinarily do not *create* this definition, even though their society often can be said to do so; ordinarily, all they do is to assess correctly what the situation ought to be form them and then act accordingly.

There is little that people can do to affect or alter the features of most social situations. What people do is dominated by the contingencies of the interaction structure surrounding them, regardless of how they define the situation.

In addition to their relative impotence in manipulating social conditions, humans are feeble information-processing instruments. Freud (1927:6) noted that humans have a naive perception of their immediate surroundings and are generally unable to estimate the contents of their own personal experiences. That is, people seldom have a clear picture of what is going on around them. The limitations of the human nervous system are well documented (see Mayhew, 1980 and references therein), and the human penchant for proliferating errors in communication networks is notorious (Campbell, 1958; DeFleur, 1962). In view of all this ineptitude, it is not surprising that research on decision-making processes in organizations finds chaos. According to James G. March (cited in Curry, 1974:29), it is often the case that:

> There exists little connection between what goes on in an organization and what the administration thinks and says is going on. . . . [T]here exists little connection between decisions made yesterday and those made today. . . . [T]here exists little connection between plans and actions, or intentions and outcomes. . . . [T]here exists little connection between overt decision processes and actual decisions (outcomes). . . . [T]here exists little connection between problems and solutions, except perhaps a temporal one: the solution was around when the problem arose.

Contrary, therefore, to what a social psychological perspective would suggest, the study of individuals is likely to tell little or nothing about the structure and operation of social systems.

When it comes to questions of organizational structure or survival, a general theory which accounts for these phenomena is not constrained to treat the thoughts, plans, strategies, etc. of individuals as anything but random. Decision making in organizations, as elsewhere, occurs under conditions of imperfect information about the environment (March and Simon, 1958:137–71). Administrators do not know what is happening in their environment: they guess. Even if all the requisite environmental information were available, humans are not necessarily capable of analyzing it and assessing its implications. They would still be guessing. A theory of organizational structure and evolution may assume that decision makers act appropriately or inappropriately at random. This will make no difference to the structure of a general theory, because knowledge of the intentions or actions of individuals is not required to explain the conditions of human social organization (Alchian, 1950:211–6).

V. SYSTEM STRUCTURE AND EVOLUTION

A. The Evolutionary Perspective

An evolutionary perspective, as in Darwin (1859) and H. Spencer (1876, 1880, 1882, 1896), accounts for the existence of certain phenomena, in part, by explaining why others are not present. In the case of social systems, the reason that other forms are not present is that they have either perished from interaction with their environments or have modified their structure while in direct interaction with their environments. The first type of event requires no further comment, but the second is easily misunderstood when applied to instrumental formal organizations. For example, it is not necessary to assume that people in organizations understand what is happening in their environment. If such knowledge were necessary, all human social systems would have perished long ago, because humans generally do not know what is happening around them. Accordingly, for some structural modification to come about in an organization adjusting to its environment, it is not necessary to assume that what happens is the result of conscious strategy. It might be in some instances, but it could as easily come about through trial and error. If organizations appear to embody rationality, this is not necessarily because someone thought up rationality and applied it to the design of organizations. Rather, random variation, structural modification for any and every reason, can lead to adaptive forms. If workable forms are hit upon, whether by accident or design, they tend to be retained. Reasons for why they work—the supposed rationality of humans—can be, and usually are, concocted at a later date. What is called organizational rationality is not a property of persons or their ideas. It is a property of social systems (Mannheim, 1935:29), and reference to the dispositions of individuals is not required to account for its existence. As indicated previously, organizations are designed by nature, not by people.

However, explaining why some forms are not present is only part of the argument. It is also necessary to indicate why things are as they are. In attempting to account for the emergence of unity of command, therefore, it is just as necessary to explain why this form exists as it is to explain why other forms do not. Furthermore, all such explanations must be formulated in such a way that they lead to falsifiable predictions. For only then can a theory claim to be an explanation of anything. Finally, the predictions must agree with the data.

Unity of command can emerge as a form of control structure in relatively small and even segmentary social systems (Gluckman, 1960). But it is even more clearly associated with high functional differentiation and large size. The formulation to be developed here probably applies to both simple and complex systems insofar as they experience similar environmnetal pressures. But grasping the long sweep of history requires an emphasis on the increases in population size, functional differentiation and technical complexity that have repeatedly emerged, driving social organization more and more in the direction of what Max Weber (1922:605–78) called "bureaucracy." This long-term trend has resulted in larger size as a function of time (Hart, 1931:438–61; Lenski, 1979:8–10) and has accelerated with the development of industrial technology (Wagner, 1892:893). Bureaucratic structure pervades every aspect of contemporary social life (Bates, 1974; Blau, 1974). It is not confined to corporations and governments. It spans nations and connects even tribal groupings to the state (Barth, 1961; Fernea, 1970). However, most social systems do not last very long, whether they are bureaucratic or not. For this reason, a preliminary consideration of system–environment interaction is a minimum prerequisite for a theory of unity of command.

B. Organizational Mortality

The history of humanity is a record of failure. The vast majority of all human societies that have ever existed have perished. In the main, they have been crushed or absorbed by other societies. These are facts of history (Lenski, 1970:90–94), facts which have been too long neglected by most social scientists. The conditions which have destroyed human societies, organizations, and groups of all kinds are not hidden under archaeological debris. They are still here, and they are just as real for organizations as they were for societies. Of the first 5,000 limited companies formed in England, 54 percent ceased to exist within a decade (Shannon, 1932:396–419). Greater longevity but similar results were reported for Italian and Swiss joint-stock companies (Lasorsa, 1928; Gaedicke, 1929). The surprising aspect of such studies is that even comparatively large systems do not last long. A study of 181 American automobile firms found that 64 percent disappeared in less than 10 years (Epstein, 1928). However, when research examined significant size variation, it usually revealed that even though most firms have low life expectancies, survival probability tends to increase with size (McGarry, 1930; Heilman, 1932; Vaile, 1932; Steindl, 1945).

In a study of 10,000 business firms in Poughkeepsie for the period 1843–1936, Hutchinson et al. (1938) found that 30 percent failed in the first year and

78 percent had vanished within ten years. In view of such statistics, it is shocking to read Starbuck's (1965b:464) statement that: "The fact of the matter is that nearly all organizations, nearly all the time, find survival easy." The opposite is true. In the United States, a business firm and a hound dog have about the same life expectancy. This condition represents an improvement for business firms. In the nineteenth century, when Adam Smith's invisible hand was more rambunctious than it is today, business firms had even shorter life expectancies (Krooss, 1966:197–8). While truly reliable statistics are not available for early periods of rapid industrialization in England and America, a reasonable estimate would place the life expectancies of business firms just ahead of alley cats during the last two centuries (Hoffman, 1940:148–9). And there is evidence to suggest that private enterprises faired even worse prior to the industrial revolution (Gomes de Brito, 1905; Braudel, 1966a:102–3).

Actually, long-term statistics being what they are, it is not entirely clear that the life expectancies of business firms have increased. Sorokin (1947:533), Starbuck (1965b:464), and Dill (1965:1092) all agreed that size enhances survival probability. If business mortality has declined, this may be due to a shift in their size distribution. Yet mortality remains high, for as Dill (1965:1072) observed: "Most firms are small. Within the United States, in 1960, there were 4.7 million business organizations. . . . [M]ore than 95 per cent had less than 100 employees; and 90 percent had gross sales of less than $500,000." Small firms do not last long. Stepanek (1960) found that the median life expectancy for firms with fewer than four employees was 4 years. To a large degree, the size distribution appears to account for high mortality, as more contemporary studies continue to show (see references in Dill, 1965). Contrary to received propaganda, America is not the land of economic opportunity; it is the land of economic failure.

Furthermore, just because business firms are ahead of alley cats is no reason to suppose that their future is secure. The environment of private enterprise is a sea of interesting cycles and is, therefore, inherently unstable (Solo, 1967). Juglar (1860) cycles of about eight to ten years' duration crush hundreds of firms, while the downswing of a Kondratieff (1926) wave destroys thousands. A 40-month Kitchin (1923) cycle may remove no more than a handful of firms, but a Braudel (1966a:92–3) cycle of 200 years swamps millions. In the context of an international division of labor (Wallerstein, 1974a), there is some rationale for the prediction that the degree of instability in the environment of business firms will be an increasing function of time (Terryberry, 1968; Wallerstein, 1974b).

While a shift in the size distribution of firms might account for some decline in business mortality, increased environmental complexity would probably offset its effects in the absence of other considerations. But there are other considerations. To the extent that business mortality has temporarily declined in the twentieth century—and it is still not clear that it has—this may simply indicate that larger firms and governments are screening small firms from severe environmental turbulence. In the United States, some small businesses exist under the umbrella of larger firms, their sole customers. Survival of the larger systems guarantees the future of their smaller suppliers. And, to the extent that a large system like the federal government subsidizes small firms directly, or indirectly through aid to large firms, the severity of environmental fluctuations is similarly attenuated, even in the presence of—and possibly because of—increased environmental complexity. In other words, to the extent that firms increase in size or lock themselves into exchange networks with larger firms or governments, they escape some of the vicissitudes of increased complexity. But the rate of failure remains high. That business firms—the darlings of the Western world—do not live as long as the average person is a striking fact.

Due partially to their larger size, political systems appear to last longer than business firms. Accurate estimates for the life spans of state systems have never been compiled (Sorokin, 1947:529–30). Some approximations have been attempted for large empires, but Quètelet's (1848:158–61) estimate of 1,461 years is unacceptable. No state system has ever lasted that long. Quètelet was confusing the over-time operation of the "Law of Cultural Dominance" (Kaplan, 1960:75) with the survival of concrete state systems. Sorokin's (1947:529) wild claim that the Chinese state lasted 4,000 years was so outrageous that he rejected it himself on the next page (1947:530). During the period to which he referred, the state system in China collapsed not fewer than seven times (Loewe, 1966:42–69). It is doubtful whether any state has lasted for even 800 years. As their life expectancies are probably also determined by their size distribution (Montesquieu, 1748:204), between 100 and 150 years would be a safer quess for the median age of state systems, and that is probably too high. States may outlive alley cats, but they probably do not outlive trees. Under Sorokin's (1947: 529–30) criteria, most existing states are comparatively young, with the United States being one of the oldest. Some political systems have lasted less than twenty years (Holt, 1970), others less than ten (Eaton, 1954; Woolman, 1968).

Like all finite organisms, humans die from aging or misadventure. And, because people are mortal by definition, their death occasions no surprise. On the other hand, that business firms do not outlast the average person is very surprising. That political organizations do not last millennia is equally amazing. For there is nothing in the definition of human social systems—except primary groups—which requires that they be mortal. Rather, they are defined so that their life spans are potentially as great as the entire human species (Blau, 1969). People may come and go, but organizations can last forever.

Why, then, do organizations disappear? Since their definition excludes a purely biological aging process, it must necessarily be the case that they perish from misadventure. Misadventures arrive in two principal forms: physical and social encounters. Natural disasters and physical changes of all kinds can and do destroy human organizations. But, as a rule, organizations destroy each other. The social environment tends on the average to be more unstable than the

physical environment (Terryberry, 1968), and it has arranged for the demise of
most organizations just as it has for most societies. If an organization has managed to survive encounters with its purely biophysical environment, it will in the
long run tend to be destroyed by its social environment.

An organization will have a social environment comprising other social
groups, communities, organizations, and societies. This is to be distinguished
from its purely biophysical environment—although the two are usually intertwined. An organization's social environment tends to be most salient in either
its political or economic aspect. Political organization is the organization of
violence (Weber, 1921:397; Collins, 1975:351), while economic organization
relates to most material goods and services except propaganda. Propaganda is a
relatively inert part of the social environmnet unless accompanied by some
political or economic arrangement.

Destructive competition between business firms is generally recognized and
well understood (Alchian, 1950; Solo, 1967). The nature of destructive competition among political systems is equally clear in the historical record, but remains
opaque in social science literature mostly from neglect and occasionally from
obscurantism. Except when isolated by distance or other physical obstacles,
states are heavily engaged in *Aussenpolitik* (Eisenstadt, 1963:317). Such external
relations may destroy states in one of two principal ways, but usually both. First,
states are directly destroyed in warfare. The Aztec and Inca empires were directly crushed by the Spanish empire (Prescott, 1843b, 1843c, 1847a, 1847b).
The Sassanian empire was directly destroyed by the Rashidun Khaliphate
(Shaban, 1971). Most states have in fact been destroyed through external warfare, or through a combination of external and internal war. Second, although it
is a by-product of warfare, states are also destroyed—if not directly by external
powers, then indirectly—by burning up their resources required for external war
or for supressing internal war: that is, in supressing rebellion (Braudel,
1966b:168–70). The Sassanian empire had been burning up its resources in war
with the Byzantine empire when it was attacked and destroyed by the Rashidun
Kaliphate. Weakness gained in the first encounter may have contributed to
collapse in the second. One way or another, warfare removed most states in
history. For any year in the twentieth century, war has been in progress somewhere in the world. The present is not different from the past in this regard
(Richardson, 1960:32–127).

At least in theory, states could be destroyed by purely commercial competition, and such competition undoubtedly plays a part in their fate (Braudel,
1966a, 1966b; Lane, 1973; Wallerstein, 1974a). Commercial competition or
similar economic considerations can be, and often have been, the basis of war
(Sombart, 1913; Steinmetz, 1929; Urlanis, 1960). Without denying the role of
commercial competition in generating international strife, it remains necessary to
insist that states have found their downfall in warfare and its immediate contingencies, for this is what the historical record shows (Lenski, 1970:91–3).

There are a few instances in which the specific nature of terminal misadventures remain hidden in the deep time of the archaeological record (Sabloff and Willey, 1967; Van Beek, 1969), but the general trend is beyond dispute.

From the preceding observations, it is clear that organizations are here conceived as being destroyed by a change in their environmental relations. Alternative views require comment to avoid misunderstandings. A common theoretical stance is that at least some forms of human social systems contain the seeds of their own destruction. That is, properties that destroy a social system are seen as purely internal, as being built into the structure of the system itself. Representatives of this view include Marx (1859), Spengler (1918), E. Weber (1934), and Toynbee (1947, 1957). Most of these theories address large, even global, systems, but their tone implies that they are generally valid—such views have been directly applied to organizations like states (Le Bon, 1912:44). A typical statement of the seeds-of-destruction school is Toynbee's claim that: "A civilization which has become the victim of a successful intrusion has already in fact broken down internally" (1947:245). Thus, as Prescott (1843a:77) seems to have believed, the Aztecs were undoubtedly the victims of moral decay, for otherwise they could not have been conquered by the Spaniards.

There is one grave defect in such explanations. It is virtually impossible to locate a system property which is not generated by or closely articulated with the environment. For this reason, these theories tend to be untestable. Even if testable when clarified, they also have the defect of resisting clarification. Possibly because these theories are embedded in polemics (Marx and Engels, 1848), mysticism (Spengler, 1918), or ecclesiastical monologue (Toynbee, 1957), they wallow in a seemingly impenetrable terminological fog.

At times, one gains the impression that the seeds-of-destruction school has mistaken population processes for other phenomena. It is true that population systems generate the conditions of their own destruction. And they do so for exactly the reasons Malthus (1798) suggested (cf. Darwin, 1952; Boulding, 1952, 1955). But their so-called destruction is usually partial; it is seldom complete. Furthermore, the destructive capacity of a population system arises from an environmental relation, not from an internal one. It is the relation between the population and the resources in its environment which precipitates crises. Food supply is not a part of a population system (Ford and De Jong, 1970:7–14). Therefore, the destructive relations in population dynamics are system–environment relations, not internal system relations. Finally, population aggregates comprise numerous segments: communities, organizations, and nations. For this reason, population-based competition tends to take the form of political struggle between the social systems comprising the aggregate. Population pressure has generated political strife in the twentieth century (Del Boca, 1965), just as it did in prehistoric times (Carneiro, 1970, 1972). Unless otherwise alleviated, population pressure is ultimately translated into warfare.

Returning to the current perspective, it is necessary to insist, along with

Terryberry (1968), that the principal effects run from the environment into the social system, whether that is an organization or a society. The randomly selected social system is less powerful than its environment and, sooner or later, will be destroyed by its environment. This observation is made because it is historically accurate. But such considerations do not imply that all analysis must be asymmetric. Whether a social system will modify its structure, survive, or perish is determined by three sets of variables. The first is the set of variables defining the system's structure, the second is the set of variables defining the state of the system's environment, and the third is the set of variables defining the system's relation to its environment (Duncan, 1964). If a social system is destroyed, this will be because certain kinds of changes have come about in its relation to the environment. Some of the most important types of changes are taken up in the next section.

C. Theory of System Processing Limits

Organizations are finite systems in the sense that, within any finite period of time, they are limited in the degree to which they can alter their form, in the amount of information they can access, and in the amount of energy they can harness. In the face of turbulent environments, these limiting conditions are sufficient to multiply the probability that organizations will either modify their structure or perish. In some instances it will not matter whether they modify their structure or not: they will perish anyway. It is instructive to examine the conditions under which these events occur.

Humans and human social systems are called "living systems" (Miller, 1978). This includes all types of social systems: groups, associations, communities, organizations, societies, and multinational empires. It is necessary to establish some elementary axioms and theorems about these systems before taking up questions of hierarchy. Although it will be necessary to proceed without a theory of the division of labor, or even of order—with all the deficiencies such voids imply—no aspect of social structure and organization can be examined without the following propositions:

System Axiom 1:   *All living systems are finite systems.*

System Axiom 2:   *All living systems process information and energy both internally and across their boundaries in exchange with the parent system or environment.*

System Axiom 3:   *Information and energy processed by living systems moves through internal channels connecting internal elements and through external channels articulating the system with its environment.*

System Axiom 4: *Information and energy have both volume and variety dimensions.*

Although it is not necessary to go into details of measurement here, the last axiom needs elaboration. It is necessary to distinguish both a volume and a variety of information. Volume refers to the number of message units or signal markers flowing through a channel—such as the number of words per minute. Variety refers to differentiation within the message units themselves—such as the number of different words per minute. Both of these will be called amounts of information. Similarly, while it is always possible to express energy in terms of a common measure of its volume (Tribus and McIrvine, 1971), the variety of forms in which it occurs is also relevant to the study of human society (Cook, 1971; Kemp, 1971; Rappaport, 1971). Volume of energy refers to the amount flowing through a channel—such as the number of kilowatt hours per year. Variety of energy refers to the number of different forms it assumes in the physical environment (cf. Rushing, 1968). The number of different energy sources—such as trees, sheep, beans, coal, oil, moving water, wind—is a measure of the variety in the energy dimension (cf. Segraves, 1974). Both volume and variety will be called amounts of energy.

Following Ibn Khaldun (1377–80; 1967c:290–1), it is easy to see that the following theorems derive from the four System Axioms:

Upper Limit Theorem 1: *All living systems have an upper limit on the amount of information they can process internally and externally in exchange with the environment.*

Upper Limit Theorem 2: *All living systems have an upper limit on the amount of energy they can process internally and externally in exchange with the environment.*

Recall that amount of information and energy refers to both volume and variety. The corresponding Lower Limit Theorems (Ibn Khaldun, 1967b:271–2) are:

Lower Limit Theorem 1: *All living systems have a lower limit on the amount of information requisite to their operation.*

Lower Limit Theorem 2: *All living systems have a lower limit on the amount of energy requisite to their operation.*

Once again, amount of information and energy refers to both volume and variety in each. All the foregoing axioms and theorems are here applied to both humans and human social systems. But to obtain human social systems it is necessary to have another axiom (Ibn Khaldun, 1967b:271–2):

Generator Axiom: *Humans are able to obtain the information and energy requisite to their survival as living systems only through interaction with other humans.*

This may not be strictly true, but since hermits and feral men are unlikely to read this essay, it will be assumed anyway. The Generator Axiom supplies a drive to interaction, and it offers a substantive rationale for applying the Lower Limit Theorems to social systems.

A social system can build structure only to the extent that it is able to harness information and energy (White, 1943; Lenski, 1970). The presence of information always presupposes a minimum amount of energy (Tribus and McIrvine, 1971:5–7). Therefore, a fundamental constraint on any social system is the amount of energy available in its environment. Of course, reorganization of existing materials can—as in breeder reactors—produce more energy than was at first apparent in the environment. But the material for such reorganization must itself be present, for otherwise no multiplication of existing sources can occur. Consequently, theoretical propositions about system–environment relations and corollary internal system relations must always be understood to refer to variation within the environmentally imposed energy limit (Falk and Ruppel, 1976).

Social systems are engaged in information and energy exchanges with their environments and among their component parts. The rate at which these transfers occur is an important determinant of their structure and operation (Blau, 1972). The rate of exchange with the environment will be called the external transaction rate. The rate of exchange between internal system components will be called the internal transaction rate. These rates are expected to be interdependent:

System Proposition 1:   *The internal transaction rate is a direct function of the external transaction rate.*

That is, internal transaction rates for energy and information in social systems tend to be direct functions of their external transaction rates. Note that this proposition is a probabilistic statement. Furthermore, it refers only to operating systems. A system in the process of collapse will at some point in time cease to be described by System Proposition 1. In any case, this proposition leads to a series of connected statements:

System Proposition 2:   *As the transaction rate for information and/or energy approaches the upper limit of the system's processing capacity, the probability that the structure of the system will undergo a change approaches one.*

System Proposition 3:   *As the transaction rate for information and/or energy approaches the lower limit of the system's processing requisites, the* *probability that the structure of the system will undergo a change approaches one.*

System Proposition 4: *The higher the rate of change in information and/or energy transactions (resulting in an increase toward the system's upper processing limit) the greater the probability that the structural change in the system will be destruction of the system.*

System Proposition 5: *The higher the rate of change in information and/or energy transactions (resulting in a shift toward the lower limit of the system's processing requisites) the greater the probability that the structural change in the system will be destruction of the system.*

While all these statements refer to both internal and external transaction rates, System Proposition 1 implies that the principal locus of change—and even destruction—resides in the external transaction rate:

System Proposition 6: *Changes in transaction rates that are sufficient to press a system toward an upper or lower processing bound are more likely to originate outside the system, through the external transaction rate.*

This proposition does not deny that significant changes may arise from within the system; it indicates where the differential probability lies. It is a recognition of the fundamental fact that the average environment (biophysical or social) contains more information and energy than the average social system.

But the internal structure of the system is quite relevant to how and whether any such changes will come about:

System Proposition 7: *The larger the population size of a social system, the higher its upper limit on information and energy capacity.*

System Proposition 8: *The more functionally differentiated a social system, the higher its upper limit on information and energy capacity.*

System Proposition 9: *The greater the complexity of a social system's material technology, the higher its upper limit on information and energy capacity.*

These refer to upper limits on both internal and external transaction rates, as well as to internal storage capacity. Functional differentiation refers to the division of labor, or the number of functionally differentiated subunits, whether these are roles, groups, or strata. Technological complexity is a risky item, but is included because the number of material components and their interrelations—technological complexity—is generally correlated with the capacity of the technology to harness information and energy. The corresponding propositions for the lower bounds are as follows:

> **System Proposition 10:** *The larger the population size of a social system, the higher its lower limit on information and energy requisite to continued operation.*

> **System Proposition 11:** *The more functionally differentiated a social system, the higher its lower limit on information and energy requisite to continued operation.*

> **System Proposition 12:** *The greater the complexity of a social system's material technology, the higher its lower limit on information and energy requisite to continued operation.*

System Propositions 7–9 show how the social system can be relatively secure from the destructive effects of radical upward shifts in the external transaction rate. Large size, functional differentiation, and technical complexity enhance the system's ability to withstand changes that would overload and perhaps even destroy smaller, less differentiated systems. However, System Propositions 10–12 show that the same structural properties make a social system more vulnerable to radical drops in the external transaction rate. Since large, complex systems require large amounts of information and energy, the external transaction rate must itself be held at a high level to avoid breaching the lower bound on survival and operating requisites. The necessity of having access to large amounts of energy and the dangers inherent in sudden drops in the external transaction rate appear to account for the tendency of larger, more complex systems to rely upon a variety of information and energy sources (Segraves, 1974). Relying upon only a few is so risky that monotone resource extraction is rarely observed even in smaller, simpler societies (Salzman, 1971).

A word of caution is required here. While large, functionally differentiated, and technically complex systems are to a degree vulnerable because they must maintain high processing requisites, it would be false to conclude that radical drops in the external transaction rates are more likely to destroy them than smaller, simpler systems. On the contrary, complex systems can lose millions of people and enormous quantities of material without being destroyed. They can suffer catastrophic losses and still be large, functionally differentiated, and technically complex systems. Herein lies a fundamental difference between these and simpler systems. Although radical drops in external transaction rates can destroy any system, large complex systems are still more likely to survive such drops. The dramatic nature of occasional cataclysms should not obscure this fact.

The principal reason for the relative durability of large, complex systems is their structural redundancy (Landau, 1969; Hannan and Freeman, 1977). That is, their redundancy is not confined to ecological generalization alone (Segraves, 1974). These systems are also redundant in technological and social system parts. They have large numbers of personnel filling the same kind of occupational positions and large numbers of standardized material parts filling links in their technology. And these repetitive elements are widely dispersed in space. Structural redundancy makes it possible for complex systems to continue operation even under heavy bombardment from hostile environments (Wilensky, 1967:28–32).

The utility of System Propositions 1–12 can be more readily seen when their specific implications are spelled out in the next section. Here, it is necessary to note that a good deal is being assumed. Variation in the degree of functional differentiation, technical complexity, and population size are being assumed, even though separate theories would be required to account for such differences. However, the number of assumptions being made is smaller than appearances might suggest. The Generator Axiom provides a basis for the development of structure, because it supplies a drive to relatively continuous interaction among humans. For this reason it permits the deduction—through Krippendorff's law— that structured social communication will occur in social systems. Krippendorff's Law of Structural Generation states that *"any communication process, once initiated and maintained, leads to the development of social structure"* (Krippendorff, 1971:171; my emphasis). The Generator Axiom guarantees that the randomly selected human will be found in an interaction network. In surviving groups, communication will occur on a continuous basis. Under these conditions—as Krippendorff's Law indicates—even random interaction is sufficient to produce structure in social systems.

D. Generality

The next question is whether System Propositions 1–12 are sufficiently general to encompass all the system and system–environment relations involved in the study of system structure and operation. The answer is that they are. There is no phenomenon in either the system or its environment whose activity cannot be measured in terms of the amount of information and energy exchanges involved. This is partly due to the definition of amount in each case, for it includes both volume and variety of information and energy. Since internal and external transaction rates are measured in amounts of energy and information exchanged, they deal with all aspects of internal system structure and operation, as well as with all measurable environmental stimuli impinging on the system.

However, this generality may not be immediately apparent, and a few concrete examples will be helpful in showing it. To facilitate illustration, it is convenient to define instances of overload and depletion in information and energy. If the amount of information or energy entering a social system exceeds the system's processing capacity, the system experiences overload. If the amount of information or energy entering a social system falls below the system's lower processing requisites, the system experiences depletion. Either of these events is sufficient—according to System Propositions 2–6—to force alteration in a system's structure or even to destroy it entirely. Nevertheless, it is well to bear in mind that overloads and depletions may impinge on only some parts of the system, rather than saturate it throughout. In these instances, structural changes or destruction will affect only some parts of the system. They need not bring about a total structural transformation or total system destruction. But even localized overloads and depletions are instructive. They give an idea of what may be expected to happen if the overload or depletion occurs on a wider front.

In 1629, the health tribunal in Milan, Italy, waited for some time before responding to reports of plague in the countryside (Tadino, 1648:24). It finally agreed to close the city on October 30, but did not issue an order until November 29, after the plague had entered the city. According to the city's official chronicler (Ripamontius, 1640) and the principal medical officer (Tadino, 1648), the plague killed at least 70 percent of the population.

In 1891, the Russian government was slow in responding to a crisis in the nation's food supply. While famine threatened, grain was still being exported. On July 28 the government issued a ban on the export of rye, but the order was not implemented at that time. In consequence: "A steady torrent of grain poured over the border into Germany. . . . The amount of grain that crossed the border into Germany was so great that more than a month later mountains of Russian grain were standing in Koenigsberg waiting for the German railroads to move them" (Robbins, 1975:59–60). The famine of 1892 killed more than 400,000 Russians (Robbins, 1975:189).

On the island of Martinique, at 7:59 A.M. on May 8, 1902, Mount Pelée erupted, sending an incandescent storm of death into the port city of Saint-Pierre 6 miles away (Wilcoxson, 1966:1). The city's usual population of 20,000 had recently been augmented to 30,000 by persons fleeing the immediate vicinity of Mount Pelée over a period of several days. Mount Pelée had already killed 40 people (Wilcoxson, 1966:3) and was beginning to sound like it might kill more. The provincial governor, fearing that the city might be evacuated before upcoming elections, had hastened to Saint-Pierre to persuade the citizens to stay where they were. When Mount Pelée erupted, the city was wiped out. Within 5 minutes it death rate exceeded 99.99 percent. There were only 2 survivors, and the governor was not among them.

These examples illustrate aspects of internal system operations as well as the nature of environmental change. It is not necessary to assume that the Milanese, Russian, and French officials were trying to protect their people. Whether they were or not is irrelevant. What matters is that an environmental source of destruction emerged, and the response was so slow, or nonexistent, that thousands of people perished. Neither the Milanese nor the Russian officials had any guarantee that they themselves would survive. Like the French governor, they might all have died, but this prospect did not hasten their response. An attempt to understand internal system operations in terms of the thoughts of these administrators would be pointless. "Man acts in spite of the fact that he thinks" (Mannheim, 1929:111), not because of it. As indicated previously, administrators generally do not know what is happening in their environment: they guess. The French governor guessed wrong and paid for it with his life. He had no way of knowing whether Mount Pelée would erupt, but even if he had known, this does not mean that he would have been able to evacuate Saint-Pierre, or even that he would have tried to evacuate it. Similarly, the Milanese officials did not know whether there really was a plague in the countryside. They were even skeptical about its existence after it had entered the city and killed thousands (Tadino, 1648:93). Even if the officials had closed the city earlier, that would not have prevented the Bubonic Plague from entering it. Closing gates has on rare occasions sealed off areas from plague, but the ecological basis of the disease (Shrewsbury, 1970:1–6) usually undermined such efforts (see examples in Shrewsbury, 1970). Russian officials responded to energy shortages not by cutting off flows of energy out of the system, but by permitting them to continue. But it cannot be assumed that they were incompetent. There were millions of poverty-striken peasants living in the famine areas, and the loss of a few hundred thousand may have been a blessing from an official point of view.

Examining the motives and knowledge (guesses) of individual officials tells nothing about these incidents. On the other hand, internal system structure is highly relevant to understanding them. The most critical factor was population size. Russia had almost 100 million people in 1892, but the famine merely shifted its death rate from around 3 to a little less than 5 percent during one year (Robbins, 1975:188). At the other extreme, Saint-Pierre with only about 30,000 people had a death rate of practically 100 percent. The intermediate case of Milan, with a population of between 120 and 160 thousand, had an estimated death toll of between 70 and 74 percent. In these three examples, the extent of population destroyed was inversely related to population size. A further critical factor in Milan was its low value on technical complexity. Seventeenth-century medical technology could not cope with the Bubonic Plague. This fact guaranteed the futility of all administrative activity. Yet the internal structure of communication in Milan was highly relevant to the spread of plague (Lampugnani, 1634:44). In the case of Saint-Pierre, technical complexity was not up to predicting volcanic eruption, nor is it in any system even today. Similarly, the lack of a centrally organized relief system in Russia, along with a low level of technical complexity, was the principal determinant of the famine's consequences (Robbins, 1975:71), just as it has been and continues to be in most countries (Robbins, 1975:175; Mayer, 1975:571). Thus, the form of administrative rationality which can matter in such instances is that which is built into the structure of the system itself (Mannheim, 1935:29).

The Milanese and Russian examples are instances of energy depletion, while the case of Saint-Pierre was one of energy overload. The energy drop in Milan was not just due to the fact that plague was accompanied by famine (Ripamontius, 1643:386), but to the dynamics of the disease itself. Bubonic Plague is a bacterial infection (Shrewsbury, 1970:1), and bacterial infections destroy an organism by depleting energy from its cells (Burnet and White, 1972:32–43). In the case of all environmental changes transmitting disease into a human system, the change in the energy or information transaction rates may occur directly from biophysical environment to human population, or through regular channels of social communication, the latter being most common (Burnet and White, 1972:105–17). Furthermore, disease is not confined to changes in the external transaction rate for energy. Viral diseases attack the organism by creating an information overload in cells, disorganizing their activity (Burnet and White, 1972:52–69, 70–87). And the input of disease into human systems can disorganize their cultural as well as their biological information patterns. The Bubonic Plague not only killed people, it terrified them (Paré, 1568; Hecker, 1832). The immediate reason lay in the etiology of the disease and the low level of technical complexity in the systems attacked. The plague followed no recognizable pattern in killing people: it appeared to strike at random (Shrewsbury, 1970:447). The Bubonic Plague killed people by the carload, sent governments flying to shelter, and shook ideological systems to their foundations (Gasquet, 1893).

Infectious diseases, then, involve changes in the transaction rates for both information and energy. As potential sources of structural change and system destruction, plagues have attenuated their ferocity in the twentieth century—in some countries—due to technological complexity, high division of labor, and the administrative implementation of both (Burnet and White, 1972:3). Famines, whether in Russia or elsewhere, are instances of energy depletion, and they have not disappeared as a significant type of environmental change. Famines are usually precipitated by a form of energy depletion called drought, and drought continues to destroy human social systems in the ninth decade of the twentieth century. The forms of energy depletion and their consequences for structural change in human social systems have been detailed by Segraves (1974). Energy overloads, like the eruption of Mount Pelée, are possibly the most frequent source of total system destruction. They arrive in a variety of forms: earthquakes, hurricanes, lightning bolts, and nuclear warheads. A hail of arrows, bullets, or artillery shells constitutes an energy overload in most circumstances, so that destruction of systems in war falls under this heading. The Third Reich, the Japanese Empire, the Aztec Empire, the Inca Empire, the Sassanian Empire, and the Government of South Vietnam, among others, were all destroyed by energy overloads. In this form, energy overloads continue to be a significant source of system destruction in the ninth decade of the twentieth century.

In spite of the examples which have been used here, to say that a social system has been destroyed is not to imply that its underlying population has died. The members need only disperse for the system to cease operation. This occurs quite commonly in bankruptcy of business firms. Money is a form of information (Duncan, 1964:65), and when the external transaction rate for this form of information drops below the system's processing requisites, the organization is destroyed by information depletion. Information depletion may account for the demise of most business firms. The members abandon the communication network—which then ceases to exist—and wander off to set up new bases for bankruptcy. Of course, a decline in the external transaction rate for money may press the system into reorganization and this type of change—noted in System Proposition 3—is probably more common than bankruptcy.

Information overloads, even in the form of money or its equivalent, can shut down a social system or force its reorganization. The New York Stock Exchange experienced a sharp increase in its external transaction rate on volume of information in 1959. The volume of transactions increased to such an extent that the system was almost overloaded and forced to shut down. But it managed a reorganization instead. The system was reorganized to handle a higher external and internal transaction rate by increasing staff size, introducing new technology, and rearranging patterns of work and communication (Meier, 1962:72–4). Systematic studies of changes in the external transaction rate on information volume and variety have been conducted to determine the effects of near-overload conditions on organizational structure. They show that System Proposition 2 tends to be verified, at least in police departments (Drabeck, 1969).

System Propositions 1–3 imply that changes in external transaction rates are relevant to a very broad class of phenomena, not just to the disasters threatened in System Propositions 4 and 5. An organization like a restaurant may, for example, experience a series of continuous cycles of growth and decay in its external transaction rates (Whyte, 1949). That is, levels of activity impinging on the system may rise and fall over regular intervals, creating a temporal order of environmental changes. The system's structure may respond by fluctuating over a regular sequence of changes in communication, work flow, and technical apparatus mobilized to meet each level of activity. System Propositions 1–3 capture this less dramatic type of environmental change and relate it directly to such structural responses. The observation that changes in the volume and variety of information and energy impinging on an organization can have direct structural effects has been incorporated in a formal theory of organizations (Blau, 1972). System Propositions 1–3 and 6 are general statements which acknowledge Blau's attempt to specify how increased volume of activity for work organizations can modify their structure. All the system propositions are consistent with Blau's theory, as well as with earlier efforts to apply the same line of reasoning to communities and nations (Zipf, 1949).

In light of these considerations, System Propositions 1–12 will—I trust—be construed as including a necessary range of differences in system and system–environment relations. They do not emphasize catastrophe, but they include it. This view is less restrictive than those which stress either a functionalist routine or a cataclysmic drama. Inclusion of the latter is less to be feared than emphasis on the former. Conflict and disaster are not less a part of social life than harmony and routine procedure (Collins, 1975). System Propositions 1–12 deal only with system and system–environment relations. They do not include environmental relations per se. However, all three sets of conditions are required for an adequate coverage of the determinants of organizational structure and operation. Numerous attempts have been made to describe organizational environments directly, or indirectly (Emery and Trist, 1965; Lawrence and Lorsch, 1967; Thompson, 1967; Terryberry, 1968; Hannan and Freeman, 1977; Aldrich, 1979). But a great deal remains to be accomplished in this area. The discussion which follows is, however, not intended to be comprehensive.

E. Environmental Ferocity

Some environments are more ferocious than others. The set of environments which was later called World War I accounted for the lives of about 13 million people, if one includes its aftermath in the Russian Revolution and Civil War (Reinhard and Armengaud, 1961:406). And intersocietal ferocity escalates with increased societal complexity: compare World War I with World War II. However, the reverse is true of intrasocietal ferocity. Intensity of internal conflict is—beyond some very high level of interdependence—a decreasing function of social system complexity (Simmel, 1923:311–3). On balance, citizens of highly industrialized social systems spend more time cheating one another than killing one another. But intersystem relations are another matter, and their destructive potential was significant long before the twentieth century opened its teeth. The Spanish invasion of Central America is a case in point. Between 1519 and 1600, the native population of Mexico fell from 11 to 2.5 million (Cook and Simpson, 1948:10–46; Borah, 1951:3). Even if this estimate is cut in half to satisfy weak spirits, the Spanish invasion still precipitated an ecological catastrophe of the first magnitude.

A low rate of change in the external transaction rate measures—indirectly—a relatively placid environment. Similarly, the differential between the transaction rate and the system's lower bounds on information and energy measures—indirectly—the relative munificence of the environment. Perhaps the interaction of these two terms may be said to measure—again indirectly—the relatively pressure of organizational environments. System Propositions 4–6 do not offer direct characterization of the environment, but they permit examination of its relative ferocity by looking at system–environment relations.

Rate of change in the external transaction rate, whether for energy or information, measures the ferocity of interchanges between an organization and its environment. Therefore, environmental ferocity itself must be the rate of change in energy and information in the environment. What is needed here is a characterization of the ferocity distribution in the environment. Whether the environment is biophysical, social, or both, it is appropriate to invoke the principle of least action: "When any change occurs in nature, the quantity of action employed for this is always the smallest possible" (de Maupertuis, 1756:36). Beginning with the purely biophysical environment, the deduction is that energy and information will appear in amounts that are inversely proportional to the frequency of their occurrence. Relatively small amounts occur frequently; relatively large amounts occur rarely. If this were not so, few living systems would be able to exist or navigate (Ashby, 1952). Just how the terms of this rank–frequency distribution interact hinges upon the underlying structures which support them. In many instances, the supporting structures are poorly understood; otherwise, prediction of earthquakes, volcanic eruptions, and storms would be more reliable. Cyclical changes, as in weather and tides, have been intensively studied, but long-term trends in the physical environment are still difficult to interpret. Insofar as the biophysical environment is concerned, this inquiry will move on in comparative ignorance. No generalizations will be made about the biophysical environment per se. However, powerful social systems can have repercussions on their physical environment. Any social environment which is powerful enough to affect an organization, can also create secondary— apolitical—instabilities by disturbing the physical environment as well. A political neighbor is a twofold menace.

Surprisingly, the supporting structures for energy and information in social environments are better understood. Since the supporting structures are other social systems, the conditions which affect environmental rates of change in energy and information are given by the same conditions that determine them within social systems. Specifically:

Environmental Proposition 1: *The higher the energy level in the social environment, the greater the rate of change in environmental energy.*

Environmental Proposition 2: *The higher the information level in the social environment, the greater the rate of change in environmental information.*

Levels of information and energy here refer to amounts as previously defined. The higher the energy level, the farther it can fall, and the farther it can fall, the greater the probability that at least some falls will be rapid. Similarly, the larger the amount of information or energy in the social environment, the greater are the potential recombinations of both to magnify volume and variety. Most upward shifts may be small, but the potential for rapid increases is far greater at higher levels.

Accordingly, environmental ferocity accelerates with increasing levels of information and energy. Furthermore, the determinants of information and energy levels in social systems, and therefore in social environments, are reasonably well known (Terryberry, 1968; Segraves, 1974). If the number of social systems providing environments for one another is fairly large, the weak form of Auerbach's (1914) Law holds:

System Proposition 13:   *The population size of social systems is inversely related to the frequency of their occurrence.*

The randomly selected social system will be comparatively small, and will likely find several other small social systems in its environment. But the multiplicity of systems forming any one environment will make them more powerful than the randomly selected organization which must deal with them. At times, the empirical adequacy of System Proposition 13 may be obscured by the fact that some social systems are nested within others or span the boundaries of others. Business firms may be contained within states or they may span state boundaries. Usually, therefore, it is necessary to distinguish between those systems which are relatively self-contained and those which are not.

System Proposition 13 says a great deal about the likely distribution of energy and information levels in social environments. This is not because energy and information are deterministic functions of population size, but because the structures which support high levels of information and energy usually presuppose large populations. A large social system might not have a high level of either information or energy. But a social system which has high levels of information or energy will be large if the system is self-contained; or if the system is not self-contained, it will be nested in a large population:

System Proposition 14:   *Technical complexity is an increasing function of population size.*

System Proposition 15:   *Functional differentiation is an increasing function of population size.*

System Proposition 16:   *Technical complexity is an increasing function of functional differentiation.*

System Proposition 17:   *Internal transaction rates on information and energy are increasing functions of technical complexity.*

System Proposition 18:   *Internal transaction rates on information and energy are increasing functions of functional differentiation.*

System Proposition 19:   *Internal transaction rates on information and energy are increasing functions of population size.*

Technical complexity, functional differentiation, and population size are expected to have the effects noted on information and energy transaction rates because they tend to reinforce one another.

System Propositions 14–16 point to the tendency of large social systems to become increasingly differentiated into subsystems. Interaction and feedback between subsystems pump up the degree of functional differentiation and technical complexity in each, contributing to the overall increase in both (Eisenstadt, 1964). The background conditions which create these interrelations are still unknown. There exists no adequate theory of the division of labor. Furthermore, current knowledge suggests that it is a mistake to assume that differentiation in social systems is generated by the action of one subsystem (B. A. Spencer, 1973).

System Propositions 17–19 point to the determinants of high levels of information and energy in the environment. Since political environments are made up of social systems, their potential ferocity is—through Environmental Propositions 1 and 2—determined by the internal transaction rates of those systems. Potential ferocity of a political environment is a direct function of the size, functional differentiation, and technical complexity of the social systems comprising that environment. And the only way to deal with ferocity is to become ferocious. If energy level and information level refer to the amounts of each flowing through social systems, then, synthesizing from White (1943, 1959), Lenski (1970), and Segraves (1974):

System Proposition 20: *The survival probability of a social system is a direct function of its energy level.*

System Proposition 21: *The survival probability of a social system is a direct function of its information level.*

System Proposition 22: *The information level of a social system is a direct function of its energy level.*

Then, from System Propositions 17–19 it is easy to see that:

System Proposition 23: *The survival probability of a social system is a direct function of its degree of technical complexity.*

System Proposition 24: *The survival probability of a social system is a direct function of its degree of functional differentiation.*

System Proposition 25: *The survival probability of a social system is a direct function of its population size.*

System Proposition 25 is a formal statement of Sorokin's (1947:533) claim. Its plausibility is suggested from the association with technical complexity, functional differentiation, and high levels of information and energy from System Propositions 14–24. However, insofar as raw survival is concerned, size should have its own independent effect. The larger a system becomes, the greater the environmental change required to destroy it. The Principle of Least Action guarantees that large changes will be comparatively rare.

F. Perspective

The weak form of Auerbach's Law holds as a result of the Principle of Least Action. The relative frequency of social systems will be inversely related to their population size. The prevalence of smaller systems is, then, not due to their greater survival probability. High frequency of small systems results from the fact that less energy is required to form them. But once formed, their mortality is high. The low frequency of larger systems is due to the tremendous amounts of energy required to form them. But once in existence, their survival probability is high. This observation should not be permitted to obscure the fact that social systems of any size generally perish. The high rate of failure for social systems is integral to understanding the forms which do persist.

As social systems increase in population size, they become internally differentiated at a declining rate (Carneiro, 1967; Blau, 1970; Mayhew et al., 1972). As a result, the average number of personnel in structural components increases with size, yielding high structural redundancy. This redundancy, along with technical complexity and ecological generalization (Segraves, 1974), gives complex systems a higher survival probability. Because they process large amounts of information and energy, large, complex systems tend to be ferocious in dealing with their environment. But it is their underlying social and technical structure which gives them resilience in the face of environmental turbulence.

From a long trend in history, social systems have expanded in size and complexity (Lenski, 1970:131). They have managed to do this primarily by becoming bureaucratic in form. But how they become bureaucratic in form is an unanswered question. In part, it must be answered by a theory of the division of labor. And, in part, it must be answered by a theory of hierarchical structure. Addressing this problem, Spencer (1882), Simon (1962, 1973), and Carneiro (1970) have suggested that increases in size and complexity can come about by connecting subgroups through hierarchy. That is, evolution in the sense of increases in size and complexity (Spencer, 1882; Starbuck, 1965b) occurs by threading components together in hierarchical order. This may be ture, but the specific process which brings it about is poorly understood. The following section takes up the problem and attempts to fill some gaps in existing knowledge.

VI. EMERGENCE OF HIERARCHY

A. Structure and Operation

Social systems which face nonproblematic environments are free to articulate, disarticulate, and rearticulate at random. What structure they assume probably does not matter. A relatively benign, munificent, placid environment will produce what boredom demands. Given enough time, the system can experiment with all possible organizational forms, or none at all. The latter possibility is unlikely. Even under low environmental pressure, structure is to be expected in human systems; random interaction will generate structure (Krippendorff, 1971). Furthermore, placid environments are relatively rare in the historical record. It is therefore necessary to examine the relation between structure and environment somewhat more specifically.

For a wide variety of environments, human organizations which survive long enough to be observed in operation will be characterized by (1) unitary action and (2) short reaction time. Most others will be eliminated by environmental turbulence. Unitary action—which may involve either simple or compound division of labor (Durkheim, 1893)—is a minimum prerequisite for keeping the organization within its upper and lower limits on information and energy. And the time interval in which an organization cycles through a sequence of actions— in relation to an environmental condition—is also critical. A reaction time longer than the corresponding environmental cycle is the same as no action. For these reasons, the structural features of communication networks which bear upon unitary action and reaction time are of considerable importance.

In line with the Generator Axiom, human groups will be mapped by connected communication networks. Under primordial conditions (relative isolation from other networks), sustained contact within connected networks will produce languages: one or more common codes of information markers. Gliding over the specific histories of these languages, some messages will be descriptive and others imperative in content or mode. For communications directed from one point to another, all network forms which can occur at size three are shown in Figure 9 with all digraphs of order three. In digraphs with a unique source (a point which can transmit messages to all other points directly or indirectly), such as out-trees and those digraphs which are at least unilateral (contain a spanning path), any set of imperatives can be diffused to all points in the network and may (without regard to their source) emerge as *standing orders* (norms) for the population contained in the network. Systems lacking a unique source are quite likely to develop a partition of norms in disjoint regions of the network (subcultures).

There is one kind of standing order which permits sequential coordination of action through imperatives: the norm which stipulates that commands will be obeyed. Without the diffusion of this norm, the effects of imperatives may be the

Figure 9.   All Distinct (Nonisomorphic) Diagraphs of Order Three, Mapping
All Distinct Configurations of Control Structure at Size Three.

same as casual conversation. But, with this norm in place, and assuming a high
degree of compliance with it, coordination by command is at least a possibility.
In fact, this norm underlies the operation of an imperatively coordinated association (Weber, 1922:29). Since instrumental formal organizations are imperatively
coordinated associations, the question of what forms coordination may be expected to assume in their networks presupposes that the indicated norm has
indeed diffused throughout the system. To the extent that this norm is a prerequisite to unitary action, it will have diffused in all surviving organizations.

Assume that the digraphs in Figure 9 map the flow of imperatives in a number
of different organizations or within the same organization at different times.
Turbulent environments will eliminate those structures which inhibit unitary
action or expand reaction time. This elimination will come about through direct
destruction of the system or through a shift from one structure to another as
indicated in System Propositions 2–6.

In spite of their relatively small size, the networks in Figure 9 provide considerable variety. Two complete asymmetric digraphs (called tournaments) appear in the upper half of the figure's fourth column. Two out-trees are shown: a maximum level hierarchy is third from the top in the third column and a maximum span hierarchy is at the top of the third column. Also shown are three disconnected networks. The nine remaining configurations either lack a common source of command or contain cycles. Now consider the options. Disconnected networks do not come into serious consideration: unitary action is not even a possibility. Of those connected structures which are neither out-trees or tournaments, all contain cycles or multiple sources of command. Since multiple sources permit conflicting directives and cycles extend the time for a random walk of any message, they inhibit unitary action and expand reaction time. Each of the two tournaments also contains a structural defect. One forms a spanning cycle, which means expanded reaction time as well as no common source of imperatives. The other permits one position to receive commands from more than one source, and since conflicting commands can inhibit unitary action, this form is also problematic. It would appear, then, that only the out-trees in Figure 9 are structurally conducive to unitary action in organizations. The same arguments can be extended to larger sizes: in fact, increases in size produce pressures which will push all imperatively coordinated associations even more sharply in the direction of out-tree hierarchies.

However, before taking up the question of size and similar system variables, it is convenient to summarize those aspects of system–environment relations which make unitary action and short reaction time crucial to system survival without regard to size. Recalling System Propositions 1–6 and the relevant definitions:

System Proposition 26: *The higher the mean rate of change in external transaction rates, the greater the probability that an organization will have a vertically differentiated communication network.*

System Proposition 27: *The higher the mean rate of change in external transaction rates, the greater the probability that vertical communication networks will be used to coordinate activity in the organization.*

System Proposition 28: *The higher the mean rate of change in external transaction rates, the greater the probability that coordination of activity will occur through out-tree hierarchies.*

These propositions connect out-trees to turbulent environments. But fluctuations in the amount of energy and information impinging on the system are not the only problematic features of environments. The absolute levels or amounts of energy and information exert pressure on organizations, quite independent of the effects of turbulence:

System Proposition 29: *The higher the mean external transaction rate, the greater the probability that the communication network will contain an out-tree.*

System Proposition 30: *The higher the mean internal transaction rate, the greater the probability that the communication network will contain an out-tree.*

System Propositions 29 and 30 indicate that pressure toward unity of command is exerted not only by the amounts of information and energy directly impinging on the system, but also by the swollen internal exchanges that occur in consequence of external saturation (consult System Proposition 1).

While these system–environment relations, and internal ramifications, are expected to hold independent of size, expanding scale and complexity of an organization should intensify their effects. Recalling System Propositions 7–25 and the relevant definitions:

System Proposition 31: *The larger the population size of an organization, the greater the probability that its communication network will contain an out-tree.*

System Proposition 32: *The greater the average distance among internal system elements engaged in communication, the higher the probability that the communication network will contain an out-tree.*

System Proposition 33: *The greater the degree of internal functional differentiation, the higher the probability that the communication network will contain an out-tree.*

System Proposition 34: *The greater the technical complexity of an organization, the higher the probability that its communication network will contain an out-tree.*

System Proposition 35: *The more continuous in time is the operation of an organization, the higher the probability that its communication network contains an out-tree.*

System Propositions 31–35 summarize certain aspects of Friedell's (1967) suggestion that organizations will shift their control hierarchies in the direction of tree-like semilattices the more their operations take on a *gesellschaftliche* as opposed to a *gemeinschaftliche* character. However, since some of the mechanisms involved in this shift are not obvious, a few remarks in clarification are appropriate.

As the size of an organization increases, the average distance among its population elements usually increases as well. But whether such changes occur simultaneously does not matter. Both will have an effect and a compound effect if they change together. As population increases additively, the number of possible communication links increases geometrically (Mayhew and Levinger, 1976b). If these possibilities are actually realized, the time per contact will decline with increasing size, ultimately to the point where only minimal messages of the yes–no variety can occur. With continued increases in size, even this minimum information will disappear from some links. Further, for each of the S population elements maintaining S − 1 links, information overload would rapidly appear with increasing size. Consequently, in organizations that survive, the network will become thinner and thinner (in relative terms) as size increases. Distance has a similar, but possibly more powerful, effect. As the distance between communicating elements increases, the amount of time and energy expended to maintain links expands geometrically. Hence, reaction time expands geometrically with each additive increase in distance. Although the effects of distance are modified by technology, they do not disappear (Mayhew and Levinger, 1976b). Consequently, at any given level of technology, surviving systems will have thinner and thinner networks (in relative terms) as distance increases. Similarly, as horizontal (compound) division of labor and technical complexity increase over the bottom level of the network, the number of stalled actions increases multiplicatively. For each functional link in both activity and technology, the downtime of larger and larger parts of the system expands rapidly. These disruptions will expand reaction time sharply. Functional and technical complexity thus place powerful constraints on operation, requiring even more stringent schedules of activity and systematic coordination. Since hyperconnectivity in the network through which activity is coordinated would simply compound, rather than attentuate, these delays, surviving systems will have thinner and thinner networks (in relative terms) as functional specialization and technical complexity increase in the horizontal dimension. Finally, the more continuous are the organization's operations, the shorter the time intervals available to take up slack from communication failures or delays from technical and functional linkage breaks. The time available between action in one part of the system and a coordinated action in another part of the system shrinks toward zero. Any hyperconnectivity in the communication network through which activity is coordinated would simply compound this effect. Consequently, in surviving systems, the control network will grow thinner and thinner (in relative terms) as continuity of operations increases.

All of the conditions indicated in System Propositions 31–35 point to the same general results for surviving systems: because time pressure increases, the relative number of links in the communication network must decrease. As Simmel (1902:2) observed, if a system increases in size, it will undergo structural alterations or cease to operate. When System Propositions 12–19 are recalled to accompany System Propositions 31–35, the pressure on system structure becomes even clearer. Population growth is usually associated with increases in the other variables indicated and with increasing amounts of information and energy flowing through the system's internal network. Coordination of action will yield unitary action and reaction times within environmentally set limits only if the network of commands grows thinner. Ultimately, this network will drop to $S - 1$ links, the minimum necessary for connecting the S elements in the system. In communication networks mapped by directed graphs, only trees have this property: out-trees, in-trees, and trees-without-uniform-direction. And, since in-trees and trees-without-uniform-direction do not permit unitary action, only out-trees remain as a possibility. Surviving systems will sharply reduce their networks to tree form in general and to out-tree form in particular.

At this point it is appropriate to consider whether an increase in the likelihood of an out-tree structure may be due to a simple increase in the a priori probability of an out-tree at each step in size. That is, as size increases, what is the a priori probability of an out-tree out of all possible command networks? Or, what is the a priori probability of an out-tree out of all possible connected command networks? Tables 2 and 3 answer these questions with a brief illustration of relations that hold generally. Whether for all possible command networks or for all possible connected command networks, the *a priori* probability of an out-tree is a rapidly decreasing function of size. This same negative relation holds for all directed graphs which are trees. So, the relation predicted in System Proposition 31, and in other propositions to the extent that their variables are empirically associated with size, is quite opposite the a priori expectation. If the observed frequency of out-trees increases with size, this cannot be simply because of increased structural possibilities: structural possibilities predict a decline in their relative frequency.

Table 2. Number of Distinct Authority Structures (Directed Graphs), Number of Unity of Command Authority Structures (Out-Trees), and Ratio of Out-Trees to Directed Graphs, for Selected Organization Sizes

Organization Size	Number of Distinct Directed Graphs[a]	Number of Distinct Out-Tree Structures[b]	Ratio of Out-Trees to Directed Graphs
2	3	1	.333
3	16	2	.125
4	218	4	.018
5	9,608	9	.0009
6	1,540,944	20	.000597
7	882,033,440	48	.00000005
8	1,793,359,192,848	115	.00000000006

[a]*Source:* Oberschelp (1967: 70).
[b]*Source:* Prins (1957: 85–86).

Table 3. Number of Distinct Connected Authority Structures (Connected Directed Graphs), Number of Unity of Command Authority Structures (Out-Trees), and Ratio of Out-Trees to Connected Directed Graphs, for Selected Organization Sizes

Organization Size	Number of Distinct Connected Directed[a] Graphs	Number of Distinct Out-Tree Structures[b]	Ratio of Out-Trees to Connected Directed Graphs
2	2	1	.5
3	13	2	.15
4	199	4	.02
5	9,364	9	.001
6	1,530,843	20	.00001
7	880,471,142	48	.00000005
8	1,792,473,955,306	115	.00000000005

Notes
[a]*Source:* Harary and Palmer (1973: 241).
[b]*Source:* Prins (1957: 85–86).

B. Embedded Out-Trees

As long as the groups in which it occurs are relatively small, face-to-face interaction permits rapid feedback in communication. This rapid feedback means that problems which would otherwise arise due to size, distance, and complexity of organization do not constrain the flow of action. This is not to say that small populations have no problems in communication or control. On the contrary, as the discussion of Figure 9 made clear, there are powerful reasons for the emergence of out-trees even in very small groups. Nevertheless, face-to-face contact *may permit* a much higher degree of connectivity in command networks than would otherwise be expected *as long as these networks contain an embedded out-tree.* A command network contains an embedded out-tree in any instance where a proper subset of its relations maps an out-tree across all its population elements. And, although a large number of such networks can be identified, only two types are of interest here: tournaments and transitive closures over out-trees. These two types are likely to occur (however infrequently) in small groups engaged in face-to-face interaction. In the absence of face-to-face contact, even these two types would have minimal survival probabilities. At size two, an out-tree, a tournament, and a transitive closure over an out-tree are identical forms; that is, only larger groups are of interest here. Indeed, tournaments and transitive closures on out-trees are unlikely to occur in groups larger than about ten people and are more commonly confined to the range $3 \leq S \leq 7$.

A tournament maps a command network in which there is exactly one asymmetric relation between each pair of positions. According to a well-known theorem, every tournament contains a spanning path (Rédei, 1934) and, therefore, a maximum-level embedded out-tree. Clearly, small, face-to-face groups mapped by tournaments *could* maintain unitary action *if* they coordinated critical activity through their embedded out-tree. However, it is not clear that they *would* do so except under a restricted condition mentioned below. Most tournaments contain a variety of cycles and, in extreme cases, are hyperconnected to the point of communicative chaos (Moon, 1968:91–5). Most tournaments would, therefore, have a survival probability somewhere in the neighborhood of zero, even in small, face-to-face groups.

If a digraph is in the form of an out-tree, there are some positions which a superior commands directly and (in most out-trees) others which he commands only indirectly through the chain of command. This, at least, is true of all supervisory positions except those exclusively commanding the bottom of the hierarchy. A transitive closure over an out-tree is formed by adding new command relations such that a supervisory position now directly commands all of the positions which it previously controlled only indirectly. This means, for example, that instead of going through the chain of command as is ordinarily done, the chief executive (or any other supervisor) can send commands *directly* to any of his subordinates. Accordingly, the network is denser than an out-tree and contains an embedded out-tree. If this occurred under limited and prescribed conditions, it would convey the advantage of short-circuiting the chain of command downward, reducing reaction time. Large-scale organizations with radio or similar long-range communications technology do at times permit this to occur under limited and prescribed (usually emergency) conditions. It occurs, for example, when the chief of a metropolitan fire department—using the radio in his office—directly commands personnel at the scene of a fire. Because this short-circuiting is prescribed by a standing order to occur under specified (and infrequent) conditions, it does not offset the unity of command hierarchy through which most of the organization's activity is directed. Rather, the control hierarchy is a simple out-tree the vast majority of the time. While this is of interest, the same short-circuiting *always* occurs in small, face-to-face groups because the person issuing the order does so in the presence of all personnel. They know the order at the time it is issued, whether it is directed to them or to anyone else in the group. If in a small, face-to-face group which overtly conducts command through an out-tree there should arise an occasion in which the chief executive simply turns to the entire group and issues an order, no problem arises even if this occurs routinely. The reason is, of course, that contrary orders, when they do occur, are immediately known to all members of the organization and can be resolved on the spot. So, the advantages of the out-tree form are not lost in face-to-face interaction mapped by a transitive closure over an out-tree. It is not at all unlikely that such systems of command will be observed in small groups, but this does not imply that they will do so when environmental pressure forces the system toward the upper or lower limits of its energy and information-processing capacities. Under those conditions, even small, face-to-face groups are likely to shift exclusively to a maximum-span out-tree (Stern, 1972).

If a transitive closure is mapped over a maximum-level out-tree, the result is a tournament called a *linear hierarchy*. This is the only tournament without cycles and—being a transitive closure on an out-tree—has the advantages mentioned above. That it lacks hyperconnectivity and contains a spanning out-tree are the two conditions which make it the most commonly observed form of "dominance" in "animal" societies and even in small, face-to-face human groups (Mayhew and Gray, 1971).

If commands are directed from one person to another in human groups, the structural problems which arise in maintaining unitary action and short reaction time are greatly attenuated by the conditions of face-to-face interaction. From the point of view of the theoretical perspective developed here, the presence of transitive closures on out-trees is not problematic. That these should occur periodically in face-to-face groups is consistent with the rationale predicting the emergence of out-trees more generally.

C. A Priori Expectations

Miller (1978) has suggested that all self-regulating systems, including human social organizations, will coordinate action through a control hierarchy. He also appears to believe that decentralization of activity in these systems will simply intensify, rather than attenuate, problems of coordination (1978:109). It is convenient to state Miller's main contention as an:

Echelon Axiom: *All self-regulating systems will coordinate their action through a control hierarchy.*

If this axiom is applied to imperatively coordinated associations mapped by all distinct (nonisomorphic) digraphs, it can be shown that it will be correct in its main contention—that the system will be stratified—with an a priori probability very close to one for most values of size. In other words, there is a simple network basis for the emergence of inequality in authority in imperatively coordinated associations. If an organization is an imperatively coordinated association, it will exhibit inequality in authority relations with a very high a priori probability. The existence of inequality in such associations is predicted by their definition. In contrast to such network determination, the principal thesis of the present essay is an:

Out-Tree Axiom: *Control hierarchies in instrumental formal organizations will be articulated in the form of out-trees.*

As the discussion of Tables 2 and 3 made clear, if this axiom is correct, it departs from *a priori* expectations. For sizes larger than two, all connected authority structures will have a low *a priori* probability of being out-trees, and the *a priori* probability of an out-tree shrinks toward zero as size increases. The Out-Tree Axiom is expected to be empirically correct the vast majority of the time. Certainly, on rare and short-lived occasions, there will be structures other than out-trees mapping authority relations in formal organizations. This much is clear from the discussion of embedded out-trees. But departures may be even more general. Across cultures and across history, possibly all digraphs have some nonzero *a posteriori* probability of appearing as control structures in organizations. What the Out-Tree Axiom implies is that environmental conditions will generally be such that, 93–99 percent of the time, instrumental formal organizations will usually have out-tree control structures. This is an empirical claim, rather than an *a priori* one, as may be seen from Tables 2 and 3.

Assume, for purposes of illustration only, that the Out-Tree Axiom is strictly true. Then it is possible to calculate *a priori* expectations for some of the important structural features of organizational hierarchies. These expectations indicate the kinds of structural variation that would occur in control hierarchies purely on the basis of knowledge that they are out-trees, while ignoring all other information. To illustrate the general procedure, Table 4 shows the *a priori* probability that an out-tree will be symmetric at selected values of size. This probability is simply the ratio of symmetric out-trees to all out-trees at a specified size of organization. The number of possible out-trees at each size was noted earlier in Table 1. Table 4 shows that in organizations with out-tree control structures—if no other factors intervene—the randomly selected organization is unlikely to contain a symmetric out-tree at sizes larger than four, and that the *a priori* probability of a symmetric out-tree is a decreasing function of size. This trend holds generally. What the illustration shows is simple. If there is an empirical tendency of control hierarchies to be symmetric, some very powerful factors must be operating to offset the *a priori* trend, factors whose strength must increase as a direct function of size.

Recall that R is the relative frequency of cut-points, or of supervisory positions, in an out-tree of given size. That is, R is the relative size of the controlling component in organizations mapped by out-trees, or the *a priori* likelihood that the command hierarchy will be broken by the random removal of a point—the disruption potential of the hierarchy. Averaging R across all out-trees at a given size provides the *a priori* expectation for these conditions or events. The result, symbolized E(R), is shown in Table 5 for selected sizes. For odd or even sizes greater than two, E(R) is an increasing function of size and approaches asymptotically the value of .5618 as size increases without bound. Thus, if organizations are coordinated through out-trees, then, in the absence of other considerations, the supervisory component will grow in relative size and so will the disruption potential, as size increases, exposing the system to greater and

Table 4. A Priori Probability of a
Symmetric Out-Tree as a Function of
Organizational Size, Under the Out-Tree
Axiom

Size	Probability[a]
2	1.0
3	1.0
4	.5
5	.22
6	.10
7	.06
8	.017
9	.007
10	.0027
11	.0011
12	.0004
13	.0002
14	.00006
15	.00003
16	.000008
17	.000003
18	.000001
19	.0000004
20	.00000015
21	.000000085

Note
[a]Probability = the ratio of all distinct (nonisomorphic) symmetric out-trees to all distinct (nonisomorphic) out-trees at this
size.

greater likelihoods of broken communication.[2] Of course, the indicated results
are quite contrary to what is generally observed in organizations. Ordinarily, the
relative size of the supervisory component is a decreasing function of size (Blau,
1970). Apparently, very powerful factors are operating to offset the *a priori*
trend. To gain perspective, recall that D is the mean cutting number of positions
in an out-tree of given size, or the *magnitude* of that structure's disruption
potential. If the *a priori* value of D increases as a function of size, then the
degree of communicative disruption portended in R is even more serious, even
more devastating, the larger the system becomes. It can be shown that an *a priori*
increase in D, symbolized E(D), accompanies increases in size, although I have
provided only a brief illustration in Table 6. Now, consistent with the line of
reasoning followed up to this point, I suggest that:

System Proposition 36: *The survival probability of an organization is
inversely related to the disruption potential of its control hierarchy.*

Table 5. Expected Relative Size of the Supervisory
Component, E(R), as a Function of Organizational Size,
S, Under the Out-Tree Axiom

S	E(R)	S	E(R)	S	E(R)
2	.5000	14	.5433	26	.5522
3	.5000	15	.5447	27	.5525
4	.5000	16	.5458	28	.5529
5	.5112	17	.5468	29	.5532
6	.5167	18	.5477	30	.5535
7	.5239	19	.5484	31	.5538
8	.5283	20	.5491	32	.5540
9	.5323	21	.5498	33	.5543
10	.5354	22	.5503	34	.5545
11	.5380	23	.5509	35	.5547
12	.5401	24	.5513	36	.5549
13	.5418	25	.5518	∞	.5618

Source: Robinson and Schwenk (1974).

System Proposition 37: *The survival probability of an organization is inversely related to the magnitude of its hierarchy's disruption potential.*

Recalling from earlier propositions that an increase in size will be accompanied by increases in technical complexity, spatial dispersion, functional differentiation, *etc.*, the communication network becomes ever more critical to operation as size increases. With each step up the size scale, environmental selection pressure will operate with ever-increasing intensity on R and D. Accordingly, System Propositions 36 and 37 permit the inference that, as size increases, if out-trees

Table 6. Expected Magnitude of a
Hierarchy's Disruption Potential, E(D), as
a Funcion of Size, S, Under the Out-Tree
Axiom

S	E(D) Exact Form	Decimal Form
2	0/2	0.000
3	2/6	0.333
4	14/16	0.875
5	74/45	1.644
6	309/120	2.575
7	1,244/336	3.702

are generated at random, the majority of them will perish in interaction with their environments, and they will do so in direct proportion to their values of R and D. Hence, the value of R which permits survival is a decreasing function of size. So:

System Proposition 38: *In organizational control networks mapped by out-trees, the relative size of the controlling component is a decreasing function of system size.*

System Proposition 38 states the exact opposite of the *a priori* expectation for out-trees. It makes an empirical claim, not a definitional one. In this regard, it is interesting that the two *a priori* expectations thus far considered for out-trees have a differential relation to size. As size increases, the *a priori* probability of a symmetric out-tree declines, but the *a priori* relative size of the supervisory component increases. If the relative size of the supervisory component is to be reduced, as in System Proposition 38, so as to minimize both R and D, this is most simply accomplished by increasing the span of control faster than the number of hierarchical levels and by making the hierarchy symmetric. It has elsewhere been suggested that hierarchical symmetry creates the trend stated in System Proposition 38 (Meyer, 1971). The line of argument followed here implies that the opposite is true: symmetry increases as a consequence of reducing R. For organizations to survive as size expands, their supervisory ratios must decline. That decline will produce a shift toward symmetry because it will come about through a differential expansion of levels and spans, such that spans increase faster than levels.[3]

It is easy to see that hierarchical symmetry in out-trees cannot by itself account for the relation stated in System Proposition 38. As Starbuck (1965a:499) observed, if spans of control are held constant while levels increase with size, then R will be a *direct* function of S in symmetric out-trees. Conversely, as Table 7

Table 7. Relation Between the Relative Size of the Supervisory Component (R) and Organizational Size (S), When Levels are Constant and Spans Increasing in Symmetric Out-Trees

Levels = 3			Levels = 4			Levels = 5			Levels = 6		
S	Span	R	S	Span	R	S	Span	R	S	Span	R
7	2	.429	15	2	.467	31	2	.484	63	2	.492
13	3	.308	40	3	.325	121	3	.331	364	3	.332
21	4	.238	85	4	.247	173	4	.260	1,365	4	.249
31	5	.194	156	5	.199	781	5	.199	3,906	5	.199
43	6	.163	259	6	.166	1,555	6	.167	9,331	6	.167
57	7	.140	400	7	.143	2,801	7	.143	19,608	7	.143

Table 8.   Relation Between the Relative Size of the
Supervisory Component (R) and Organizational Size (S),
When Levels Increase at a Faster Rate than Spans in
Symmetric Out-Trees

S	Levels	Spans	R
3	2	2	.333
9,841	9	3	.333
2	2	1	.500
8,191	13	2	.500
4	2	3	.250
87,381	9	4	.250

shows, if levels are held constant which spans increase, R will be an inverse function of S in symmetric out-trees. Or, as Table 8 shows, if both spans and levels increase with size, but levels increase at a much faster rate than spans, R can be a *constant* function of S in symmetric out-trees. And, as Table 9 shows, if spans and levels increase at the same rate as a function of size, R will be an *inverse* function of S in symmetric out-trees. Generally, therefore, the relation between R and S can be positive, negative, or constant in symmetric out-trees, depending upon the rates of change in spans of control and levels of authority. Now, without assuming symmetry, if spans and levels increase together with size such that spans increase faster than levels, then in organizations with out-tree hierarchies, not only will System Proposition 38 be correct, but also as a consequence of these conditions, the hierarchies will shift in the direction of symmetry. Thus, an appearance of symmetry or at least tendencies toward symmetry can easily be a consequence, rather than a precondition, of relations yielding System Proposition 38. In fact, there are grounds for suggesting that as size increases, organizations will increase their spans faster than their levels, and, in consequence, conform to System Proposition 38.

Before taking up the grounds for this empirical expectation, it is convenient to note the *a priori* expectations for the number of hierarchical levels, L, and the chief executive's span of control, M. The latter corresponds to the number of major hierarchical divisions. Averaging across these values for all out-trees at a given size provides the random expectation for the number of levels, E(L), and the random expectation for the number of major divisions, E(M), shown for selected sizes in Tables 10 and 11, respectively. As these tables show, both E(L) and E(M) are direct functions of size.[4] Both relations can be shown to hold generally. To my knowledge, mathematicians have yet to determine the *a priori* expectation for the mean span of control, X, in out-trees. For very small values of size, E(X) is an increasing function of size, but the general nature of the function is unknown. Because E(R) is an increasing function of S, it is doubtful that E(X) increases very much with size, and may even stabilize or reverse direction in the upper reaches of size. On the other hand, the *a priori* expectation for the number of hierarchical levels shown in Table 10 is consistent with empirical observations, including the fact that the number of levels does not appear to vary across a wide range. As distinguished from levels, spans of control in real organizations exhibit a very wide range (Evan, 1963:471).

Returning to the question of R, the number of hierarchical levels and the span of control are of specific theoretical importance. As size increases, if levels alone increase, reaction time expands rapidly, exposing the organization to the risk of failure in maintaining unitary action within environmentally set limits. As size increases, if spans alone increase, recalling Upper Limit Theorem 1, population elements will rapidly approach a condition of information overload. Consequently, as size increases, both levels and spans must increase according to a

Table 9. Relation Between the Relative Size of the Supervisory Component (R) and Organizational Size (S), When Levels and Spans Increase at the Same Rate in Symmetric Out-Trees

S	Spans	Levels	R
7	2	3	.42857
40	3	4	.32500
341	4	5	.24927
3,906	5	6	.19995
55,987	6	7	.16666
13	3	3	.30769
85	4	4	.24706
781	5	5	.19974
9,331	6	6	.16645
137,649	7	7	.14286
21	4	3	.23810
156	5	4	.19872
1,555	6	5	.16656
19,608	7	6	.14285
3	1	3	.66667
15	2	4	.46667
121	3	5	.33058
1,365	4	6	.24982
19,531	5	7	.19999

ratio that minimizes these real operational problems. If it is acknowledged that reaction time is more critical to system survival, and that problems of overload can often be overcome through division of labor and other standardization procedures, then the empirical expectation would be that spans will increase much faster than levels. Accordingly, the relative size of the supervisory component will decrease as size increases, hierarchies will shift toward symmetry, and all of these conditions will enhance the organization's survival probability: they imply a minimization of both the degree and the magnitude of the hierarchy's disruption potential.

On a priori and substantive grounds, it is expected that:

System Proposition 39: *In organizational control networks mapped by out-trees, the number of hierarchical levels is an increasing function of size.*

On a priori and possibly on substantive grounds as well, it is expected that:

System Proposition 40: *In organizational control networks mapped by out-trees, the number of major hierarchical divisions is an increasing function of size.*

Table 10. Relation Between the Expected Number of Hierarchical Levels, E(L), and Organizational Size, S, Under the Out-Tree Axiom

	E(L)	
S	Exact Value	Decimal Value
2	2/1	2.00000
3	5/2	2.50000
4	12/4	3.00000
5	31/9	3.44444
6	78/20	3.99999
7	206/48	4.29166
8	530/115	4.60869
9	1,446/286	5.05590
10	3,894/719	5.41585
11	10,592/1,842	5.75027
12	28,955/4,766	6.07532
13	79,758/12,486	6.38779
14	220,493/32,973	6.68707
15	612,537/87,811	6.97562
16	1,707,835/235,381	7.25561
17	4,778,444/634,847	7.52692

Table 11.   Expected Number of Major
Hierarchical Divisions, E(M), as a
Function of Organizational Size, S, Under
the Out-Tree Axiom*

	E(M)	
S	Exact Value	Decimal Value
2	1/1	1.00000
3	3/2	1.50000
4	7/4	1.75000
5	17/9	1.88888
6	39/20	1.95000
7	96/48	2.00000
8	232/115	2.01739
9	583/286	2.03846
10	1,474/719	2.05006
11	3,797/1,842	2.06134
12	9,864/4,766	2.06966
13	25,947/12,486	2.07808
14	68,546/32,973	2.07885
15	183,612/87,811	2.09099
16	493,471/235,381	2.09647
17	1,334,147/634,847	2.10151
18	3,624,800/1,721,159	2.10602
19	9,893,860/4,688,676	2.11016
20	27,113,492/12,826,228	2.11391

*M is the chief executive's span of control.

On substantive grounds—and possibly on a priori grounds—it is expected that:

System Proposition 41:   *In organizational control networks mapped by out-trees, the mean span of control is an increasing function of size.*

On substantive grounds, it is expected that:

System Proposition 42:   *In organizational control networks mapped by out-trees, the rate of increase in the mean span of control as a function of size is greater than the rate of increase in the number of hierarchical levels as a function of size.*

While all these relations will yield a shift toward hierarchical symmetry, this shift is no more than an epiphenomenon.

VII.   EMPIRICAL CONSIDERATIONS

A.   Unity of Command

Table 12 shows a range of social systems which are reported to have coordinated their action through unity of command hierarchies. The time period represented, from the sixth century B.C. to the twentieth century A.D., ranges over 2,500 years. A variety of cultures represents all continents. Table 12 suggests that out-trees have a wide dispersion in both space and time. Of course, I cannot vouch for the accuracy of the reports cited, nor should the illustrations be taken to imply that out-trees are universal. Rather, the extent of out-tree representation and the conditions under which they occur can only be determined through systematic comparative analysis (Durkheim, 1895:165). Nevertheless, the wide range in space and time shown in Table 12 is highly suggestive. If out-tree hierarchies have the kind of survival advantages that I have suggested, the widespread representation they display in Table 12 is exactly what would be expected (Durkheim, 1895:73).

I suggested that there will be departures from unity of command on rare and short-lived occasions. Without regard to the specific conditions generating such departures, if they do occur they will result in internal conflicts, delayed messages, stalled actions, and, ultimately, disaster. Any kind of hyperconnectivity in the structure of control creates a lack of clarity in authority relations so that conflicting claims will generate friction in the scheduling of activity (Sterling, 1965). Especially striking are those instances in which the shift creates dual control, where subordinates can receive commands from more than one superior. This is all the more problematic when it occurs at the apex of the hierarchy. Under these circumstances—dual control in the upper echelon—the organization navigates by random collision, lending the appearance of a headless chicken.

Of course, if the organization shifts to dual control, remains temporarily in that state, and then shifts back to unity of command, the result may be no more than temporary delays, stalled actions, and partial disasters in the interval, with the organization emerging somewhat battered but still intact. This, at least, is suggested by the few examples available in the literature. Writing ca. 144–129 B.C., Polybius (1922:254) reported such a temporary instance of dual control at the apex of the Roman army fielded against Hannibal during the Second Punic War. The folly of the Roman Senate's action was apparent to both of the generals given supreme command. At first they considered alternating their command on a daily basis, but finally divided their troops into two separate forces. In any case, the overall result was disaster in combat. The disaster was partial, rather than complete. The Roman army survived by reuniting under one commander, that is, by returning to unity of command (Polybius, 1922:256–7).

Departure from unity of command may be even more generalized, involving several levels of authority. Maccia and Maccia (1971:170–3) reported an instance of such a generalized departure in a New York City school district. The departure was followed by disrupted activity and a quick return to the original out-tree form. Chandler (1962) reported the same result when Sears and Roebuck instituted (temporarily, as it developed) a policy of multiple superiors for each subordinate.

In all three of the instances cited above, the pattern is the same. An organization with a unity of command structure shifts to a more hyperconnected network; conflict and disruption of activity ensue; and then the organization returns to the out-tree form. No doubt, there have been instances in which these shifts occurred and the scale of disaster was large enough to remove the organization entirely; hence, no return to unity of command. Some students of civilization have even suggested that hyperconnectivity in control networks may have prevented newly born systems from lasting long enough to leave a trace in the archaeological record (Flannery, 1972).

The preceding cases may serve to illustrate what can happen in the space of a few weeks, a few months, or even one year. Other instances of departure from the out-tree formation may last no more than a few days. For example, Lambton (1968:235–9) reported that the core of the Saljug Empire's administrative system was an out-tree under Malik-Shah (from 1072 to 1092 A.D.) in Iran. However, Lambton (1968:238) noted that the Sultan would at times play one Amir off against another by assigning them to the same district simultaneously. The result was conflict between the Amirs, with one ultimately assuming his rights by force. In Lambton's view, this was the outcome intended by the Sultan. Rather than being a policy of structuring routine administration, these overlapping assignments to reward retainers in a patrimonial system were means of paying two debts with one coin. And, since it may take no more than a few days for one band of armed retainers to destroy another band of armed retainers, these departures from unity of command were probably temporary in the extreme.

In contrast, there are environmental conditions which could produce and sustain hyperconnected administrative system for a much greater period of time, perhaps even for years. This could come about within a society undergoing radical changes in the broad contours of its social structure, the period of the French Revolution being a case in point. De Tocqueville (1856:111) described an out-tree control structure in the Ancien Régime extending from the central government in Paris down to the provinces. However, he said (1856:318–23) that reforms in 1787 included departures from unity of command. The result was mass confusion and a general slowing down of the whole administrative process: internal conflict and expanded reaction time. In a society undergoing violent revolution, it would be astonishing to find anything else. Furthermore, if the revolutionary process lasts years, or even decades, the administrative chaos associated with it could continue for the same period of time.

The literature search which resulted in Table 12 produced only five instances of departure from the out-tree structure. Four were temporary variations which

(*text continued on page 213*)

Table 12. Administrative Hierarchies with Unity of Command Control
Structures, by Location, Century, and Source

System	Location	Centuries	Sources
Manchu Empire	China	16–17th	Lee (1970: 24–27)
Republic of Turkey	Asia Minor	20th	Stirling (1953: 41)
Samanid Empire	Central Asia	9–10th	Frye (1965: 44–46)
Mamluk Empire	Egypt	13–16th	Ziadeh (1964: 16–18, 77–78)
School District in New York City	U.S.A.	20th	Maccia and Maccia (1971: 170–173)
Greek Army under Antiochus	Syria	3rd B.C.	Polybius (circa 127 B.C.; 1923: 195)
Columbus, Ohio, Police Department	U.S.A.	20th	Drabeck (1969: 54)
Baban Pashalik	Southern Kurdistan	20th	Barth (1953: 61)
China Merchant's Steam Navigation Company	Ch'ing China	19–20th	Feuerwerker (1958: 102,115)
University of Minnesota Institute of Technology	U.S.A.	20th	Caplow (1964: 73)
Association Internationale du Congo	Belgian Congo	19th	Fieldhouse (1966: 357–358)
Russian Empire	Central Asia	19–20th	Fieldhouse (1966: 335–336) Wheeler (1974: 272–275)
Military Expedition under Hernando Cortes	Mexico	16th	Diaz del Castillo (1632: 139-141)
Bakufu and Tokugawa States	Japan	14–19th	Sansom (1958: 67–70; 1961: 145–148; 1963: 21–24)
Japanese Empire	Multiple Continents	19–20th	Steiner (1965: 43–49) Allen (1971: 18–19) Kim (1962: 54–56)
Russian Agricultural Estate	Russian Baltic Province of Kurland	18th	Plakans (1975: 10)
C.S.A. Navy Department	Confederate States of North America	19th	Wells (1971: 118–119, 138–146)
Rifian State of Abd el Krim	Northern Morocco	20th	Woolman (1968: 147–151)
Azande Kingdom of Gbudwe	Eastern Sudan	19–20th	Evans-Pritchard (1963: 142–144)
Agricultural Estate	Hungary	19th	Blum (1948: 101)
Hebrew Army in Galilee	The Levant	1st	Josephus (circa 77; 1927: 545)
Oyo Empire	West Africa	18–19th	Atanda (1973: 14–24)
Kingdom of Buganda	East Africa	19–20th	Southwold (1966: 84)

(continued)

Table 12. *(Continued)*

System	Location	Centuries	Sources
E. I. Du Pont de Nemours & Company	U.S.A.	20th	Chandler (1962: 74–77)
Bandit Gangs led by Caudillos	Latin America	19th	Wolf and Hansen (1967: 175)
Two Textile Mills	India	20th	Chowdhry and Pal (1957; 13)
Umayyad Khaliphate	Multiple Continents	7–8th	Shaban (1970: 63–86; 1971: 113)
Frontier Outposts of the Han Empire	China	1–2nd B.C.	Loewe (1967a: 58–98; 1967b: 385–386)
Ch'ing Empire	China	19th	Chu (1962: 5) Twitchett (1963: 98–106)
Sung Empire	China	10–11th	Kracke (1953: 47–51)
Spanish Empire	Multiple Continents	16–19th	Fieldhouse (1966: 18–19, 143) Burling (1974: 149–152)
British Empire	Multiple Continents	16–20th	Smith (1960: 264–265) Dyson-Hudson (1966: 8–10) Abrahams (1966: 130–132) Jones (1966: 57–58) Cunnison (1966: 10–11, 103–110) Barrow (1967: 4–19) Tepperman (1975: 165)
Portuguese Empire	Multiple Continents	16–20th	Fieldhouse (1966: 31, 40)
French Empire	Multiple Continents	18–20th	Fieldhouse (1966: 37)
Department of Agriculture in Lahj	Arabia	20th	Maktari (1971: 65)
Habe Government of Zazzau	West Africa	18–19th	Smith (1960: 34–72, 333–343)
Zulu Empire	South Africa	19th	Omer-Cooper (1966: 17–18, 34–35)
Swazi State	South Africa	19th	Omer-Cooper (1966: 50–51)
Jere-Ngoni Empire	South Africa	19th	Omer-Cooper (1966: 70–71)
Gaza Empire	South Africa	19th	Omer-Cooper (1966: 58–59)
Khumalo State	South Africa	19th	Omer-Cooper (1966: 134–135)
Almohad Empire	North-West Africa	12–13th	Julien (1964: 98–102)

(continued)

Table 12.   *(Continued)*

System	Location	Centuries	Sources
Hafsid State	Tunisia	13–15th	Julien (1964: 145–150)
Ottoman Empire	Multiple Continents	15–20th	Evans-Pritchard (1949: 94–95)
			Julien (1964: 294–295)
			Inalcik (1973: 76–118)
The Medici Bank	Italy	14–15th	de Roover (1966: 83)
Achaemenid Empire	Mesopotamia and Persia	6th B.C.	Olmstead (1948: 59)
Charhar Mongols	Mongolia	20th	Aberle (1957: 8–15
Byzantine Empire	Multiple Continents	6–8th	Ostrogorsky (1940; 1969: 31–35, 43, 245)
Army of the Rashidun Khaliphate [During Invasion of the Sassanian Empire]	Greater Mesopotamia	8th	Levy (1969: 5)
Army of the Abbasid Khaliphate [During a Siege of Baghdad]	Greater Mesopotamia	9th	Levy (1969: 426)
Inca Empire	South America	15–16th	Metraux (1961: 100–107)
Mali Empire	West Africa	13th	Trimingham (1962: 76)
Sanusi of Cyrenaica	Libya	19–20th	Evans-Pritchard (1949: 26–27, 80)
Empire of the Culhua Mexica [Aztec]	Valley of Mexico	15–16th	Katz (1969: 365–366)
Fulani Empire [Sokoto Khaliphate]	West Africa	19–20th	Smith (1960: 82–92, 190)
			Last (1967: 53–57)
			Low (1972: 9–19, 213)
Army of Sheikh Mahammad 'Abdille Hassan	East Africa	20th	Lewis (1961: 226–227)
Kingdom of Kongo	Central Africa	14th	Kimambo (1968: 29–30)
Hawaiian State	Hawaii	18–19th	Sahlins (1958: 14)
Saljug Empire	Iran	11th	Lambton (1968: 235–239)
Ismaili State of Alamut	Iran	11–13th	Hodgson (1968: 425)
Bulamogi State	East Africa	19–20th	Fallers (1965: 134–139)
Busambira State	East Africa	19–20th	Fallers (1965: 134–139)
Ife State	West Africa	19th	Bascom (1969: 360–361)
Belgian Empire	Belgian Congo	20th	Fieldhouse (1966: 360–361)
30 Factories	Israel	20th	Samuel and Mannheim (1970: 218, 224–225)
Swat State	Northern Pakistan	20th	Barth (1959: 129)
Thonga Tribe [Military]	South Africa	19th	Junod (1927: 455–457)

(continued)

Table 12. *(Continued)*

System	Location	Centuries	Sources
Prussian-German State [Civil service and Army]	Prussia and Greater Germany	18–20th	Hintze (1910: 494–495) Lotz (1914: 579–665) Taylor (1958: 417–432) Hermann (1966: 164, 386–388, 497)
Roman Catholic Church	United States	20th	Peterson and Schoenherr (1978: 798)
Roman Republic and Empire	Multiple Continents	2nd B.C.– 5th A.D.	Polybius (circa 127 B.C.; 1923: 310–366) Caesar (circa 51 B.C.; 1917: 592–605) Josephus (circa 77; 1927: 597–609) Abbott (1926: 55) Grant (1974: xxxi-xxxii)
Metropolitan Fire Department	U.S.A.	20th	Stern (1972)
Mahdist State in the Sudan	North-East Africa	19th	Holt (1970: 119–121; 246–248) Shibeika (1966: 492)
Maratha State under Shivaji	India	17th	Pandey (1965: 126–127; 1967; 416)

(text continued from page 209)

quickly returned to the original form. Even these four routinely operated through unity of command.

B.   Shape of Hierarchy

Meyer (1971) suggested that administrative hierarchies may be symmetric—a practice, he suggested, which may have been adopted from military organization. Blau (1971) noted that the hierarchies he studied were not symmetric. The literature survey undertaken here agrees with Blau. Asymmetric out-trees are documented for numerous cultures, and especially for military organizations (MacKinnon, 1833; Maurice, 1934; Pandey, 1965:127; Levy, 1969:412; Dyson-Hudson, 1966:10). Although there have been attempts to impose hierarchical symmetry—in one army under the first Islamic Empire (Levy, 1969:426) and in the military organization of the Inca Empire (Métraux, 1961:103)—whether these attempts were successful is unknown.[5]

C.   Fluctuation in Form

Recall that C is the intensity of indirect control in out-trees. If C increases, the hierarchy is shifting toward a high proportion of indirect control relations, the extreme case being the maximum-level hierarchy. If C declines, the hierarchy is shifting toward a high proportion of direct control relations, the extreme case being a maximum-span hierarchy. For small values of size—two through nine—the *a priori* expectation, E(C), is a decreasing function of size. Mathematicians have yet to show whether this function holds generally. But the range for which it does hold is sufficient for the present discussion.

Stern (1972) studied the structure of a metropolitan fire department, giving special attention to the forms of hierarchy appearing in each fire station. These stations varied in size up to eight, so the E(C) is known for each case considered. Of particular interest were the hierarchical forms in the fire station and at the scene of fires. The observed values of both S and C shifted down when the fire crews moved from the station house to the scene of a fire. Indeed, the hierarchy shifted to a maximum-span out-tree at the scene of a fire, making all control relations direct. This is the exact opposite of the random expectation. But it confirms the reasoning in this essay: this form minimizes D, R, and reaction time. As the environment becomes more turbulent, the hierarchy shifts to a flatter form, with direct control minimizing most communication problems.

VIII.   CONCLUDING COMMENT

The conditions which generate "bureaucracy" are undoubtedly various. But at least two of them are the division of labor and hierarchy. This essay has focused on hierarchical differentiation and has merely assumed the division of labor along with other conditions relevant to both. In general, it has been suggested that imperatively coordinated associations articulate their communication networks in forms that are primarily determined by environmental relations. Fundamentals include: (1) the finite nature of all human organisms and social systems; (2) the constraints on communication generated by the requisites of unitary action and short reaction time; and (3) the fact that the randomly selected organization is less powerful than its environment. All organizations perish. It is simply a question of how soon they will disappear, not of whether they will disappear. Ultimately, organizations will disappear regardless of the form they assume. In the interim, it is instructive to consider which forms of organization and which side conditions will enhance survival probability more or less. For a host of reasons indicated in previous sections, organizations which articulate their command networks in the form of out-trees are expected to have higher survival probabilities than those which do not. This is why—the argument maintains—unity of command is almost universally observed. However, even assuming unity of command, organizational form can still vary a great deal.

Some kinds of out-trees should have higher survival probabilities than others. Other things being equal, the taller the hierarchy, the longer the reaction time. Other things being equal, the higher the proportion of cut-points, the greater the likelihood of communicative disruption. And, since communicative disruption directly cancels unitary action, it is even more problematic than expanding reaction time. Accordingly, as size increases, the system is increasingly exposed to a double risk through interaction with its environment: (1) loss of unitary action directly through broken communication, and (2) loss of unitary action indirectly through expanding reaction time across hierarchical levels. Size will increase through both an increase in the span of control and an increase in the number of hierarchical levels. However, hierarchical levels will increase at a lower rate than spans of control. The consequences of this trend are several: (1) the network's disruption potential (relative number of cut-points) will decline as size increases; (2) the magnitude of the network's disruption potential (average cutting number) will decline as size increases; and (3) the relative size of the controlling component (administrative positions) will be a decreasing function of size. A direct consequence of these trends is a shift toward symmetry, although this is a matter of degree.

In imperatively coordinated associations mapped by out-tree command networks, the activity of the organization is directed from supervisory positions. The personnel occupying these positions constitute the system's controlling component. This component exercises control through the positions it occupies, that is, through the structure of the network. At very small sizes, the controlling component *may* constitute half or even more than half of all personnel. However, as size increases, the relative number of cut-points (supervisory positions) will decline in *surviving* organizations. The general result will be that—for most sizes of organization—the controlling component will be a minority of all personnel, a minority which shrinks in relative size as the total size of the organization increases. Thus, most imperatively coordinated associations will be governed by a minority, a minority whose power becomes increasingly concentrated as size increases. It is important to emphasize that these conditions are the exact opposite of what would be expected on an *a priori* basis.

The sociological perspective of this essay is quite traditional in several respects. I have relied on "intention free" mechanisms in explaining both (1) the generation of structure and (2) the selection of structures in organizations facing turbulent environments (Schmid, 1981). The view that structural outcomes are primarily a result of the interaction between a social system and its environment is well known (H . Spencer, 1882; Michels, 1911; Segraves, 1974; Hannan and Freeman, 1977; Aldrich, 1979). The notion that unitary action is necessary to order in imperatively coordinated associations is one of the oldest in the sociological literature (Ibn Khaldun, 1967a:337; Fayol, 1917:27). Also, the phenomena I have been attempting to explain are long-standing sociological concerns. The commonly noted result that the relative size of an organization's controlling component (supervisory component) is inversely related to its population size harks back to Mosca's (1923:55) observation on that same relation at the level of the community or society.

What is different in the approach outlined here is simply the elaboration of structural possibilities—the different forms which can occur—and an examination of how they vary along dimensions that can have explanatory power. But even this is no more than an extension of standard sociological reasoning. And, because the point of view expressed here is sociological, it is quite contrary to those of van den Berghe (1974) and Collins (1981), among others. Social differentiation and hierarchical relations are here conceived as system determined phenomena, not as derivatives of individual urges or emotions.

Finally, as I am inclined to agree with Natorp's (1910:14–5) view that knowledge about any subject is not a "fact" but only part of an ongoing "process" of inquiry, I recall my observation that this essay offers no more than a *first approximation* to a theory of vertical control in organizations. Whether the propositions advanced here will ultimately be retained, reformulated, or rejected remains to be seen.

ACKNOWLEDGEMENTS

An earlier version of this essay was presented at the conference on "Formal Theories of Organization" at the Werner-Reimers-Stiftung in Bad Homburg, West Germany, March 6, 1981. I thank Professor Wolfgang Sodeur and his colleagues for their many helpful comments. I thank the members of the Structuralist Group at the University of South Carolina for comments on the earlier version as well, particularly Peter Mariolis, J. Miller McPherson, Patrick D. Nolan, Lynn Smith-Lovin, and John V. Skvoretz. I thank Alice Nolan, Siebold Noland and Grendel Fritz for assistance in typing the manuscript and I acknowledge partial support of this work by National Science Foundation Grant Number SOC 7905695.

NOTES

1. Where foreign language sources are cited, the translation into English has been supplied. In this case, "imperatively coordinated association" is Weber's *Herrschaftsverband*. Since I have taken this from Weber, a word of clarification is in order. Neither this nor any other term in sociology requires a "subjective" definition. Neither the flow of commands from one point to another, nor the differential rates of compliance with them (differentiating points into authority positions) require any *subjective* definition, assumption, or interpretation (cf. Frege, 1892:29). All terms I use in constructing arguments about organizational hierarchies rely on objectivist assumptions about the nature of the phenomena discussed (cf. Zimen, 1973). Any "subjectivist" interpretation of my terminology is incorrect. Furthermore, arguments which claim that sociological theories must incorporate so-called subjective phenomena (e.g., Collins, 1981:1011) rest upon a non sequitur (Mayhew, 1980:363).

2. All the a priori illustrations in the text are based on distinct, nonisomorphic out-trees, that is, unlabeled out-trees. For labeled out-trees, Rényi (1959) has shown that E(R) is also an increasing function of size.

3. A shift toward symmetry could come about in either of two ways. First, the number of symmetric hierarchies could increase as a proportion of the total. Second, a shift in the direction of

symmetry can occur—without producing actual symmetry—through a decline in the *variance* around the lengths of out-tree branches. Both could occur simultaneously. I suspect, however, that to the extent that a shift toward symmetry does occur, it is simply in the declining variance mentioned. Except for sizes two and three, where all out-trees are symmetric by definition, it is rare to see a symmetric out-tree. And, due to the definitional symmetry at small sizes, and the prediction here concerning size, the degree of symmetry in out-trees may have a nonmonotonic curvilinear relation to size.

4. For labeled out-trees, Moon (1970) has shown that E(L) is also an increasing function of size.

5. Simmel (1920) described an Italian secret society which had the general aspect of a symmetric out-tree. This case is not listed in Table 12 because Simmel's source was a newspaper report. Newspapers are among the least reliable data sources, so I mention this case only as a possibility. Of course, a primary characteristic—indeed a defining characteristic—of secret societies is the minimization of communication flows. Since they can minimize information flows by assuming a tree form, there is considerable reason to credit Simmel's view. However, it is not immediately obvious that secret societies would assume a *symmetric* out-tree form.

REFERENCES

Abbott, Frank F.
1926 "Civitates liberae et immues and civitates stipendiariae." Pp. 39–55 in F. F. Abbott and A. C. Johnson (eds.), Municipal Administration in the Roman Empire. Princeton: Princeton University Press.
Aberle, David F.
1957 Chahar and Dagor Mongol Bureaucratic Administration, 1912–1945. New Haven: HRAF Press.
Abrahams, R. G.
1966 "Succession to the chiefship in northern unyamwezi." Pp. 127–141 in Jack Goody (ed.), Succession to High Office. Cambridge: Cambridge University Press.
Alchian, Armen A.
1950 "Uncertainty, evolution and economic theory." Journal of Political Economy 58:211–221.
Aldrich, Howard E.
1979 Organizations and Environments. Englewood Cliffs: Prentice-Hall.
Allen, Louis
1971 Japan. New York: American Heritage Press.
Ashby, W. Ross
1952 Design for a Brain. London: Chapman and Hall.
Atanda, J. A.
1973 The New Oyo Empire. London: Longman.
Auerbach, Felix
1914 "Das gesetz der bevölkerungskonzentration." Petermanns geographische Mitteilungen 59:74–76.
Barrow, Thomas C.
1967 Trade and Empire. Cambridge: Harvard University Press.
Barth, Fredrik
1953 Principles of Social Organization in Southern Kurdistan. Oslo: Brødrene Jørgensen.
1959 Political Leadership among Swat Pathans. London: London School of Economics.
1961 Nomads of South Persia. Oslo: Universitetets Etnografiske Museum.
Bartos, Otomar J.
1967 Simple Models of Group Behavior. New York: Columbia University Press.

Bascom, William
1969 The Yoruba of Southwestern Nigeria. New York: Holt, Rinehart & Winston.
Bates, Frederick L.
1974 "Alternative models for the future of society." Social Forces 53:1–11.
Berge, Claude
1958 Théorie des graphes et ses applications. Paris: Dunod.
Blau, Peter M.
1964 Exchange and Power in Social Life. New York: John Wiley.
1969 "Objectives of sociology." Pp. 43–71 in Robert Bierstedt (ed.), A Design for Sociology. Philadelphia: American Academy of Political and Social Science.
1970 "A formal theory of differentiation in organizations." American Sociological Review 35:201–218.
1971 "Comment on two mathematical formulations of the theory of differentiation in organizations." American Sociological Review 36:304–307.
1972 "Interdependence and hierarchy in organizations." Social Science Research 1:1–24.
1974 On the Nature of Organizations. New York: John Wiley.
1977 Inequality and Heterogeneity. New York: Free Press.
Blum, Jerome
1948 Noble Landowners and Agricultute in Austria, 1815–1848. Baltimore: Johns Hopkins University Press.
Bono, Salvatore
1964 I corsari barbareschi. Torino: Edizioni rai Radio-televisions.
Borah, Woodrow
1951 New Spain's Century of Depression. Berkeley: University of California Press.
Boulding, Kenneth E.
1953 The Organizational Revolution. New York: Harper and Brothers.
1955 "The malthusian model as a general system." Social and Economic Studies 4:195–205.
Braudel, Fernand
1966a La Méditerranee et le monde méditerranéen à l'époque de Philippe II. Seconde édition. Paris: A. Colin. Tome I.
1966b La Méditerranee et la monde méditerranéen à l'époque de Philippe II. Seconde édition. Paris: A. Colin. Tome II.
Burling, Robbins
1974 The Passage of Power. New York: Academic Press.
Burnet, Macfarlane and David O. White
1972 The Natural History of Infectious Disease. Fourth edition. Cambridge: Cambridge University Press.
Caesar, G. Julius
1917 De bello Gallico. London: Heinemann.
Campbell, Donald T.
1958 "Systematic error on the part of human links in communication systems." Information and Control 1:334–369.
Caplow, Theodore
1964 Principles of Organization. New York: Harcourt, Brace & World.
Carneiro, Robert L.
1967 "On the relationship between size of population and complexity of social organization." Southwestern Journal of Anthropology 23:234–243.
1970 "A theory of the origin of the state." Science 169:733–738.
1972 "From autonomous villages to the state, a numerical estimation." Pp. 64–77 in Brian Spooner (ed), Population Growth. Cambridge: MIT Press.

Chandler, Alfred D.
  1962   Strategy and Structure. Cambridge: MIT Press.
Chowdhry, Kamla and A. K. Pal
  1957   "Production planning and organizational morale." Human Organization 15:11–16.
Chu, Tung-tsu
  1962   Local Government in China under the Ch'ing. Cambridge: Harvard University Press.
Collins, Randall
  1975   Conflict Sociology. New York: Academic Press.
  1981   "On the microfoundations of macrosociology." American Journal of Sociology 86:984–1014.
Cook, Earl
  1971   "The flow of energy in an industrial society." Scientific American 225:134–144.
Cook, Sherburne F. and Lesley B. Simpson
  1948   The Population of Central Mexico in the Sixteenth Century. Berkeley: University of California Press.
Cunnison, Ian
  1966   Baggara Arabs. Oxford: Clarendon Press.
Curry, John R.
  1974   "Presentation by james g. march." Seminars on Organizations. 1:29–31.
Darwin, Charles
  1859   On the Origin of Species by Means of Natural Selection. London: Murray.
Darwin, Charles G.
  1952   The Next Million Years. London: Rupert Hart-Davis.
DeFleur, Melvin L.
  1962   "Mass communication and the study of rumor." Sociological Inquiry 32:51–70.
Del Boca, Angelo
  1965   La guerra d'Abissinia, 1935–1941. Milano: Giangiacomo Feltrinelli.
Diaz del Castillo, Bernal
  1632   Historia verdadera de la conquista de la Nueva España. Madrid: Imprenta del Reyno.
Dill, William R.
  1965   "Business organizations." Pp. 1071–1114 in James G. March (ed.), Handbook of Organizations. Chicago: Rand McNally.
Drabeck, Thomas E.
  1969   Laboratory Simulation of a Police Communication System Under Stress. Columbus: College of Administrative Science.
Duncan, Otis D.
  1964   "Social organization and the ecosystem." Pp. 36–82 in Robert E. L. Faris (ed.), Handbook of Modern Sociology. Chicago: Rand McNally.
Durkheim, Émile
  1893   De la division du travail social. Paris: Alcan.
  1895   Les règles de la méthode sociologique. Paris: Alcan.
Dyson-Hudson, Neville
  1966   Karimojong Politics. Oxford: Clarendon Press.
Eaton, Clement
  1954   A History of the Southern Confederacy. New York: Macmillan.
Eisenstadt, S. N.
  1963   The Political Systems of Empires. New York: Free Press.
  1964   "Social change, differentiation and evolution." American Sociological Review 29:375–386.
  1971   Social Differentiation and Stratification. London: Scott, Foresman.

Emery, F. E. and E. L. Trist
1965   "The causal texture of organizational environments." Human Relations 18:21–31.
Epstein, Ralph C.
1928   The Automobile Industry. Chicago: Shaw.
Evan, William M.
1963   "Indices of the hierarchical structure of industrial organizations." Management Science
       9:468–447.
Evans-Pritchard, E. E.
1949   The Sanusi of Cyrenaica. Oxford: Clarendon Press.
1963   "The zande state." Journal of the Royal Anthropological Institute 93:134–154.
Fallers, Lloyd
1965   Bantu Bureaucracy. Second edition. Chicago: University of Chicago Press.
Falk, Gottfried and Wolfgang Ruppel
1976   Energie und Entropie. Berlin: Springer.
Fayol, Henri
1917   Administration industrielle et générale. Paris: Dunod.
Fernea, Robert A.
1970   Shaykh and Effendi. Cambridge: Harvard University Press.
Feuerwerker, Albert
1958   China's Early Industrialization. Cambridge: Harvard University Press.
Fieldhouse, D. K.
1966   The Colonial Empires. New York: Delacorte.
Flannery, Kent V.
1972   "The cultural evolution of civilizations." Annual Review of Ecology and Systematics
       3:399–426.
Ford, T. R. and G. F. De Jong (eds.)
1970   Social Demography. Englewood Cliffs: Prentice Hall.
Freud, Sigmund
1927   Die Zukunft einer Illusion. Wien: Internationaler psychoanalytischer Verlag.
Friedell, Morris F.
1967   "Organizations as semilattices." American Sociological Review 32:46–54.
Frege, Gottlob
1892   "Über sinn und bedeutung." Zeitschrift für Philosophie und philosophische Kritik
       100:25–50.
Frye, Richard N.
1965   Bukhara. Norman: University of Oklahoma Press.
Gaedicke, Herbert
1929   "Altersaufbau, abgangsordnung und lebensdauer von aktengesellschaften." Allgemeines
       statistisches Archiv 19:513–529.
Gasquet, Francis A.
1893   The Great Pestilence. London: Simpkin, Marshall.
Gluckman, Max
1960   "The rise of a zulu empire." Scientific American 202:157–168.
Goffman, Erving
1974   Frame Analysis. Cambridge: Harvard University Press.
Gomes de Brito, Bernardo
1905   Historia tragico-maritima. Lisboa: Bibliotheca de classicos portuguezes. Tomo VIII.
Grant, Michael
1974   The Army of the Caesars. New York: Charles Scribner's Sons.
Grousset, René
1939   L'Empire des steppes. Paris: Payot.

Hannan, M. and J. Freeman
1977   "The population ecology of organizations." American Journal of Sociology 82:929–964.
Harary, Frank
1967   A Seminar on Graph Theory. New York: Holt.
1969   Graph Theory. Reading: Addison-Wesley.
Harary, F., R. Z. Norman and D. Cartwright
1965   Structural Models. New York: Wiley.
Harary, F. and P. A. Ostrand
1971   "The cutting center theorem for trees." Discrete Mathematics 1:7–18.
Harary, F. and E. M. Palmer
1973   Graphical Enumeration. New York: Academic Press.
Hart, Hornell
1931   The Technique of Social Progress. New York: Holt.
Hecker, Justus F. K.
1832   Der schwarze Tod in vierzehnten Jahrhundert. Berlin: Herbig.
Heilman, Ernest A.
1932   Mortality of Business Firms in Minneapolis, St. Paul and Duluth, 1926–1930. Minneapolis: University of Minnesota Press.
Hermann, Carl H.
1966   Deutsche Militärgeschichte. Frankfurt am Main: Bernard & Graefe.
Hickson, D. J., C. R. Hinnings, C. A. Lee, R. E. Schneck and J. M. Pennings
1971   "A strategic contingencies theory of intraorganizational power." Administrative Science Quarterly 16:216–229.
Hintze, Otto
1910   "Der commissarius und seine bedeutung in der allegemeinen verwaltungsgeschichte." Pp. 493–528 in Mario Krammer (ed.), Historische Aufsätze. Weimar: Böhlaus.
Hodgson, M. G. S.
1968   "The ismaili state." Pp. 422–482 in J. A. Boyle (ed.), The Cambridge History of Iran. Volume V. Cambridge: Cambridge University Press.
Hoffmann, Walther G.
1940   Wachstum und Wachstumsformen der englischen Industriewirtschaft. Jena: Fischer.
Holt, P. M.
1970   The Mahdist State in the Sudan, 1881–1898. Second edition. Oxford: Clarendon Press.
Hume, David
1739   A Treatise of Human Nature: I. Of the Understanding. London: John Noon.
Hutchinson, A. R., R. G. Hutchinson and M. A. Newcomber
1938   "A study of business mortality." American Economic Review 28:497–514.
Ibn Khaldun, Abd-ar Rahman
1967a The Muqaddimah. Translated by F. Rosenthal, second edition. Princeton: Princeton University Press. Volume 1.
1967b The Muqaddimah. Translated by F. Rosenthal, second edition. Princeton: Princeton University Press. Volume 2.
1967c The Muqaddimah. Translated by F. Rosenthal, second edition. Princeton: Princeton University Press. Volume 3.
Inalcik, Halil
1973   The Ottoman Empire. New York: Praeger.
Jones, G. I.
1966   "Chiefly succession in basutoland." Pp. 57–81 in Jack Goody (ed.), Succession to High Office. Cambridge: Cambridge University Press.
Josephus, Flavius
1927   Istoria Ioudaikou Polemou Pros Romaious. London: Heinemann. Volume 1.

Juglar, Clement
  1860   Des crises commerciales. Paris: Guillaumin.
Julien, C.-A.
  1964   Histoire de L'Afrique du Nord. Deuxième édition. Paris: Payot.
Junod, Henri A.
  1927   The Life of a South African Tribe. Second edition. London: Macmillan. Volume 1.
Kaplan, David
  1960   "The law of cultural dominance." Pp. 69–92 in M. D. Sahlins and E. R. Service (eds.),
         Evolution and Culture. Ann Arbor: University of Michigan Press.
Katz, Friedrich
  1969   Vorkolumbische Kulturen. München: Kindler.
Kemp, William E.
  1971   "The flow of energy in a hunting society." Scientific American 225:104–115.
Kim, C. I. E.
  1962   "Japanese rule in korea (1905–1910)." Proceedings of the American Philosophical Soci-
         ety 106:53–59.
Kimambo, Isaria
  1968   "The rise of the congolese state systems." Pp. 29–48 in T. O. Ranger (ed.), Aspects of
         Central African History. Evanston: Northwestern University Press.
Kitchin, Joseph
  1923   "Cycles and trends in economic life." Review of Economic Statistics 5:10–16.
Kondratieff, N. D.
  1926   "Die langen wellen der konjunktur." Archiv für Sozialwissenschaft uns Sozialpolitik
         56:573–609.
Kracke, E. A.
  1953   Civil Service in Early Sung China, 960–1067. Cambridge: Harvard University Press.
Krippendorff, Klaus
  1971   "Communication and the genisis of structure." General Systems 16:171–185.
Krooss, Herman E.
  1966   American Economic Development. Second edition. Englewood Cliffs: Prentice-Hall.
Lambton, A. K. S.
  1968   "The internal structure of the saljug empire." Pp. 203–282 in J. A. Boyle (ed.), The
         Cambridge History of Iran. Cambridge: Cambridge University Press.
Lampugnani, Agostino
  1634   La pestilenza seguita in Milano, l'anno 1630. Milano: Carlo Ferrandi.
Landau, Martin
  1969   "Redundancy, rationality, and the problem of duplication and overlap." Public Admin-
         istration Review 29:346–358.
Lane, Frederic C.
  1973   Venice, A Maritime Republic. Baltimore: Johns Hopkins Press.
Lasorsa, Giovanni
  1928   "Indagini sulla mortalità della società italiane per azioni." Giornale degli economisi e
         revista di statistica 68:838–858.
Last, Murray
  1967   The Sokoto Caliphate. New York: Humanities Press.
Lawrence, P. R. and J. W. Lorsch
  1967   "Differentiation and integration in complex organizations." Administrative Science Quar-
         terly 12:1–47.
Le Bon, Gustave
  1912   La Révolution francaise et la psychologie de révolution. Paris: Flammarion.

Lee, R. H. G.
1970   The Manchurian Frontier in Ch'ing History. Cambridge: Harvard University Press.
Lenski, Gerhard E.
1970   Human Societies. New York: McGraw-Hill.
1979   "Directions and continuities in societal growth." Pp. 5–18 in Amos H. Hawley (ed.), Societal Growth. New York: Free Press.
Levy, Reuben
1969   The Social Structure of Islam. Second edition. Cambridge: Cambridge University Press.
Lewis, I. M.
1961   Pastoral Democracy. London: Oxford University Press.
Loewe, Michael
1967a Records of Han Administration: I. Cambridge: Cambridge University Press.
1967b Records of Han Administration: II. Cambridge: Cambridge University Press.
Lotz, Albert
1914   Geschichte des deutschen Beamtentums. Zweite auflage. Berlin: von Decker.
Low, Victor N.
1972   Three Nigerian Emirates. Evanston: Northwestern University Press.
Maccia, E. S. and G. S. Maccia
1971   "Use of siggs theory model to characterize education systems as social systems." Pp. 159–182 in M. D. Rubin (ed.), Man in Systems. London: Gordon & Breach.
MacKinnon, David
1833   The Origin and Services of the Coldstream Guards. London: Bentley.
Maktari, A. M. A.
1971   Water Rights and Irrigation Practices in Lahj. Cambridge: Cambridge University Press.
Malthus, Thomas R.
1798   An Essay on the Principle of Population. London: Johnson.
Mannheim, Karl
1929   Ideologie und Utopie. Bonn: Cohen.
1935   Mensch und Gesellschaft im Zeitalter des Umbaus. Leiden: Sijthoff.
March, J. G. and H. A. Simon
1958   Organizations. New York: Wiley.
Marx, Karl
1859   Zur Kritik der politischen Oekonomie. Berlin: Duncker.
Marx, K. and F. Engels
1848   Manifest der kommunistischen Partei. London: Burghard.
Maupertuis, Pierre-Louis M., de
1756   "Recherche des loix du mouvement." Pp. 29–42 in Oeuvres de Mr de Maupertuis. Nouvelle édition. Tome IV. Lyon: Bruyset.
Maurice, Frederic
1934   The History of the Scots Guard. London: Chatto & Windus.
Mayer, Jean
1975   "Management of famine relief." Science 188:571–577.
Mayhew, Bruce H.
1973   "System size and ruling elites." American Sociological Review 38:468–475.
1980   "Structuralism versus individualism, Part 1." Social Forces: 59:335–375.
1981   "Structuralism versus individualism, Part 2." Social Forces 59:627–648.
Mayhew, B. H. and L. N. Gray
1971   "The structure of dominance relations in triadic interaction systems." Comparative Group Studies 2:161–190.
1972   "Growth and decay of structure in interaction." Comparative Group Studies 3:131–160.

Mayhew, B. H. and R. L. Levinger
 1976a "On the emergence of oligarchy in human interaction." American Journal of Sociology
   81:1017–1049.
 1976b "Size and the density of interaction in human aggregates." American Journal of Sociology
   82:86–110.
Mayhew, B. H., R. L. Levinger, J. M. Mcpherson and T. F. James
 1972 "System size and structural differentiation in formal organizations." American Sociological Review 37:629–633.
McFarland, David D.
 1970 "Review of blalock's theory construction." Social Forces 48:543–544.
McGarry, Edmund D.
 1930 Mortality in Retail Trade. Buffalo: University of Buffalo.
Meier, Richard L.
 1962 A Communications Theory of Urban Growth. Cambridge: MIT Press.
Métraux, Alfred
 1961 Les Incas. Paris: Seuil.
Meyer, Marshall W.
 1971 "Some constraints in analyzing data on organizational structure." American Sociological
   Review 36:294–297.
Michels, Robert
 1911 Zur Soziologie des Parteiwesens in der modernen Demokratie. Leipzig: Klinkhardt.
Miller, James G.
 1978 Living Systems. New York: McGraw-Hill.
Montesquieu, Charles, de
 1748 De l'Esprit des loix. Tome I. Geneve: Barrillot et fils.
Moon, John W.
 1970 Counting Labelled Trees. London: Clowes.
Mosca, Gaetano
 1923 Elementi di scienza politica. Seconda edizione. Torino: Bocca.
Natorp, Paul G.
 1910 Die logischen Grundlagen der exacten Wissenschaften. Berlin: Teubner.
Oberschelp, Walter
 1967 "Kombinatorische anzahlbestimmungen in relationen." Mathematische Annalen
   174:53–78.
Olmstead, A. T.
 1948 History of the Persian Empire. Chicago: University of Chicago Press.
Omer-Cooper, J. D.
 1969 The Zulu Aftermath. Evanston: Northwestern University Press.
Ostrogorsky, George
 1940 Geschichte des byzantinischen Staates. München: Beck.
 1969 History of the Byzantine State. Translated by J. Hussey. New Brunswick: Rutgers University Press.
Pandey, Awadh B.
 1965 Society and Government in Medieval India. Allahabad: Indian Universities Press.
 1967 Later Medieval India, 1526–1761. Allahabad: Indian Universities Press.
Paré, Ambroise
 1568 Traicté de la peste. Paris: Wechel.
Pearson, Karl
 1911 The Grammar of Science. Third edition. London: Black.
Peterson, R. W. and R. A. Schoenherr
 1978 "Organizational status attainment of religious professionals. Social Forces 56:794–822.

Plakans, Andrejs
1975   "Peasant farmsteads and households in the baltic littoral, 1797." Comparative Studies in Society and History 17:2–35.
Polybius
1922   The Histories. Translated by W. R. Paton. London: Heinemann. Volume 1.
1923   The Histories. Translated by W. R. Paton. London: Heinemann. Volume 3.
Popper, Karl
1935   Logik der Forschung. Wien: Springer.
Prescott, William H.
1843a History of the Conquest of Mexico. London: Bentley. Volume 1.
1843b History of the Conquest of Mexico. London: Bentley. Volume 2.
1843c History of the Conquest of Mexico. London: Bentley. Volume 3.
1847a History of the Conquest of Peru. New York: Harper. Volume 1.
1847b History of the Conquest of Peru. New York: Harper. Volume 2.
Prins, Geert C. E.
1957   On the Automorphism Group of a Tree. Doctoral dissertation. Department of Mathematics. University of Michigan.
Quètelet, Adolphe J.
1848   Du Système sociale et les lois qui le régissent. Paris: Guillaumin.
Rappaport, Roy A.
1971   "The flow of energy in an agricultural society." Scientific American 225:116–132.
Rédei, L.
1934   "Ein kombinatorischer satz." Acta Litterarum ac Scientiarum 7:39–43.
Reinhard, M. H. and A. Armengaud
1961   Histoire générale de la population mondiale. Paris: Montchrestien.
Rényi, A.
1959   "Some remarks on the theory of trees." A Magyar Tudományos Akadémia Mathematikai Kutató Intézetének Közleményei 4:73–85.
Richardson, Lewis F.
1960   Statistics of Deadly Quarrels. Pittsburg: Boxwood.
Ripamontius, Iosephus
1640   De pest quae fuit anno MDCXXX. Mediolani: Malatestas.
Robbins, Richard G.
1975   Famine in Russia, 1891–1892. New York: Columbia University Press.
Robinson, R. W. and A. J. Schwenk
1974   "The distribution of degrees in a large random tree." Department of Mathematics, University of Michigan.
Roover, Raymond, de
1966   The Rise and Decline of the Medici Bank, 1397–1494. New York: Norton.
Sabloff, J. A. and G. R. Willey
1967   "The collapse of may civilization in the southern lowlands." Southwestern Journal of Anthropology 23:311–336.
Sahlins, Marshall D.
1958   Social Stratification in Polynesia. Seattle: University of Washington Press.
Salzman, Phillip
1971   "Movement and resource extraction among pastoral nomads." Anthropological Quarterly 44:185–197.
Samuel, Y. and B. F. Mannheim
1970   "A multidimensional approach toward a typology of bureaucracy." Administrative Science Quarterly 15:216–228.

Sanson, George
  1958   History of Japan to 1334. Stanford: Stanford University Press.
  1961   History of Japan, 1334–1615. Stanford: Stanford University Press.
  1963   History of Japan, 1615–1867. Stanford: Stanford University Press.
Schlick, Mortiz, von
  1931   "Die kausalität in der gegenwärtigen physik." Die Naturwissenschaften 19:145–162.
Schmid, Michael
  1981   "Struktur und selektion." Zeitschrift für Soziologie 10:17–37.
Segraves, B. Abbott
  1974   "Ecological generalization and structural transformation in sociocultural systems." American Anthropologist 76:530–552.
Shaban, M. A.
  1970   The Abbasid Revolution. Cambridge: Cambridge University Press.
  1971   Islamic History, A.D. 600–750. Cambridge: Cambridge University Press.
Shannon, H. A.
  1932   "The first five thousand limited companies and their duration." Economic History 2:396–424.
Shibeika, Mekki
  1966   "The fiscal administration of the mahdist state, 1881–1898." Pp. 491–492 in C. Issawi (ed.), The Economic History of the Middle East, 1800–1914. Chicago: University of Chicago Press.
Shrewsbury, J. F. D.
  1970   A History of Bubonic Plague in the British Isles. Cambridge: Cambridge University Press.
Simmel, Georg
  1894   "Le Problème de la sociologie." Revue de métaphisique et de morale 2:497–504.
  1902   "The number of members as determining the sociological form of the group, I." American Journal of Sociology 8:1–46.
  1907   "Soziologie der über- und unterordnung." Archiv für Sozialwissenschaft und Sozialpolitik 24:477–546.
  1920   Soziologie. 2. Auflage Leipzig: Duncker & Humblot.
  1923   Soziologie. 3. Auflage Leipzig: Duncker & Humblot.
Simon, Herbert A.
  1962   "The architecture of complexity." Proceedings of the American Philosophical Society 106:467–482.
  1973   "The organization of complex systems." Pp. 1–27 in H. H. Pattee (ed.), Hierarchy Theory. New York: Braziller.
Smith, M. G.
  1960   Government in Zazzau. London: Oxford University Press.
Solo, Robert A.
  1967   Economic Organizations and Social Systems. Indianapolis: Bobbs-Merrill.
Sombart, Werner
  1913   Krieg und Kapitalismus. Leipzig: Duncker & Humblot.
Sorokin, Pitirim A.
  1947   Society, Culture, and Personality. New York: Harper.
Southwold, Martin
  1966   "Succession to the throne of buganda." Pp. 82–126 in Jack Goody (ed.), Succession to High Office. Cambridge: Cambridge University Press.
Spencer, Berkley A.
  1973   "Community differentiation and the fallacy of intersectoral causation." Human Organization 32:59–71.

Spencer, Herbert
1876 Principles of Sociology. London: Williams & Norgate. Volume 1.
1880 Principles of Sociology. New York: Appleton. Volume 2-Part 4.
1882 Principles of Sociology. New York: Appleton. Volume 2-Part 5.
1896 Principles of Sociology. London: Williams & Norgate. Volume 3.
Spengler, Oswald
1918 Der Untergang des Abendlandes. München: Beck. 1. Band.
Starbuck, William H.
1965a "Mathematics and organization theory." Pp. 335–386 in J. G. March (ed.), Handbook of Organizations. Chicago: Rand McNally.
1965b "Organizational growth and development." Pp. 451–533 in J. G. March (ed.), Handbook of Organizations. Chicago: Rand McNally.
Steindl, Joseph
1945 Small and Big Business. Oxford: Blackwell.
Steiner, Kurt
1965 Local Government in Japan. Stanford: Stanford University Press.
Steinmetz, S. Rudolf
1929 Soziologie des Krieges. Zweite Auflage. Leipzig: Barth.
Stepanek, Joseph E.
1960 Managers for Small Industry. Glencoe: Free Press.
Stern, Robert N.
1972 Two Models of Structural Differentiation in Organizations. Master's thesis. Department of Sociology, Vanderbilt University.
Stirling, Paul
1953 "Social ranking in a turkish village." British Journal of Sociology 4:31–44.
1965 Turkish Village. New York: Wiley.
Tadino, Alessandro
1648 Ragguaglio dell'origine et giornali successi della gran peste contagiosa. Milano: Ghislifi.
Taylor, Telford
1958 The March of Conquest. New York: Simon & Schuster.
Tepperman, Lorne
1975 "Demographic aspects of career mobility." Canadian Review of Sociology and Anthropology 12:163–177.
Terryberry, Shirley
1968 "The evolution of organizational environments." Administrative Science Quarterly 12:590–613.
Thomas, W. I. and D. S. Thomas
1928 The Child in America. New York: Knopf.
Thompson, James D.
1967 Organizations in Action. New York: McGraw-Hill.
Tocqueville, Alexis, de
1856 L'Ancien régime et la révolution. Deuxième édition. Paris: Levy.
Toynbee, Arnold J.
1947 A Study of History. Abridgement of vols. 1–4 by D. C. Somervell. London: Oxford University Press.
1957 A Study of History. Abridgement of vols. 7–10 by D. C. Somervell. London: Oxford University Press.
Tribus, M. and E. C. McIrvine
1971 "Energy and information." Scientific American 255:179–188.
Trimingham, J. Spencer
1962 A History of Islam in West Africa. London: Oxford University Press.

Twitchett, D. C.
1963   Financial Administration under the T'ang Dynasty. Cambridge: Cambridge University Press.
Urlanis, Boris T.
1960   Voiny i narodonaselenie Evropy. Moskva: Sotsial'no-ekonomicheskom.
Vaile, Roland S.
1932   Studies in Economics. Minneapolis: University of Minnesota Press.
Van Beek, Gus W.
1969   "The rise and fall of arabia felix." Scientific American 221:36–46.
van den Berghe, Pierre L.
1974   "Bringing beasts back in." American Sociological Review 39:777–788.
Wagner, Adolf
1892   Grundlegung der politischen Ökonomie. Dritte Auflage. Leipzig: Winter.
Waissman, F.
1959   "The decline and fall of causality." Pp. 84–154 in A. C. Crombie (ed.), Turning Points in Physics. Amsterdam: North-Holland.
Wallerstein, Immanuel
1974a   The Modern World System, I. New York: Academic Press.
1974b   "The rise and future demise of the world capitalist system." Comparative Studies in Society and History 16:387–415.
Walter, Benjamin
1966   "Internal control relations in administrative hierarchies." Administrative Science Quarterly 11:179–206.
Weber, Erich
1934   Beiträge zum Problem des Wirtschaftsverfalls. Wien: Deuticke.
Weber, Max
1921   Gesammelte politische Schriften. München: Drei Masken Verlag.
1922   Wirtschaft und Gesellschaft. Tübingen: Mohr.
Wells, Tom H.
1971   The Confederate Navy. University: University of Alabama Press.
Wheeler, Geoffrey
1974   "Russian conquest and colonization of central asia." Pp. 264–298 in T. Hunczak (ed.), Russian Imperialism. New Brunswick: Rutgers University Press.
White, Leslie A.
1943   "Energy and the evolution of culture." American Anthropologist 45:335–356.
1948   "Mans control over civilization." Scientific Monthly 66:235–247.
1959   The Evolution of Culture. New York: McGraw-Hill.
Whyte, William F.
1949   "The social structure of the restaurant." American Journal of Sociology 54:302–310.
Wilcoxson, Kent H.
1966   Chains of Fire. Philadelphia: Chilton.
Wilensky, Harold L.
1967   Organizational Intelligence. New York: Basic Books.
Wirsing, Rolf
1973   "Political power and information." American Anthropologist 75:153–170.
Wolf, E. R. and E. C. Hansen
1967   "Caudillo politics." Comparative Studies in Society and History 9:168–179.
Woolman, David S.
1968   Rebels in the Rif. Stanford: Stanford University Press.

Ziadeh, Nicola A.
1964   Damascus under the Mamluks. Norman: University of Oklahoma Press.
Zimen, Karl-Erik
1973   Strukturen der Natur. Frankfurt am Main: Fischer.
Zipf. George K.
1949   Human Behavior and the Principle of Least Effort. Reading: Addison-Wesley.

ORGANIZATIONAL DECLINE

Leonard Greenhalgh

I. INTRODUCTION

Organizational decline is receiving increasing attention from students of organizations. The increased attention results from a growing recognition of the importance and complexity of the phenomenon. Organizational decline is important because it is proving to have costly organizational and social consequences. Its importance is expected to increase as we enter an era of decline that some believe will last into the next century (Boulding, 1975; Levine, 1978; Whetten, 1979, 1980b). Organizational decline is also proving to be more complex and interesting than previous conceptualizations suggested. The phenomenon and its manifestations are multidimensional (see Miller and Friesen, 1980) and when approached as such can enrich understanding of the dynamics of organizational life cycles.

Most students of organizations are likely to have experienced or at least observed organizations during a decline phase, and thereby gained some appreciation of the complex, interrelated, sociological and sociopsychological dynam-

Research in the Sociology of Organizations, vol. 2, pages 231–276
Copyright © 1983 by JAI Press Inc.
All rights of reproduction in any form reserved.
ISBN: 0-89232-203-9

ics. Surprisingly, however, the usual scholarly conceptualizations of organizational decline seem simplistic and sterile. The focus is usually on shrinkage of some size dimension, such as work force, market share, net total assets, profit, or such market assessments of the organization as stock price or securities ratings. Rarely are these manifestations related to underlying processes. As a result, the existing literature does little to illuminate experience; it draws attention away from the diverse facets of organizational decline, and focuses on some narrow and often uninteresting subset.

Shrinkage-based definitions may be not only conceptually impoverished, but actually misleading. They are likely to focus attention on *manifestations* of decline rather than on the phenomenon itself. It is necessary to reach beyond obvious symptoms to the underlying process if the phenomenon is to be understood in any depth and novel and nontrivial consequences predicted and investigated.

This paper proposes a definition which will provide conceptual clarity by distinguishing the phenomenon from its manifestations. Specifically, organizational decline is viewed as deterioration in the organization's adaptation to its environment. Decline occurs when the organization fails to maintain the adaptiveness of its response to a stable environment, or when it fails to either broaden or increase its domination of a niche which has a diminishing carrying capacity.

The converse of decline, thus defined, is not growth, as is often implied, but adaptation. The shrinkage/growth dimension is easy to operationalize but lacks the conceptual richness of the decline/improved adaptation dimension, and it therefore is less appropriate as well as potentially misleading. Of course, these two dimensions are related in a variety of ways. Maladaptation sooner or later leads to changes in organizational attributes, many of which can be measured in terms of size. In turn, changes in size may be, in a particular case, a fundamental cause of maladaptation.

Defining organizational decline in terms of adaptation establishes an important linkage with the related concept of organizational effectiveness. A reduction in adaptation is seen by many writers as equivalent to or at least a determinant of organizational effectiveness (Goodman and Pennings, 1977). Indeed, Steers (1975) found "adaptability-flexibility" to be the dominant criterion of organizational effectiveness in his review of the literature. Pondy (1977:229) suggests that adaptation is central to organizational effectiveness because:

> Given a series of random ecological changes, the type of organizing model most likely to survive is one based on evolutionary mechanisms. Within such an evolutionary organizing model, the most natural performance criterion is the capacity for adaptation.

J. P. Campbell (1977) adds the observation that while many have written about the adaptation dimension, few have attempted to measure it. Instead, data collection has tended to focus on size dimensions, as is the case with organizational decline.

Although the adaptation-based definition is conceptually richer than its size-based competitors, it is not without problems. First, organizational researchers have always been perplexed by the difficulty of defining the organization's boundary (see, e.g., Aldrich, 1979). In the case of organizational decline, the researcher might encounter a declining subunit within a healthy, adaptive parent organization. Such situations are not unusual in conglomerates, for instance. Imposing different boundaries in such cases will lead to different assessments of decline. Second, different time horizons may produce different assessments of the effectiveness of the organization's response. An organization may make adaptive responses to a long-term scenario at the expense of short-term adaptation. Third, evaluation of an organization's effectiveness in responding to a given environment depends on the perspective of the evaluator. For instance, the adaptive value of substituting capital for labor during a recession may be evaluated negatively by labor leaders who wish to preserve jobs, and positively by stockholders who want to increase efficiency and thus maximize future profits.

Scholars must deal with these problems and also with the inadequacy of static models. Such models dominate the study of organizations, for obvious reasons, and tend to foster the use of cross-sectional research. Static models and cross-sectional research do not lead the researcher to examine organizational phenomena that change over time. They may, in fact, actually mislead the research by causing Type II errors in which research hypotheses are rejected that would have been confirmed had a longitudinal design been used (Ford, 1980a; Freeman and Hannan, 1975; Whetten 1980a). In the case of organizational decline, problems arise when comparing organizations that are more adapted with organizations that are less adapted. An important complementary approach would be to compare organizations at times when they are more adapted with the same organizations when they have subsequently become less adapted, preferably studying the processes that occur during the decline.

An additional challenge is the lack of a knowledge base on which to build an understanding of organizational decline. Extrapolation from what is known about adaptation is limited and dangerous, which raises serious questions about the usefulness of terms which encompass both adaptation and decline, such as organizational change. It will be evident from the succeeding discussion that change involving adaptation is not the converse of change involving decline. Many organizational processes and relationships are asymmetrical between the two conditions, and many decline processes are irreversible. Adaptation and the growth that typically accompanies it are therefore in some respects qualitatively different from decline and shrinkage; as a result, overarching concepts include heterogeneous phenomena. Thus, for instance, it would be an error to research adaptation and growth and then make generalizations about organizational change that are thought to apply to decline and shrinkage situations.

The conceptual base is lacking also because the literature on organizational decline remains sparse despite its importance, reflecting the general neglect of this area of inquiry (Easton, 1976; Ford, 1980b; Hannan and Freeman, 1980; Hartley and Cooper, 1976; Levine, 1978; Scott, 1974; Whetten, 1980a). Researchers have instead given most of their attention to organizations that are adapting well. The differential attention is partly attributable to a growth orientation which pervades and biases the study of organizations (Ford, 1980b; Whetten, 1980a). Convenience has also been a factor. Whetten (1980a) notes that shrinking organizations are scarce in a rapidly growing economy, and researcher access is relatively difficult at all times; as a result, growth in the body of knowledge has been somewhat constrained by the availability of researchable sites. His point explains why most of what has been written about decline and shrinkage appeared in the era of the Great Depression of the 1930s. Hanlon (1979) casts doubt on the generalizability of data from that era to the 1970s and 1980s; thus, there is even more cause to suggest that the current state of the art in theory and research appears to be quite primitive.

This paper will review and synthesize the literature relevant to declining organizations, and will then assess the state of the art in this subject area. Section II focuses on the effects of decline at the organizational level of analysis; then in Section III we move to the (sociopsychological) level of the organizational participant who reacts to organizational-level changes. In Section IV, these literatures are integrated into a model of the dynamics and consequences of organizational decline. The model shows that the consequences of decline interact and subsequently accelerate decline through positive-feedback loops. The resulting vicious cycle has important implications for those making administrative and managerial decisions in organizations, and for those trying to change organizations or regulate them. The paper also defines the mission of organizational researchers who must provide greater knowledge of the etiology, dynamics, and consequences of organizational decline.

II. THE SOCIOLOGY OF ORGANIZATIONAL DECLINE

This section explores the phenomenon of decline at the organizational level of analysis, in contrast to the individual-level, sociopsychological focus of the section that will follow. Furthermore, attention will center on short-run changes that accompany decline in individual organizations, in contrast to the "population ecology" approach, which examines longer-run morphological changes within populations of organizations (Aldrich, 1979; D. T. Campbell, 1969; Hannan and Freeman, 1980; Pennings, 1980). While a population-level understanding of decline may be important to policymakers, it is likely to be less useful to practitioners, who must work in, manage, stabilize, and perhaps change a particular organization. The restriction of scope excludes concepts that emerge at the population level of analysis; such emerging phenomena must be considered when there is an effect on the focal organization. Given this focus, the basic question addressed in this section will be: What do current paradigms in organizational theory contribute to the understanding of organizational decline?

The model adopted in this section envisions a dynamic equilibrium between an organization and its open system environment. Changes in either the organization or its environment give rise to organizational responses that tend to be oriented toward restoring the equilibrium. The equilibrium has two facets that are at least conceptually separable; namely, the organization–environment equilibrium (to which the notion of adaptation is relevant), and the intraorganizational equilibrium of organizational properties. The discussion which follows concerns the interactions of these two facets of organizational equilibrium. A change in organizational size is one possible response to a disturbed organization–environment equilibrium; it leads to adjustments in other organizational properties. Increases or decreases in size do not necessarily produce symmetrical corresponding adjustments in other properties. Embryonic empirical research suggests asymmetry may be more prevalent than symmetry, as many organizational properties are more responsive to growth than to shrinkage, and many adjustments to growth are essentially irreversible.

Five major organizational attributes are affected by decline and the organizational shrinkage that usually accompanies it; namely, organizational structure, slack, leadership, innovation, and work force composition. Decline would also induce changes in relationships between the organization and important elements of its environment. The effect of decline on each of these phenomena and the symmetry of such effects are discussed next.

A. Organizational Structure

Ford (1980a) identifies four structural properties that are affected by shrinkage: formalization, centralization, differentiation, and administrative intensity. Various changes in organizational structure affect each other as well as other organizational variables. Cross-sectional research suggests that increases in size generally bring increases in both vertical and horizontal differentiation, which in turn produce coordination problems (Blau, 1970; Ford, 1980a; Freeman and Hannan, 1975). The organization responds to such problems through formalization; that is, by introducing new programs for dealing with them, by centralization, and by increasing the size of the administrative component which handles the coordination function (Ford and Slocum, 1977). Since coordination involves indirect costs that are weighed against the benefits accruing from coordination, equilibrium points exist–at least in the minds of decision makers. These equilibrium points may be fairly clearly defined, as in the case of span of control norms, or poorly defined, as in the case of ad hoc appointments to handle unique coordination problems. For a given technology and market condition, two questions arise that students of organizations often combine: (1) Is the equilibrium curve for structural properties during shrinkage the same as during growth? and (2) Do empirical characteristics of organizations approximate the equilibrium points during growth and shrinkage or do they deviate systematically?

Empirical research to investigate the effects of shrinkage on structural variables is very sparse, and what little research has been done has focused on administrative intensity in school districts. A prominent variable in cross-sectional research on organizational size (see, e.g., Blau, 1970; Blau and Schoenherr, 1971; Pondy, 1969; Rushing, 1967), administrative intensity has received disproportionate attention from students of organizational shrinkage. Several researchers have noticed that administrative intensity seems to be asymmetrical between growth and shrinkage, but only a few empirical studies have addressed this issue.

Tsouderos' (1955) data from 10 voluntary organizations show that during growth, administrative expenditures grow at a lower rate than does income, whereas administrative expenditures and number of office workers increase rapidly after the downturn toward shrinkage. Akers and Campbell (1970) studied a set of occupational associations and investigated administrative intensity, measuring size in terms of association membership, and the administrative component in terms of the number of full-time staff in each association's national office. In addition to cross-sectional analysis, these authors performed a longitudinal comparison of 1949 data with 1964 data for 75 organizations and were able to separate the set into growers and shrinkers. They found that the administrative component grew when the organization grew, but at a slower rate. Only 4 of the 75 organizations retrenched, and 2 of these showed an increase in the administrative component, similar to Tsouderos' (1955) findings. (The third retrenching organization showed no change, while the fourth reduced its administrative staff.) Freeman and Hannan (1975) analyzed changes in sizes of personnel categories in 805 school districts in California. They found that growing and shrinking districts were alike in the ratios of the direct component (i.e., teachers) to demand levels, but different in the ratio of the administrative component to the same demand levels. The growth/shrinkage difference in administrative intensity, thus defined, would be asymmetrical.

Ford (1980a) conducted an empirical study of 24 school districts in Maryland. He subjected the data to both cross-sectional and longitudinal analysis and was led to different conclusions about shrinkage depending on the method used; only the more valid longitudinal results are of interest here. Ford found that the shrinking school districts in his population not only showed asymmetry, but actually had *growing* administrative components while enrollments were dropping.

The structural asymmetry found by these researchers appears to be explainable in terms of both asymmetry of equilibrium points and systematic deviation from equilibrium points due to a lag in structural response. Several factors could account for asymmetry of equilibrium points during shrinkage. First, it can be argued that other structural variables display an asymmetry of equilibrium points, since organizational procedures, once institutionalized, show strong resiliency (Allison, 1971; Lodahl and Mitchell, 1980). This resiliency has been described as structural inertia (Burns and Stalker, 1961; Hannan and Freeman, 1980; Stinchcombe, 1965). Continuation of the process of formalization (Freeman and Hannan, 1975; Tsouderos, 1955) would require a certain minimum administrative component, since specialists are not divisible. In support of this threshold view, Ford's (1980a) data indicate that the number of administrators is more responsive to the number of schools comprising the school district than to either enrollments or revenues. Thus an asymmetry of equilibrium points in the case of differentiation and formalization would be expected to lead to a concomitant asymmetry of equilibrium points in administrative intensity.

Another factor tending to produce asymmetry of equilibrium points is political in nature. Incumbents within the administrative component are likely to be more powerful than in the direct labor component. Freeman and Hannan (1975) suggest that the former may be particularly formidable in public school systems, since they can control access to information that could be used to support a decision to displace them and, in addition, tend to form coalitions to preserve their interests.

In the case of *temporary* asymmetry due to a lag in response, Freeman and Hannan (1975) cited data collected by Hendershot and James (1972) as evidence that the size/structure relationship is different between school districts that grew rapidly and districts that grew slowly. It can be concluded from these data that relationships are lagged at least during growth, which could itself produce an apparent asymmetry, depending on the timing of measurements, even if the relationships followed the equilibrium path during shrinkage.

The lag in the administrative component's response to changes in organizational size can be the result of asymmetrical outcomes of short-term decision making to effectuate change during growth and shrinkage. In the private sector, there seems to be a tendency to delay adding staff, especially "indirect" workers, during growth that may well be a throwback to a "principle of management" popular in the 1950s known as "optimal undermanning." In the public sector, the lag is more likely to be on the down side, since short-term decisions may favor continuing to operate organizations below their capacity rather than closing them (Freeman and Hannan, 1975). Both phenomena would produce apparent asymmetry that would be expected to disappear over time.

B. Organizational Slack

Organizational slack is a surplus of resources over what is required to maintain equilibrium in an environmental niche (Cyert and March, 1963). Slack is seen as necessary in protecting the organization's technical core from environmental adversities (Thompson, 1967). It is a key variable in the case of organizational decline, since it can be both an effect and, ultimately, a cause. Yet the phenomenon of slack, much less its relationship to decline, has not been adequately empirically investigated.

An organization that is adapting well to its environment can be expected to increase its size in order to more fully exploit its niche. As it grows, there is likely to be a modest overall increase in organizational slack (Bourgeois, 1981). The progression is unlikely to be smooth, however: the overall upward trend in slack will show fluctuations over time because opposing tendencies of slack creation and consumption (Galbraith, 1973) shape the growth/slack relationship.

The relationship of slack to size is complex during organizational decline. Slack is a multifaceted organizational property. Whereas the various forms of slack are affected the same way by growth, they are differentially affected by decline so that a resource imbalance arises. Specifically, slack working capital becomes scarce while human resources and the less liquid capital assets tend to become excessive for the scale of operations.

The typical decline scenario illustrates these dynamics. An efficient market, sensitive to maladaptation, soon leaves the declining organization's output units saturated with product (see Hirschman, 1970; Kolarska and Aldrich, 1980), well beyond what is needed to buffer the organization's technical core (Thompson, 1967). The transformation process is curtailed, leaving productive resources underutilized. At the same time, working capital becomes tied up in the form of inventory. Thus, while there is an excess of slack overall, virtually none of it is likely to be in the form of "uncommitted and easily recommittable resources" (Thompson, 1967:150). Ironically, the maladapted organization first loses slack in the resource it needs most to restore its level of adaptation.

Each major category of resources must be considered separately when assessing the symmetry of the slack/size relationship during growth and decline. Slack liquid resources disappear with the onset of decline and are unlikely to reappear unless and until the organization recovers. Capital assets remain underutilized throughout the decline period, with slack increasing until they are sold off. The overall effect of decline on the amount of slack in human resources depends on the organization's reaction. The basic tendency is for human resource slack to increase as the organization shrinks. If the organization does nothing other than cut back production, slack in human resources will simply grow. A series of cutbacks, as the organization reduces its scale of operations during shrinkage, might produce an alternating pattern of having workers stretched to their limits, then in abundance. In such circumstances, the size/slack relationship during shrinkage might be sinusoidal, oscillating between excess slack and very little slack. Furthermore, there are likely to be contrasting trends within the work force. The administrative component is more resistant to the shrinkage that accompanies decline than is the production component of a work force. It will be pointed out below that the work force also undergoes qualitative shifts during decline such that the employees most crucial to organizational adaptation are likely to be the first to leave a declining organization.

The effects of organizational decline on slack resources, though complicated and underresearched, are important because different degrees of slack affect other organizational processes, and decline itself. First, excess slack in committed resources implies inefficiency (Bourgeois, 1981), which at best decreases the chance of generating the uncommitted resources needed for recovery, and at worst impairs the organization's ability to compete in the market, thereby reenergizing the decline cycle. Second, the combination of limited slack in liquid resources and scarce opportunities increases the likelihood of divisive organizational politics (Cyert and March, 1963; V. Schein, 1979), which erodes the social fabric of the organization and makes recovery less likely. Finally, slack in liquid and human resources is necessary for innovation (Miles and Randolph, 1980), which in turn is necessary to reverse decline.

C. Organizational Leadership

In a declining organization, the responses of leaders will depend on their attitudes toward change, their definitions of the decline situation, their reactions to stress, and the availability of slack resources. With regard to attitudes toward change, Whetten (1980b) classifies leaders according to two dimensions: whether they positively or negatively value change, and whether they proactively or reactively approach decline. He suggests that the two dimensions will interact so that the dominant pattern will be for leaders who are indifferent or ambivalent about change to be reactive, while those who have either a strong affinity or a strong aversion to change will tend to be proactive.

A second factor affecting leadership is that leaders respond to their definition of the situation. Situations are often defined in terms of existing programs to deal with problems. The typical leader will encounter decline as a novel predicament, and thus he or she will have no solution available to deal with it. Search behavior would be expected to home in on the solution to a familiar problem that approximates features of the decline situation, so that decline becomes defined in terms of that solution. Thus the leader's response repertoire inhibits adaptation by imposing cognitive blinders.

Tunnel vision is exacerbated to the extent that leaders tend to seek less input from subordinates under decline conditions (Whetten, 1980a,b; See also Staw et al., 1981). Levine (1979) points out that while leaders are aware that participation facilitates change, they also soon learn that subordinates' participation in their own demise is not a viable process; it seems to lead inexorably to conflict.

Leaders' behavior, particularly their decision making, is also affected by the stress that decline creates. First, decline is threatening, and the resulting stress produces a general tendency towards rigidity among leaders (Staw et al., 1981). Second, leaders are likely to show a preference for quick responses to relieve the tension they experience (Whetten, 1980b), which may preclude the careful problem statement and diagnosis usually essential for adequate solutions; and, definition of the situation as being critical may lead to neglect of crucial elements. Stress also tends to foster problemistic search (Smart and Vertinsky, 1977), whereby solutions are sought in the vicinity of the symptoms (Cyert and March, 1963; see Hall, 1976, for an application of this concept to a specific case situation of decline). This tendency has implications for the *content* of response (discussed in the next subsection) as well as for leader behavior.

The absence of recommittable slack during organizational decline compounds the effects of stress on managerial decision making. Levine (1978:317) notes that resources are unavailable for planning, control, and information systems when these tools are perhaps most needed to help to minimize the risk of making mistakes.

Finally, decline may affect leadership by creating the impetus to displace the current leaders with a new cadre. This response is especially likely when power elites attribute the decline to intraorganizational problems. The rationale may be more instrumental in nature. New leaders are often specifically introduced into the organization for the purpose of making painful cuts. Such agents of change would not be constrained by loyalty to existing coalitions. It is also possible that leaders are replaced in recognition of the need for different skills in managing a downturn, just as different skills are needed in the routinization of charisma (Weber, 1947) as the leader's function changes from entrepreneurial development to institutionalization (Kimberly, 1980a). Staw and his colleagues (1981) note that the impetus to change leaders may come from the led.

The above discussion identifies four sets of dynamics by which leadership becomes less adaptive during organizational decline. Using shrinkage/growth as a surrogate for the decline/adaptation dimension, there is asymmetry in the relationship between adaptability of leadership and organizational size as the organization progresses from growth to shrinkage. More specifically, leader adaptiveness would be expected to be at its highest when the organization is young and beginning to grow. As time goes on, there is likely to be a shift from innovation to routinization as the organization grows. As decision making becomes increasingly programmed, organizational leaders become more reliant on standard operating procedures and less adaptable, hence the reduction in adaptability from an initial high point to a point of program saturation. Leader adaptability plummets with the onset of decline and shrinkage for the reasons noted above. There is likely to be some point of desperation, at which leaders may or may not abandon the decision programs that are not stemming the decline. The leaders can either continue their maladaptive behavior to the point of organizational termination (see, e.g., Kolarska and Aldrich, 1980) or try to regain the initial level of adaptability.

D. Organizational Innovation

The previous discussion of leadership focused on the way key decision makers respond to organization–environment disequilibria. The discussion will now move from the adaptability of the *patterns* of response (e.g., participative vs. autocratic, proactive vs. reactive) and the conditions that elicit such patterns (e.g., stress, slack resources, change aversion, reality construction) to the *content* of response.

Response content is best evaluated in terms of its contribution to organizational adaptation. In general, organizations that have become poorly adapted to their niches must *vary* their technologies (including their programs, human and nonhuman capital, and resources) and then *select* and *retain* organizational properties that increase adaptation to their environments. These are the basic elements of the organizational innovation process. This view is derived from the population-level evolutionary metaphor, however, so extreme care is warranted when discussing the adaptation of particular organizations to their environments. For example, organizational actors rather than an impartial environment may determine the subprocesses of variation, selection, and retention, and their actions may be guided by their predictions of future environmental states rather than by immediate environmental press.

There is a general inverse relationship between decline and innovation. A plot of overall innovation as a dependent variable against organizational size as a surrogate for the decline/adaptation dimension would resemble the relationship between leadership adaptability (an obvious correlate of innovation) and organizational size. That is, innovation would be at its highest soon after birth, but would become displaced by routinization as the organization grows. The onset of decline dries up slack liquid resources and inhibits creativity and risk taking. Thus innovation is likely to become frozen until the power elite launches a crash program to stimulate recovery. The symmetry of relationships between organizational size and each innovation subprocess is examined next.

The variation element is inherently problematic, and can inhibit innovation in all organizations, not just those that are declining. The chronic difficulty arises from the tension between tendencies toward stability and conservatism and the conflicting tendencies toward change and adaptation. Under the stressful conditions of decline, when variation is perhaps most needed, the conservative tendencies tend to be exacerbated (Schuler, 1980; Staw et al., 1981), which can result in a state of program paralysis that precludes innovation.

Under conditions of decline, variation is affected by changes in the work force and by reduced experimentation. As explained below, the work force becomes more homogeneous as a result of retrenchment, with the more valuable workers being the first to leave. Reduced experimentation is the result of scarce slack in liquid resources and in greater risk aversion. The changes in the work force are difficult to reverse, as is risk aversion, which tends to produce asymmetry between adaptation and decline. The patterns of slack generation and consumption during these two states was discussed in an earlier section.

Innovation may also be inhibited by a maladaptive change in the selection subprocess. More specifically, decline seems to induce a myopic commitment to increased efficiency of the existing transformation process (Staw et al., 1981). Whetten (1979) explains that since decline increases the pressure of accountability, organizational actors are likely to pursue courses of action having consequences that are both visible and measurable. The latter become criteria that guide the selection subprocess. The pressure of accountability may shape the selection process in a way that not only may be dysfunctional to the organization, but may be known to the decision makers to be dysfunctional.

In addition, a preoccupation with the efficiency of the existing transformation process leads to its general rationalization. Rationalization is a global selection criterion that leads to increased control, standardization, and reduced program redundancy. These strictures may increase the exodus of creative workers. The result is less organizational variety (Weick, 1979), whereby adaptation has been achieved at the expense of adaptability. Thus the rationalization constraint on the selection process cycles back to inhibit variation.

Effects on the selection process should also show opposite tendencies during growth and shrinkage. During growth, one would expect a greater emphasis on effectiveness than on efficiency, since ends would be defined better than means (see Thompson, 1967:86). The result would be that organizational actors would select variations according to a more global definition of adaptation, which would include adaptability to anticipated future environmental changes. In contrast, efficiency would receive overt emphasis during decline and shrinkage as insecure actors frame their situations and responses in the most favorable light for self-protection. This emphasis would diffuse to lower-seniority cohorts of organizational actors through the process of socialization (see Lodahl and Mitchell, 1980) and produce an asymmetry of equilibrium points.

Other organizational processes would contribute to asymmetry in the size/selection relationship. Merton (1957) points out that a general drift in orientation toward means rather than ends occurs over time in large organizations. Since organizations can be expected to have grown before they shrink, selection will naturally and irreversibly tend to be oriented more toward effectiveness (i.e., ends) during growth and more toward efficiency (i.e., means) during shrinkage.

Finally, innovation may be inhibited in the retention phase because the declining organization lacks the mix of resources needed to actually develop and introduce selected variations as new programs. Human resources may be plentiful, but working capital is likely to be scarce. All changes in routines involve at least some startup costs. The declining organization may have to defer the changes even though they are critically needed. Alternatively, committed resources may be liquidated to implement adaptive changes, and this may precipitate further decline in the deprived subsystem. These dynamics are essentially irreversible.

E. Work Force Composition

As suggested previously, the best and most creative workers are likely to be attracted to smaller, low-routine organizations which provide career advancement opportunities and creative outlets. Such people become harder to attract as the organization grows and innovations are routinized to ensure retention. Organizational decline, especially the first sign of shrinkage, causes a sudden acceleration of this trend. It will be shown in the next major section that voluntary turnover of all employees increases with the onset of decline, and that it is usually the most valuable workers who leave first. The residual pool of poorer-quality workers will at best inhibit recovery, and at worst, accelerate the decline. Thus the trend in the quality of the work force is likely to be asymmetrical as the organization proceeds through a cycle from birth to adaptation and growth, and then to decline.

The growth and shrinkage that accompanies adaptation and decline has other effects on the organization's work force composition. During growth, the newer cohorts of workers will be larger than previous cohorts, thus skewing the age and experience distributions toward the younger side. The class composition of the work force will change, too, in the direction of more variety: proactively, the organization can take advantage of increased opportunities for affirmative action programs during growth; reactively, the organization may have to dig deeper into the local labor market during growth, since its demand will have increased relative to supply. Finally, under norms of rationality, the organization will minimize transaction costs in allocating workers within its internal labor market. This will result in "fresh talent" being injected into the higher growth and presumably more adaptive organizational subunits, where that talent is most needed.

Decline and shrinkage affects the age, experience, and class distributions, plus patterns of allocation within the internal labor market. Programs to adjust the work force by altering the flows of individuals into and/or out of the organization directly affect work force composition. The two primary managerial techniques for adjusting a work force are attrition and layoff programs (see Greenhalgh and McKersie, 1980). Attrition programs usually involve a hiring freeze. The effect of such programs is to eliminate a cohort of entrants. This usually alters the organization's age distribution (see Dembowski, 1980) and certainly alters its experience distribution. In the case of layoffs (which typically also involves a hiring freeze), individuals are usually terminated in the inverse seniority order. The effect on the age and experience distributions is greater, because several cohorts may be eliminated. Since minority groups and women will tend to be disproportionately represented in the lower-seniority groups, the sex and racial composition of the work force will be reduced. The result is a low variety (i.e., fairly homogeneous in terms of race, sex, and age) work force that has a fairly uniform education and socialization history. Its capacity for innovation will be low due to its homogeneity and the consequences of hiring freezes which preclude the infusion of individuals who bring an awareness of new technology or stimulate a search for novel solutions to existing problems (Ettlie, 1980). At the same time, workers' motivation to participate and contribute will be low due to the constriction of career opportunities (Levine, 1978; Whetten, 1980b).

Levine (1979) reports an alternate work force reduction mechanism that can have equally serious consequences for future organizational effectiveness. A common procedure in the public sector is to distribute cutbacks proportionally across all units. While this approach has advantages in terms of political palatability, its negative impact on the units affected tends to be proportional to their efficiency prior to the cutbacks. The inefficient, poorly managed, excessive-slack units take the work force cuts in stride, whereas the well-managed, efficient units have to cut back resources needed for future productivity growth and service delivery.

When the organization is shrinking, its demand is low relative to supply in the local labor market. Even under the hiring freeze of an attrition program, the organization replaces crucial workers. Power elites can take advantage of the situation in two ways, depending on which values they wish to serve. Pursuing increased effectiveness, they can take advantage of the opportunity to upgrade the work force and thereby increase the organization's stock of human capital. Dembowski (1980), for instance, found that declining school districts were more likely to require teacher certification in more than one subject area. Pursuing increased efficiency, power elites can ''exploit the exploitable'' (Levine, 1978). Exploitation involves taking advantage of the weakened demand conditions by hiring workers on unfavorable terms, denying them career opportunities they would have enjoyed under more balanced labor market conditions, and perhaps even separating them when their time in grade has made it more economical to replace them with entry-level workers.

The changes in the variety of work force composition would be truly asymmetric between growth and shrinkage. This asymmetry would result from the difficulty of replacing age cohorts (indeed, an employee-selection criterion that was designed to do so would violate Equal Employment Opportunity guidelines regarding age discrimination) as well as from the difficulty in recruiting minorities to a declining organization (Goodman and Salipante, 1976).

F.   Changes in Organizational Relationships

In addition to changes in the properties of organizations, decline and its antecedent conditions can affect an organization's relationships with its workers, with unions, with other organizations, and with regulatory agencies. Each relationship is briefly discussed.

1. Relationship with Organizational Participants

Decline has a great effect on the relationship between the organization and its participants. Much of this effect takes the form of individuals' reactions to their perceptions of the changes. These reactions are dealt with in the next major section. At the group/organizational level of analysis, however, the relationships with and between coalitions (Bacharach and Lawler, 1980), and changes in the organization's compliance structure (House, 1975) are important phenomena.

The political model of organizations focuses on the competition of interest groups for resources. The relationship between interest groups is by definition conflictful, and the intensity of the conflict (Dahrendorf, 1959) is at least partly determined by the scarcity of valued resources. As a result, the amount of organizational slack tends to determine the dynamics of the organization's political structure. Scott (1974:245) states the situation very simply: the existence of slack allows "management to buy off internal consensus from the potentially conflicting interest group segments that compete for resources in organizations" (see also Cyert and March, 1963).

Managing in a declining organization is made difficult by the double disadvantage of having interest groups perceive very high stakes—and perhaps even an end-game situation—and minimum slack resources with which to ameliorate conflict. Adaptation means change, and change has different consequences for the various interest groups. The declining organization can hardly afford resistance to innovation; nor, due to the shortage of liquid resources, can it afford the increased side payments to compensate disadvantaged groups. As a result, the organization may find adaptation too costly.

Conflict between interest groups appears to be somewhat symmetrical between adaptation and decline periods. During organizational adaptation and growth, interest group conflict would probably follow an "inverted-U-shape" pattern when plotted against organizational size. In the very early stages, interest groups would not have coalesced and mobilized their power. Over time, however, interest groups work out differences through intraorganizational bargaining (Walton and McKersie, 1965) and are able to articulate a unified stand. With the further passage of time, management develops some skill and experience in dealing with the groups and is able to manage the conflict by appropriate allocations of an increasingly large pie. The result is (ideally) a political equilibrium at the lower right side of the "inverted U."

The organization's political system would probably be quite responsive to the onset of decline, due to the speed of the rumor mill and its tendency to differentially amplify bad news. The issues would probably crystallize almost instantaneously around partisan interests (Levine, 1978). Coalitions would close ranks, and the parties would begin manipulating perceptions to protect their interests in anticipation of scarcity, thus polarizing their positions. Therefore, one would expect a retracing of the "inverted U" at a much steeper angle, indicating a sharp rise in the intensity of political conflict. The rise would only be reversed if the parties were able to engage in integrative bargaining to solve mutual problems rather than distributive bargaining to divide up the shrinking pie (Walton and McKersie, 1965), a shift in stance which usually occurs too late.

The second aspect of the relationship of the declining organization to its participants is the change that would be expected in the basis of compliance. Etzioni (1961:12) provides a typology of compliance relations that shows the congruency of organizational power types with alternative types of participant involvement. A passage from the state of adaptive growth or at least stability to decline and shrinkage would represent a breach of the implicit employment contract (see Greenhalgh and Kaestle, 1981). That is, workers exchange their labor not only for accrued wages, but also for a stream of future opportunities. The resulting positive involvement takes the form of a general commitment to the organization and its mission. It induces the worker to exert more than the minimum necessary to "work to rule." The onset of decline and shrinkage curtails the perceived stream of future benefits. The effect is a shift from positive involvement to neutral or negative involvement (Ford, 1980b). The shift changes the quality of involvement from more committed toward more calculative or alienated; the power typically exerted on the organization's members from more moral and social toward remunerative and possibly coercive; and the organizational type away from normative (Etzioni, 1961).

The relationship between compliance structure and organizational size (as a surrogate for adaptation/decline) is quite complex. There is probably a tendency to drift from normative to remunerative during growth, with an acceleration of this process during shrinkage (see Hanlon, 1979:101). A strong lag effect would be expected because the compliance structure is such a central variable that the multifaceted adjustments necessary to regain intraorganizational equilibrium would be very slow.

2. Relationship with Unions

A declining organization's relationship with a union is complex, and its effects can only be summarized here. The relationship will obviously depend on whether a union represents the employees at the start of the decline period. If there is no union, the probability of a unionization campaign will increase as employees become preoccupied with their powerlessness to maintain continuity of employment.

The discussion which follows assumes the presence of the union throughout the organization's life cycle. During prosperous times of adaptation and growth, accomplishment of the union's mission of optimizing organizational inducements (March and Simon, 1958) for its members is relatively easy, due to the steadily increasing surplus and plentiful opportunities. Furthermore, when market opportunities exceed the organization's ability to meet the demand, managements tend to concede union and worker security provisions (such as restrictive work rules) in order to avoid lost production through strikes. Such provisions might provide a feeling of security during prosperity, but may reduce de facto security during decline by hindering adaptation.

As the organization moves into a period of decline and shrinkage, two distinct but related types of problems arise, namely, internal problems of the union as an organization per se, and problems in the relationship between management and the union.

The basic source of internal union problems is the inability to protect members' job security in a declining organization. The disequilibrium of an excessive work force must be corrected. Thus, in the long run, the union can only control the means by which the work force is reduced, at best insisting on an attrition program which ensures that no worker will involuntarily lose his or her job (see McKersie et al., 1981). If the union cannot prevent layoffs, it loses member support and often engenders overt member hostility (cf. Staw et al., 1981). Member involvement becomes alienated or at least calculated, rather than committed (Etzioni, 1961). Even when the union is able to negotiate an attrition program rather than layoffs, it still has its own organizational shrinkage problem in the form of membership (and hence overall resource) decline. As a result, the union's power elite is vulnerable to internal conflict due to the withdrawal of member confidence and support. Scarcity fuels the conflict.

The union's internal problems are an important aspect of the context of the relationship between the union and the declining employer. The union's response to the employing organization's predicament is a public event that has consequences for the union's power elite. Responses that help the organization adapt and recover may not be politically wise: they may contradict members' expectations. For example, the union's socialization process may have led members to expect their leaders to show intransigent resistance in a crisis. Adaptive departures from this stance may be perceived in terms of weakness and co-optation, making leaders vulnerable to displacement. Leaders' explanations of the difficult trade-offs that must be made may be unpalatable to a membership that has been previously led to believe that simple, unambiguous solutions exist for complex, ambiguous organizational problems.

Routinization of response is yet another factor which limits any role the union may play in helping the organization recover. Much of a union's interaction with management can be explained by its repertoire of standard operating procedures (Allison, 1971). In the United States, these standardized responses are based on distributive bargaining (Walton and McKersie, 1965): that is, each situation tends to be viewed first as a zero-sum game in which either management gains, or the union and the workers gain. This view triggers some form of highly visible aggressive defense. Allison (1971) points out that the rationality of such responses is irrelevant in explaining the actions taken. But even if the union recognizes its response as being irrational, there is likely to be a history of negative exchange that would preclude cooperative action.

The formidable combination of impediments makes the positive-sum approach of integrative bargaining (Walton and McKersie, 1965) likely only at the point of desperation. The U.S. experience stands in sharp contrast to the experiences of its principal industrial competitors, Japan and Germany. In those countries, adaptation is a predominant value governing the relationship between organizations and unions (and government, as a third partner); therefore, organizational decline in those countries occurs in spite of the unions, rather than with added impetus from them, as in the United States.

To summarize this subsection, the relationship of the organization with its union tends to be maladaptive, and changes little with the fortunes of the organization. Only in some crisis situations does this pattern change, often too late.

3. Relationship with Other Organizations

The other organizations in the environment of the declining organization can be categorized for the present purposes as suppliers of inputs, receivers of outputs, and competitors. Decision makers in supplier organizations will display conflicting tendencies. They will want to support the declining organization in order to protect their own output function, but will also be concerned with finding alternate markets for their outputs. In the process, they will be generous to the declining organization's competitors, which will tend to hasten the decline by making the niche less hospitable. At the same time, supplier decision makers will take action to protect their own input function by imposing more stringent credit policies on the declining organization than on its competitors, which will likewise tend to hasten the decline. The tight credit policy will likely continue until the declining organization is on the brink of collapse, at which point suppliers may actually reverse the policy in order to preserve the market for their own outputs.

Thompson (1967:32) views such actions as a generic rational response: ''Under norms of rationality, organizations seek to minimize the power of task-environment elements over them by maintaining alternatives.'' Thus if supplier support were plotted against the surrogate variable organizational size, the relationship would be asymmetrical. An analogous relationship would be expected for recipients of the organization's outputs.

The relationship expected between the organization and its competitors would depend on whether the declining organization was losing market share or the total market was shrinking. In the former case, no change in interorganizational relationships would be expected. In the latter case, the competing organizations might at some point establish joint programs to distribute the costs of innovation

(Whetten, 1980b). The competitor cooperation/size relationship would be reminiscent of the union–management cooperation/size relationship described earlier. By contrast, however, any cooperation that emerged would probably not be a last-ditch effort. The joint innovation programs would more likely be institutionalized in the form of industry associations. Thus the competitor cooperation/size relationship would be asymmetrical between adaptation and decline periods.

4. *Relationships with Regulatory Agencies*

The vigor of the regulatory process appears to be directly (and symmetrically) proportional to the health of the organizations being regulated. One could offer three reasons for this proposition, although no empirical data were found to support such reasoning. First, the power elites of declining organizations do not hesitate to attribute their predicament to constraints imposed by regulatory agencies. This bad publicity reduces the status of regulatory agencies and their staffs, providing a disincentive for zealous regulation. Second, organizational members articulate their interests in the form of political pressure to reduce environmental stress, and regulatory agencies have budgetary vulnerability which tends to make them responsive to political pressure. Third, it is contrary to the interests of regulatory agencies to lose the organizations they regulate, since the latter are (or likely affect) inputs that determine their own survival and prosperity.

5. *Other Changes in the Organization's Environment*

Finally, organizational decline has a multiplier effect. Like any system, it is vulnerable to the demise of one of its elements, which would trigger a series of responses throughout the network. Such responses will be summarized by five propositions. In the event of organizational decline, the greater will be the impact on the system: (1) the more important the declining organization is in the total economy of system; (2) the greater the magnitude of its decline; (3) the more the system is tightly coupled; (4) the more alternative recipients exist for the organization's outputs; and (5) the fewer alternative sources exist for the organization's inputs.

6. *Summary*

The focal organization is affected by a complex set of interrelated processes that occur during organizational decline and shrinkage. The effects cannot be understood or predicted from what is known about adaptation and growth, since there is little symmetry between the effects of up-side and down-side changes. Asymmetry is encountered in organizational structure, as evidenced by what Ford (1980b) calls "structural hysteresis" in administrative intensity; in organizational slack (with similar up-side relationships in the cases of liquid resources, human resources, and capital assets, but quite different down-side patterns of asymmetry, and even differences within the human resources category); in leader adaptiveness, as a result of the essentially irreversible tendency for entrepreneurial skills to be displaced by institutionalization skills during adaptation and growth, followed by the need for stress-resistant reroutinization or even deroutinization skills during decline; in innovation, in much the same way—and for many of the same reasons—as in the case of leader adaptability; in the work force composition, in terms of quality, experience distribution, and heterogeneity; and in the declining organization's relationships with workers, unions, regulatory agencies, and competitors.

III. THE SOCIAL PSYCHOLOGY OF ORGANIZATIONAL DECLINE

The previous section examined decline at the organizational level of analysis; the focus will now shift to the individual level to consider the effect of perceived organizational decline on the relationship between individuals and objects in their environment.

Individual-level effects of decline are important because they have organizational-level consequences, the major two being reductions in efficiency and in innovation. Inhibiting organizational efficiency has the effect of accelerating decline because the organization becomes less fit to compete in its niche. Reduced innovation precludes recovery to the necessary level of adaptation. Thus sociopsychological variables are involved in positive-feedback loops which operate in concert with the effects of sociological variables discussed in the preceding section.

This section begins by considering the typical context in which employee perception occurs; namely, the preoccupation with decline scenarios, the scarcity and ambiguity of official information, and rampant rumors. The section then enumerates the various sociopsychological reactions to decline.

This section will not examine the symmetry of the effects of adaptation and growth versus decline and shrinkage on each variable. Asymmetry would be expected to occur, but the asymmetry would not be expected to be different for each variable considered. A general statement will avoid repetition.

Sociopsychological reactions depend on the phenomenology of adaptation and decline rather than on objective organizational reality. An adaptive organization that is stable or growing offers workers a set of inducements to participate and contribute (March and Simon, 1958). The onset of decline and shrinkage threatens the continued availability of inducements and thereby abrogates the existing psychological contract. The perceived discontinuity in the psychological contract alters organizational participants' relationships to the organization. The affected variables include job security, propensity to leave, job involvement, job effort, and organizational commitment. Asymmetry arises in the sense that other factors being equal, decline would have a negative (from the organization's perspective) effect on each of these variables, whereas conditions of adaptation and growth or stability would be expected to have a positive or at least neutral effect.

Concerning the context of perception, the literature on organizational change consistently reports that employees become preoccupied with how changes could affect them (see Greenhalgh, 1978). Paradoxically, a common management practice is to deliberately withhold information regarding changes as long as possible. The result of these two phenomena is that employees in a perceived change situation tend to feel starved for information.

Evidence of the dearth of needed information is apparent from the results of survey research conducted in urban drug abuse agencies being phased out (Greenhalgh and Jick, 1978) and in the relocation of a rural hospital (Jick and Greenhalgh, 1978). In each organization, more than two-thirds of the employees reported that they had to rely on informal sources for information regarding continuity of employment. Rumors were by far the best informal source. In fact, several employees of the rural hospital reported that the psychiatric patients were more reliable sources of information than state personnel officials, supervisors, and union officials.

In such environments, reality construction can be a haphazard process. The onset of rumors of impending layoffs disrupts employees' taken-for-granted assumptions about the stability of their lives. In the absence of adequate, unambiguous, consistent, and believable information from official sources, they turn to fellow workers to negotiate definitions of the situation that can be reconciled with whatever information was gleaned from informal sources. Greenhalgh (1979a) explored this process and found some evidence which suggests that shared metaphors may shape how groups of employees in a declining organization evolve and respond to a definition of the situation. The dominant response was embodied in the metaphor of "disinvolvement," or withdrawal of the self from the organization, an apparently generic grief reaction to losses of objects which have high ego involvement (Greenhalgh, 1979b; Marris, 1974; Strange, 1977). The shared metaphor is probably transmitted through what Sykes (1965) describes as the "oral tradition" of the workplace.

Workers evolve cognitions concerning the viability of the organization before symptoms of decline (such as shrinkage of some size dimension) become evident to the organizational researcher. These cognitions can be measured in terms of perceived job security. The construct and its correlates will be explored in the next section, followed by an investigation of individual cognitions and attitudes regarding the experience of layoff per se.

A. Job Security

Job security is most usefully defined in terms of power to maintain career continuity. It could involve such anticipated organizational events as the blockage of career progress, demotion, obsolescence of skills, the disappearance of a mentor, the prospect of an unfavorable reorganization, or the ascendancy of a rival coalition. Viewing power as the obverse of dependence (Emerson, 1962), one would expect an individual with high intra- and/or interorganizational career mobility to be less dependent in any one specific job context, and thus feel more able to maintain career continuity.

Thus defined, job security is likely to be an important issue whenever an organization undergoes change. Since recent years have been almost universally characterized as an era of rapid change, one would expect job security to be a basic variable in the sociopsychological study of organizations. It is not. It appears occasionally in the literature but is rarely given central focus; instead, it usually appears as a component of other constructs, such as job satisfaction.

The result is that the pervasive organizational phenomenon of low job security has remained underresearched. There has been virtually no conceptual development, so that the concept has been treated as a unitary global variable that is "somehow" related to job satisfaction. Content validity has been a problem because job security has been operationalized as a global rather than a multifaceted variable, and is usually scaled on the basis of its consistency with facets of job satisfaction. Furthermore, its explanatory power has not been shown to be outstanding, because it has been used in research conducted primarily in stable organizations where the construct has low salience.

B.   Correlates of Job Security

As described above, the job security variable measures the worker's perception of and affective reaction to organizational decline (and other organizational change situations) based on the perceived implications of the change for that individual. Changes in organizational inducements result in changes in the exchange relationship. Thus one can expect different levels of job security to have correlates representing what the individual views as a fair exchange for the opportunities for career continuity offered by the organization. Barnard (1938) classified decisions made by employees in an exchange relationship with an employing organization into two categories: decisions to participate and decisions to contribute. Decisions to participate involve employee vs. nonemployee status, whereas decisions to contribute presuppose participation and involve such constructs as degree of effort and level of commitment. Rice et al. (1950) introduced a model which suggests that such exchange decisions are not homogeneous, but may be qualitatively different depending on the stage of the worker's career within the organization (a point also made by E. H. Schein, 1980). Greenhalgh (1980) combined the Barnard model with the model of Rice and associates and added preemployment stages. His exchange-based model, summarized in Figure 1, is useful in organizing the correlates of job security one would expect in the context of organizational decline.

In the pre-employment stage (Stage 1 of the model), one would expect the organization's image to affect the initial decision about whether to apply for

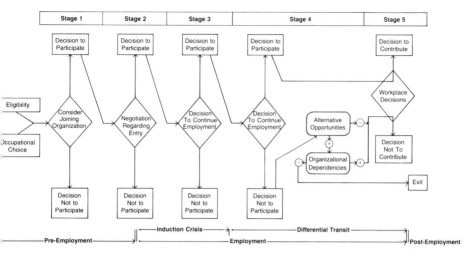

Figure 1. Decisions to Participate and Decisions to Contribute During the Life Cycle of the Employment Relationship. (Source: Greenhalgh, 1980.)

employment. A declining organization would be likely to have gained an image of low job security for its employees. Workers having a high need for security and labor market alternatives would be expected to self-select into organizational careers offering greater security. This tendency would leave the declining organization with a decline period cohort of employees having a low need for security or limited labor market alternatives.

During the second stage, the individual and the employer meet to explicitly or implicitly negotiate the terms of exchange, arriving at a psychological contract (E. H. Schein, 1980). An important element of the psychological contract is its time horizon, and one would expect the duration to be somewhat reciprocal: an organization offering little hope of continuity of employment should not expect the employee to have a strong or lasting commitment to participate. Thus, one would expect that, compared to their counterparts in more adaptive organizations, recruits in a declining organization enter the organization with low a priori job security and low intention to continue participation.

Two points should be made concerning the above hypothesis. First, the literature brings no empirical evidence to bear on the hypothesis. Second, the hypothesis assumes the applicant knows that the organization is declining. If the individual knows about the organization's decline in Stage 1, he or she can either self-select into a more adaptive organization or bring up the decline issue during negotiation of the psychological contract in Stage 2. If the individual does not know about the decline situation at the beginning of Stage 2, there is evidence to suggest that the organization is unlikely to provide accurate information. In a study of recruits entering a declining organization, Jick and Greenhalgh (1980) found that employees had received realistic job previews in the sense that the job content they were led to expect matched their subsequent experience on the job. By contrast, however, information about the future of the organization was absent or tended to be optimistic, and was a poorer match with the definitions of the situation that evolved on the job (see Jick and Greenhalgh, 1981).

In Stage 1, the decision to participate led potential applicants to take the next step and apply for employment. That step, described as Stage 2, led to a reaffirmation or cancellation of the decision to participate, based on a tentative psychological contract. Stage 3 represents the individual's initial experience of participation. It is described by Rice and his colleagues (1950) as the "period of induction crisis," since employees get a "*real* job preview" and reevaluate the exchange relationship.

Goodman and Salipante (1976) studied the induction crisis experience of companies that were trying to employ individuals classified as hard-core unemployed. They found a positive relationship between job security and short-term retention. However, no other studies were found to illuminate the effects which varying degrees of job security have at this stage in the organizational career. In fact, there is a general paucity of research at this career stage. This neglect is surprising since researchers acknowledge, at least implicitly, that employees relate differently to the organization during their early months on the job. For example, researchers frequently exclude recent hires from samples of "normal" employees.

It is probably safe to generalize beyond the Goodman and Salipante (1976) population of labor market marginals to propose that employees who by the end of Stage 2 have not come to share the dominant scenario of the organization's future will have a problem of dissonant cognitions. Reduction of their expectations about the organization's future is likely to raise the basic question of whether they will continue participation.

At the conclusion of the period of induction crisis, employees who have decided against participation will have left or will be in the process of leaving. Those who have decided to continue to participate will progress to Stage 4. This stage is called the "period of differential transit" (Rice et al., 1950), recognizing that while there is no longer a participation crisis, there is still attrition. Organization members probably do not continually raise the issue of whether or not to continue participation during this stage; they do so only in response to some stimulus, such as rumors.

The discussion has thus far assumed that the onset of decline occurred prior to entry. When this is so, it would appear that decline should not be a factor in reevaluating the organizational inducements (March and Simon, 1958) half of the psychological contract. However, E. H. Schein (1980) warns that the contract is not static, but rather is reevaluated whenever needs change. Thus if the employee's need for job security changed, the presence of continuing decline might imbalance the exchange relationship. (A change in need for security may not involve a *trait* change: increased dependencies such as new debts or additional family members may cause a *state* change.)

The effects of impaired job security during the fourth ("differential transit") stage are summarized in the subsections that follow.

1. Propensity to Leave

Under conditions of changed needs in the face of a continuing decline situation or a new decline threat, the exchange disequilibrium serves as the stimulus to once again confront the decision to participate. While most of the research on turnover has focused on this fourth stage, only a small fraction of that research has been conducted in declining organizations or has involved job security as a focal variable.

Chinoy (1955) reports a negative relationship between job security and propensity to leave in his interviews with auto workers, but does not provide empirical data. Gow et al. (1974) found a positive correlation between satisfaction of need for security and tenure, the latter being the inverse of turnover and thus a very rough index of propensity to leave (one can postulate that propensity to leave is a prerequisite for turnover). Two studies used exit interview data to relate voluntary resignations to job security concerns (Ronan, 1967; Smith and Kerr, 1953). In addition, Stogdill (1965) found dissatisfaction with job security in high-turnover stores he studied.

The relationship was more explicitly studied in research reported by Greenhalgh (1979b) and Jick (1979). The two studies used different measures of job security and propensity to leave, and different samples of the same declining and shrinking hospital system. Both reported a significant negative correlation between the variables. Additional research revealed that the more valuable workers, who tend to have the better labor market alternatives, are likely to be the first to leave (Greenhalgh and Jick, 1979; Greenhalgh and McKersie, 1980; see also Levine, 1979; Whetten, 1980a).

A set of macro-level studies corroborates the above findings concerning the relationship between job security and propensity to leave. Cross-sectional analysis conducted by Fry (1973:49) determined that "industries with high layoff rates also experience high quit rates since individuals will voluntarily move from companies or industries which possess a high degree of instability." Fry's findings are generally supported in the research of Stoikov and Raimon (1968) and Block (1977).

Some of the studies cited above involved an index of propensity to leave rather than a direct measure of the concept. The reason for highlighting the distinction is that the model views turnover as a two-stage process (March and Simon, 1958), in which propensity to leave will be actualized in exit behavior only when there are alternative opportunities (Price, 1977) and no strong dependencies. An employee who has decided against further participation, but is constrained from

leaving by either opportunities or dependencies, will enter Stage 5 with a substantially redefined psychological contract (Rabinowitz and Hall, 1977).

Stage 5 involves ongoing workplace decisions to contribute or withhold contribution. An employee who had made a positive decision to participate in Stage 4
would normally be expected to decide to contribute in Stage 5. The reluctant
participant, or "psychological quit" (March and Simon, 1958; Quinn, 1973) is
the more interesting case. That individual's degree of intended contribution
would be sufficient to balance her or his perception of the exchange relationship,
subject to a lower bound representing the minimum contribution necessary to
avoid dismissal. An employee's contribution is multifaceted, and can be differentiated into six operational categories: job involvement, productivity, work
group loyalty, organizational commitment, acceptance of goal-oriented changes,
and union loyalty (the relevance of this last category to the set is explained
below). The remainder of this section discusses the evidence of the effect of a
declining organization on each facet of contribution.

2. Job Involvement

Very little progress has been made in clarifying the conceptual and operational
difficulties of job involvement (Rabinowitz and Hall, 1977), much less the effect
of a declining organizational context on the variable. Only two studies have
explored the latter relationship; neither represents a definitive test of it. Hall and
Mansfield (1971) used a shortened version of the Lodahl scale (see Lodahl and
Kejner, 1965) to measure the effects of organizational stresses on researchers in
three R&D (research and development) laboratories. Job security was a key
element of these stresses. Their hypothesis, based on balance theory, that the
researchers would reduce their involvement in their work, was not empirically
confirmed. Greenhalgh (1979b) also used a shortened version of the Lodahl
scale, but correlated job involvement with a three-item job security scale in a
study of a declining hospital system. As hypothesized, he found a positive
correlation between job security and job involvement, but the magnitude was low
and failed to reach significance.

Gannon et al. (1973) compared two groups of defense-industry engineers that
had worked for the same company. The first set had been laid off and later
reemployed, while the second set had never been laid off. The 2 groups showed
no significant differences on any of the 12 Lodahl scale items used, but job
security was not measured. Instead, Gannon and his colleagues (1973:331) assumed that because "both the managers and their engineers knew that reductions
in force were highly improbable . . . the current engineers should not be influenced in any appreciable manner by the reduction in force while the terminated
engineers should be attitudinally affected in a negative manner." The implication is that the survivors constituted an appropriate control group. However, the

assumption of high job security of the survivors is questionable (Greenhalgh, 1979b, 1982), since individuals' assessments of job security seem to be based on a constructed reality that can be in direct contradiction to ''objective'' reality. Thus it is quite likely that both of the groups studied by Gannon and his colleagues were equally insecure; those who left, because of the direct experience of job loss, and those who survived, because of the vicarious experience of job loss. As a result, the study must be viewed as inconclusive.

These sets of results, obtained using less than ideal measures of the variables, lead one to question whether job involvement is an aspect of the psychological contract and therefore vulnerable to adjustments of exchange imbalances. Hall and Mansfield (1971) found that individuals' scores on the scale were fairly stable compared to the variation across subjects; they suggested that the construct may represent more a personality trait than an attitude, a possibility raised in the original Lodahl and Kejner (1965) article, and in several papers since (Lawler and Hall, 1970; Rabinowitz and Hall, 1977; Schwartz, 1980).

Schwartz's conceptualization of job involvement is particularly provocative. He presents evidence to suggest that, as measured on the Lodahl scale, job involvement may well represent an obsession/compulsion dimension rather than an attitudinal reaction to job characteristics. Based on this view, people who score high in job involvement would be oriented toward work as a socially valued outlet for their obsessions rather than being oriented toward a *particular* job or organization. Thus decline of a particular organization would not be expected to greatly affect obsessive/compulsive personalities, since other organizations and activities could provide the context in which they respond to their obsessions. Therefore, such people might react to the inability to maintain continuity of activity rather than continuity of employment. No existing job security constructs incorporate the continuity-of-activity dimension. Certainly further research using more sophisticated measures is needed to determine whether and how organizational decline is related to involvement in work.

3. Job Effort

Job effort is the most basic contribution in an exchange relationship. Thus when an organization is perceived to reduce the inducement of continuity of employment, one would expect workers to put in less effort, at least where the consequences of reduced effort have low visibility. The empirical evidence linking job security to job effort, however, is mixed.

One prevalent reaction to potential job loss, particularly when the employee first hears the rumors or news, is anxiety. Several articles have been written on the relationship of anxiety to productivity, mostly involving lab experiments (see, e.g., Taylor and Spence, 1952); they indicate a general impairment of performance associated with high levels of anxiety.

More relevant to field settings is the work of Roethlisberger and Dickson (1946:153), who attributed to layoff anxiety some aberrations in their data from the Hawthorne plant:

> The . . . decline in output . . . was . . . related to the operators' anxieties over the uncertain future of the mica splitting job. The decline began shortly after the first rumors . . . appeared, and it progressed as . . . fears . . . became more acute. This experience showed the effect of interfering preoccupations on the attitudes of the operators and, in turn, on their output.

These findings do not constitute rigorous support for the hypothesized positive relationship between job security and productivity, since low job security was inferred rather than measured. If "hard" measurements rather than observations had been made, however, the results would have been very useful, since the quasi-experimental design, even though applied fortuitously to a natural field experiment, had some strengths: there were pre-, during-, and postobservations on the experimental population and a matched control population, with the effect not appearing in the control or pretreatment observations, and attenuating in the posttreatment observation. Thus the Hawthorne findings can be considered basically supportive.

More direct support was found by Greenhalgh (1979b), who found a significant negative correlation between job security and effort. Both variables involved self-reports; the effort variable encompassed current work effort and behavioral intentions concerning effort. Hanlon's (1979) interviews of workers laid off in the New York City fiscal crisis corroborated these findings.

Restriction of output is also related to job security. Guest and Fatchett (1974) noted that a threat to job security often resulted in a conscious decision by workers to restrict their productivity, thereby alleviating the threat by "stretching out the job." Finally, Beynon (1973) found evidence of the relationship between job security and productivity in his nonparticipant observations over a five-year period in the British motor industry.

Three additional studies which bore directly on the hypothesis found no relationship between job security and productivity. Hershey (1972) compared piece rates of matched groups in the same organizations; the "experimental group" (this was a natural experiment) had been notified of layoff, while the control group had not. All four companies where the research was conducted had histories of layoffs, and control subjects were chosen on the basis of their being vulnerable to layoffs. Thus, Hershey's data do not refute the present hypothesis, since Greenhalgh (1979b) shows that there should be little difference between the threat (i.e., the vicarious experience) experienced by the control group and the threat experienced by the experimental group. Hershey's research would only represent a test of the hypothesized relationship between job security and productivity had he considered his two groups alternative treatment groups, and compared these with matched control groups consisting of nonvulnerable employees in companies with a history of perfect job security.

The second relevant study was conducted by Hackman and Lawler (1971). As an incidental output of their study of job dimensions and internal motivation, they correlated satisfaction with job security (using a single item) with supervisors' ratings of respondents' quantity and quality of work, plus overall effectiveness. The correlations were all positive, but they were very low and did not reach significance.

Finally, Hall and Mansfield (1971) studied reaction to job security stress among researchers in R&D laboratories and found "no significant differences in self-rated performance or effort" between their affected and control groups.

4. Organizational Commitment

Job involvement and job effort are employee contributions in an exchange relationship which share the same referent; namely, the worker's specific organizational role. In the case of organizational commitment, the referent is the organization, a reified abstraction to employees. It is hypothesized that in a declining and shrinking organization, employees will adjust their psychological contracts by reducing their commitment to the organization (see Hanlon, 1979:105) in addition to making the adjustments previously described.

The concept of organizational commitment has long been recognized as important in the study of organizations, although much confusion exists as to what is involved in the construct (Becker, 1960; Buchanan, 1974). The present conceptualization of organizational commitment, based on exchange theory, has its roots in the work of Chester Barnard, who viewed his roughly equivalent concept, loyalty, as "an essential condition of organization" (1938:84). In a similar vein, Porter et al. (1974:608) pointed out that "the development of organizational commitment appears to require an individual to think in fairly global terms about his or her relationship to the organization. . . ." Consistent with Barnard, and Porter and his colleagues, "cooperative" behavior of employees is viewed as going beyond the content of supervisory instructions, job descriptions, and standard operating procedures, to becoming involved in the organization's mission. Thus employees who have decided without reservation to contribute would be expected to be willing to participate in the give and take of an organization's contingent reactions to its environment: in other words, they would tolerate some degree of organizational change since they would be identified with its general goals.

From this line of reasoning, there emerge two dimensions to organizational commitment: organizational identification and resistance to (i.e., absence of) change. The distinction between organizational identification and resistance to change is more obvious in operational terms than it is in conceptual terms. In the case of identification, one in effect asks directly whether respondents feel a sense of organizational belonging (i.e., with the organization, its management, and the work group). In the case of resistance to change, one asks whether changes which may not maximize respondents' interests are viewed favorably.

Only one study was found which investigated the relationship between job security and organizational identification. Greenhalgh (1979b) found a significant positive correlation, confirming his hypothesis that decline engenders psychological withdrawal.

The relationship between organizational decline and resistance to change is conceptually complex because one would expect to find four factors that can work simultaneously to overdetermine the relationship. First, organizational decline leads to organizational change, and employees who perceive themselves to be affected by it could be expected to resist the change per se. This prediction is based on the contention of Fink et al. (1971) that perceived changes mobilize maintenance forces within the psyche that arise to reestablish homeostasis.

Second, there should be a simple direct relationship between decline-induced change, as perceived by employees, and their resistance to the change. March and Simon (1958) contend that resistance will occur if the changes reduce the surplus of inducements over contributions in the employee's assessment of the exchange relationship, representing an effort to hold the organization to the terms of the psychological contract.

Finally, as noted earlier, decline increases stress, which in turn makes organizational actors less adaptive, relying doggedly on standard operating procedures (Allison, 1971) when the organization most needs to change them. Fox and Staw (1979) have confirmed this "trapped administrator effect" in a laboratory study, finding that as job security decreased, there was a significant main effect on subjects' commitment to a previously chosen course of action.

These distinctions obviously have greater conceptual clarity than operational discriminability. The same recalcitrant attitudes and behaviors can be the result of each or all of the above factors. Nonetheless, researchers studying declining organizations can expect: (1) some resistance to any change; (2) resistance to the specific changes that are altering the exchange relationship; and (3) resistance to changes not directly related to decline.

There is a substantial literature on resistance to change which supports the hypothesized relationship between organizational changes, psychological contracts, and employee resistance to change. Much of this literature involves the broad spectrum of technological changes (e.g., Coch and French, 1948), although other studies involved reactions to reorganizations (e.g., Rothman et al., 1971).

Merton (1962) proposed an inverse relationship between job security and resistance to change. Greenhalgh (1979b) measured the relationship specifically and found a significant negative correlation between the variables. The resistance-to-change scale loaded on the same factor as his organizational identification scale discussed in the previous subsection, supporting the posited theoretical linkage between organizational identification and resistance to change as facets of organizational commitment.

C. Summary

Employees construct a definition of their employment situation. Perceived risk of discontinuity is augmented by traditional managerial secrecy, rumors, ambiguity, and the rhetoric of interest groups. Employees' attitudinal reactions to their perceptions take the form of impaired job security. A secure job is an organizational inducement (March and Simon, 1958); therefore, the perception of diminished security is viewed as a violation of the psychological contract and a resulting imbalance of the exchange relationship. Employees restore the imbalance by reducing their willingness to continue participation, or by reducing their contributions if exit is constrained. Thus the correlates of impaired job security include propensity to leave, job involvement, job effort, and organizational commitment. Those dynamics have organizational-level consequences, primarily through their effects on efficiency and innovation. Thus the sociopsychological reactions of employees are involved in powerful positive-feedback loops, and must be understood and dealt with.

The sociopsychological reaction of workers who are *actually* laid off also has organizational consequences: The experience leaves attitudinal scars, and most laid-off workers are subsequently rehired. Although a discussion of the effects of layoff is beyond the scope of this paper, it is worth noting that the actual experience produces a qualitatively different type of sociopsychological reaction than the vicarious experience (i.e., job insecurity). The effects of actual job loss are better explained in terms of the grief paradigm than of exchange theory (see Greenhalgh, 1979b).

IV. GENERAL SUMMARY AND IMPLICATIONS

In this final section, a diagram is presented and explained that summarizes the relationship of decline to other variables of interest to organizational scholars. These relationships' implications for both researchers and practitioners are explored.

A. Summary of Relationships

Figure 2 summarizes the interrelationships between organizational decline and other organizational and environmental variables discussed in previous sections. Three aspects of the diagram deserve particular attention. The first is the impor-

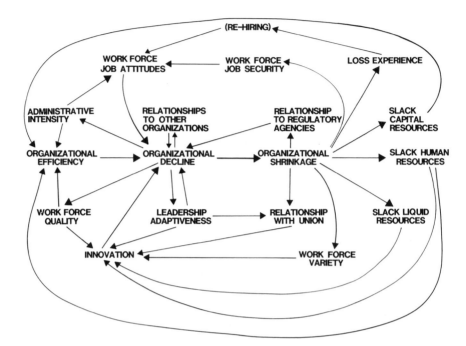

Figure 2.   Summary of Relationships of Organizational Variables and
Organizational Decline.

tance of organizational shrinkage, innovation and efficiency as central variables
linking decline with related phenomena. The second is the interrelation of sociological and sociopsychological factors which produces organizational-level
effects. The third is the predominance of positive-feedback loops that give new
impetus to the decline process. The interrelation of the variables is briefly explained next.

The original impetus for decline in an organization could, for the sake of
clarity, be attributed to some exogenous event. For instance, a key customer
could suddenly go bankrupt. Latent maladaptation in this scenario would take the
form of overdependence on a single receiver of the organization's outputs, and
actual maladaptation would be having a scale of operations in excess of what the
niche will support.

The maladapted organization would be in a state of decline and could no
longer support the previous scale of operations; in response, the organization
would shrink. Shrinkage would be unlikely to occur instantaneously and uniformly throughout the organization; rather, resources would be expected to diminish at different rates. The differential shrinkage would likely create increased
slack in capital and human resources, and reduced slack in liquid resources. The

increased slack in capital and human resources would decrease organizational efficiency.

The tendency for the organization's better workers to quit in the face of decline would also reduce organizational efficiency, as would the expected increase in administrative intensity. These effects would probably be minor, however, compared with the loss in efficiency that would result from dysfunctional work force attitudes.

The negative attitudinal climate would be shaped by three factors. The most important would be the job security crisis that would arise from the rumors and ambiguity of the decline milieu. Low job security would result in minimum contributions for the level of inducements (March and Simon, 1958). A subset of the work force having equally dysfunctional attitudes would include employees who had been rehired after experiencing layoff. The scars left by that experience would likely take the form of alienated, or at best calculative, involvement (Etzioni, 1961). Negative attitudes would be reinforced as a result of the tendency for administrative intensity to increase during shrinkage. The greater misfortune befalling the production component would cause equity problems, which would tend to further curtail contributions, and consequently reduce efficiency.

Organizational efficiency is thus determined by several interacting factors which are in turn engendered by organizational decline. Reduced organizational efficiency accelerates organizational decline because it reduces the surplus generated by the organization's operations. Less surplus means less capacity for buffering, and thus greater vulnerability to environmental shocks (Thompson, 1967). Thus organizational efficiency is a key element in a powerful positive-feedback loop.

The increased slack in human resources has been considered only as an impediment to efficiency in the scenario presented thus far. These slack resources would also provide a potential benefit: human resources could be reallocated from routine tasks to innovation programs, the latter being an antidote to decline. Other decline phenomena would constrain the organization from taking full advantage of this opportunity, however. The change in composition of the work force during decline and shrinkage would be one such constraint. The lower quality and variety of the work force would diminish its contribution to innovation despite its increased availability. Furthermore, working capital is usually a necessary condition for innovation. With little slack in recommittable resources, the organization could not take full advantage of its slack human resources.

The decision making behavior of members of the power elites would also constrain innovation. Decline engenders tunnel vision, vulnerability to stress, authoritarianism, failure to involve others in decision making, and expediency at the expense of creativity. Such behavior would be dysfunctional in three ways. First, it would lead to maladaptive rather than innovative decisions, which would have a separate main effect in accelerating decline. Second, the response of leaders would create a climate of negativism, risk aversion, and lack of support, which would inhibit innovation. Third, the leaders' behavior would reduce the probability of developing a constructive relationship with the union. Having to deal with a myopic management adds to other difficulties the union would experience during decline. The union must cope with internal problems caused by membership shrinkage. In the face of these adversities, the union would be likely to revert to the primitive standard operating procedure of resisting changes initiated by management. Except as a last resort, the union would be unlikely to become a partner with management in adaptive innovation for their mutual benefit.

The union is likely to be only one of several interest groups that would exert power that would have the effect of inhibiting innovation. Coalitions would form to defend special interests within the organization. Their emergence would coalesce other interest groups, and innovation would be displaced by conflict.

Innovation in an organization is thus determined by several factors, each of which is affected by decline. The innovation/decline relationship completes a positive-feedback loop that consists mainly of inhibiting tendencies. The assumption is made that constant change occurs in the organization's environment. Examples of such changes would be increases in government regulation, advances in technology, and rising costs of labor or energy. Innovation is a change in organizational routines, broadly defined; some level of innovation is necessary to keep pace with normal environmental flux. The condition of decline requires increased innovation to readjust the organization to its environment. However, decline gives rise to forces that inhibit even the normal level of innovation, so that the organization becomes less and less adapted to its environment. In this sense, there is positive feedback which accelerates decline.

Two sets of organizations in the declining organization's environment would also be affected by, and in turn affect, the decline process. Customers and suppliers would obviously be affected by the organization's decline but would not tend to hasten the process until some threshold point had been passed. Up to that point, they could be a crucial source of liquid assets by extending credit. Beyond that point, they would likely reduce the organization's market share by transferring business to competitors.

The organization's relationship with regulatory agencies would show an opposite pattern. Regulatory agencies would tend to make the environment more stringent for the organization until decline had progressed to the point where organizational survival became unlikely. Regulatory pressure would probably then be eased.

These last two factors stand out because they are the only factors that are not involved in a strong positive-feedback loop. All of the other factors discussed earlier are effects of decline which accelerate further decline. Furthermore, most of the effects are irreversible, in the sense that they lead to the establishment of new equilibrium points in the organizational system rather than being temporary departures from existing equilibrium points.

B. Implications for Researchers

Given the complex nature and limited current knowledge of organizational decline, the basic implication for organizational researchers is that their work has just begun. Decline is possibly the least understood of the important organizational phenomena. The neglect is partly attributable to the relative convenience of cross-sectional research, which is not ideal for studying organizational changes and may actually be misleading (Ford, 1980a; Freeman and Hannan, 1975; Whetten, 1980a).

Where attention has been devoted to changes, researchers have focused on growth (Ford, 1980b). There are several reasons for this, which can be summarized by Whetten's (1980a) observation that three assumptions pervade the literature and bias organizational research towards a growth orientation.

The first assumption is that size is positively correlated with age. This assumption envisions a progression from small size at founding to some terminal size determined by environmental constraints at maturity. The history of Control Data Corporation exemplifies this progression. Begun by an 8-person group in 1957, the organization had grown in 10 years to more than 10,000 employees and had evolved an extensive hierarchical structure designed to carefully maintain coordination (Quinn, 1976). Many large organizations have histories like that of Control Data Corporation, and resemble the prototype envisioned in the size/age assumption. Despite such prominent examples, the assumption may not be generalizable to all large organizations. Starbuck (1980) contends that: (1) large organizations are usually created on a large scale (Volkswagen–U.S.A. may be an example of this: the dealer and service network was formed before the organization began the systematic importing of cars); (2) small organizations usually remain small (the "Mom and Pop" grocery store rarely becomes a supermarket chain); and (3) both large and small organizations can fail without going through an atrophy stage. One can extend Starbuck's reasoning by considering cases in which organizations change size through acquisitions and divestments without undergoing linear growth and shrinkage.

Empirical research is needed to settle the question of whether organizations typically or atypically experience a growth phase. Meanwhile, it can be assumed that while growth has probably been overemphasized in the study of organizations, it is still an important process for many organizations, it is more likely to be an index of adaptation than of maladaptation, and it provides a useful contrast for shrinkage conditions.

The second assumption Whetten notes is that size is a desirable organizational property, due to the resulting increases in economies of scale and resiliency to environmental shocks. This second assumption obviously hinges on the first one: to foster a growth orientation, greater size would have to be perceived to result from growth rather than creation or metamorphosis through merger or acquisition. In other words, the growth orientation results from a size orientation.

The third and possibly most important assumption is that growth is an index of organizational effectiveness (see, e.g., Katz and Kahn, 1966; Negandhi and Reimann, 1973; Thompson, 1967), reflecting the influence of a broader social ideology.

Despite their orientation towards growth, researchers and practitioners must understand other organizational states. In this regard, the life-cycle model has some potential to extend thinking beyond a preoccupation with growth, static models, and cross-sectional research. The major benefit claimed for the life-cycle approach is that it directs researchers' attention to the history (and even prehistory) of organizations and to the environment, which provides an exchange context and a selection mechanism (Aldrich, 1979) that determine the focal organization's progress and continuity.

The life-cycle model (or any similar multistage model) can lead one to ask richer questions about organizations and their activities and relationships, such as whether these are constant across life-cycle stages (cf. Greenhalgh, 1980; Quinn and Cameron, 1981) and whether (and how) attributes in an earlier stage affect the status of those and other attributes in a later stage. There may be subtle qualitative differences. For instance, an organization may be secretive during the creation or growth stage to foster innovation, as well as during shrinkage to protect its access to inputs (for example, information which might reduce the chance of securing working capital may be suppressed). The behaviors involved may be objectively identical, but are quite different in terms of their meaning to organizational actors (cf. Geertz, 1974) and effects on future organizational states and relationships.

A first priority for researchers who adopt a life-cycle rather than a static conceptualization is to develop a satisfactory operational definition of organizational decline, in order to facilitate cumulative research. Ease of measurement, lack of ambiguity, potential for replication, applicability across sectors of the economy, and comparability of the resulting data with findings in related paradigms are all important criteria for an adequate operational definition.

Based on the aforementioned criteria, work force size is the leading candidate to operationalize decline, even though it only involves one possible manifestation. The construct is objective, relatively unambiguous, easily quantified, applies equally well to public and private sector organizations, and in many cases involves public information. It is also the predominant definition of organizational size (Kimberly, 1976), which has received considerable research attention and has convergent validity with other operationalizations of changing size (Child, 1973).

The construct is also versatile in that it readily encompasses reductions in force, plant closings, and organizational termination. A reduction in force would involve the elimination of some but not all positions in an organization or subunit thereof; a subunit closing would involve the elimination of positions in a subunit while the rest of the organization survives (as in the case of a multiplant corporation closing one of its plants); and organizational termination would indicate the elimination of all positions throughout the organization.

The work force–based definition fares less well when judged against the criteria of construct and content validity. The concept of reduced adaptation to the organization's environment provides a richer understanding of the complex, interrelated processes which probably lead to a reduction in several size dimensions. The construct validity problem arises because the use of work force size as an operational definition means that researchers are measuring one possible symptom rather than decline per se. Indeed, one can imagine organizational decline situations in which the work force and other size dimensions are not decreasing, but are actually increasing: For instance, a government or monopoly can become increasingly maladapted, in the sense of becoming unresponsive to the needs of its constituency or market, while growing rapidly.

The content validity problem arises because many elements of the concept are omitted from the operational construct. A more comprehensive construct might have to jointly address several criteria for decline. A multifaceted construct might avoid, say, interpreting a situation as decline when capital is being substituted for labor, and the organization is thereby adapting to state-of-the-art technology that will capture the market with greater efficiency and quality. In such a situation, the shrinking work force would evidence adaptation rather than maladaptation and a multifaceted construct would be required to avoid being misled.

A multifaceted construct would require a multidisciplinary approach to investigate it. For instance, organizational slack, an important element in the decline process, appears as a fairly simple concept in the organizational theory literature. However, to go beyond the grossest generalizations in using the concept requires incorporating concepts from other disciplines, such as financial and human resource accounting, production and operations management, industrial and organizational psychology, and business policy. Thus to investigate decline, and its etiology and consequences, researchers will have to blend different disciplines at a common level of analysis.

Development of the definition of organizational decline would be aided greatly by conceptual development of the notion of organizational adaptation, of which decline is a special case. Many writers use the notion of adaptation, at least implicitly, in explaining organizational phenomena, but adaptation has received very little attention per se. One important reason for the neglect was noted above: the dominant approach to studying organizations, involving static models and cross-sectional research, is not well suited to dealing with phenomena such as adaptation that occur over time.

C. Implications for Practitioners

An understanding of the relationship of decline to other organizational phenomena, as summarized in Figure 2, would benefit organizational decision makers. Adequate diagnosis of managerial problems requires that symptoms be distinguished from causes, and rational choice among action alternatives requires that impacts be predicted. The latter point is particularly important in declining organizations because of the vulnerability of managerial actions to unintended side effects which accelerate decline.

Intervention requires that managers and other change agents understand the system they are trying to change. For instance, it is crucial to know whether a temporary displacement from an equilibrium point needs to be restored, or a displaced equilibrium point needs to be returned to its previous level. An opposite force or removal of the displacing force will restore the previous equilibrium in the former case. Given irreversible processes, restoration of a previous equilibrium point in the latter case may necessitate realignment of a network of relationships.

It is most critical that managers be able to identify positive-feedback loops. These are crucial points of intervention in a declining organization. To accomplish this, managers need to have a general understanding of the etiology, dynamics, and consequences of organizational decline. In addition, they should be aware of three specific areas in which steps can be taken to arrest the decline process.

First, managers can develop contingency plans for decline and shrinkage. In practice, few organizations have such plans. At best, generous buffers are provided to cope with environmental turbulence under a worst-case, steady-state scenario. When maladaptation occurs and decline processes become activated, managers tend to take stopgap measures intended to deal with the most visible symptoms, particularly those for which the managers are accountable. Such interventions probably serve as further shocks on the system, and managers find the positive-feedback loops accelerating decline. The increasingly desperate managers then attempt increasingly drastic stopgap measures. Entropy ensues.

Contingency planning for decline should ideally include all phenomena involved in positive-feedback loops. Four areas are crucial; namely, providing slack liquid resources, work force planning, survival of innovation programs, and involvement of the union in solving decline problems.

Planning for the provision of slack liquid resources is probably the best developed of the four areas. Accountants have evolved elaborate techniques for cash flow planning and management. Financial planners likewise have techniques for optimizing the liquidity and profitability of a portfolio of assets. In the field of business policy and strategy, analogous analytical procedures exist for assembling a portfolio of companies within a conglomerate. However, the above planning processes are oriented more toward growth, or at least stability, than toward shrinkage.

Work force planning is also fairly well developed, but is rarely used during shrinkage, a surprising fact given the reactivity of this form of resource. Most work force reductions represent expedient adjustments when organizational problems have reached a critical stage. Adjustments are frequently accomplished through layoffs, yet in many of these cases, involuntary separation is simply unnecessary to accomplish the work force reduction. The consequences of the job security crisis and the scars of job loss are very costly to the organization; prevention is usually feasible and less costly. Managed attrition programs work in most cases and can be effective in minimizing the job security crisis (Greenhalgh, 1982). They can also avoid problems of reduced work force variety and quality, and of increased administrative intensity.

Another critical area for intervention is innovation. A frequent candidate for cutback is the research and development function and other nonproduction organizational units necessary for innovation. The cutbacks represent a stopgap measure to raise efficiency, but they come at a time when the organization also needs to boost innovation as an antidote to decline.

Finally, managers usually fail in their dealings with the union during organizational decline. Mutual problems can be addressed outside of the usual forum of adversarial collective bargaining, through the use of such devices as a labor–management committee (see McKersie et al., 1981; Shultz and Weber, 1966). As a result, the union becomes (or continues to be) part of the problem rather than part of the solution, so long as managers view plant closings and other cutbacks as opportunities to escape from a union that is hard to deal with.

Policy makers represent another group of practitioners that can benefit from a better understanding of the complexities of decline. The basic lesson to be learned is that there are no "quick fixes" for decline in societally important organizations. Policy makers are dealing with a complicated open system. The typical first reaction of "throwing money at the problem" does not address the spectrum of adversities confronting the declining organization. At best, an infusion of funds might temporarily provide some slack in liquid resources. Another public policy initiative that has been advanced is to impose an exit tax on organizations trying to close an organizational subunit. From what is known of decline, it is hard to see how such a constraint would do anything to stem decline and shrinkage. Indeed, it would be more likely to increase decline by precluding one potentially adaptive option by the parent organization.

It should be obvious that an understanding of the process of and related to organizational decline is equally important to managers making decisions in organizations as to policy makers making decisions affecting organizations. To improve that understanding and the resulting decisions, organizational sociologists must develop the current embryonic knowledge of organizational decline into an advanced paradigm.

ACKNOWLEDGMENTS

I would like to acknowledge the guidance of Steve Mitchell, Dave Whetten, Howard Aldrich, John Hennessey, Charlie Levine, and Bob McKersie on earlier drafts of this paper.

REFERENCES

Akers, R. and F. L. Campbell
    1970   "Size and the administrative component in occupational associations." Pacific Sociologi-
            cal Review 13:241–251.
Aldrich, H. E.
    1979   Organizations and Environments. Englewood Cliffs, NJ: Prentice-Hall.
Allison, G. T.
    1971   Essence of Decision. Boston: Little Brown and Company.
Bacharach, S. B. and E. J. Lawler
    1980   Power and Politics in Organizations. San Francisco: Jossey-Bass.
Barnard, C. I.
    1938   The Functions of the Executive. Cambridge: Harvard University Press.
Becker, H. S.
    1960   "Notes on the concept of commitment." American Sociological Review 66:32–40.
Beynon, H.
    1973   Workin for Ford. London: Allen Lane.
Blau, P.
    1970   "A formal theory of differentiation in organizations." American Sociological Review
            35:201–218.
Blau, P. M. and R. A. Shoenherr
    1971   The Structure of Organizations. New York: Basic Books.
Block, R. N.
    1977   "The impact of union-negotiated employment security provisions on manufacturing quit
            rate." In Proceedings of the Twenty-Ninth Annual Winter Meeting, Industrial Relations
            Research Association, Madison.
Boulding, L. J.
    1975   "The management of decline." Change (June):8–9; 64.
Bourgeois, L. J., 3rd.
    1981   "On the measurement of organization slack." Academy of Management Review 6:29–39.
Buchanan, B.
    1974   "Building organizational commitment; the socialization of managers in work organiza-
            tions." Administrative Science Quarterly 19:533–546.
Burns, T. and G. M. Stalker
    1961   "Variations and selective retention in socio-cultural evolution." General Systems
            16:69–85.
Campbell, J. P.
    1977   "On the nature of organizational effectiveness." In P. S. Goodman, J. M. Pennings &
            Associates, New Perspectives on Organizational Effectiveness. San Francisco: Jossey-
            Bass.
Child, J.
    1973   "Parkinson's progress; accounting for the number of specialists in organizations." Admin-
            istrative Science Quarterly 18:328–346.
Chinoy, E.
    1955   "Automobile Workers and the American Dream. Boston: Beacon.
Coch, L. and J. R. P. French
    1948   "Overcoming resistance to change." Human Relations 1:512–532.
Cyert, R. M. and J. G. March
    1963   A Behavioral Theory of the Firm. Englewood Cliffs, NJ: Prentice-Hall.
Dahrendorf, R.
    1959   Class and Class Conflict in Industrial Society. Stanford: Stanford University Press.

Dembowski, F. L.
1980 "The effects of declining enrollments on the instructional programs of public, elementary and secondary schools." Paper presented at the Annual Conference of the American Educational Research Association, Boston.

Easton, A.
1976 Managing for Negative Growth. Reston, VA: Reston Publishing Company.

Emerson, R. M.
1962 "Power-dependence relations." American Sociological Review 27:21–41.

Ettlie, J. E.
1980 "Manpower flows and the innovation process." Management Science 26:1086–1095.

Etzioni, A.
1961 A Comparative Analysis of Complex Organizations. New York: Free Press.

Fink, L., J. Beak, and T. Taddeo
1971 "Organizational crisis and change." Journal of Applied Behavioral Science 7:15–37.

Ford, J. D.
1980a "The administrative component in growing and declining organizations: a longitudinal analysis." Academy of Management Journal 23:615–630.
1980b "The occurrence of structural hystersis in declining organizations." Academy of Management Review 5:589–598.

Ford, J. D. and J. W. Slocum, Jr.
1977 "Size, technology, environment and structure of organizations." Academy of Management Review 2:561–575.

Fox, F. V. and B. M. Staw
1979 "The trapped administrators: effects of job insecurity and policy resistance upon commitment to a course of action." Administrative Science Quarterly 24:449–471.

Freeman, J. and M. T. Hannan
1975 "Growth and decline processes in organizations." American Sociological Review 40:215–228.

Fry, F. L.
1973 "More on the causes of quits in manufacturing." Monthly Labor Review (June):48–49.

Galbraith, J.
1973 Designing Complex Organizations. Reading, MA: Addison-Wesley.

Gannon, M. J., C. Foreman, and K. Pugh
1973 "The influence of a reduction in force on the attitudes of engineers." Academy of Management Journal 16:330–334. Geertz, C.
1974 The Interpretation of Cultures. New York: Basic Books.

Goodman, P. S. and J. M. Pennings
1977 "Perspectives and issues: an introduction." In P. S. Goodman, J. M. Pennings & Associates, New Perspectives on Organizational Effectiveness. San Francisco: Jossey-Bass.

Goodman, P. S. and S. Salipante, Jr.
1976 "Organizational rewards and retention of the hard-core unemployment." Journal of Applied Psychology 61:12–21.

Gow, J. S., A. W. Clark, and C. S. Dossett
1974 "A path analysis of variables influencing labor turnover." Human Relations 27:703–719.

Greenhalgh, L.
1978 A Cost-Benefit Balance Sheet for Evaluating Layoffs as a Policy Strategy. Ithaca: New York State School of Industrial & Labor Relations, Cornell University.
1979a "Guiding metaphors, communication, and behavior." Paper presented at the annual meeting of the Academy of Management, Atlanta.
1979b Job Security and the Disinvolvement Syndrome: An Exploration of Patterns of Worker

Behavior Under Conditions of Anticipatory Grieving Over Job Loss. Ph.D. dissertation, Cornell University.

1980   "A process model of organizational turnover: the relationship with job security as a case in point." Academy of Management Review 5:299–303.

1982   "Maintaining organizational effectiveness during organizational retrenchment." Journal of Applied Behavioral Science 18(2):155–170.

Greenhalgh, L. and T. D. Jick
1978   The Relocation of a Rural Hospital Unit: The Impact of Rumors and Ambiguity on Employees. Ithaca: New York State School of Industrial & Labor Relations, Cornell University.

1979   "The relationship between job insecurity and turnover, and its differential effect on employee quality level." Paper presented at the annual meeting of the Academy of Management, Atlanta.

Greenhalgh, L. and R. B. McKersie
1980   "Cost effectiveness of alternative strategies for cutback management." Public Administration Review 6:575–584.

Greenhalgh, L. and J. M. Kaestle
1981   "Severance pay in the public sector." Paper presented at the annual meeting of the Academy of Management, San Diego.

Guest, D. and D. Fatchett
1974   Worker Participation: Individual Control and Performance. London: Institute of Personnel Management.

Hackman, J. R. and E. E. Lawler, III
1971   "Employee reactions to job characteristics." Journal of Applied Psychology 55:259–286.

Hall, D. T. and R. Mansfield
1971   "Organizational and individual response to external stress." Administrative Science Quarterly 16:533–547.

Hall, R. I.
1976   "A system pathology of an organization: the rise and fall of the old 'Saturday Evening Post'." Administrative Science Quarterly 21:185–211.

Hanlon, M. D.
1979   Primary Groups and Unemployment. Ph.D. dissertation, Columbia University.

Hannan, M. I. and J. H. Freeman
1980   "The population ecology of organizations." In J. R. Kimberly and R. H. Miles (eds.), The Organizational Life Cycle. San Francisco: Jossey-Bass.

Hartley, J. and C. L. Cooper
1976   "Redundancy: a psychological problem?" Personnel Review 5(3):44–48.

Hendershot, G. E. and T. F. James
1972   "Size and growth as determinants of administration-production ratios in organizations." American Sociological Review 37:149–153.

Hershey, R.
1972   "Effects of anticipated job loss on employee behavior." Journal of Applied Psychology 56:273–275.

Hirschman, A. O.
1970   Exit, Voice and Loyalty. Cambridge: Harvard University Press.

House, R. J.
1975   "Etzioni's theory of organizational compliance." In H. L. Tosi (ed.), Theories of Organization. Chicago: St. Clair.

Jick, T. D.
1979   Process and Impacts of a Merger: Individual and Organizational Perspectives. Ph.D. dissertation, Cornell University.

Jick, T. D. and L. Greenhalgh
  1978 The Closing of Urban State Agencies: Impact on Employee Attitudes, Perceptions, Careers, and Economic Security. Ithaca: New York State School of Industrial & Labor Relations, Cornell University.
  1980 "Realistic job previews: a reconceptualization." Paper presented at the annual meeting of the Academy of Management, Detroit.
  1981 "Information processing of new recruits in a declining organization." Paper presented at the annual meeting of the Academy of Management, San Diego.
Katz, D. and R. L. Kahn
  1966 The Social Psychology of Organizations. New York: Wiley.
Kimberly, J. R.
  1976 "Organizational size and the structuralist perspective: a review, critique, and proposal." Administrative Science Quarterly 21:571–597.
  1980a "Initiation, innovation, and institutionalization in the creation process." In J. R. Kimberly and R. H. Miles (eds.), The Organizational Life Cycle. San Francisco: Jossey-Bass.
  1980b "The life cycle analogy and the study of organizations: introduction." In J. R. Kimberly and R. H. Miles (eds.), The Organizational Life Cycle. San Francisco: Jossey-Bass.
Kolarska, L. and H. Aldrich
  1980 "Exit, voice and silence: consumers' and managers' responses to organizational decline." Organization Studies 1:41–58.
Lawler, E. E., III, and D. T. Hall
  1970 "Relationship of job characteristics to job involvement, satisfaction, and intrinsic motivation." Journal of Applied Psychology 54:305–312.
Levine, C. H.
  1978 "Organizational decline and cutback management." Public Administration Review 38:316–325.
  1979 "More on cutback management: hard questions for hard times." Public Administration Review 39:179–183.
Lodahl, T. M. and M. Kejner
  1965 "The definition of measurement of job involvement." Journal of Applied Psychology 49:24–33.
Lodahl, T. M. and S. M. Mitchell
  1980 "Drift in the development of innovative organizations." In J. R. Kimberly and R. E. Miles (eds.), The Organizational Life Cycle. San Francisco: Jossey-Bass.
McKersie, R. B., L. Greenhalgh, and T. D. Jick
  1980 "Economic progress and economic dislocation." Working paper, Sloan School of Management, Massachusetts Institute of Technology.
  1981 "The CEC: labor-management cooperation in New York." Industrial Relations 20:212–220.
March, J. G. and H. A. Simon
  1958 Organizations. New York: Wiley
Marris, P.
  1974 Loss and Change. New York: Pantheon.
Merton, R. K.
  1957 Social Theory and Social Structure. Rev. ed. New York: Free Press.
  1962 "The machine, the worker, and the engineer." In S. Nosow and W. H. Form (eds.), Man, Work and Society. New York: Basic Books.
Miles, R. M. and W. A. Randolph
  1980 "Influence of organizational learning styles on early development." In J. R. Kimberly and R. H. Miles (eds.), The Organizational Life Cycle. San Francisco: Jossey-Bass.

Miller, D. and P. Friesen
  1980   "Archetypes of organizational transition." Administrative Science Quarterly 25:268–299.
Negandhi, A. R. and B. C. Reimann
  1973   "Task environment, decentralization and organizational effectiveness." Human Relations
         26:203–214.
Pennings, J. M.
  1980   "Environmental influences on the creation process." In J. R. Kimberly and R. H. Miles
         (eds.), The Organizational Life Cycle. San Francisco: Jossey-Bass.
Pondy, L. R.
  1969   "Effects of size, complexity and ownership on administrative intensity." Administrative
         Science Quarterly 14:47–61.
  1977   "Effectiveness: a thick description." In P. S. Goodman, J. M. Pennings, & Associates
         (eds.), New Perspectives on Organizational Effectiveness. San Francisco: Jossey-Bass.
Porter, L. W., R. M. Steers, R. T. Mowday, and P. V. Boulian
  1974   "Organizational commitment, job satisfaction, and turnover among psychiatric techni-
         cians." Journal of Applied Psychology 59:603–609.
Price, J. L.
  1977   The Study of Turnover. Ames: Iowa State University Press.
Quinn, J. B.
  1976   "Control Data Corporation." Case No. B.P. 45–0123, The Amos Tuck School of Busi-
         ness Administration, Dartmouth College.
Quinn, R. E. and K. Cameron
  1981   "Organizational life cycles and shifting criteria of effectiveness: some preliminary evi-
         dence." Working paper, Graduate School of Public Affairs, State University of New York
         at Albany.
Quinn, R. P.
  1973   Locking-In as a Moderator of the Relationship Between Job Satisfaction and Mental
         Health. Ann Arbor: Survey Research Center, University of Michigan.
Rabinowitz, S. and D. T. Hall
  1977   "Organizational research on job involvement." Psychological Bulletin 84:265–288.
Rice, A. K., J. M. M. Hill, and E. L. Trist
  1950   "The representation of labor turnover as a social process." Human Relations 3:349–372.
Roethlisberger, F. G. and W. J. Dickson
  1946   Management and the Worker. Cambridge: Harvard University Press.
Ronan, W. W.
  1967   "A study of and some concepts concerning labor turnover." Occupational Psychology
         41:193–202.
Rothman, R. A., A. M. Schwartzbaum, and J. H. McGrath, III
  1971   "Physicians and a hospital merger: patterns of resistance to organizational change." Jour-
         nal of Health and Social Behavior 12:46–55.
Rushing, W.
  1967   "The effects of industry size and division of labor on administration." Administrative
         Science Quarterly 12:273–295.
Schein, E. H.
  1980   Organizational Psychology. 3rd ed. Englewood Cliffs, NJ: Prentice-Hall.
Schein, V.
  1979   "Examining an illusion: the role of deceptive behaviors in organizations." Human Rela-
         tions 32:287–295.
Schuler, R. S.
  1980   "Definition and conceptualization of stress in organizations." Organizational Behavior
         and Human Performance 25:184–215.

Schwartz, H. A.
1980 ''Job involvement, job enrichment and obsession-compulsion.'' Paper presented at the annual meeting of the Eastern Academy of Management, Buffalo.
Scott, W. G.
1974 ''Organizational theory: a reassessment.'' Academy of Management Journal 17:245–254.
Schultz, G. P. and A. R. Weber
1966 Strategies for the Displaced Worker. Westport, CT: Greenwood Press.
Smart, C. and I. Vertinsky
1977 ''Designs for crisis decision units.'' Administrative Science Quarterly 22:640–657.
Smith, F. J. and W. A. Kerr
1953 ''Turnover factors as assessed by the exit interview.'' Journal of Applied Psychology 37:352–255.
Starbuck, W. H.
1980 ''How success spoils organizations.'' Paper presented at the annual meeting of the Academy of Management, Detroit.
Staw, B. M., L. E. Sandelands, and J. E. Dutton
1981 ''Threat-rigidity effects in organizational behavior: a multilevel analysis.'' Administrative Science Quarterly 26:501–524.
Steers, R. M.
1975 ''Problems in the measurement of organizational effectiveness.'' Administrative Science Quarterly 20:546–558.
Stinchcombe, A. L.
1965 ''Social structure and organizations.'' In J. G. March (ed.), Handbook of Organizations. Chicago: Rand-McNally.
Stogdill, R. M.
1965 Managers, Employees, Organizations. Columbus: Ohio State University Press.
Stoikov, V. and R. L. Raimon
1968 ''Determinants of differences in the quit rate among industries.'' American Economic Review 58:1283–1298.
Strange, W. G.
1977 Job Loss: A Psychological Study of Worker Reactions to a Plant-Closing in a Company Town in Southern Appalachia. Ph.D. dissertation, Cornell University.
Sykes, A. J. M.
1965 ''Myth and attitude change.'' Human Relations 18:323–337.
Taylor, J. A. and K. W. Spence
1952 ''The relationship of anxiety level to performance in serial learning.'' Journal of Experimental Psychology 44:61–64.
Thompson, J. D.
1967 Organizations in Action. New York: McGraw-Hill.
Tsouderos, J. E.
1955 ''Organizational change in terms of a series of selected variables.'' American Sociological Review 20:206–210.
Walton, R. E. and R. B. McKersie
1965 A Behavioral Theory of Labor Negotiations. New York: McGraw-Hill.
Weber, M.
1947 The Theory of Social and Economic Organization. T. Parsons (ed.). Trans. A. M. Henderson and T. Parsons. New York: Oxford University Press.
Weick, K. E.
1979 The Social Psychology of Organizing. 2nd ed. Reading, MA: Addison-Wesley.

Whetten, D. A.
  1979   "Organizational responses to scarcity: difficult choices for difficult times." Working
          paper, College of Commerce and Business Administration, University of Illinois at Ur-
          bana-Champaign.
  1980a   "Organizational decline: a neglected topic in organizational science." Academy of Man-
          agement Review 5:577–588.
  1980b   "Sources, responses, and effects of organizational decline." In J. R. Kimberly and R. H.
          Miles (eds.), The Organizational Life Cycle. San Francisco: Jossey-Bass.

LIBRARY
OF
MOUNT ST. MARY'S
COLLEGE
EMMITSBURG, MARYLAND

Research Annuals in
SOCIOLOGY

Consulting Editor for Sociology

Samuel B. Bacharach
Department of Sociology and School
of Industrial and Labor Relations
Cornell University

**Advances in Early Education
and Day Care**
Series Editor: Sally Kilmer,
Bowling Green State University

**Advances in Health
Economics and Health
Services Research**
(Volume 1 published as Research in
Health Economics)
Series Editor: Richard M.
Scheffler, George Washington
University. Associate Series Editor:
Louis F. Rossiter, National Center
for Health Services Research

**Advances in Special
Education**
Series Editor: Barbara K. Keogh,
University of California,
Los Angeles

**Advances in Substance
Abuse**
Series Editor: Nancy K. Mello,
Harvard Medical School—
McLean Hospital

Comparative Social Research
Series Editor: Richard F.
Tomasson, The University of
New Mexico

**Current Perspectives in Social
Theory**
Series Editors: Scott G. McNall
and Gary N. Howe, University of
Kansas

**Knowledge and Society:
Studies in the Sociology of
Culture Past and Present**
(Volumes 1-2 published as Research
in the Sociology of Knowledge,
Sciences and Art)
Series Editors: Robert Alun Jones,
University of Illinois
Henrika Kuklick, University of
Pennsylvania

**Perspectives in
Organizational Sociology**
Series Editor: Samuel B.
Bacharach, Cornell University

**Political Power and Social
Theory**
Series Editor: Maurice Zeitlin,
University of California,
Los Angeles

**Research in Community and
Mental Health**
Series Editor: Roberta G.
Simmons, University of Minnesota

**Research in Economic
Anthropology**
Series Editor: George Dalton,
Northwestern University

**Research in Law, Deviance
and Social Control**
(Volumes 1-3 published as Research
in Law and Sociology)
Series Editors: Rita J. Simon,
University of Illinois and Steven
Spitzer, Suffolk University—
Boston

**Research in Political
Economy**
Series Editor: Paul Zarembka,
State University of New York,
Buffalo

**Research in Race and Ethnic
Relations**
Series Editors: Cora B. Marrett,
University of Wisconsin, and
Cheryl Leggon, University of
Chicago

**Research in Social
Movements, Conflicts and
Change**
Series Editor: Louis Kriesberg,
Syracuse University

**Research in Social Problems
and Public Policy**
Series Editor: Michael Lewis,
University of Massachusetts

**Research in Social
Stratification and Mobility**
Series Editors: Donald J. Treiman,
National Academy of Sciences,
and Robert V. Robinson, Indiana
University

**Research in Sociology of
Education and Socialization**
Series Editor: Alan C. Kerckhoff,
Duke University

**Research in the Interweave of
Social Roles**
Series Editor: Helena Z. Lopata,
Loyola University of Chicago

**Research in the Sociology of
Health Care**
Series Editor: Julius A. Roth,
University of California, Davis

**Research in the Sociology of
Work**
Series Editors: Ida Harper
Simpson, Duke University,
and Richard L. Simpson,
University of North
Carolina, Chapel Hill

Studies in Communications
Series Editor: Thelma McCormack,
York University

**Studies in Symbolic
Interaction**
Series Editor: Norman K. Denzin,
University of Illinois

Please inquire for detailed brochure on each series.

 JAI PRESS INC.

Advances in
Industrial and Labor Relations

Edited by **David B. Lipsky**

New York State School of Industrial and Labor Relations, Cornell University

This series will publish major, original research on all subjects within the field of industrial relations, including union behavior, structure, and government; collective bargaining, in both the private and public sectors; labor law and public policies affecting the employment relationships; the economics of collective bargaining; and international and comparative labor movements. Reflecting the multidisciplinary nature of industrial relations, its contributors will include economists, sociologists, and other social scientists as well as lawyers and specialists in labor relations. Although there are now several journals that publish research on industrial relations, the space limitations of these journals preclude their publishing longer—and possibly more reflective—studies. Many industrial relations scholars have sought a forum for the publication of research that is too long for a journal article but not enough for a book or monograph.

Volume 1, 1983
ISBN 0-89232-250-0

CONTENTS: Organizations and Expectations: Organizational Determinants of Union Membership Demands, *Samuel Bacharach and Stephen M. Mitchell, Cornell University.* **Perceptions of Academic Bargaining Behavior,** *Robert Birnbaum, Columbia University.* **The Unionization Process: A Review of the Literature,** *Richard Block and Steven L. Premack, Michigan State University.* **Unionization in Secondary Labor Markets: The Historical Case of Building Services Employees,** *Peter Doeringer, Boston University.* **Public Sector Impasses Procedures: A Six State Study,** *Paul Gerhart and John Drotning, Case Western Reserve University.* **The Effects of Civil Service Systems and Unionism on Pay Outcomes in the Public Sector,** *David Lewin, Columbia University.* **The Relationship Between Seniority, Ability, and the Promotion of Union and Nonunion Workers,** *Craig A. Olson and Chris J. Berger, State University of New York at Buffalo.* **Towards a Theory of the Union's Role in an Enterprise,** *Donna Sockell, Columbia University.* **Union Organizing in Manufacturing: 1973-76,** *Ronald Seeber, Cornell University.*

University libraries depend upon their faculty for recommendations before purchasing. Please encourage your library to subscribe to this series.

INSTITUTIONAL STANDING ORDERS *will be granted a 10% discount and be filled automatically upon publication. Please indicate initial volume of standing order.*

INDIVIDUAL ORDERS *must be prepaid by personal check or credit card. Please include $2.00 per volume for postage and handling on all domestic orders; $3.00 for foreign.*

JAI PRESS INC., 36 Sherwood Place, P.O. Box 1678
Greenwich, Connecticut 06836
Telephone: 203-661-7602   Cable Address: JAIPUBL

MAR 1 9 1985